THE PEOPLE ON THE BEACH

ROSIE WHITEHOUSE

The People on the Beach

Journeys to Freedom After the Holocaust

HURST & COMPANY, LONDON

First published in the United Kingdom in 2020 by
C. Hurst & Co. (Publishers) Ltd.,
41 Great Russell Street, London, WC1B 3PL
Copyright © Rosie Whitehouse, 2020
All rights reserved.

Printed in Great Britain by Bell and Bain Ltd, Glasgow

The right of Rosie Whitehouse to be identified as the author
of this publication is asserted by her in accordance with the
Copyright, Designs and Patents Act, 1988.

Distributed in the United States, Canada and Latin America by
Oxford University Press, 198 Madison Avenue, New York, NY 10016,
United States of America.

A Cataloguing-in-Publication data record for this book
is available from the British Library.

ISBN: 9781787383777

This book is printed using paper from registered sustainable
and managed sources.

www.hurstpublishers.com

CONTENTS

ACKNOWLEDGEMENTS

I think of myself as a "road trip historian", but much of the research for this book was actually done sitting on my sofa and in bed late at night.

Without modern technology, this book could not have been written and the protagonists could not have been found. It was on one of those nights when I was burning the midnight oil that Rachel Judah, my daughter, offered a helping hand and found a list of the *Josiah Wedgwood*'s passengers that had been published in the newspaper *Lakkarow w'Larahok*, when the ship arrived in Palestine. My luck was finding that I could click and translate. We danced around the room.

My biggest thanks go to the survivors and their families. I thank them not just for their time but also for their hospitality and kindness. My greatest sadness is that I never met in person those I have encountered in the virtual reality of Holocaust testaments. I have watched enough of these to know that recording them is a hard thing to do and I thank the survivors who did just that, spending hours in front of the camera for posterity.

Since this is a road trip, I thank the trusty family car for getting me around Europe and for offering a haven in which to think as I ate up the miles. When it got me to Warsaw, I went to have a coffee at the apartment of the Polish journalist and Jewish activist Konstanty Gebert. He gave me invaluable advice and set me off on an unforgettable journey around his country.

In Germany, the guiding hand behind my quest for the people on the beach was Father Cyrill Schäfer at St Ottilien monastery in Bavaria. He prompted me to look for the children of Zalman Grinberg, the first and main doctor at St Ottilien when it served as a DP camp after the war. I had only one clue to go on, though: I had read that his son Yair was a doctor on the east coast of the US, but knew no more. I thank all those receptionists I bothered at the many hospitals and clinics I called until I found him. After that, Father Cyrill's hospitality brought me, Yair and his family together at St Ottilien. There, at a reunion, we spent many happy hours, not only with those born in the monastery to survivor mothers, but also with Robert Hilliard, the journalist who had, as a young man, prompted a change in US policy towards the DPs. The monastery has a special place in Jewish history and the monks could not have been kinder.

In Italy my mentor was the historian Marco Cavallarin. Without his help, large sections of this book would not have been written. He always has a fascinating story in his back pocket, and many he told me that do not feature in this book have instead become newspaper stories giving traction to the wider narrative of what happened to survivors in Italy immediately after the war. I am grateful to the team at *Haaretz*, *The Jewish Chronicle* and *Tablet* for publishing them. They attracted the attention of the journalist Anshel Pfeffer, whose grandparents were survivors who had followed the Bricha route and ended up in Milan. He offered me an invaluable helping hand by introducing me to my agent Deborah Harris, who became this book's fairy godmother.

I am also grateful to Robert Baldock, formerly of Yale UK, for his encouragement. Writing this book was a journey into the unknown. I had to write it to find out exactly what the story was, and so I first produced a manuscript without an agent or a publisher. It was a lonely task in which his support was invaluable. The same goes for Ed Serotta, the director of Centropa, an amazing repository of memory and pictures of central and eastern European Jewry. Sitting in his office in Vienna, he sketched out the overall arc of what I was to do—as if he was pitching an idea for a Hollywood movie! It fired me up on the drive over the Alps into Italy.

In Israel it was our cousin Tami Lowenthal who kept my spirits up with bowls of ice cream and Friday night drinks with her friends.

Huge thanks go to my publisher Michael Dwyer, who took the manuscript on, and the amazing team at Hurst who turned it into a book during the coronavirus lockdown. Many thanks to my editor Lara Weisweiller-Wu and all the people who have worked on it.

My final thanks go to my husband Tim Judah and my children Ben, Esti, Rachel, Jacob and Eve, who read numerous versions of this story and kept me company as I drove thousands of miles looking for the people on the beach. I am sorry dinner time was reduced to an endless round of takeaway pizzas.

LIST OF ILLUSTRATIONS

For their kind permission and assistance with reproducing their family photographs, the author and publisher would like to thank Yechiel Aleksander (YA), Orli Bach (OB), David Buirski (DB), Dani Chanoch (DC), Haim Confino (HC), Emanuella and Yair Grinberg (EYG), Amos Klausner (AK), and Menachem Kriegel (MK).

LIST OF ILLUSTRATIONS

INTRODUCTION

On a summer's night in 1946 over a thousand Holocaust survivors secretly travelled to a secluded beach on the Italian Riviera. They stood in silence in the moonlight as they waited for a ship disguised as a banana boat to collect them. They had survived Auschwitz, hidden in forests, endured death marches, and now they were about to take on the Royal Navy. In charge of the operation were a dainty Italian Jewish aristocrat called Ada Sereni and an agent code-named Alon, who worked for the Jewish Agency in Tel Aviv. The affair was top secret. Also trying to board the ship on that midsummer's night was a well-known American journalist, I.F. Stone, who was slightly deaf and often wore a hearing aid with an antenna that made him look like a bespectacled Martian.

The ship was a former Canadian corvette that had hunted down German U-boats during the Battle of the Atlantic and had been bought by a secret Jewish underground organisation in New York. Most of the crew had never been on a boat before. The ship, which was named after Josiah Wedgwood, a member of the House of Lords who had died in 1943, was about to run the British naval blockade off the coast of what is now Israel but was then the British Mandate of Palestine. Despite the horrors of the Holocaust, and their commitment to the establishment of a Jewish state made in the 1917 Balfour Declaration, the British were determined to limit the number of Jewish refugees entering their territory.

As soon as the trucks arrived, the passengers jumped down quickly, feet crunching on the pebbles; their faces tense and drawn, they stood huddled together on the shore in silence. The Italian police arrived and took the aristocrat, the agent and the journalist away for questioning. Once the police had left, the survivors quickly boarded the ship, and it stole away, out of sight and out of mind.

This book is the story of the people on the beach, of how they survived the Holocaust and how they came to sail away to Palestine. In part it is a detective story. It is an account of how I found out who they were, where

1

they came from, what had happened to them during the Holocaust, how they had survived, and why they felt that their future belonged in Palestine.

To find answers to these questions I travelled to Ukraine, Lithuania and on to Poland. I visited the places where they had lived for generations, the camps in which they had suffered and the forests where they took up arms. I followed the route they took when they decided there was no future for them in Europe. I drove through Bavaria in southern Germany and over the Alps into Italy. This book is the story of that journey and the people I met along the way who remember the story of the Holocaust and its aftermath.

This is not a story of characters from a distant past but of real people who live with the Holocaust every day of their lives—people who found themselves confronted with the worst inhumanity imaginable. It is an intimate, personal story of the Holocaust, and I believe that is why it matters: it tells the story of the survivors in their own words conveyed to me not in the clinical surroundings of a museum or institute, but in their own homes. I believe this is the way the story should be heard. The Nazis dehumanised the Jews. They took away their individuality by giving them numbers instead of names. As the people I met tell their story in the pages that follow, they do so as they make me coffee in their kitchen, put biscuits on a plate or give me a lift to the station. One survivor became so distracted by the tale he was telling while he made a cup of tea that he put the kettle in the fridge by mistake, only to retrieve it seconds later, much to his embarrassment. I pretended not to have noticed. It was a frailty that revealed much. The Holocaust is still living history.

This is also a story of the present. For the families of the people involved, it is a living trauma. I was one of many mothers who confronted the difficulty of telling my children that people disliked their great-grandmother so much that they murdered her in Auschwitz simply because she was a Jew. The daughter of one survivor I met says that her father talked so much about what had happened to him that she grew up in fear of the SS and still jumps when there is a knock on the door.

The story the survivors told me of why they left their homes to build a new life in Palestine is a tale that has largely been forgotten. It is an odd one to have fallen through the cracks, as it is part of a larger tale, one that sits between two crucial historical events—the Holocaust and the declaration of the State of Israel in 1948. It is the link between the two. This is one of the reasons that it needed to be recorded.

History is often written with stereotypes. The people I met were not downtrodden, angst-ridden survivors of a weak and passive people who went like lambs to the slaughter, nor were they aggressive imperialists off to conquer a foreign land, as they are often portrayed.

Overlooking the suffering and desperation of the survivors in those vital years has allowed a false history to grow up around the story of how Israel was born. It is lack of knowledge that allows history to be distorted. If the facts are forgotten, it leaves those who want to hijack history free to do so.

The book focuses on those survivors who travelled on the illegal immigrant ship the *Wedgwood*, which set sail from the tiny port of Vado Ligure in June 1946, but it also tells a much larger story. Seventy thousand Holocaust survivors passed through Italy between 1945 and 1948, and the *Wedgwood* was just one of many ships that took them to Palestine. They left not just from Italy but from ports all along the Mediterranean and the Black Sea. This is more than just the story of one boat; it is an account of that biblical exodus. It looks at why so many Holocaust survivors felt they could not return to or remain in the places where their families had lived for generations, and how Zionism offered them a future.

My journey to find the survivors began in Vado, a ferry port in the north-west of Italy. The coast road runs to the docks past decaying Art Nouveau villas and scrubby-looking apartment blocks. The red-and-white towers of the Tirreno power station dominate the skyline. Condemned as a health hazard, its coal-fired burners sit idle. Vado is a workaday place with no air of mystery about it and is an unlikely spot to be hiding a dramatic story. There is a stunning view across the Gulf of Genoa to Monte Portofino, but Vado is far from a millionaire's playground. Lorries and carloads of tourists heading for Corsica and Sardinia queue up on the quayside and boats unload at the new container port.

I am a guidebook writer by trade and Liguria is my patch. When I wrote the first edition of the *Bradt: Liguria* guide, I ignored Vado as I thought there was nothing interesting to say about it. Updating the second edition of the book online, I stumbled across a press clipping that mentioned the mysterious *Wedgwood*, which had sailed from here in 1946. I assumed that, as this was a Jewish story, my husband, who is Jewish, would know about it. He had never heard of the *Wedgwood*. It was all the more surprising as my father-in-law had represented Italian shipyards and the family liked to holiday on the coast.

On the beach in Vado I approached a couple of elderly people who shrugged their shoulders and shook their heads when I asked if they had heard of the *Wedgwood*. Then I tried my luck with a group of fishermen tidying their nets. The young ones looked blank and carried on cleaning their equipment, but 84-year-old Domenico Farro was happy to take a break and chat with a stranger. He told me that Vado still looks much as it did when he was a child, but in those days the port had just one quay. He remembered the Jews coming from Germany, although in fact they came from fourteen different countries and from as far away as Belarus and Lithuania. "They were like this," he said sucking his cheeks and pulling his thumb and fingers down on each side of his face, indicating that they were gaunt and sorrowful-looking. "They came in the night and they pulled up the gangplank and went. It was fast!" He waved his hand indicating speed. "There were lots of things going on in those days, lots of comings and goings and illegal business. I remember, but the young ones do not. It is forgotten. When the Jews came, people didn't come out to look. There was so much else going on here. Jews leaving was just one of many things. It was nothing special, but I remember looking at them." I can imagine the scene: the moon lighting up the bay, the rugged mountains framing it like a stage.

Farro was seven when he started fishing and has lived in Vado all his life. In the middle of the night, the fishermen would have been just about to return from hauling in their catch. "I was born in that yellow house there," Farro told me, adding, "There were two boats that left with Jews, you know, not one. One was white and I can't remember the colour of the other. They came and went quickly. The *carabinieri*, I don't know what they did, but they just came and then they let them go." Farro did not say if they were bribed but waved his hand to indicate that they didn't care. "It was always communist here and times were hard after the war. We traded salt and olive oil to get flour from the north. It was tough back then."

The image of this anonymous group of huddled people stuck in my mind, along with a thousand unanswered questions. As I drove back along the winding coast road from Vado, I naively assumed the answers must exist in a book that I could order with a single online click. In fact, there was no one-stop history book to explain how these survivors from thousands of miles away made it to an obscure beach in northern Italy and were prepared to smash through a Royal Navy blockade.

To find their story I had to begin by reading piles of books, each one devoted to an isolated moment or story that in turn contained intriguing references to other events in which, as I slowly began to discover, the people on the beach had played a part.

Many of the books and memoirs I read were remaindered from libraries or had neat little stickers inside, the kind you put on the back of an envelope with your name and address. The owner had probably died and was often someone with a Jewish name who had lived in Florida. I supposed that his or her once precious library had been sold or given away by relatives uninterested in the stories they contained. Maybe the person who owned them had never told their family the true tale of what happened to them in the Second World War, let alone its aftermath. I began to piece together a vast and colourful story peopled with extraordinary characters who had been forgotten, a number of whom were among the silent crowd on the beach. Some of the books were dry and dull but others were vivid personal memoirs and hinted at the intimate personal story I would uncover.

I was intrigued by why these people felt they had no other choice than to spend days in an overcrowded and dangerous boat that would take on the Royal Navy, but I had one enormous problem to solve before I could set out to find the answer. Who were they and what were their names? There were no passenger lists for illegal boats full of refugees.

I eventually discovered that the names, ages and countries of birth of the people on the beach were recorded in the detention centre near Haifa where they were taken on arrival in Palestine. It was a camp guarded by British soldiers and surrounded by barbed wire and watchtowers. I copied down the names of over 1,300 people listed in the archives of the former Atlit detention camp from each of the separate entries, although the reports say there were 1,257 people on board the *Wedgwood*.

My problems were only just beginning. There were endless spelling mistakes, probably made as their names were transcribed into Hebrew and then into English. To complicate matters, a number of passengers changed their names to Hebrew ones when they arrived in Haifa and for this reason some were mistakenly recorded twice. Eventually I found the recorded stories of a handful of the people who had made their way to Vado. Some had spoken publicly about their wartime experiences and had been important underground leaders in war-torn Europe. Some died in the battles against the Arabs in the war of 1948, others left tantalising clues, but the majority remained anonymous. It is for that reason, more than any other, that at the back of this book can be found the list that I compiled of those who sailed on the *Wedgwood*. I am still looking for people and hope that someone who reads this book might recognise one or two names.

The Romanian Jews on my list have proved to be the most difficult to identify. One reason is that often, and oddly, their names have been changed to Slavic versions. Abramovici becomes Abramovich, for example. The Nazi genocide of the Romanian Jews centred on an area called

Transnistria. It was an artificial creation and covered the lands between the Bug and Dniester rivers, stretching down to Odessa on the Black Sea, which the Nazis awarded to the fascist leader of Romania, General Ion Antonescu. According to the US Holocaust Memorial Museum, it is thought that between 150,000 and 250,000 people were murdered or died of starvation and exhaustion there, but the true figure will probably never be known.

Stark facts jumped out at me as soon as I printed out the list of names. Only twenty-one of the people on the beach were over the age of 40 and the youngest was 13. These were mostly young people aged between 18 and 30. Two-thirds were men. Women, children and the elderly had been the first to die in the Nazi camps, but other trends were not so easy to fathom. They came from fourteen countries, but two-thirds of them were from Poland. Was this just because more Jews had lived in Poland or was there another factor at play? Why had they decided not to return to their homes or to leave them in such large numbers?

This is also the story of those who helped the Jewish survivors on their way out of Europe. That journey began in eastern Europe where the Jewish partisan and poet Abba Kovner came to the conclusion that there was no future for his people in their traditional homelands after he had witnessed the murder of the Jews of Vilnius. His partisan group began to look for an escape route to Palestine and in the process linked up with a unit of the British Army, the Jewish Brigade, which had been recruited in Palestine and which fought their way up Italy. When they realised the extent of the horrors of the Holocaust, the Brigaders disregarded army commands and set out to help the survivors in eastern Europe.

But Kovner was consumed by a thirst for revenge and failed to realise his dream of uniting the survivors into a single group with one voice. That task fell to an unlikely Moses—a 30-year-old bespectacled American army chaplain called Abraham Klausner. Klausner found an ally in a young doctor, Zalman Grinberg, who had survived the Kovno Ghetto in Lithuania and Landsberg concentration camp, a sub-camp of Dachau. Under the guidance of Klausner and Grinberg there was a Jewish revival in the American-occupied sector of Germany and the survivors found their voice. Klausner also became the linchpin between the survivors flooding out of eastern Europe and the Jewish Brigade, which helped them travel on to Italy.

Across the Alps, the Milanese Jewish leader Raffaele Cantoni, another forgotten Jewish hero, set up the infrastructure that would accommodate the 70,000 Jewish refugees who crossed into Italy in the aftermath of the Holocaust. Few had any desire to stay there and the vast majority were determined to get to Palestine even if that meant making the journey in a dangerously overcrowded, illegal immigrant ship.

That final journey was made possible by the two secret agents who waited for the *Wedgwood* to arrive in Vado in June 1946. Yehuda Arazi and Ada Sereni were a highly effective pair of conspirators and under their guiding hands thousands of survivors set sail for Palestine.

The Holocaust plays into contemporary politics, and that is why I decided to pursue this story on foot, not in an archive, because there are stories about the present here, not just about the past. In order to understand what made these people leave Europe, I visited the places they had left behind to discover what had happened there and to find out how they were remembered.

To my surprise, as I travelled the route of their exodus, I discovered that from Kaunas in Lithuania to Arenzano in Liguria there were people just like me uncovering the survivors' stories. And it mattered to them, not just because they wanted to give the survivors a name and a face and to restore their humanity, or set the historical record straight, but because they felt that telling this story was simply an important thing to do and could change the world around them for the better.

OUT OF THE EAST

1

RIVNE

BANDERA'S VICTORY

It is late February when the train pulls out of Kiev's central station. The
snow is starting to fall. The train's carriages rattle and roll along the tracks,
past large fields waiting to be sown and through dense forests and spindly
glades where bare trees are dressed in thick balls of mistletoe. I am heading west to Rivne. It is now a Ukrainian city but was once in Poland.

Rivne was the first city in Poland to be liberated by the Red Army in
February 1944 and was then known by its Russian name of Rovno and its
Polish one of Rowne. Unlike the surviving Jews in Soviet Ukraine to the
east, the Jews of Rivne were at this point regarded as Polish citizens, as
Rivne had, in 1939, been part of pre-war Poland, so, as far as the Soviet
authorities were concerned, survivors here were free to do as they wished.

I am making the journey to Rivne because this is where the story of
the people on the beach in faraway Liguria begins. Here a small group of
influential partisans decided that there was no future for the Jewish
people in Europe and took it upon themselves to organise an escape
route to Palestine. That exodus is known by its Hebrew name of Ha
Bricha, the Flight.

I am also here to discover the story of Yitzhak Kaplan. He is one of the
3,000 survivors out of the 37,000 Jews who lived in Rivne at the outbreak
of the war. He was just 16 when he sailed on the *Wedgwood*. Knowing that
the story of the Bricha starts in Rivne, I have looked for him again and
again, typing his name endlessly into the Internet search engine, but so far
he has eluded me. I know that I need to find him, as my plan is to travel to
Israel and talk to the last of the *Wedgwood* people who are still alive and to
record their stories before it is too late. But first I have to find out what

11

that story is. As Kaplan was one of the youngest people on the ship, there is a strong possibility that he might still be alive. But there is no guarantee that he even lives in Israel or is still called Yitzhak Kaplan for that matter. Why did he decide to leave? Was it simply impossible to stay in a place where your friends and family had been murdered or was there something about the post-war world that made him decide he had no future in eastern Europe? I hope Rivne will provide some answers.

The train stops at Berdychiv, almost 200 km to the west of the Ukrainian capital. It is the birthplace of the Soviet journalist Vasily Grossman, the author of the epic novel *Life and Fate*, published in the West decades after his death. The book's accounts of the Holocaust are unforgettable. Grossman made his name by following the Red Army on their assault westwards towards Berlin and spent years reporting from the front lines. Kiev was liberated in November 1943 and there Grossman heard the stories of the massacre of 33,771 Jews at Babi Yar, which had taken place in September 1941 in a ravine on the outskirts of the city. The offensive westwards from Kiev was launched on 24 December 1943 and, after heavy fighting on 5 January 1944, the Red Army arrived in Berdychiv. Grossman interviewed eyewitnesses, both the few Jewish survivors and Ukrainians. He was shocked to discover the major role that his former Ukrainian neighbours had played in the murder of his mother, his relatives and the thousands who lost their lives in Berdychiv. Although Stalin's policy towards the Jews was changing as the war came to an end and he was to become more and more anti-Semitic in the years to come, he had previously permitted the establishment of a Jewish Anti-Fascist Committee. It was under its auspices that Grossman and fellow writer Ilya Ehrenburg began to collect testimonies from survivors for what was to become their *Black Book* chronicling the fate of Soviet Jews at the hands of the Nazis.

It seems appropriate to travel into such a dark story in the pitch black of a cold winter's night. I watch the blue dot on the map on my mobile phone to track the route as the train shudders on. After recapturing Kiev, it took the Red Army a month to reach Rivne. It takes me three and a half hours by train from Berdychiv.

The Battle of Rovno was fierce and left much of the city in ruins. On the night of 4 February 1944, the partisans, who had links to the Red Army, were the first to arrive. Among them were about 500 Jews. In town there was chaos. Rivne stood in the borderlands of eastern and central Europe. Poles, Ukrainians and Soviets were all keen to claim ownership here and of the surrounding countryside. Bandits and partisans scoured the villages. Followers of the Ukrainian nationalist Stepan Bandera murdered Jews along with Poles.

Borders have often moved in this part of the world. When Hitler and Stalin invaded Poland in September 1939, Rivne was in Poland, but according to a secret clause of the Molotov–Ribbentrop Pact that Nazi Germany and the Soviet Union had signed in August, Poland was to be divided between them. By November the Soviet zone was annexed to the USSR, but it was then lost to the Nazis when they attacked the Soviet Union in June 1941. At the Tehran Conference of the Allies in 1943, Stalin demanded that, in the post-war dispensation, this territory should be part of the Soviet Union again. However, at the time of liberation in 1944 these lands and the people there were briefly recognised as Polish again, until 1945, when most of them were formally reincorporated into the Soviet Union at the Potsdam Conference; Poland was compensated with former German lands to the west and in East Prussia. It is a complicated story, but in this way Rivne became part of Soviet Ukraine and, when the Soviet Union collapsed in 1991, part of independent Ukraine.

Immediately after the liberation, a small group of about thirty partisans chose to stay in Rivne as the Red Army continued to roll westward. They took shelter in the synagogue on Shkolnaya Street. I have read the story recounted by the Israeli historian Yehuda Bauer of two brothers among the partisans, Abraham and Eliezer Lidovsky. They had grown up in the tiny village of Zhetl, now in Belarus, where their father was a carpenter. Both men had been campaigning Zionists before the war and had had close contacts with Zionist activists in Warsaw. The war had not changed their views but rather reinforced their convictions. Eliezer Lidovsky had lost his wife and two children. Rivne was a dangerous place and the brothers did not take long to come to the conclusion that life for Jews in the area was a practical and psychological impossibility.

On 17 March 1944, the Lidovsky brothers called a meeting with the other partisans at the home of Dr Erlich, a partisan battalion doctor and now director of the hospital in Rivne. Here they laid out their plan for taking the survivors to Palestine. Most of their fellow partisans thought that they were crazy to consider such a move while the war was not yet over. Dr Erlich's home served as a kind of community centre and most Jews who passed through Rivne went there. It was also the nerve centre for the rescue of Jewish children who had been hidden during the war or had survived by living in the forests. Up to three hundred were found by

Lidovsky's partisan unit. The brothers soon became famous as the tale of Jews helping Jews became a newspaper story but, on a fundraising trip to Moscow, they were tipped off that Zionism was not compatible with the Soviet way of thinking. They decided that, despite the risk, it was best to move westward and quickly. So once they had gathered their flock, the brothers moved them to Lublin, then the acting capital of Poland. With them may have been another of the *Wedgwood*'s passengers, 22-year-old Hayah Yomshtik. Clicking around on the Internet, I have found out that she escaped a death march and had hidden in the forests. Like many local Jews, she sought safety in the city after the liberation and then travelled to Lublin in the months after the end of the war.

Although they were not from Rivne, the Lidovsky brothers acquired considerable authority among survivors in the town, who accepted them as leaders. They were well-known partisans and the majority of those who had survived the war had done so because they had been members of the various partisan groups that operated across this part of Poland. Now, after the liberation, survivors looked at each other and asked, "What next?" Where did the future lie? It was the partisans who gave them the answer.

It is significant that a number of the people on the beach in Vado who waited to board the *Wedgwood* were former partisans. Among them was 22-year-old Pesach Abramowicz. He was one of the first people on my list whom I started to search for, simply because he is almost at the top of it. I quickly found his name on the website of the Ghetto Fighters' House museum in Israel. He had fought with the Bielski brothers in the Naliboki Forest in what is now Belarus. Unlike other Jewish partisan groups, they took friends and family with them when they fled into the countryside and they moved through the forest as a virtual tribe of people, up to 1,200 in number at one point. After the liberation, the Bielskis refused to join the Red Army and led those who wanted to follow them westward. As the train rattles on through the dark, I wonder if there is a similar story behind Yitzhak Kaplan's departure from Rivne. Did he leave with the partisans?

Rivne is a surprise. Its main square is clean and tidy and the Hotel Ukraine next to the opera house is unexpectedly welcoming. I eat supper in the "Ayrish" [Irish] bar in the basement. The city is strikingly prosperous compared with other Ukrainian provincial towns. It has a Wild West feel to it and I am not surprised when I discover that the tills in its shops and smart bars are full of money made from illegal amber mining in the nearby forests.

From the Sky Bar at the top of its tallest building in the centre of town, you can see from one end to the other of Boulevard Soborna, the main street that runs from west to east. Before the Second World War, Rivne had been for centuries a thriving commercial centre. It was a predominantly Jewish city and so a lively hub of Jewish life. Some of the grand villas of the town's wealthy merchants stand as a reminder of the elegant and sophisticated Jewish community that once lived here, including what is now the Amber Museum, painted baby blue and decorated with delicate flower motifs.

At the eastern end of Boulevard Soborna, with its Stalinist and Khrushchev-era buildings, on a slight incline, stands a church with glittering domes. In the square around it, in the freezing early hours of 7 November 1941, the majority of Rivne's Jews were called together by a German Einsatzgruppe (SS paramilitary death squad), one of the many mobile units that systematically exterminated Jews in the east from July that year. The Jews of Rivne were marched out of the city to the nearby Sosenki pine forest. In an orgy of killing that lasted for two days, 17,500 adults were shot or thrown alive into a large pit that had been specially prepared; 6,000 children suffered the same fate in an adjacent pit. The slaughter is known as the second Babi Yar. The massacre was timed to be carried out before the ground froze. It was probably also no coincidence that the killing began on the anniversary of the Bolshevik Revolution. Many local Ukrainians supported the Germans as their liberators from their brief experience of what they were told was Jewish-created communism both there and in Soviet Ukraine, which had suffered through the great man-made famine of 1932–3. This "intimate" Shoah by bullets, as it is called, contrasted with the organised and industrial massacre carried out in the gas chambers of Auschwitz. What's more, their experience of communism had strengthened many Ukrainians' dislike of the Jews. The social dynamics on the ground had thus changed and were to make it too difficult for most Jewish survivors to later pick up the pieces of their lives and start again.

After the Second Word War, memorial books, known as yizkor books, catalogued the history of Jewish communities across eastern Europe. In the Rivne yizkor there is an account given by a man called Abraham Kirschner, who was not selected to make that fateful walk to Sosenki. In testimony given after the war he said:

> Those of us who had stayed behind kept meeting people who told us of that horrible night, and that in the forest lay thousands of murdered bodies. There were still some among the dead in the trenches who were still alive but who were slowly choking to death from lack of air. On the third day [after the massacre] thirteen of us drove out to the forest without our arm-

15

bands [which identified them as Jews], using a borrowed automobile. Our eyes were welcomed with a hellish sight. Thousands of bodies were already beginning to turn black in the mud. In one area there were hundreds of Soviet passports, in another an abandoned boot, pieces of human bodies. I did not find my own family, but only my beautiful 17-year-old female friend, who was lying next to her parents with a bullet hole in her cheek.

This is the horror that the people on the beach decided to leave behind. I realise that it has to play a part in the family story of the *Wedgwood*'s Yitzhak Kaplan.

Turn and look west, and the view from the Sky Bar takes your eyes across the River Uste past the former ghetto area, where the few Jews who survived the massacre, because they had jobs that exempted them from death, once lived. Across the street is the formerly Jewish-owned beer factory, the initials of its one-time owners spelt out in the wrought iron gates and fences along the red-brick building. It is still in business but no longer a Jewish firm.

Nearby on Dubinskaya Street was the home of the wealthy Mussman family. Most of the well-off inhabitants of the city lived opposite the former Polish barracks. Hertz Mussman was a mill owner who had the foresight to move to Palestine in 1934. Fania, one of the family's three daughters, was to grow up to become the mother of the Israeli novelist Amos Oz. The large red-brick building and its courtyard and outhouses is at number 29 but, oddly, a plaque commemorating the family has been placed on a small grey stone house at number 31. Vik Chymshyt, a local town archivist, a slim, intense woman in her forties, is baffled as to why the authorities and the Russian-speaking Jewish organisation who arranged the commemoration did not ask her for help in identifying the house before the visit by the novelist's daughter in 2014, when the plaque was unveiled.

It seems fitting that the surreal, haunting memories of life in Rivne that tormented his mother and that Oz described in his memoir *A Tale of Love and Darkness* are clouded in a blur. Fania was driven mad by her inability to overcome what she imagined had become of the rest of the family and friends they had left behind. She committed suicide when Amos was just 12 years old. Even if the plaque is on the wrong house, it is a positive sign to see any kind of memorial. Fania Oz-Salzberger, Oz's daughter, must have felt the same, as she said nothing when she was taken to celebrate its unveiling. The house lacks the cellar and the large gardens that figure so strongly in her father's memoir. The real house is ugly; the wrong one is much prettier if smaller. The real one is something of a let-down. The garden, kitchen garden and orchard have been concreted over and the house appears dismal and lifeless, unlike the one Oz describes in his book.

Chymshyt and I take a taxi for a ten-minute ride down the main street and out of the city to the Sosenki Forest. The Sosenki death pits also exist in a twilight zone. The taxi takes a small turning just past the brand-new showrooms that sell cars to the gangsters making money out of illegal amber mining. A padlocked bar blocks the road to the Sosenki memorial and we walk the last few metres up the hill to a concrete menorah which is not visible from the main road. From here steps lead down into the memorial park on top of the death pits. It is a surprise to see the memorial. Across Ukraine in big cities and small, there are more often than not no monuments whatsoever to the Jews who once lived there. A dead dog lies on a mound of melting snow in the centre of the small paved entrance. Perhaps it is a reminder that some in Rivne still find the memory of the dead a threat, that the Shoah here in Ukraine has yet to fade into the history books and that anti-Semitism is still an issue.

If I had survived the pit, I am not sure that I would have lingered here. Bandera and his followers, who fought both the Nazis and the Soviets for an independent Ukraine during and after the Second World War, are local heroes and there are shrines to them dotted all over western Ukraine. They were a controversial group that murdered Jews and Poles across the region in their quest for a purely Ukrainian Ukraine. It is understandable why the Jewish community decided they would not replace the sign on the main road indicating the presence of the memorial when it was vandalised. Chymshyt has an air of desperation when she explains that at school her three sons have learned nothing about Sosenki but only about the Holodomor, the man-made famine in Ukraine of the Stalin years, which did not affect Rivne because it was then in Poland. The memorial park is a depressing, bleak place. Rivne is still on the front line where history is wielded as a weapon. It is raw and frightening. It is easy to see what convinced the Jews to leave. Memories aside, after the war it was simply not safe to live here.

I have heard stories that Jewish ghosts haunt the main road. According to these tales, they can be seen walking back home into town. Chymshyt, a Russian-speaking Ukrainian who is not Jewish, helps the survivors' families trace their loved ones. She has never heard these tales. She shrugs her shoulders but says: "I feel that it isn't just the families, who now live all over the world, who ask me to identify the victims, but it is as if those who were murdered are calling out to be remembered." I have asked Chymshyt to help me search in the town archives for Yitzhak Kaplan but she has found no record of him. I understand what Chymshyt is saying. As I search and search for the people on the beach, there are occasions when, despite having input someone's name ten, twenty or even thirty times to no avail, they then suddenly appear. It is as if they have been hiding and have finally agreed to come out and tell their story.

We take the taxi back into town. The Great Synagogue still stands on Shkolnaya Street although it is now tucked away behind a shopping centre. It is a dumpy yellow building with two porticoed doors over which are two arched and elegant windows. Today, it is the Avantgarde sports centre. Chymshyt answers my question before I have asked it. No, we cannot go in. "The people inside become very angry if I come inside with Jews who are visiting. It's not a good idea." I wonder if they are worried about property restitution cases.

I ask Chymshyt about the Lidovsky brothers, the partisans who believed that the Jews must escape from Rivne to Palestine. She has never heard of them, but she has heard of the story of how the survivors and the partisans buried the Torah scrolls that they found in a big trunk in the basement of the synagogue as well as those that had been desecrated and left lying around the building. The survivors gathered them together and one of the partisans put their guns beside the scrolls and swore to remember what the enemy had done to them. "They then carried out a symbolic funeral," she tells me, and they walked with the Torahs to the graveyard through the ruined streets and there they dug a grave for them. "Many of the tombstones in the graveyard were missing," she adds. "They had been used to pave the city's pavements."

Chymshyt walks me the short distance across town to the former graveyard. She points out the indented brickwork on some buildings that was characteristic of Jewish houses. I wonder where young Yitzhak Kaplan grew up. We pass large villas that once belonged to important Jewish families and there are still a few tiny and impoverished-looking Ukrainian houses that must have stood there in 1939 huddled next to them. We arrive at the town hall, where she works, behind which rises a small steep hill. "The Torah scrolls are in there somewhere," she says gesticulating vaguely in the direction of the hill which is covered in rubbish. "The Soviets bulldozed the Jewish cemetery to make way for the city hall." I will later read that the scrolls were exhumed and are no longer in Ukraine.

In the twilight world of modern-day Rivne, it is also clear that Yehuda Bauer's conclusion that Jewish life was completely obliterated in the city and that the Jews who live here come from elsewhere is not completely true. Ephraim German runs a laundry and drycleaning business close to where the cemetery once stood. His family has lived in Rivne for hundreds of years and he is a chubby, prosperous-looking man.

The Germans were very wealthy before the war broke out. His grandmother had been in Karlovy Vary in 1939, taking a cure. The year before, this famous Czechoslovak spa town, being part of the Sudetenland, had been seized by the Nazis. So fearful had the experience made her that in 1941, before the Nazis invaded this part of Poland, she insisted that the family move to Uzbekistan. Those who did not listen to her died in Sosenki. So, German's immediate family survived and moved back to live in their large elegant house close to the synagogue, weeks after the liberation. German's parents married in 1946. His mother, another Rivne Jewish survivor, was a communist and felt that the family should stay behind in Rivne and build a socialist city. As a small boy German attended synagogue with his father, but once it was closed by the Soviets the family continued their religious life in secret.

His parents worked in the town archives and his father spent his spare time gathering details of the families who had perished in Sosenki. That archive, in Russian and Hebrew, is now in the Rivne synagogue. "It was my father's calling," he says sitting at his large brown desk in his wood-panelled, first-floor office. He has never heard of the name Lidovsky and is baffled when asked about the story of the service at the Sosenki memorial which the brothers organised and where they told those who had gathered to follow them on the long road to Palestine. "Those who stayed were not there, I suppose," he jokes. "It is not true that Jewish life died here completely. There were a number who came back, and even though people have left since, we still have five families in the city who have been here for generations. That the community is exclusively made up of those who came from elsewhere is not true."

It is time to meet the rabbi and German insists that he drive us back to Shkolnaya Street. A few metres from the Great Synagogue-cum-sports centre is a much older building that was once a yeshiva, a Jewish religious school, hence the name of the street. Today, the eighteenth-century building is Rivne's synagogue and has a congregation of about fifty. Rabbi Schneor Schneersohn meets us at the door and is keen to point out the unusual wooden mezuzah, some hundreds of years old, in the door frame before he bustles off to organise his children, who have been home-schooling on a computer in the large room that doubles as synagogue and meeting room. It is divided in two by a small screen, so men and women can worship separately. One wall is covered with a huge poster of the Wailing Wall, against which is positioned a metal tea trolley with its kettle, mugs and teabags.

We settle down at the formica table in front of the Wailing Wall. Rabbi Schneersohn's grandfather was one of the partisans who liberated Rivne, and he was a local man. The small, soft-spoken rabbi slowly recalls what his grandfather told him.

> He was in the forest with ten others and they had the feeling that they were the only ones left. They thought no one else had survived. It was just like the Torah story of Lot's daughters [who thought that everyone in the world had been killed after the destruction of Sodom], but soon, because Rovno was to Jews the capital of Jewish life in the area, anyone who had survived began to make their way here.

Those who arrived were mostly young adults and, as the rabbi explains, the most pressing problem was to find the children who had been hidden.

> Search parties went out looking for them in the forests and knocking on doors in the villages as the children did not know that the war was over and were too scared to come out. It was the same with adults as well. It was important that the children did not lose their connection to Jewish life.

Rabbi Schneersohn has been in Rivne for thirteen years; he was born in 1977 in Israel on the anniversary of the Sosenki massacre. He feels it was fate that brought him here. If anyone here knows anything about the Lidovsky brothers, it would be him, but he shakes his head and says wisely that whoever they were, they were right to tell those who were not vital for the continuation of Jewish life to leave and go to Palestine. Holding his plump hands together, he adds sagely: "Life here is like the Second Temple. When the old people saw the Second Temple they cried. They remembered the majesty of the old times, but the young people were simply happy they just had a temple." His message is upbeat, but being the rabbi in Rivne is a tough job. He explains, with a sad expression, that the job of gathering in the Jews who had survived the Holocaust was not a task that was completed in a few months, so you simply could not say that all those Jews who had lived here left with the partisans in 1944.

"People still come to me telling me that they were children who were not found. They were brought up as part of the family but, as they have grown older, they have realised that this was not the case and want to be recognised." For the rabbi the problem is that these survivors do not have any documents to prove who they are, and it leaves him in a personal conflict. "In Halachic law there is black and white but between there is a lot of grey." After the fall of the Soviet Union the Israeli authorities had to be very strict, as many people who wanted to leave came forward claiming to be Jewish. But, when he knows in his heart that people are Jewish, Schneersohn says he will do all a rabbi can do to help them.

> Those who are born a Jew have a Jewish soul and cannot stop being a Jew. A son can change his name, but he cannot change who his real father is. The catastrophe of the Shoah has not finished. I see it in Jewish life around me. All my life my grandfather searched for members of his family and maybe one day I will find them.

I ask what it is like explaining to his children what happened here. It is an emotional topic and the rabbi gets up suddenly and leaves the room mid-sentence. He returns five minutes later with a wad of paper napkins that he places on the table and then busies himself preparing a mug of hot water. I worry I have overstepped the mark but, a few minutes later, he is composed and sits down again. As he nurses the mug in his hands, he talks about the difficulties of explaining to his seven children what happened in Rivne. "I hear stories that are not in the history books. There are different levels of knowing the truth. I have heard stories that are unimaginable. Remembering is a symbolic victory over Hitler, this is why we must not forget."

At this moment his mobile phone next to the napkins vibrates and his face breaks into a smile as the news arrives that a cousin in Israel has just had a baby daughter. With renewed vigour he says: "Every time I hear these tragic stories from the war it motivates me to do more for Jewish life here." He apologises that he does not live close by and would have liked to invite me to lunch. "What can I do? We have no kosher restaurant, but now I am determined I will open one. Visitors spur me on!"

Back in the Hotel Ukraine, I start to search again for any lead on Yitzhak Kaplan. Months later I have still not tracked him down. It is late at night. "Do you really need to find him?" my husband asks. But I do. The rabbi was right. Finding him would be part of the symbolic victory over evil. I do not even know if Yitzhak Kaplan is alive. If he is and I do not carry on looking for him, he might die. I continue putting the names from the list of passengers into my search engine time and time again. Then, frustrated, and despite the fact that I do not speak Hebrew, I translate his name with Google Translate and then search anew. He is the first person I try this with. I click on a couple of irrelevant pages and then open an article from an Israeli paper in which there is a large picture of an elderly man and his granddaughter; she is in military uniform and has clearly won some kind of award. The translate button reveals her name and I discover that she lives in Haifa. I start to hunt for her on Facebook, matching profile pictures with the image in the paper. It does not take long to identify her and I send her a message with my contact details. Later that night Kaplan's son Ronan contacts me on WhatsApp.

* * *

A year after being in Rivne, I am finally in Israel. Previously I had decided that I would gather all the information I could before speaking to the survivors, so I know exactly what to ask them. Some Holocaust survivors say that people's ignorance has deterred them from speaking about their experiences and that as a result they are selective about what they choose to say.

I catch a taxi in downtown Haifa. It drives up behind the Baha'i Gardens and into the hills above town. Yitzhak Kaplan's house has a stunning view south across the coast towards Atlit, the British detention centre, where he was held when he arrived in Palestine. The living room is modern, with bright white tiles. There are pictures of Kaplan's children and grandchildren by the television. In the corner there is a table laid with cakes. "We are Polish. We have to have cakes," says Ronan, who is not only here to help with the translation but to listen to his father's story. Kaplan has never before spoken in such depth about the past, not even to his family.

Kaplan, dressed in a smart blue shirt and jeans, does not look as if he is 88. He is keen to offer me something to eat and makes coffee, while he explains he was born 15 km east of Rivne in a small village where his parents had a shop. This is probably why there was no record of him in the Rivne archives. The Kaplans were one of two Jewish families who lived in the village of Babyn. Kaplan was sent to the Hebrew school in Rivne, which was close to Amos Oz's family house. Kaplan had two brothers and four sisters. His older brother had been conscripted into the Red Army when the war broke out and was never heard of again. Although he says the family were "50–50" in favour of Zionism, one of his sisters, Chaya, left for Palestine in 1936. When the Germans invaded in 1941, Kaplan, his parents, two sisters and a brother fled before them, moving ever deeper into the Soviet Union as the Nazis advanced.

His sister Fani, however, chose to stay in Rivne to wait for her husband, who was in the Polish Army. She was one of those murdered in Sosenki along with her two small children, who were taken from her and shot at the separate death pit. In Rivne the Sosenki massacre had seemed to me like history, but now it is part of the present. What Kaplan's sister went through before she died, let alone her children, is unimaginable. I am so stunned when he tells me this that I do not stop him to ask how he discovered what had happened to them. What does become clear as he tells his story is that this is not the reason the family left for Palestine.

The warm winter sun streams in through the window as Kaplan quickly moves on to tell me how his surviving family was torn apart by the war. His father fell sick and died, and his other brother became a pilot in the Red Army. He would not see him again until the 1980s. Kaplan had wanted to enlist too, but a broken wrist changed the course of his life. He did not become a Red Army soldier and a Soviet citizen like his brother. "In the summer of 1944, the war was finally over in Rovno and my sister Pola, who was 25, decided that she would go back to find out if it was safe to return." He speaks slowly and matter-of-factly. "There she met and married a partisan, Iser Glazer, who had lost his family. He was one of the partisans who had liberated the city. It was dangerous to travel, so she sent her new husband to come and collect us. One day he just appeared. We had no idea he was coming or who he was." Nevertheless, the remaining members of the family returned with Glazer. They intended to go home and carry on with their lives. It was, however, too dangerous to go back to their house in Babyn, lest they be lynched by their former neighbours. "The village was full of Banderists and someone else was living in our house," Kaplan tells me. Many decades later Kaplan was to return to the village again, only to discover that the house had been destroyed and, where it had once stood, there was now just an empty lot.

Rejected by their neighbours, the Kaplans decided to start a new life in Rivne. It is clear that the story that the Lidovskys led all the Jews out of the city is something of a myth. Glazer, who was now head of the family, was hopeful that they could build a future in Rivne. Kaplan makes it clear that as the months passed, his brother-in-law decided that the family had no choice but to leave because everyday life was simply too dangerous. In the early spring of 1945, a few months before Rivne reverted to formal Soviet rule, while it was still possible to leave, they decided to try to reach Palestine. Their personal story reflects the larger one for Jews as a whole in Rivne. It was a place where it was not safe to be Jewish in the years after the war.

There were no survivors from the death pits in Sosenki that I have heard of. Yitzhak Kaplan cheated death and now sits across the table drinking a cup of Nescafé in his bright, sunny living room. It is a victory to record his story here. This is a hunt, not just for the names of those who sailed on the *Wedgwood*, but for their faces, their personalities and their humanity. It is Purim in a few weeks' time. The festival celebrates how Queen Esther saved the Jews in another close call with annihilation by the Persian Empire in the fourth century BC. Kaplan urges me to eat a hamantasch before I leave. It is a biscuit eaten at the celebrations, which are full of triumphant fun and merry-making.

2

AUSCHWITZ

WHO IS FOR LIFE?

I always said I would never go to Auschwitz. I had my own picture of what happened there in my mind's eye. I had read books about it; I had seen the movies just like everyone else. But being surrounded by a culture of Holocaust memory does not necessarily equate to an understanding what happened in the Shoah—far from it—even if members of your family met their deaths in the horrors of the Second World War.

In Rivne the Jews died in a hail of bullets, but in what is modern-day Poland many were murdered in the death camps. Alongside these were a plethora of forced labour camps. This journey through the industrialised mass murder of the Holocaust and meeting those who survived is a history lesson unlike any other. It teaches me much about the people who founded the State of Israel. It is a lesson in the importance of oral history. The camps of Sobibor and Belzec are rarely mentioned because they have no survivors. It is testimony that keeps history alive, and only by speaking to those who endured the Holocaust can we actually begin to understand it.

The wild, untamed River Bug, designed by nature to soak up floodwaters, slips into marshy woodland and forms a natural border between Poland and Belarus. Today this is a real political frontier where the European Union comes to an end. Across the water, Belarus is in a world of its own, yet until the end of the Second World War much of it was part of the Polish heartland and there was no border here at all. Away from the river, the pretty, low-lying spindly bushes give way to russet-trunked pines and sandy groves. An empty road winds through the tall trees to a small village clustered around a lonely little siding 96 km east of Lublin. The station at Sobibor was built after the war but the tracks that cut through the forest are original. They come to an abrupt end next to the village.

The Sobibor death camp opened in March 1942 but began work in earnest in May. It was a surreal, systematised world where people were quickly herded from the cattle trucks, then stripped naked, even shorn of their hair, and funnelled into gas chambers pumped full of carbon monoxide. In the *Black Book*, Ehrenburg and Grossman record the story of a German guard, a boxer from Berlin who could slay a man with one hand, but who patted the naked children on the head as they walked into the gas chamber and even gave them candy.

Branches were woven into the perimeter fence and the camp was surrounded by both a minefield and flocks of geese that were stirred up to create a cacophony while the slaughter was carried out, in the belief it would hide the reality from the local population. It failed, and the Jewish underground soon had word of what was happening.

By July 1942, 100,000 Jews mainly from the Lublin region had lost their lives in this hellhole. Some of the 34,313 Dutch Jews brought here are commemorated along a walkway through the trees lined with small rocks on which little plaques, the type you see on park benches, record their names. I wish I knew more of the only Dutchman on the *Wedgwood*, Leo Oberstein, who was 47 years old in 1946. Moments before death, the western Jews were asked to write postcards home. It was a trick to reassure them and make them believe that there was a future for them here, and it meant they made no fuss as they did not realise that death was around the corner. In all it is thought that 250,000 people were murdered at Sobibor until a Jewish rebellion prompted the camp's closure in 1943. The gas chambers were quickly demolished and covered by an asphalt road; trees were planted to disguise the site. When the Red Army arrived in this part of Poland, there was nothing to see and no reason to make a diversion into the lonely forests where few people lived.

Although the rumours of the murders at Sobibor were well known and the uprising was quickly documented by testimony of what had taken place, Sobibor still seemed like a sick man's dream in the winter of 1944– 5. In the post-war population exchange that began in the following months, in which Ukrainians were sent east and Poles moved west, the former were housed in the barracks of the old camp's guards, which were then demolished in 1947. Until the 1960s the site was abandoned and forgotten. When I arrive, two tractors are clearing a site for a new visitors' centre, and where the gas chambers once stood in a forest glade there is now a mound of ashes covered artistically in white stones. Sobibor is slipping out of the mist and is being memorialised. Standing on the side of the railway tracks, I can almost see the people being unloaded from the trains.

Two hours south along the road, past endless small villages and lakes, is Zamosc. When Poles talk about the Holocaust, especially those who are keen to record it and remember the Polish Jewish culture that thrived in their country for generations, they invariably talk about what they have lost. They talk about a Poland that was once open and multicultural. The map of Europe is still scarred by the Cold War and the centre of European life has yet to fall back on its central European axis. To compound this, modern-day south-eastern Poland is in a nowhere zone on the edge of the EU and is populated almost exclusively by Poles. It is easy to assume that this is the way things have always been. Five minutes in Zamosc, however, shines a bright light on Polish history. This small, compact town would feel at home on the plains of Lombardy. Zamosc was designed for the nobleman Jan Zamoyski as the ideal Renaissance town by the Italian architect Bernardo Morando in 1580. It was his private fiefdom and sat on an important trading route between the Baltic and the Black Sea. It had a cosmopolitan population including Armenians, Germans, Greeks, Italians, Jews and Scots. Records in the town hall show that officials were busy learning Hebrew in the seventeenth century, as it was important for trade. The town's beautiful Renaissance synagogue has been carefully restored but is used as a visitors' centre as there is no minyan—the required ten men for worship; the handful of Jews here pray at home, if they pray at all. In 1939, 45 per cent of the people of Zamosc were Jewish, and this was the birthplace in 1871 of the radical socialist Rosa Luxemburg. Here Nazi occupation policy, above and beyond murdering 12,000 of Zamosc's Jewish citizens, was to drive the Poles off their rich fertile fields and give them to German settlers. A few hundred Jews survived the war in the Soviet Union and fifty in the city itself. Two of those survivors, Hinda and David Korenbilt, sailed on the *Wedgwood*. This is all I know about them despite hours of searching and emailing organisations in Israel and even their family. Zamosc is a closed book.

From here the main road to Ukraine leads south to Tomaszow Lubelski, a nondescript town that was also once part of the Zamoyski empire and is named after its founder's son. In the suburbs is the site of the Belzec extermination camp, which was a template for those to come. It stands on the main road to Lviv. Local trains pass by between the road and the camp, which was deliberately built right next to the mainline between Lviv and

Lublin. Nazi extermination sites are not all the same. This one is just the size of a few football pitches and must have been such a scene of intense activity that no one passing by could have failed to notice it. When experimental gassing was carried out here in February 1942, the victims had little idea of what awaited them. As the murder machine began to work in earnest, selections were made on the station ramp. As the weeks passed by, the victims arrived knowing more and more about what was going to happen to them, and the unloading and processing became increasingly frantic. By December, 500,000 people had been consumed by the killing machine. This was the fate of many of the families of those who sailed on the *Wedgwood*. It is thought that fewer than ten people escaped from Belzec. Only two gave any testimony of what had happened there. One of them was murdered after the war and another made it to the safety of Canada.

Although the Germans had at first made no attempt to hide the camp, at the end of 1943 it was decided that it would be destroyed and the evidence eradicated. Holocaust denial began in the Holocaust itself. Where the camp had been, the Nazis built a new country house with landscaped gardens and planted crops around it. Belzec remained like this until the 1960s when a small memorial was erected in what, by then, was a run-down park. In 2004, Belzec edged back into the national consciousness. A museum was opened, and an imposing memorial was built on the site of the camp, which is covered in twisted wire and industrial slag. It rises up a hill, and a straight path is cut through the middle. It follows the original path to the gas chambers, which had proved a design flaw. It was too easy for the victims to see where they were being taken and this is the reason why at Sobibor the path twists in order to conceal the destination. There was no return from Belzec, and without a core of survivors the camp has found it hard to attract people and it gets few visitors. There are no widely available or bestselling memoirs written by survivors of the camp. It has no Primo Levi. As a result, it does not figure in popular culture and, like many aspects of the Holocaust, is a forgotten story. The museum and the monument have failed to change the tide of history. When I visit, two elderly couples and a family peruse the exhibits but the guards are relaxed and chat over tea. There is little to keep an eye on here.

Although Belzec and Sobibor are now little known, the Polish Jews had no illusions when they arrived at the death camps. There were often episodes of violence as they fought for their lives. The existence of the camps was common knowledge—brought out of Poland by the underground—and the Allies were aware of them too. But what was it like to survive the camps?

Were these survivors different from Yitzhak Kaplan, who had spent the war in the Soviet Union, or from the partisans who had fought for their lives? Were these survivors destroyed as people by their experiences?

Looking for an answer, I drive on to Auschwitz. The place swarms with tourists. Cars and coaches fill the carparks and locals quick to make a few zlotys try to divert day-trippers from the free parking to their private paying lots. Next to Auschwitz-Birkenau, the heart of the killing machine, is a carpark and visitors' centre that looks like a motorway service station. Under the umbrellas outside the cafe you can gaze at the huge stone gate. At its height the camp housed well over 100,000 people. Here the Nazis gassed or otherwise murdered at least a million people, the vast majority of them Jews. Tourists queue for hours in high season at the main entrance of Auschwitz I—to see this part of the museum you must join an official tour. But the most significant part of the complex, Birkenau, is off on a limb and there are no queues.

Despite the fame of Auschwitz today, the news of its liberation struggled to make it onto the front pages of newspapers in January 1945. The liberation of Majdanek the previous summer had been covered in the Soviet press and a trial had quickly followed, but Auschwitz was largely ignored. The Soviets had no interest in highlighting Jewish suffering, and so the Red Army's arrival in Auschwitz was treated as an incidental event in the push westwards.

Auschwitz is a huge complex and is made up of three large sites: Auschwitz I, the original camp which was a political prison and labour camp; Auschwitz II-Birkenau, which was both a concentration camp and the main extermination camp; and Auschwitz III-Monowitz, which was a labour camp attached to the IG Farben factory. Auschwitz also had 45 satellite camps, which meant that it was the largest of the Nazi concentration camps, but it is not only the size of the place and the enormity of the crime that attract the visitors. Auschwitz has not been forgotten, because the mass murder here was an international event. People were brought from all over occupied Europe, and when it was all over there was a significant number of survivors left to tell the story of what had happened.

It is not just the memory of Auschwitz that needs preserving. There is also a fight to save the buildings. Auschwitz was not built for posterity, and in the months after the war, 200 of the wooden barracks were taken down so that the materials could be used for reconstruction. Fearful that the evidence of what happened would disappear, Polish survivors took the initiative and set up a museum in June 1946, and a group of guards was organised to protect the former camp from looting. The museum centred on the original camp at Auschwitz I, where political prisoners had been held. It received 100,000 visitors in 1946 alone, mainly Poles. It was officially opened by a decree of the Polish parliament in July 1947, and since then 44 million people have come here. Auschwitz is also unique as a historical site for the sheer number of personal items that need to be preserved. Scientists in white coats battle to preserve suitcases, keys and clothes while archivists scan yellowing documents and work to preserve the crumbling paper that chronicles the horrors. Money is a constant challenge, but all the cash in the world cannot preserve the seven thousand kilograms of victims' hair that is brittle and fading. It will soon turn to dust.

The museum tour of Auschwitz I that I join is extensive but takes a break before it moves on to Auschwitz-Birkenau. Visitors are told that they can catch the shuttle bus and join the guide there. I drive. Within moments, I am overwhelmed by the heat and the size of the place and sit on some steps to recover. I find myself looking at the famous ramp where the trains from all over Europe arrived, but I overhear a number of tourists ask each other what they are looking at. They ask: "What is this place? Haven't we just toured the camp?" Even here there is not enough being done to tell the truth and spell out exactly what happened. I retreat to the cafe in the carpark. Many of the people who made it to Vado had the distinctive bluish numbers of an Auschwitz prisoner tattooed on their arms, but the visit has not brought me any closer to understanding what I've seen.

I buy a copy of Primo Levi's *The Truce* in the bookshop. The 25-year-old Italian chemist was in the "Infectious Diseases Ward" running a high temperature with scarlet fever when the Russians arrived at Auschwitz. His simple prose captures the emptiness of the moment.

> The first Russian patrol came in sight of the camp about midday on 27 January 1945. Charles and I were the first to see them: we were carrying Somogyi's body to the common grave, the first of our roommates to die. We tipped the stretcher on the defiled snow, as the pit was now full, and no other grave was at hand: Charles took off his beret as a salute to both the living and the dead.

> They were four young soldiers on horseback, who advanced along the road that marked the limits of the camp, cautiously holding their sten-guns. When they reached the barbed wire, they stopped to look, exchanging a few timid words, and throwing strangely embarrassed glances at the

sprawling bodies, at the battered huts and at us few still alive … They did not greet us, nor did they smile; they seemed oppressed not only by compassion but by a confused restraint, which sealed their lips and bound their eyes to the funeral scene.

Some of the prisoners covered their heads in shame and wept. The liberation, Levi recalled, "rang out grey and muffled" and was accompanied by a desire to wash the memory away and by an "attack of mortal fatigue". The book is called *The Truce* because after the liberation, that fatigue slipped away and the survivors embarked on a second round of fighting for their lives when, imbued with the Zionist dream, they arrived in Palestine. Despite the promise of the Balfour Declaration that the Jews would be given a home in Palestine, the survivors found that the British had left them alone to fight for it.

* * *

It is only six months later that I begin to understand the story of what happened at Auschwitz. I am on a bus in Israel on the way to a small hilltop village called Karmei Yosef. It is January and the weather is stormy. When I realise that it takes half an hour to walk up the hill from the main road where the bus has dropped me, I decide it is time to hitchhike. Within seconds a young woman in her thirties picks me up. She asks me where I am going, but there is no mobile signal here, so I cannot check the address. I tell her I am here to see a man called Dani Chanoch. She knows who he is and tells me he spoke at her school. Everyone knows where he lives.

Chanoch is the youngest person who sailed on the *Wedgwood*. He is a miracle survivor. He greets me outside his house with a warm handshake and reminds me that it is 18 January, the anniversary of the day he was death-marched out of Auschwitz. He is smiling and affable as he ushers me into his messy office at the top of the house. "It's an archive," he says pointing at the shelves. "I have records of everything here." The wind whistles round the building.

Chanoch was born in 1933 in Kovno in Lithuania into a wealthy family. His father owned a factory and they lived on the pretty picture-postcard main square opposite the town hall of what is now known as Kaunas. His life was, he says, "like living in a candy box" and I wonder, even as he tells me that the family were Zionists, if he and his older brother would ever have left had the Nazis not invaded. In the first days of the German occupation, which began in 1941, Lithuanians killed and murdered Jews at will. It was too dangerous for the family to go out, but Chanoch with his Baltic looks and blond hair was sent to collect food and run errands. "I saw it with my own eyes," he says, "I saw what they did."

The Jews of Kovno were rounded up into a ghetto and, in a series of selections, murdered in the Tsarist-era forts that surround the city. Before one such selection targeting the children, his brother Uri, who worked for the underground, warned him what was going to happen and told him to hide. Dani was discovered. When Uri saw his younger brother in the clutches of a German soldier, he thought he was going to die. Somehow Dani managed to wriggle out of the German's grip and fled as the soldier fired shots at him. Uri was stripped naked and beaten but refused to say where his younger brother had gone. "This was the moment that changed me and when I realised that I had to fight to live," Chanoch says. He is a tall, thin man with small shining brown eyes. His comment says much about what formed men like him, the generation who became the first Israelis.

When the Kovno Ghetto was destroyed in July 1944, the Chanoch family was deported. "At Stutthof, they decided to hide me with the men as it would give me a chance to stay alive. This is the point that the family ended. I did not say goodbye to my mother," he says. "But if you want to survive, if you want to stay alive, there is no time for pain or sorrow." Perhaps this is why so many survivors like Chanoch did not talk publicly about their experiences until they knew they really had survived, when they retired and their children were grown—when they had lived life to the full.

In Stutthof Chanoch's mother and sister left the train and the men were taken to a sub-camp of Dachau in Landsberg. "We thought we were lucky as we were in a labour unit and I got a job in the SS kitchen, but they decided that we young boys were unfit for work and they took us in trucks to Dachau and then by train to Auschwitz." There were 131 boys in the group. They were ghetto kids who knew each other. Chanoch does not know why they were not immediately gassed, but instead put to work on the ramp emptying the cattle trucks of the bodies of those who had died on the journey along with the belongings that the people had been told to leave behind. Chanoch was 11 years old. One transport brought his father to be gassed, but at the time he had no idea of this.

At first I think his story illustrates the randomness of survival, but as we eat the classic Lithuanian Jewish kranz cake I am corrected. Chanoch escaped two selections on Rosh Hashanah and Yom Kippur in which 90 of the children in the group were murdered. "The high holidays were the selection season. Once they came with a stick and, if you were shorter than the stick, that was it." He tells me: "We tried to hide those who were too short. We were all friends and we had a solidarity. You survive if you keep together. We watched the whole group. Thirty-eight of us survived and they took us to a corner of hell called Gunskirchen, where we were liberated. We witnessed cannibalism, everything. We were guarded by 16-year-old Nazi girls who were terrible, but we watched each other's backs and during this period no one died."

Chanoch is feisty and a bit of a showman. "I have a BA, you know! A Bachelor of Auschwitz," he jokes. But it is not a joke—it is an explanation. It is the answer to the question why this young boy had no home to return to when the Americans arrived, why he had to find a new place to call home. In 2008, he retraced the route of his Holocaust experiences with his two grown children. In the film *Pizza in Auschwitz*, his daughter Miri says that he started talking to them about the Holocaust when her elder brother was born, and has never stopped. It is a funny film about a terrible subject and is called *Pizza in Auschwitz* because when her father insists on spending the night on his old bunk, Miri goes to buy a takeaway pizza so she is sure he has eaten something. The viewers see him lying on his bunk eating a slice of pizza.

Over coffee in his high-ceilinged, whitewashed sitting room Chanoch tells me he is writing a thesis for his degree at the Hebrew University, on solidarity. "It is the key to survival," he says. "There is no one who survived without support and solidarity, without help." Being able to make friends in the first place is also a key to surviving. Studying for a degree at 85 is part of his determination to achieve what the Nazis tried to stop him from doing.

Chanoch is a funny and warm person and knows everyone involved in Holocaust commemorations. Back in his office we are soon on the phone to his contacts. He has a cheeky smile and he offers me a glass of tequila. He has a large bottle in the cupboard of his desk. I feel bad that I decline the offer. Life is about enjoying things. You can pass through hell and laugh at a joke. He returns to the theme of his thesis. "You know, not one of us died from January to May 1945, because we stuck together," he says before we move on to talk about how he found his brother Uri, which is a story that belongs later in this book.

Chanoch offers me a lift to Ramlah bus station. I am in a hurry to catch the last bus back to Tel Aviv before Shabbat starts. Before I leave, I say goodbye to his wife, a psychologist, who is busy working at her desk in the sitting room. I thank her for the coffee and say I hope that I did not disturb her. She takes my hand and says: "Thank *you* for coming. Talking about the Holocaust keeps him going. It keeps him alive."

Chanoch decides not to take the main road but to drive through the woods to show me the flowers. I wonder how many there can be in January. We pass a monument made of bricks from Auschwitz. "I am one of the founders of Karmei Yosef. It is our village," Chanoch says proudly as the car winds down a country road to a graveyard. The car is making a terrible noise and we stop to inspect the back wheel. "This is where I am going to be buried. I wanted you to see it. I have even already staged my own funeral here," he says. That is exactly what he means—he has had a mock funeral service. I can see he likes shocking people. "I want to know exactly where I will be buried and what will happen to me. So many did not. My family did not have the luxury of a grave." There are no flowers in the woods. He brought me here to show me his grave. This is the lesson of the ramp he wants me to learn. Chanoch is grandfatherly and calls me later to check that I made it back to Tel Aviv safely. When he hangs up I wonder if he is unique in retaining his zest for life and an ability to be himself. I soon find out he is not.

It is discovering the story of the *Wedgwood*'s Eliezer Eisenschmidt that really makes me realise I had a false, sanitised memory of Auschwitz, which I have been protecting by saying I would not visit the camp. It has until now prevented me from understanding how the survivors were affected by the camps. Eisenschmidt must have stood out among the people on the beach waiting for the *Wedgwood* to come to shore. He was a 26-year-old man with completely white hair. Eisenschmidt, who had been transported with his family, was brought up in Lunna near Grodno, then a small Polish village, which is now in Belarus. His father had taken it as a good sign that the train did not turn in the direction of Treblinka. It was December 1942. Eisenschmidt was detailed to work in a Sonder-kommando; that is, he was forced to work in the undressing rooms, clean the gas chamber and incinerate the bodies. He was interviewed twelve times by Gideon Greif for his book *We Wept without Tears*. It is an account of the surviving Sonderkommando members' stories. Eisenschmidt's first job was to load carts outside a building, with what he was not told. Then the doors opened. "A dead woman stood there, naked, her body doubled up. We froze. We couldn't grasp what was happening there. We saw the bodies in the gas chamber. When we began to remove the bodies, we saw how they'd become a single mass." At first he was too revolted to touch them. "Such a thing had never happened to me … I couldn't work until someone hit me hard on the back with a rod. Then I realised that there was no escape, that I couldn't back away." It took Eisenschmidt years to talk openly about his experiences and then hesitantly, as many people regarded the Sonderkommando members as criminals after the war.

In October 1944, Eisenschmidt was part of the Sonderkommando uprising and was one of the few survivors. He owed his life to a Polish family who nursed him back to health after he had been shot in the leg escaping from a death march in the last months of the war. Gideon Greif found Eisenschmidt optimistic and funny. The survivors I meet are exactly the same. But when I read the account in Greif's book of the murder of a group of boys in October 1944, I recall the words of the rabbi in Rivne, who told me that the more you find out about the Holocaust, the more horrific you realise it was. They were mad with fear and knew exactly what was going to happen to them. Among them were Dani Chanoch's friends. Chanoch was tall, and it was his height that saved his life. Just a bit shorter and he would have been dead when the Nazis made their selection with a stick.

In 1945, just after the end of the war, Eisenschmidt married Yehudit Wolbrom, who had also survived Auschwitz, and they sailed on the *Wedgwood* to start a new life. Eisenschmidt's memories vividly bring to life the anonymous faces of the dead. The Sonderkommando members were allowed to take what they could from what was left in the undressing room. The Polish Jews had virtually nothing, but in the bags and pockets of the Jews from further afield there was often food. The Greeks brought olives, which the Poles ate thinking they were plums, only to be shocked by their bitter taste. They also brought cornbread. The Dutch, he said, brought dainty sandwiches like the ones served on aeroplanes. As he had never been on a plane at this point in his life, I can only imagine that he came across them years later. In the early autumn of 1943 my husband's grandmother arrived in Auschwitz. She was born in Berlin and was arrested in Nice. Did Eisenschmidt go through the pockets of her coat? Did she have any idea of what was going to happen to her? Eisenschmidt said that the Greeks had no idea of what awaited them. Most of those who arrived after the long journey were disoriented, confused and ill. Of the 46,091 Greek Jews who arrived in Auschwitz from Salonika, only 1,950 survived.

Forty-two of the Greek survivors sailed on the *Wedgwood*. One of them, Moshe Ha-Elion, now 93, lives in Bat Yam, south of Jaffa. He has a smart modern flat on the fourteenth floor that overlooks the beach. The Mediterranean stretches out before us as I admire the view with him. There is weak winter sunshine and a mist is rising. Moshe Ha-Elion is tiny and slightly stooped. He has documents and books set out on the coffee table ready to show me. His carer brings tea and he starts to tell me about himself. He knows exactly what he wants to say, and it is difficult to stop him and ask a question. He picks up his memoir. It is a slim black volume. I also have a copy in my bag. It is called *The Straits of Hell*. Ha-Elion is a poet, and the title of his book comes from Psalm 116:3. He points to the words on the inside page: "The pangs of death compassed me, And the straits of Hell got hold upon me, I found anguish and sorrow." Four and a half months after the liberation, in Italy, he began to record dates and notes of what had happened to him but soon abandoned the project as the task of building a new life took over. As Chanoch has said, there was no time for pain and sorrow if you wanted to survive.

After the war, Ha-Elion met and married a fellow Auschwitz survivor, Hanna Waldman, who sailed with him on the *Wedgwood*. When he arrived in Palestine, he fought and was wounded in the 1948 war. He was a soldier in the Israeli Defence Force (IDF) for over twenty years after which he worked in the Ministry of Defence. Keeping his family safe was a priority. In the 1980s Ha-Elion decided that he must try once more to write down what he had seen and experienced. He has an impish smile and senses the absurd in the story he tells of being saved by a Polish classics professor, who was a prisoner, and who wanted lessons in modern Greek. In return he shared his food with Ha-Elion. As a political prisoner, the professor received packages from relatives, and without his help Ha-Elion is convinced he would not have had the strength to carry on.

Ha-Elion was born in Thessalonika in 1925. Salonika, as he still calls it, was one of the great Jewish cities of Europe. The Salonika Jews were different, and in Auschwitz they were considered exotic and tough. They spoke Ladino, not Yiddish, were Sephardim, and many of the men were extremely strong as they had worked as stevedores in the port. Ha-Elion's father, who had been a bookkeeper, had died in the ghetto and the family, which was made up of his grandparents, mother, sister, uncle and his uncle's wife and baby, had believed that they were going to be resettled in Poland and, in April 1943, had volunteered to go there as they thought life might be better. He tells me again and again that they had no idea what was happening to them. I sense in his account not anger but bewilderment.

Ha-Elion was separated from his mother and sister Nina on the ramp and sent to work in Auschwitz I as a labourer. "You could not comprehend the place. I was there weeks and I did not know what was going on until one day a friend pointed at the smoke and told me my family were dead." His friend, Yona Yaakov, had been at school with him and also survived to make the journey to Palestine on the *Wedgwood*. "I thought he had lost his mind, something had happened to him. I simply could not believe the Germans could do this," Ha-Elion says, leaning closer to me. I can see he is still shocked. I wonder if he knew that Eisenschmidt was on the boat. It is possible that he was in the undressing room when his mother and sister arrived at the gas chambers. Ha-Elion is a frail old man, but I do not feel it is appropriate to ask. Being polite and civilised is a victory in itself.

Not long after he arrived in Auschwitz, Ha-Elion was sent to be trained as a bricklayer thanks to the intervention of a fellow Greek prisoner, 14-year-old Jacob Maestro, who saved well over a hundred of his compatriots. Maestro spoke German and as a result got a job in the SS employment office. Maestro survived and he too sailed on the *Wedgwood*. Ha-Elion has recently received copies of documents from Auschwitz that detail how he was condemned to twenty-five lashes after it was found that he had sent a note to a girl from Salonika, who was in the women's section of the camp, in an attempt to find out if his mother and sister were really dead. It is as if he is showing me vital evidence that corroborates his story.

In his memoir he writes that his daughter simply could not understand how he had gone of his own free will to have the sentence carried out. Was he a docile victim? He later saw in Tel Aviv the man whose job it was to carry out the punishment. Ha-Elion says he does not know if he let him off lightly as this was a unique experience. "You don't know how it was if you were not there," he says. "You cannot understand the unimaginable." I am glad I did not ask about Eisenschmidt, as it would have been a foolish question, showing that I did not understand anything.

This is the problem with the story of the Holocaust as it fades into history. It is so unfathomable that it can easily be disbelieved. Ha-Elion has, since his retirement in 1996, become a tireless campaigner against Holocaust denial and sat on the board of Yad Vashem, Israel's official Holocaust memorial, for ten years. It was important to make this journey to meet him.

He talks about his liberation at the Ebensee concentration camp in Austria, and the long journey that took him to Palestine. At that point all he wanted to do was to return to Greece. Although his family were

Zionists, he says that they never thought of going to Palestine to live. He says he has pictures of the liberation. He asks if I would like to see them, much as he might be offering to show me a collection of prints or stamps. He walks slowly but steadily to his study in a small room at the back of his flat and settles down in front of a giant computer screen that dwarfs him. He has translated, maybe aptly, the *Odyssey* into Ladino. He does not answer my question about why he did this, as he is concentrating on the task at hand and is busy looking at the computer screen. He taps at a picture of survivors sitting on bunks that he has opened up. "That's me! Do you recognise me?" I do not. He chuckles and then he looks at me steadily and says in his heavily accented English, "I have written a poem for my sister." Through his large glasses he studies the enormous screen, looking for a file. He has set the poem to music. We watch a video of a beautiful young Israeli soldier singing it in Hebrew. He hums along, but I am not sure what is being sung. When the film finishes, he clicks on an English translation. There is a pause while he studies it. Then he starts to sing in a shaky, frail voice:

> The beautiful young maiden, the most beloved daughter
> to whom always her parents, all best in life they gave her.
> They bought her silken garments, with golden jewels adorned her,
> and shielded her from sadness, from crying even further.

He pauses and then selects a verse further down the page:

> One day the evil Nazis, far from her nest they stole her,
> together with her parents, they took her to the lager.
> They stayed six days in wagons, locked up by day and night,
> in darkness they remained there, without seeing daylight.

He stops and turns to me. "It's called 'The Maiden in the Lager'. You know what a 'lager' is?" I nod and he seems surprised. He is silent and looks as if he is studying the words, working out how to improve them. Out of the window the lights of Tel Aviv, its skyscrapers and beachfront, twinkle in the distance. In the sitting room he has told me that when he and his wife Hanna arrived here, he built them a lean-to shack behind a laundry where they worked on Levinsky Street.

His unsteady voice takes up the song again:

> But when to Birkenau, the camp of death, arrived,
> immediately, her fate at once was then contrived.
> They shout to her, they beat her, each hit assaults her frame,
> the number on her left arm, from now becomes her name.

I think in this part of the poem he is actually writing about himself and that he has processed the trauma in a different way from the other survivors I have met. Sitting next to Ha-Elion and listening to his faint, frail voice, I can only think what an extraordinary journey his life has been.

> *She's possibly awake? She possibly is dreaming?*
> *Her soul can hardly fathom, the terror she is feeling,*
> *in seeing guards and soldiers, the fences and barbed wire,*
> *the troops with dogs and weapons.*
> *The circumstance was dire.*
>
> *She knew, from now and onward, her life changed forever,*
> *her world has been destroyed, not free she will be ever.*
> *With evening came the darkness.*
> *She feels sad like no other.*

Everyone who was a prisoner in Auschwitz was the same: struggling to remain human and alive, to fathom what had happened to them, and to keep being who they were before. At one point Eisenschmidt found a small bag of flour in the undressing room and the Sonderkommando made matzo for Passover. By hanging onto the threads of normality, they survived.

I ask Ha-Elion if I can take his photograph. I show him the picture on my phone. "I didn't look that old even yesterday," he laughs. It is time to leave. "We must never stop talking about the Holocaust," Ha-Elion says as he holds my hand while I bid him farewell. "Never." He stands by the door waving as I call the lift. I understand that the Holocaust is a fact of life.

On the bus back to Tel Aviv I read the appendix to his memoirs in which his daughter Rachel wrote: "We were born in the State of Israel in the first years of its establishment. During our childhood you were in uniform, we were proud to be the children of an officer in the IDF, the army that protects our country and ensures our independence." Yet she continues: "We knew from pictures that you wore the striped clothes, which we had already imagined as a symbol of submission and of helplessness." The story of the *Wedgwood* is also the story of how the survivor in the striped pyjamas became a sun-tanned Israeli soldier with a gun.

3

VILNIUS

HARMATZ'S CHOICE

The question that is most commonly asked about the Holocaust is why the Jews allowed themselves to be murdered. It is a question that not only shifts the blame onto the victim but shows a misunderstanding of what actually happened during the Second World War. Many survivors have asked me, "What were we supposed to do?" It is a rhetorical question which they answer by saying that they had nowhere to run and no one in authority would lift a finger to help. Many of the local police forces were in cahoots with the Nazis. We were trapped, they say. Yet there were Jews who fought back, and not just in the Warsaw Ghetto. Resistance was far more widespread than is understood.

I drive past wild forests to Vilnius and into the heart of the Lithuanian capital to uncover the story of those who fought back and of their leader, Abba Kovner. The story of the Jews of Vilnius illustrates the link between the Holocaust and the founding of the State of Israel. The city's Jewish partisans not only took up arms against the Nazis but, under Kovner's guidance, set up the first escape routes out of Europe. Once in Palestine they picked up their guns again and fought for the State of Israel. What they had witnessed during the Holocaust and afterwards made them committed Zionists.

Vilnius is called Vilna in Yiddish and Russian, but in 1918, it had a large Polish population and was forcibly incorporated into the new Polish state in 1920. It was also one of the iconic Jewish cities of eastern Europe. Sixty-five per cent of the population were Jews. It was the first base of YIVO, the global centre for the study of Yiddish language and culture, and is famed as the home of the eighteenth-century rabbinic sage known as the Vilna Gaon.

What also matters for this story is that Vilnius was the birthplace in 1897 of the socialist and Jewish Bund movement and was also a major Zionist centre, which gave Theodor Herzl, the movement's founding father, an ecstatic welcome in 1903. The Jews of Vilnius were engaged in a major debate in the interwar years about where their future lay. For some it was in Palestine and for others it was in a socialist utopia which they would build at home in Vilnius. The divide was reflected in the lively political life of the city's youth. Socialist and Zionist youth groups were extremely popular in the first half of the twentieth century, and their members continued to meet in secret during the war. The experiences of the war and its aftermath would impact on the debate and turn many towards Zionism.

When Hitler and Stalin divided Poland between them in 1939, Vilnius fell under Soviet control, but the city was soon transferred to Lithuania, which in turn was annexed by the USSR. When Hitler broke the pact and invaded the Soviet Union on 22 June 1941, German forces took just five days to reach Vilnius. In September 1941 the city's Jews were rounded up into a ghetto in the old town.

Among them was the Harmatz family, who until the beginning of the war had led a happy and cultured family life in the small town of Rokiskis over the border in Lithuania. The family were highly educated and many of them had studied at university in Berlin and St Petersburg. Abraham and Dvora Harmatz had three sons, Zvi, Josef and Ephraim, but their family began to fall apart when Zvi was called up to fight in the Red Army and the family's factory was confiscated by the new communist authorities. Abraham Harmatz moved the family to Vilnius in hope of finding work. Once locked inside the ghetto, his world shattered, and he found it impossible to go on. He abandoned his family and disappeared. Most likely he committed suicide. Dvora Harmatz was left to care for 16-year-old Josef and 14-year-old Ephraim.

Josef Harmatz would become a leading figure in the local partisan movement and a close friend of its leader, Abba Kovner. Kovner had been part of the Zionist youth movement before the war and in the 1930s had dreamed of a future in Palestine. After the war he would become one of the first Bricha leaders. Although Harmatz would eventually sail to Palestine on the *Wedgwood*, he was an unlikely Zionist and ally of Kovner. Despite his background, the young Harmatz looked down on his family's achievements and was a committed communist. He was, he said, "infatuated with the idealism—future dreams and promises of a New World".

Despite the fact that the Soviets invaded Lithuania in 1939, his sympathies lay with the Russians and were reinforced as Jewish refugees brought tales of persecution in German-occupied territory. After the war he would be faced with a stark choice: would he stay in Lithuania and build a communist state or would he follow his Zionist friends, who were all he had left in the world?

In the ghetto the youth movements' leaders formed the United Partisan Organisation on 21 January 1942. The ghetto was deeply divided over the question of armed resistance, and more often than not it was the youth who argued that it was time to fight back. At its inaugural meeting Harmatz's future friend and ally, 24-year-old Abba Kovner, his sharp features tight and his eyes flashing, delivered what was to become a famous speech. He told the audience: "Let us not go to the slaughter like sheep. We are not strong, but the butchers can be answered in only one way: self-defence." Harmatz, who was now 18 years old, joined up immediately. Kovner was a small, wiry man with wild, curly black hair and deep brown eyes. He was a noted poet who had already been writing poetry in Hebrew before the war. He cast himself in the role of the Hebrew and Yiddish poet Bialik, whose *City of Slaughter* had blamed the Jews of Kishinev for their docility during the violent pogrom of 1903.

Yitzhak Wittenberg was the United Partisan Organisation's first leader, and when the Germans discovered its existence, they demanded that he be handed over. They took eight hostages whom they threatened to kill in his place. Harmatz was one of them and he was badly beaten before Wittenberg eventually gave himself up and committed suicide. Kovner then took over. At this point he decided that they had no choice but to flee into the forest and fight the Germans from there. The partisans who sailed on the *Wedgwood* were Jews armed with guns long before they set foot in Palestine. Browse through the passenger list at the back of this book and you will find the names of young men and women who were prepared to fight for their lives in ghettos that have been long forgotten.

Kovner had a canny understanding of the predicament he and his fellow Jews were in. In an early round-up he had seen a German soldier tear a baby from its mother's arms and smash its head against a wall, not once but three times, as the mother begged for mercy. Kovner had no illusions about German intentions towards the Jews of Vilnius, but it was the events in the Paneriai Forest that convinced him they intended to exterminate not just the ghetto but all of European Jewry. In the stories of the people on the *Wedgwood* it is clear that many other young Jews thought this as well and, regardless of their political persuasions, it turned many of them into fighters.

The Paneriai Forest, or Ponar Forest as it is called in Yiddish, is just past the airport, 16 km south-west of Vilnius. Paneriai was and still is popular with day-trippers hunting berries and mushrooms, but it is also the site of one of the Shoah's horrific killing fields. Trains clank by, eerily hidden by the trees in the dank forest. There is a steady trickle of Sunday afternoon tourists heading for the visitors' centre. The events are well documented and an enthusiastic curator in the information centre thrusts a massive book about the Holocaust in Lithuania into my hand, assuring me it is a "good *kniga*", a good book. He points to the donation box. I cover the book with my cardigan to protect it from the rain as I walk around the death pits where some 75,000 people, mostly Jews but also Poles and Soviet prisoners, were murdered between 1941 and 1943. I hold the book tight to my chest as if it can somehow protect me from the horror. It is too frightening to really put yourself there. Empathy does not work in understanding the Holocaust. One cannot empathise with the unimaginable. The Germans did not hesitate before carrying out the crimes with the help of Lithuanian collaborators. A month after the invasion, 13,000 of Vilnius's Jews lay dead in this forest; and 22,000 more had joined them before the year was out.

In their *Black Book* Ehrenburg and Grossman devote a small, piercing paragraph to Paneriai. "The Germans fell in love with the site," they write; "on the right there was a road along which the victims could be conveniently hauled, and on the left was the Vilna–Warsaw railway just a quarter of a kilometre away. From there the Germans laid rails leading to a large pit." The Red Army had dug several huge round pits during the Soviet occupation to store aircraft fuel. There are death pits across mile upon mile of eastern Europe, some marked, others forgotten, but Paneriai is one of the most important, because the eyewitness accounts that Kovner heard, of what happened in the forest, not only convinced him that armed resistance was the only way forward, but it also sowed the seeds in his mind of the belief that there was no future for any Jews in Europe.

It was an unusually cold, frosty October night in 1941, when 19-year-old Sara Menkes crawled out of a Paneriai death pit and stole back into the ghetto. Sara was not the first person to make this return trip nor was she the first to be disbelieved. The Jews hung on to the hope that those who had been taken away, allegedly to work, had been resettled in camps, and there was a general reluctance to hear what she or others had to say. She was taken to meet Kovner. Ashen and ghostly, she told him her story. Killings were still going on there in April 1943 when Harmatz was working as a ghetto policeman and was ordered with his colleagues to go to Paneriai to tidy up after a massacre. Harmatz returned to the ghetto and told Kovner what he had seen. "There were three huge ditches, full of corpses," he recalled in oral testimony given to the Imperial War Museum in London. "Dozens of additional corpses lay spread-eagled around them, helpless souls shot trying to escape. Our group was assigned to clean up all these remains and throw them into the ditch." In his soft accented voice, he says: "I saw a lot of massacres. It is difficult to see bodies with brains spread about outside of people's heads and young couples embracing in death, and mothers with their babies. These are things you can't forget."

I drive back to Vilnius trying to understand not only why partisans like Harmatz and Kovner became the first of the Jewish leaders to decide that the Jews should leave eastern Europe but also why, before they left, they had to carry on the fight and settle their scores with the Nazis. To this end the two men would, after the war, embark on a plan to kill six million Germans in revenge for the crimes that had been committed against their people. Harmatz died in 2016 just as I began my research, but he did write his memoirs and provide testimony. There is now a race against time to find the individual stories of what happened in those crucial years after the war.

Vilnius reveals little, though. The city is a chameleon that has changed its colours. Today, unlike before 1945, it is overwhelmingly Lithuanian. It is like a stage set in which new actors play their roles after the previous ones have departed, never to return. These days Vilnius is a popular week-end destination. The cobblestoned former ghetto is neatly restored and its winding streets are full of tourists on walking tours. Unsure where to go, and regardless of the drizzle, I follow one of the tour guides, who leads his flock along its narrow alleyways.

Under communism the city's Jewish heritage was erased from the history books and rarely discussed. Since the collapse of the Soviet Union, the Holocaust has been a controversial issue in Lithuania, and the role Lithuanians played in it has only just begun to be addressed. In contemporary Lithuania, locals who fought with the Germans against the Red Army are widely revered as patriotic freedom fighters. From Poland to Ukraine to Lithuania, a new surge of nationalism and pride over having broken free from communism is growing. Few have patience with narratives that depict cooperation with the Nazis as anything more than a fringe phenomenon. Whereas Western countries have been coming to terms with their wartime culpability, in eastern Europe there is persistent and widespread denial of individual or institutional complicity in anti-Semitic violence against their country's Jewish citizens during the Nazi era. What happened after the Second World War is widely ignored.

The United States Holocaust Memorial Museum estimates that 90 per cent of Lithuania's Jews were murdered during the Holocaust, and some estimates go even higher. The crimes committed by Lithuanian collaborators during the Second World War seem irrefutable, but the country's collective memory has been muddied by its anti-communist nationalism. The Soviet Union occupied the country first in the wake of the Nazi–Soviet pact and then again in 1944. Lithuania only became an independent country in 1990. Soviet crimes against Lithuanians are widely equated with Nazi crimes against the Jews and, in line with much right-wing thinking all over Europe between the world wars, many Lithuanians still associate Jews with Bolshevism. This was a strain of anti-Semitism that was stoked by Nazi propaganda.

One of the most controversial books to have appeared in Lithuania in recent years is Ruta Vanagaite's *Our People*. To research the book she travelled across her homeland with Nazi-hunter Efraim Zuroff, director of the Simon Wiesenthal Center's Israel office, and set out to prove that Lithuanians were an integral part of the Nazi killing machine. The book, which was published in 2016, was a bestseller, but it sparked a heated debate and Vanagaite has been labelled a traitor. She has received death threats, and her book has since been withdrawn from sale. The furore caused in 2018 by Polish legislation making it a crime to ascribe responsibility to Poles for crimes committed by the Nazis is part of a wider story.

But back to Vilnius. Its former ghetto is now clearly marked, but it seems that that the Jewish past is slipping into the world of postcards and kitsch memorabilia; it is not revealing any of its secrets to me. When Harmatz returned here with his son Ronel in 1994, he found it impossible to convey to him the horror of wartime Vilnius, and he left the city "empty-hearted". He wrote in his memoirs: "I could barely believe myself that it had happened … It is impossible to transport oneself back to those days when terror reigned and fear eclipsed every single day of our lives." Many survivors have said to me that often the story seems unreal even to them.

I struggle to connect with a world that no longer exists. The Vilna Gaon museum is an endless display of information boards and a scattering of candlesticks in glass cases. The Choral Synagogue, where Kovner made a famous rousing speech after the liberation at Jewish New Year, is closed for restoration. I walk along the street towards the Jewish Cultural Centre. Standing outside is Rosa Bieliauskiene, who is waiting to meet me. She is a tiny woman who comes up to my chest, and is in her early seventies. She bustles me into the centre's cafe. It serves hummus bagels and falafels. In the hope of tasting something authentic, I opt for a cherry bun. She chooses the same. We have come to meet one of the Jewish community's celebrities, 95-year-old Fania Brantsovskaya, a former partisan, who fought in the forests.

Bieliauskiene is gentle, unassuming and organised. She has arranged to meet me with forty-five minutes to spare, to make sure that I do not keep Brantsovskaya waiting. Charmingly, she is armed with a bunch of delicate white flowers for the former ghetto fighter. We have time for coffee and cakes. Bieliauskiene tells me that both her parents spent the war years in the Soviet Union. Like the Kaplan family from Rivne, many Jews in Vilnius fled eastwards when the Germans attacked the Russians. Her parents met in Vilnius after the liberation and were both convinced that the only safe place to live was in a big city, as the shtetl life they had known before the war had been wiped out and the countryside was a dangerous place. Lithuanians who had taken Jewish property, she says, had no wish to see their neighbours return.

Bieliauskiene was born in 1946, and the borders closed too quickly, once the country was absorbed into the post-war Soviet Union, for her parents to decide if they had a future there. I get the impression that given more time they would have left. She says she is surprised that I am interested in her story but is quick to answer my questions and make sure that I understand that Jewish life in Vilnius did not come to an end in 1944 and that traces of the world I am looking for still exist. Bieliauskiene tells me she was brought up speaking Yiddish in a secular household that kept the high holidays and held a Jewish identity. She is certain that the situation for Jews in Lithuania has changed for the better since the fall of communism and is almost defensively proud of the Jewish school where she teaches history. She has a sweet, almost childish face and does not touch the fruit bun in front of her but carefully wraps it in a paper napkin and pops it in her handbag before we leave, betraying her experience of the difficult communist years.

The Jewish community centre was once a school and has a grand entrance. Its big marble staircase has a sturdy polished wooden bannister that Bieliauskiene taps as we walk upstairs. "You can imagine the children

47

sliding down, can't you?", she asks me smiling, and in an instant the world of Jewish heritage tourist trails slips away and I can almost hear the childish laughter of those people on the beach who were born in Vilnius. The labyrinth of corridors passes old classrooms where they might have battled with conjugations and calculus. It leads to the Ghetto Survivors' Office. We wait outside on black plastic chairs while Fania Brantsovskaya finishes her discussions with a lady from Brazil.

The former partisan is business-like and pleased that I greet her in Russian. She is immaculately dressed in a pale green short-sleeved shirt and looks no older than 70. She is keen to talk and signals for me to take the chair across the table. She has a small H&M plastic bag in her hand, and the moment I sit down she places it on the table and takes out a photograph of her mother's family. There are sixteen people in the sepia-toned picture. They sit neatly in three rows dressed in their best clothes. She quickly runs through who they are, speaking in Yiddish as Bieliauskiene translates. In the picture Brantsovskaya is 17 years old. She wears a demure dark-coloured dress with a white collar, ankle socks and clumpy shoes. She is an attractive young woman who looks older than her years. Next to her is her sister Riva, a pretty, delicate child, on whose lap sits a cousin, a little girl with pigtails called Hinda, who was later shot in Paneriai. In the middle of the back row is her mother, Rachel. Brantsovskaya taps the picture emphatically as she talks. It was taken in 1939 and sent to family in Palestine, she tells me. It was given to her in 1990 by relatives. She is matter-of-fact as she concludes her story. Her father died in Klooga, a concentration camp in Estonia. Her mother was at the Kaiserwald camp in Riga, where all the women were drowned in the Baltic. Her mother was then 42. Her younger sister, Riva, was murdered at Stutthof concentration camp. She puts the picture back in the plastic bag designed for shoppers buying hair clips and socks.

Brantsovskaya sits back in her chair and folds her hands together neatly and begins her story without prompting. She has bright blue eyes that sparkle. She is the gate through which I can reach the world of the people on the *Wedgwood*. When Kovner ordered the partisans out of the ghetto, she was one of the first to leave. It was her job, along with eleven other girls, to make contact with Lithuanian partisans. "My friend who was to go with me had no one to say goodbye to as her family had been killed, so she sat in the library while I went home and told my mother that I was going. After half an hour she came to tell me that it was time to go." Brantsovskaya plays with her Star of David necklace as she continues with her story and does not give me time to question her about their parting. "I took a handbag, a little perfume and some soap. I attached my yellow star so I could easily take it off. So, if anyone saw me they would simply see just a girl who was out for the evening." As they left, they saw that the ghetto was surrounded by police. The hour had come. It was about to be destroyed.

In the hours after their departure, Kovner and Harmatz and their fellow partisans slipped out of the ghetto through the sewers. All of the partisans talk of the guilt of leaving their mothers, and Harmatz was no exception. In the confusion he searched for his younger brother, Ephraim. Ephraim had begged Harmatz to help him join the United Partisan Organisation but their mother had told Harmatz that under no circumstances should he do so. She wanted Ephraim to live. Ephraim was to die in the concentration camp in Klooga two days before the Red Army arrived. It was decision that would haunt Harmatz forever.

Harmatz was one of the last to go down into the sewer. "The diameter of the pipes was barely the width of our bodies," he recalled in his memoirs, "so we had to crawl on our knees, and in some areas even to slither along on our stomachs." It was a rainy day and the stench was unbearable. "Often those in front would pass out, asphyxiated by the gases rising from the water, and block the route." Many of the partisans were caught when they finally crawled out of the drains. Two of them, 19-year-old Rachel Halperin and Leibke Distal, would spend the rest of the war in concentration camps but soon afterwards would meet up with Kovner and Harmatz. Both Halperin and Distal would sail to Palestine on the *Wedgwood*.

Once the partisans arrived in the forest, they were divided into four units. Brantsovskaya tells me she spent time in the same unit as Abba Kovner. It was called Revenge, or Nakam in Hebrew. Sitting in the Ghetto Survivors' Office is like being transported back in time. She still talks about Kovner as you would about a contemporary. "Abba was not a military person," says Brantsovskaya, "but he was a very nice man and had his heart in the right place." Kovner was inseparable from his two deputies. The first was the long-limbed Vitka Kempfner, whom he was later to marry. She was famous for having blown up a German troop train, one of the first acts of sabotage of its kind, killing 200 soldiers. The second was the tiny Ruzka Korsczak. "Vitka was, in my opinion, a more heroic person and we were very close, but Kovner gets all the attention. People always ask about him," she says, dismissing him with the wave of her hand. I am sure her opinions have something to do with the fact that the female partisans often took the greatest risks because, if they were caught, it was easier for them than the men, who had been circumcised, to hide their identities. "Us girls would go to the labour camps and bring people to the partisans. We brought news to the partisans and engaged in sabotage."

One of the bravest of the female partisans was Zelda Treger, who was also on the *Wedgwood* with her future husband, another of the partisans, Senka Nisanilevich. Her story illustrates how ordinary people's lives were turned upside down by the Holocaust. She was a skinny 23-year-old nursery school teacher. When she and Nisanilevich finally settled down in Palestine, she would return to her previous job teaching little children, but in the winter of 1943–4 she carried a gun and took incredible risks working as a courier. Her blonde hair and blue eyes gave her the perfect cover.

While they were hiding in the forest, Treger was dispatched eighteen times to Vilnius to collect weapons and medicines and to gather information on German movements. She travelled alone, dodging death at each step. Disguised as a peasant with a heavy bundle, she even lugged a machine gun into the forest. Food was often taken by force from peasants in the villages, and Brantsovskaya has, since independence, been on a list of those that the Lithuanian government has considered prosecuting for war crimes. Lithuanian nationalists regard the Jewish partisans as communist collaborators because they fought alongside the Russians. These were tough women, but their vulnerability in those years is almost unimaginable, as was that of all the young women who sailed on the *Wedgwood*. It is a reason why there were more men than women on the ship.

The conditions in which the partisans lived were appalling. Forest is not a word that adequately describes the virtual jungle in which they hid. I have driven past miles of the forest on the journey here, but this particular one, Rudniki, is in another league. It is a tangle of ancient ash, birch and pine trees growing over rotting trunks and roots. The woods are home to wolves, elk, lynx, bears and eagles. The partisans, because they fought with the Red Army, were heroes in Soviet times and, as a result, theirs was a story that every Soviet school child learned. Local Pioneers, members of the Soviet communist youth organisation, were all taken here to pay homage at what remains of the old partisan bunkers. Brantsovskaya used to take visitors herself but is now too old. As the present Lithuanian government has no interest in commemorating Soviet heroes, the spot no longer appears on maps, so I am forced to hire a driver.

The road leads us past the airport and heads for the border with Belarus. In 1943 the forest was impenetrable. The asphalt road is a new addition as are the dirt tracks. The car follows one that leads to a small glade in the heart of a woodland of swampy bogs and primeval trees, called *puscka* by the locals. When Harmatz returned here in 1994, he was shocked by how it had been tamed, but our driver clearly regards it as hostile territory even now. He jumps out and runs along the pathway, returning minutes later. Leaping back into the car and slamming the door, he shouts: "Yes! This is the place." He slaps the mosquitoes biting his face. The cloud of insects is thick and we are covered with them in minutes. Bieliauskiene jokes that they are descended from those that bit the partisans, before describing the fear of betrayal by the local Lithuanian peasantry, who fought the Soviet authorities well into the 1950s.

On 1 July 1944, the Red Army finally arrived. The bombardment was intense. The ground shook and the sky lit up as if there was sheet lightning. The partisans were sent orders to join the Red Army in the liberation of Vilnius. Brantsovskaya remembers that scattered along the road were the bodies of dead Soviet and German soldiers whose boots had swiftly been stolen by the peasants. Treger was given the job of transferring the wounded partisans who had been left in the forest, lest they be found and killed by Polish nationalist partisans also operating there.

When Vilnius was liberated on 13 July, just 200 Jews remained in hiding in the city. Brantsovskaya says that when she saw a woman with a Jewish face, she would go up and kiss her. It was a wonder that anyone had survived. The caretaker in the building where her family had lived gave her photographs she had salvaged from their apartment. In the Ghetto Survivors' Office she tells me that she went around the city day after day with these pictures, asking if anyone had seen her family. "One day I met a woman who had lived in the ghetto and she told me that my little sister had survived, so every day after that I went to meet the trains. I had a ration card for a winter coat. I did not trade it in and I waited, as I wanted to buy it for my sister. But a month later I met this woman again, and this time she told me she had made a mistake and that my sister was actually dead. It was terrible—it was the second time I lost my sister. I cried so much."

In Vilnius, the ghetto was a ghostly, empty place. Kovner went to his pre-war family home at 7 Poplavska Street, which was not in the ghetto, and sat on the doorstep in desolation. A neighbour came up to him and said: "Are you still alive? We hate you, go away!" Harmatz also hoped to find someone alive, but discovering that not a single person in his family had survived was "the greatest shock" he could have had. His brother Zvi was killed during the defence of Moscow when he was 19 years old, and his mother had disappeared. After the Germans had rounded up the Jews in his home town of Rokiskis, Lithuanians looted their houses. The men were separated from the women and fought back against the Nazis. "The carnage continued for two days," Harmatz writes. "No one gave in willingly. They all resisted, but the murderers dragged them one by one, breaking their arms and legs until they had finished the crime ... These were my people."

After the war, he said, "we were free, but morale was low. Memories were painful, the war had ruined everything, and our families were no more." In 1994, when he took his son to Rokiskis to show him the house where he grew up, the owners refused to let them in. Harmatz assumed that they feared he would try to reclaim the house. "Who would ever dream of returning to a life in a graveyard?" he asked. It is important to note that Harmatz said in his oral testimony that Lithuanian cooperation with the Germans, and the hatred that some of them showed towards the Jews, "was a terrible surprise". Society had changed since 1939 and one reason he left for Palestine was that "we did not fit in anymore".

Harmatz gave his testimony in 1998 and spoke with hindsight, but in the days after the liberation the future of the survivors was unclear. Although many families across eastern Europe had possessed the blue tin boxes of the Zionist organisations into which they dropped what little they could afford to donate, not everyone was a committed Zionist with a burning desire to leave for Palestine. Harmatz himself says that at this point he was just intent on finding a job "to ensure some kind of existence". The Soviet authorities were keen to hire the partisans with communist affiliations because they trusted them. Harmatz went to work for the NKVD, the Soviet security services.

Brantsovskaya had fallen in love with a fellow communist partisan and their marriage, on 27 July 1944, was one of the first to be celebrated after the liberation. By this time, she had already been allocated a job in a government ministry. Brantsovskaya is clearly very proud that she and her husband attended the victory parade in Red Square in Moscow in May 1945. She is also keen to tell me that Kovner never said a word against the Red Army. Even though it is clear that she did not have much time for him, once she was free to travel they often met in Israel. I wonder if her ambivalence stems from the fact that he had left and she had stayed. When I ask why she did not leave, she looks steely and says: "You live in London, don't you?" I was not convinced by the comparison, but she smiles at her own joke and Bieliauskiene nods in agreement. The two women laugh and speak Yiddish, as if to emphasise that the Jewish world lives on in Vilnius. Brantsovskaya then suddenly looks tired and, before ending the conversation, she drops her guard, showing her wounds. "We waited and hoped that our relatives would come. That is why we stayed in Vilnius." After that the walls went up and for decades it was too late to leave, even if she had wanted to.

After the interview, I stop for an espresso at the McDonald's at Gedimino Prospecktas 15. It is the city's main shopping thoroughfare. Post-war life for the former partisans was centred on a private flat above what is now the fast food restaurant. It was the headquarters of the Jewish committee. Brantsovskaya has told me that here they made a list of the survivors' names, and there was a wall where people could write their names and leave messages. Testimonies were taken down according to a set questionnaire with the intention that they would be used at future trials. There was also a list at the Choral Synagogue. I will find out later that similar lists were made in other parts of Lithuania, in Kovno, now Kaunas, and across Poland. It is the first I have heard of these lists. It is revealing that no one mentioned them in Rivne. The post-war world there must have left no time for such things or no people to list on them. There was clearly a more significant post-war revival in Vilnius and a hope that Jewish life could be reorganised. These lists were gathered in by the American Jewish Joint Distribution Committee, a New York-based Jewish relief organisation, and distributed across Poland before being sent to the United States and Palestine. They are now filed in archives across the world. They are painfully simple, typed documents on now-fading brownish-coloured paper with bald headings like "Women in Bergen-Belsen". They are made up of rows of names listed alphabetically with, in some cases, a year and place of birth, but more often simply the person's age. Some lists are frighteningly short. I have searched them while trying to identify the survivors on the *Wedgwood* and have seen how difficult it is to trace someone by using them. The confusion of who was where was made worse by the fact that survivors were constantly on the move.

There was another important project that was organised in the office on Gedimino Prospecktas. To my astonishment Brantsovskaya told me that the survivors were busy setting up a museum. When I heard this, I assumed that it had been a mistake in the translation, as, under the circumstances, setting up a museum did not sound like a priority. I quickly stood corrected. Vilnius had a Jewish museum before the war and what could be preserved of Jewish culture was saved in the ghetto. The collection was still called the museum. The Nazis had not simply wanted to kill the Jews but also to eradicate their culture. Saving what remained of Jewish life in

Vilnius was a priority, and all the survivors brought objects and papers to the museum, which was opened at the end of 1944. The museum was also used as a base by one of the authors of the *Black Book*, Ilya Ehrenburg. It was he who warned Kovner that there was no future for Zionists in the Soviet Union and that he would be in danger if he stayed. Ehrenburg stored the material he gathered at the museum because he was too scared to keep it in his rooms. When the museum was closed in 1949, Brantsovskaya and her husband took these papers on the night train to Moscow as they felt he should have them. At the time, she says, she did not understand the danger he was in. The Soviet message was that the Second World War was a fight between capitalism and communism, which was defending the working class. The Nazi targeting of the Jews did not fit the narrative, and while the plates were being prepared for the printing of the *Black Book*, it was banned when Stalin adopted a virulently anti-Semitic policy.

Within weeks of the liberation, Kovner, who, at 27, was older than the others, was already reaching out to Palestine. In September 1944, the newspaper *Haaretz* published a poem of his that had reached Tel Aviv via Moscow. 'Your Heart Will Be a Lyre' had been written in the forest. At this point Kovner had two immediate goals. Firstly, to gather in all the books and important papers that had been hidden in the ghetto and, secondly, to bring all the survivors together in Vilnius. Kovner was still very much the leader, but in order to lead them to safety he had to ascertain where his people were and how many had survived. Ruzka Korsczak was dispatched to Kovno, a hundred miles west. In the shattered city Korsczak saw that the ghetto had been razed to the ground. She reported that she had come across a handful of lost and demoralised survivors who had found no lives to return to and brought tales of empty buildings, rubble and burned-out tanks.

In August 1944, Romania, which had sided with the Third Reich, surrendered to the Red Army. Suddenly the idea of escaping to Palestine became a possibility, not just a pipe dream. Kovner spent hours looking for a way out of Europe by studying maps and papers and working out the best way to get to the seaports of the Black Sea, the Adriatic and the Mediterranean. The partisan bush telegraph was still working and Kovner heard rumours that a handful of envoys from Palestine had been parachuted behind enemy lines into Romania and were now operating in the capital, Bucharest. Kovner decided that Korsczak would set out on her travels again.

It was not an easy journey. Trains stopped in the middle of nowhere as the tracks had been blown up and halted every fifteen or twenty minutes at stations or in sidings. In Rivne, Korsczak met the Lidovsky brothers, and it was decided that fellow partisan Shmuel Armant, with whom she had travelled, would return to Vilnius with news of the route so far and their plans to leave for Romania while she carried on southwards with Abraham Lidovsky. On the journey to Bucharest, surviving members of the pre-war youth groups Hanoar Hatzioni and Hashomer Hatzair, who were gathering their own people together, helped them on their way. Zelda Treger was sent to Bialystok in Poland and Lviv, now in western Ukraine, as a scout, and Vitka Kempfner to Grodno, now in Belarus.

As the winter of 1944 drew in, life was becoming increasingly dangerous as the Soviets tightened their control. After the Nazi slaughter only a handful of Jews had survived, but Stalin's attitude now made rebuilding their community even more difficult. Soviet policies also made it imperative that those survivors who were Zionists leave as fast as they could. Harmatz was ever more concerned about his association with Kovner. Despite the danger, Kovner stayed in Vilnius trying to convince the surviving Jews to join him when he finally left. He asked Harmatz again and again: "What kind of future will you face here?" Eventually, Kovner decided he had to flee to Lublin, the acting capital of Poland, until Warsaw was also liberated. In his official capacity as a Soviet NKVD officer, Harmatz gave him the necessary documents. To cross borders, special papers were needed. Kovner left just in time. As the Soviet authorities came to arrest him, he fled wearing a Polish Army uniform. Harmatz now decided to follow with Treger's boyfriend, Nisanilevich, because "the friendships created in the underground were so strong"—in other words, stronger than his commitment to communism. He had made his choice, and it was Stalinism that finally drove him out.

4

POLAND

THE HOMECOMING

The partisan leaders Kovner and Harmatz arrived in the Polish heart-lands just as the liberation marked the start for many of the Holocaust survivors of a new, heart-breaking process of finding they were unwelcome in their home towns and realising that their future lay elsewhere, most probably in Palestine.

Initially, the vast majority of survivors hoped they could return home and that they might find family members or at least some remnants of the lives they had lived before the Holocaust. But the stories of the return home are about Jews being rejected by their neighbours. In modern-day politics, as arguments rage about the role that Poles played in the Holocaust, the survivors' homecoming is an important story. Many survivors found that not only were their neighbours not happy to see that they had returned, but they had no physical home to return to. Again and again, survivors say that they left Poland because they feared for their lives and were not welcome in the towns and villages where their families had lived for generations.

But the story is not as black and white as many believe it to be. What happened after the Shoah needs to be recorded, but it also has to be understood and put in its historical context. Only then can Poland move forward.

Kovner's arrival in Lublin in December 1944 was to present the survivors with a choice. Eliezer Lidovsky, one of the partisan brothers from Rivne, was already in the city. Vitka Kempfner soon joined them and her romance with Kovner blossomed. Kovner wanted to open an escape route out of Europe and unite the survivors into one group that was capable of articulating its desires and interests. Yet, as young and dynamic as the partisans were, they had no resources. To help thousands cross borders, buy false papers and food, and sail away over the Mediterranean required money and manpower.

At this crucial point two men who could help appeared on the scene. As the Red Army rolled across eastern Europe, the Allies landed in Normandy and Paris was liberated on 25 August 1944. The scent of victory brought the American Jewish Joint Distribution Committee, a key Jewish player, back onto the game board in Europe. The Joint Distribution Committee was not a Zionist organisation, but the European operation was under the control of Joe Schwartz, a learned and ordained rabbi who had been born in Odessa but brought up in Baltimore. An elegant handsome man with sparkling eyes, in the autumn of 1944 he moved the Joint Distribution Committee's HQ back to Paris from its wartime home in Lisbon. Schwartz had a different view from head office in America, which saw the organisation's post-war brief as re-establishing Jewish communities. Schwartz saw emigration to Palestine as the only solution to the Jews' troubles in the light of the restrictions placed by the US and other countries on Jewish immigration. Although Schwartz had the contacts and the money from the Joint Distribution Committee's US revenue, he lacked the personnel who could gather survivors together and organise their journey out of Europe.

He was to find an ally in Shaul Avigur, who also arrived in Paris in the autumn of 1944. The two men were to offer the survivors a lifeline. They were the shadowy figures behind what was to become the vast escape network known as the Bricha. Avigur was the head of the organisation known as Aliyah Bet, which had been set up in 1939 by the Haganah, the underground Jewish paramilitary organisation in Palestine. To make *aliyah* means to move to the Holy Land, Eretz Israel, and at this point legal immigration was called Aliyah A. But in a 1939 White Paper the British had severely limited legal immigration into the Palestine Mandate. Nevertheless, the Haganah, despite its lack of funds, had landed 26,000 immigrants in Palestine without legal papers between 1937 and 1940, so it already had the experience to run an operation to save the survivors. Aliyah B, or *Bet* in Hebrew, was the name given to the illegal option. It was to offer survivors an alternative to living a life in persecution or choosing to hide their identity in order to survive, as many of those who remained in Poland chose to do.

As the war turned against Hitler, Avigur, an austere loner, quiet unlike Schwartz, began preparing emissaries for European missions, whom he managed to persuade the British to drop into Nazi-occupied Europe. Avigur had a finely tuned system of giving operatives in the field autonomy for on-the-spot decision-making while in theory closely supervising the overall effort from Tel Aviv and then Paris. His recruits, however, tell another story. There was a lack of instructions and briefings. It was a sink-or-swim operation. Romanian-born Yeshayahu Trachtenberg, known as Shaike Dan, who was parachuted over Arad in western Romania in June 1944, was ideally suited to this kind of leadership. Dan was born in a small, impoverished town on the Russian–Romanian border but had left for Palestine at the age of 15. The deal with London was that he would help captured British pilots escape, and once that mission was completed, he was free to do as he wished. He was a spunky character and managed to connect with local Zionist youth group activists, who were involved in rescuing Jews in Romania. In August 1944, after Romania switched sides to support the Allies, Dan started chartering boats that could take a 100 or 150 Jews out of the Black Sea port of Constanta. Dan quickly developed a network of contacts across the country, convincing people to leave. When the Red Army arrived in Bucharest on 1 September, he redoubled his efforts and chartered two more boats, the *Saladin* and the *Turos*. The *Turos* set sail in November 1944 with 900 survivors on board, among them 445 children. The Joint Distribution Committee's Joe Schwartz had paid the $3 million bill for the project.

Among the passengers were Abraham Lidovsky and Ruzka Korsczak, the partisans from Rivne and Vilnius, who had met Dan's contacts in Czernowitz and been taken to Bucharest, where they were immediately dispatched by train to Constanta to catch one of the boats. They were the first refugees to bring news of the situation in Poland. By December the pair were in Haifa, and soon Korsczak was writing her memoirs, *Flames in the Ashes*, the first Holocaust book to be published in Hebrew. In January 1945 Dan, who was on leave in Palestine, attended a Haganah meeting that was to be addressed by Lidovsky. When Lidovsky saw Dan, he hugged him hysterically. For Dan and the members of the Haganah, it was proof of what could be achieved. This was Kovner's great moment. He had a route along which he could lead his people to Palestine. But how many Jews were there left to be saved? And how many would choose to leave Europe for Palestine?

* * *

To find out I drive half an hour north-east of Auschwitz to Chrzanow. It is a journey back into pre-war Poland, now a land of the imagination that lives on in the mind of the *Wedgwood*'s Alter Wiener. He survived a string of labour camps and, like so many others, his first instinct was to return home to find out what had become of his family. The welcome that he would receive made it clear that Chrzanow was no longer his home.

In 1939, Wiener was 13 years old and was one of the 20,000 people who lived in the small town of Chrzanow. Many of them made a living working in its locomotive factory. Half the population were Jewish, like Wiener. His father was a pious storekeeper and landlord, and the family, which included his stepmother, brother and half-brother, lived in the town centre above his father's shop. Wiener and the rest of the family had fled in advance of the German Army, but his father was ordered by the authorities to stay behind and supply the military. Upon their return in mid-winter, they discovered he had been murdered. Wiener's father was shot on the street by the Germans alongside 36 others, simply to instil fear among both Poles and Jews.

Wiener later lived in Oregon on America's Pacific coast and wrote a book about his life called *64735: From a Name to a Number*. He also had a Facebook profile, and this was how I made contact with him in 2017. He replied to my Facebook message saying that he had lost his hearing but was happy to answer questions on email. We started corresponding. It was a slow but important process and I soon learned that if I asked too many questions, half of them would be ignored. I reread his book a number of times, as it is easy to miss things. Despite the obvious limitations of our communication, I began to piece his story together. The first thing that Wiener wrote to tell me was that he was still traumatised by his experiences. As he told me the story of what happened to him, I began to realise that Wiener was a man who lived in the present, and it was immediately clear that what mattered to him was the act of telling and the impact his story had.

After the founding of the State of Israel, Wiener was advised by a doctor to move to a country where life was more peaceful. He worked for years in New York as an accountant, and when he retired he moved to Oregon to be closer to his children. He told me that he had hardly spoken about his experiences because the people he tried to tell simply could not take in what had happened to him. In Oregon, however, he was asked to pro-vide testimony by the local Jewish museum and, as a result, he was invited to speak at a school. A week later, the teacher gave him a hundred letters from the students who had heard him speak. Some of them told him that he had changed their lives, made them appreciate their parents and the value of their education. "Then I realised that I am doing something important and that is why I am making an effort to tell my story," he wrote. "It is indeed an effort as I am over 90 years old!" Wiener received over 88,000 letters from people who had heard him speak or read his book. At least 120 were from high school students who told him they had contemplated suicide until they heard him speak. He sent me a link to one of his talks. He was a witty and engaging speaker. He told his audience that it was also Holocaust denial that drove him forward and prompted him to write down his story for posterity. "The first copy of my book went to Ahmadinejad, then president of Iran," he told the audience. "I went straight down to the post office and sent him a copy!"

In late 1939, after Wiener's father's murder, the local Polish authorities asked his stepmother if she could identify her husband's body. He was buried in a mass grave. It was so early in the war that strange elements of normality continued in parallel with the brutality that was enveloping the country. Wiener went with her. He remembers that the body was so badly decomposed that she was only able to identify him from the few things he had in his pocket. Wiener said: "I was 13 years old. I have nightmares to this very day of looking at my father's partially decomposed face." Each one of the survivors I have met has a moment that haunts them and stands out above others. This was Wiener's such moment.

In June 1942, German soldiers came to the house, and Wiener was forcibly taken to the Sosnowiec Ghetto, now half an hour's drive away from Chrzanow. His stepmother was knocked to the ground as she tried to stop the guards from taking him away from her. He never saw his family again and has no idea what happened to them. From Sosnowiec, he was moved to a series of forced labour camps. In September 1944, in the camp at Waldenburg (then in Germany but now Walbrzych in Poland), Wiener became prisoner number 64735. Here his new identity was sewn onto his cap and jacket. Finally, in March 1945, Wiener arrived at a camp whose name at the time he did not know, as by this point he was exhausted and near collapse. Deemed useless, he was sent to die. He was standing in line for the gas chamber, the smell of burning flesh from the crematorium hanging in the air, when, all of a sudden, he was extracted from the queue and put back to work. He was so thin that he could put his hand all the way around his thigh.

On 9 May 1945, he was among the prisoners waiting for the roll call, to be counted and marched to work, but no guards showed up. It felt like an ominous trick, he recalls. "A Russian tank approached the gate of our camp. An officer stepped out from his tank and told us: 'We have come to liberate you!' We couldn't understand his Russian language, but we obviously understood that Germany had indeed been defeated." The camp residents were then told they had three days to rape, rob and even kill Germans. Wiener was unable to move and had no inclination for revenge. "I looked at the Russian soldiers as my heroic liberators. We expected them to remove our mountains of despair." As for so many of the people on the *Wedgwood*, illness, loneliness and destitution summed up liberation for Wiener, who owned only the prison clothes he was standing in, and had no money and not even a slice of bread to call his own. He had no idea where he was or how to get home. "It was like having successful surgery, but the surgeon had walked away and left me on the operating table," he wrote. Local Germans were brought into the camp to see what the Nazis had done, and on one occasion Wiener heard an ambulance and imagined it was coming to help the survivors. It was in fact on its way to care for a German visitor who had fainted.

Wiener comes across in his memoirs as a man who seized opportunities. He admitted that his vices were chocolate and women. On the way to Vado the 19-year-old had an extraordinary number of amorous affairs that seem only to illustrate the emptiness of his new life, which began when a middle-aged German woman, who visited the camp, offered to take him in. Once recovered, he immediately went home. The journey from Germany back to Poland took him through "pulverised" towns, he recounted. "There were charred and mangled vehicles everywhere. A putrid mess of a devastating war spoiled the beautiful countryside." He finally reached Chrzanow jaded and hungry. He walked anxiously to his childhood home. "The staircase leading to my apartment witnessed my joy mixed with anxiety. I knocked at the front door and told the Polish occupant that I had survived the war, and would like to look at my former home. The man slammed the door in my face. I was dumbfounded. I did not know where to turn."

Not knowing where to go, he went to visit his parents' graves, his mother having died before the war. "On the way back, I noticed a little house where the patio was paved with tombstones from the Jewish cemetery. It was a painful and shameful sight." It was an illustration of how complicity with evil made returning survivors dangerous witnesses to the theft and expropriation of Jewish property. It turned a half-starved 19-year-old orphan boy into a threat. "Most Poles seemed to be ostracising me," Wiener said. "I felt as if I was pulling a sled with no snow on the ground. I fretted that one bad move might have fateful consequences." He toyed with the idea of starting a new life in Chrzanow but "Poles who noticed me turned their heads. Some of them threw hostile glances at me." Finally, Wiener came across two cousins, who had also survived. The girls knew where the family had hidden some jewellery. They shared the pitiful find and, carrying a couple of gold chains, Wiener left his home for a second time. He sold the gold and bought some food and a train ticket to Krakow, where he found lodging in a house run by the American Jewish Joint Distribution Committee.

About 4,000 Jews were living in the city, many refugees from elsewhere, and although it had been spared destruction and the streets were as beautiful as ever, the city was tense. Food was in short supply. Soviet officials, who were now in charge, were worried about law and order as anti-Semitism was rife. Krakow was a tinderbox waiting to catch fire. The streets were buzzing with the old blood-libel tales of Jews murdering Christian children to use their blood to bake matzo. On 11 August 1945, Jews at the Kupa Synagogue tried to catch a 13-year-old boy who was throwing stones at the congregation. The boy fled, claiming that the Jews had tried to kill him. An angry crowd rapidly assembled, attacking the worshipers and burning the Torah scrolls. Riots broke out in Kazimierz, the old Jewish area of the city. A hostel where survivors had taken refuge was also attacked and the Jews beaten up. Not satisfied with having injured them, thugs followed them to hospital and beat them while nursing staff offered the minimum of care. A 56-year-old woman who had survived Auschwitz lost her life, and there were a large number of injured. The Polish intelligentsia were shocked that this could have happened in the historic university town of Krakow, the seat of Polish learning and sophistication, but the event was mirrored on a smaller scale right across the country.

This was a typical survivor's experience in Poland. Wiener's homecoming would have been identical to that of many of his shipmates, who must also have passed through a period of drifting confusion, no longer belonging and frightened for their lives. This is what drove so many of the people on the beach to decide that Palestine was the only future they had.

Yet how could this have happened just six months after the liberation of Auschwitz? What does this tell us about Poland in 1945 and present-day Polish society? Looking for an answer, I drive north from Krakow to Kielce. While Krakow is a booming tourist centre and its former Jewish quarter is full of Jewish-themed bookshops and restaurants, the buildings of Kielce's Jewish heart were ripped out of the city entirely. Opposite the Ibis hotel, on a traffic island in the middle of a busy road, is a large white building that looks like a library or a theatre. It is odd for such a building to be in the middle of a dual carriageway. But it was once the synagogue. Further along the road is a memorial that marks the spot where the ghetto stood. It consists of a menorah that is either sinking or rising out of the ground, depending on which way you look at the story of what happened here. The money to erect it was raised by local activist Bogdan Bialek, who has worked relentlessly for thirty years to get Poles to face up to what happened immediately after the Holocaust.

He could not have chosen a more difficult spot to fight his cause. Kielce is notorious as the site of a far bloodier pogrom after the war than the one that took place in Krakow. It too was sparked by tales of Jews kidnapping a child to use its blood to make matzo. On a warm summer's day in July 1946, rumours of such a kidnapping spread like wildfire, and within an hour a huge frenzied crowd of police, soldiers and workers from the nearby steelworks surrounded the American Jewish Joint Distribution Committee's office and hostel, where the survivors were being cared for. The building was just 150 metres from the police station, but before sunset 42 Jewish men, women and children were killed and 80 were left seriously wounded. Among the victims were pregnant women with their stomachs ripped open. Although most of the violence took place at the Joint Distribution Committee building on Planty Street, Jews were attacked all over the city and even on passing trains. Among the victims were some of the 500 survivors of Kielce's pre-war Jewish population, which had numbered 18,000 when the war broke out. At the former building on Planty Street, Bialek now runs a museum and educational centre.

Sixty-three-year-old Bialek, a small, gentle man, is a psychologist who was born in Bialystok on the Belarus border but he moved to Kielce in 1978. When he arrived in the city, he was surprised by the silence that surrounded the events of July 1946 and by the fact that nobody wanted to talk about them. When communism fell in 1989, locals in Kielce held a memorial for the victims of the pogrom, but for Bialek it was insufficient and much too official. A devout Catholic, he decided that he was going to single-handedly force the town to acknowledge its past. He has endured death threats and had a hand grenade thrown into his office but he has never given up and, after thirty years, he claims his educational campaign has worked. Kielce, he says, is devoid of anti-Semitic graffiti, has a low incidence of racist crimes, and local football fans do not engage in racist chants, as they do in the rest of the country. But there are still plenty of locals who do not support him and voice their dislike.

I ask him what went wrong in Kielce and in Poland as a whole, so that survivors could see no future in the country where their families had lived for hundreds of years. He is quick to point out that all of Europe was anti-Semitic in the 1930s, but by telling the tale of how 60 pregnant Jewish women were stripped and brutally murdered in Kielce by the Nazis for all to see, he explains the depth of horror inflicted on Poles during the war. "Violence became an everyday thing in Poland and was normalised. We can see in veterans returning from Afghanistan and Iraq how exposure to violence changes behaviour, and in Poland we see this on a mass scale. Those veterans meet with psychologists, but there was no psychologist for the Polish people." He also points out that most of Poland's elite had been destroyed by the war and were among the first victims of the Nazis. "In 1946 there were twenty million people in Poland but only about 300,000 had finished high school. Not only this, but there was a famine in Poland in 1946 and the country was overrun with a gangster culture." "Poland was a country in moral and material ruin." Before I leave, he adds that it was not just the communists but the Catholic Church which refused to help the Polish people confront their past. Bialek has a zeal that is unnerving and is keen to show me his own Wailing Wall, where locals can atone for their sins and leave messages, which he sends on to be placed in the real wall in Jerusalem.

* * *

From Kielce I travel on into the Polish heartland to a remote village called Jedwabne, 163 km north-west of Warsaw, to discover more about why the survivors felt they had no choice but to leave the country. This Poland is worlds apart from the capital with its swanky new office blocks. The country road passes fields of corn and runs through small villages where the houses sit in a line along the road. Wrought iron railings surround each property and there are fruit trees and daisies in the gardens. Kids on bikes make their way to the small village store. It is the Feast of the Assumption, 15 August, in honour of the Virgin Mary. In the warm late-afternoon sun, the people of Jedwabne are in their Sunday best heading to the church on the marketplace, where many of its former Jewish inhabitants once made their living. It is a grey, nondescript small town, which until 2000 was as obscure as it now looks. The Polish historian Jan Gross thrust Jedwabne into the headlines by writing an account of what happened here on a similarly warm summer's day in July 1941 when half the town murdered the other half—1,600 Jews. The majority of them were burned in a barn on the edge of the town.

In August 1939, when Hitler and Stalin divided Poland, Jedwabne was assigned to the Russians. Across those parts of Poland occupied by the Soviets, it was widely believed that Jews had collaborated with the Red Army at the expense of the Poles. It was a sentiment that played into Nazi hands once the Germans invaded Soviet territory in June 1941 and Jedwabne fell under German control. The town's population had been subjected to a campaign of Sovietisation and so all but the Jews welcomed the German soldiers. What made, and continues to make, Gross's revelations about the events that followed in Jedwabne so shocking is that for decades the locals claimed that the Germans carried out the massacre, and a stone monument even stated this for all to see.

Half a century after it happened, Jedwabne became a major story and prompted much soul-searching in Poland in the run-up to the anniversary of the murders. Gross's book, *Neighbours*, challenged the national myth of the Polish experience in the war—that a small, vulnerable nation picked on by powerful neighbours had fought for what was right. In this tale of heroic martyrdom Gross exposed a dark thread running through the story.

When President Aleksander Kwasniewski went to Jedwabne in 2001, on the sixtieth anniversary of the massacre, to unveil a new monument and apologise to the Jewish people, many of Jedwabne's residents stayed at home. It is easy to say Polish society was evil and rotten to the core, and many a Jew will tell you this, but although anti-Semitism was rife and institutionalised in Poland in the 1930s, nothing like Jedwabne had happened before the Germans arrived. The explanation of why things changed is chillingly logical. Poland was a poor country and rural life was hard; the countryside was overpopulated and the people were hungry. When the rules and regulations of normal life were destroyed in 1939, people took advantage of this lawlessness for personal gain. The people of Jedwabne moved into the homes of the Jews they had murdered and ate off their dinner plates and slept in their beds. Even when neighbours were not complicit in murder, they took advantage and helped themselves to what the Jews had left behind. Homes were not left standing empty with warm winter coats hanging in the wardrobes. Wartime was harsh and the devastation of Poland was the worst on the continent. Although the majority of the three million Polish Jews who died were lower middle class or working class, their neighbours had little opportunity for self-advancement other than by picking on Jews whose social position was being rapidly eroded by the Nazis and who were being marginalised from society as a whole. It is a lesson the present government in Poland does not want to hear. Internal Polish politics are a matter beyond this book, and attitudes in Poland to the truth of what happened during the Holocaust tell a sorry story, but the argument actually distracts from the main issue and from the question of who created the situation in which this could happen in the first place.

At the edge of Jedwabne, where scruffy fields begin beneath pylons, is the massacre site, where the barn once stood. It is shockingly small. There are five young Poles in biking gear taking pictures. They are in their mid-thirties. They are part of the generation of Poles who have started asking questions about what their parents and grandparents actually remember about the Second World War and its aftermath. The bikers pose next to the large Israeli flag and memorial candles that cluster around the stark stone monument. Within minutes, they are on their motorbikes and gone. The streets of Jedwabne are empty as I drive back towards to main road. Everyone is in church now, and I suspect that opportunities are still limited here and that many of the young people live in Germany and England.

On the way to Lublin, I stop at Treblinka, where between 780,000 and 900,000 Jews were murdered. So convinced was the local peasantry that Jews were richer than they were that what is now a peaceful place of contemplation carefully laid out with memorials and mown grass was, immediately after the liberation, a scene of frenzied excavation as the locals arrived with shovels and dug up the remains of the murdered in search of hidden treasure or at least a gold tooth. Some of the earliest photographs of the site show freshly dug holes with human bones scattered around.

* * *

It is important to remember that the current debate about the Holocaust in Poland is taking place in a country where surprisingly little is actually known about its Jewish history. Searching for a reason for this amnesia, I drive on to Lublin. The city is 170 km south-east of Warsaw and is a small, unassuming place. It is clear, however, that there is something odd about its urban geography. Lublin has an unusual and imposing white neo-Gothic castle built by the Russians when they controlled this part of Poland in the nineteenth century. It sits on the hill where the Polish kings once held court, but any child might ask where the buildings are that usually huddle at the base of a castle. Alongside the low rectangular castellated facade runs a dual carriageway, as straight as a die, and in front of the castle is a half-empty parking lot. Every day the city's commuters drive over the site of Lublin's sixteenth-century Great Synagogue, once home to one of Europe's most important yeshivas. But most of them have no idea of what was once here. The synagogue was used as an assembly point for rounding up the city's Jews, before they were sent to the extermination camp at Belzec, after which the Nazis destroyed the building in 1942. The carpark and the curve of seemingly old houses that face the castle were erected after the war on the area that was once the Jewish quarter of Lublin, which was also wiped off the face of the earth by the Germans.

Above the carpark sits the pretty sand-coloured Grodzka Gate, which is the entrance to the old town. In 1990 this historic building, which dates from 1342, was derelict and was taken over by the theatre group NN. The young actors set about restoring the building and discovering its history. To their shock and amazement, they found out that the Grodzka Gate was also known as the Jewish Gate and led from the Christian area, now Lublin's attractive old town, to the Jewish sector, which sat below the castle and is now the carpark and the noisy highway. The young thespians had no idea that Jewish Lublin was once one of the most important centres of Jewish life in the world. It was a vibrant city, both in a religious and secular sense. The Jews were long-term residents and had been granted special privileges and allowed to settle below the castle outside the city walls in 1336. Hundreds of years of history became a breaking news story for the team of the NN.

The tourists who browse the fridge magnet stalls on the old town's main thoroughfare mostly walk past the NN Teatr, and if they do stop, they may have a bite to eat in theatre's Café Szeroka 28, which, out of context, seems a rather kitsch 'Jewish' restaurant, on the ground floor of the building. The gate was once the meeting place of Christian and Jewish Lublin, and the organisers of the NN looked upon the concept positively, seeing not a door that could be shut but a portal for understanding. The NN project has been funded by the local authorities in Lublin since 1994. From the time it was set up, its team took on the enormous challenge of bringing alive the memory of Jewish Lublin, which, under communism, slipped out of public consciousness and into the black hole of forgotten memories. It is not easy to evoke a place that no one remembers, that no longer exists and whose people are all long gone. Undaunted, the young people of the NN began to collect the stories of those who had once lived in Lublin.

Blond-haired Piotr Nazaruk is an archaeologist and has spent much of the last few years identifying local mass graves. He walks me around the labyrinth of medieval buildings that is the NN's home. "We are an orphanage of stories," he tells me. "It's about the smells of that city, the rivers, the food, the first love … everything that happened here. The Jewish community in Lublin is like Atlantis." Along the walls of his office run parallel shelves of files. There are 43,000 thin brown files on the higher shelf, and on the lower one are white ones dedicated to each of the buildings of the Lublin Atlantis. In 1939, 43,000 Jews lived in Lublin out of a total population of 120,000, and the NN team are trying to discover as much information as they can about each of the Jews who lived in the city. There is a brown file for every person. "We want to bring back the faces of the lost city," Nazaruk explains, picking a file off the shelf at random. It has a name and a date of birth but inside it is empty. I feel for him. My list of passengers on the *Wedgwood* has many such entries.

The Germans occupied Lublin on 18 September 1939 and originally had plans to turn the area into a Jewish reservation. The Nisko Plan for the Jews' deportation here was abandoned in early 1940, but the locality remained central to Nazi planning and became the heart of a mass murder operation known as Operation Reinhard. Of the 43,000 people that the NN team want to document, it is believed that less than 300 survived. I have yet to trace one of those survivors to the *Wedgwood*, but at least one of the passengers was in the Lublin Ghetto and others came from the locality.

In between the files runs a strip of photographs, 2,700 of them, which were developed from glass negatives found in the attic of one of the city's former tenements when it was being restored. The team believe that they were taken by a single photographer, who worked in the city between 1914 and 1939. "Visitors sometimes recognise people," says Nazaruk, who is keen to show me the pictures of Jews in the Polish Army. "It shows the important part they played in the Polish state," he says.

The NN is more than an archive, it is also an imaginative educational centre. The Letters to the Ghetto project, held for the first time in 2001, is typical of their work. School children are invited to send letters to randomly chosen addresses in the Jewish quarter that have disappeared and to recipients who are long dead. The letters obviously have no real destination and the post office returns them marked "recipient unknown" or "no such address".

We settle down at a table surrounded by files with Nazaruk's colleagues Jagek Jeremcz and Teresa Klimowicz. The threesome would look at home in Shoreditch. They have an evangelical enthusiasm for their subject. I do not mention that it is precisely Lublin's fame as a Jewish city that has brought me here, as I do not want to deflate their excitement about the novelty of Lublin's past, but I also feel ashamed that I know nothing about the history of the city after 1946. We are reverse sides of the same coin.

In 1939, Poland was home to the largest Jewish community in the world and the centre of the diaspora. The first Jews had arrived at the end of the eleventh century. In the Second World War, 90 per cent of Poland's Jewish citizens were forced out of their homes and murdered. Their deaths left behind a huge void in Polish society, and what are called "traces" of their once vibrant culture are being rediscovered by the new generation sitting in front of me. Under communism this was a topic that was rarely discussed, and as a result Polish understanding of the Holocaust has been distorted.

When the Red Army arrived in Lublin, it set up a left-wing provisional Polish government, the Polish Committee of National Liberation, which was to evolve into the Polish communist government. "When Lublin was 'liberated' by the Red Army in July 1944,"Teresa begins, making sure that I understand "liberation" is in quotes by drawing them in the air as she speaks, "Jewish life started to evolve immediately," she says. That new Jewish life centred on a building in Rybna Street which is in the old town, just a few hundred metres from the NN, where the Central Committee of Polish Jews had its headquarters. The committee was active for just six years, but from its inception it was the key to Jewish life as it was the only Jewish body that the communist government would deal with. It organised social care, helped survivors and lobbied the authorities. Significantly, its second meeting on 13 August 1944 was dominated by questions of security and, although it received some funds from the embryonic government, the committee immediately sent a telegram to the American Jewish Joint Distribution Committee asking for help.

Teresa clicks on her phone for figures. "There are 300 recorded Jews in Lublin in September 1944 but only 15 of them were originally from Lublin. But later in the autumn of 1944 there were 2,000," she tells me, and then adds, "Lublin was also one of the most dangerous places in Poland. What we see in Lublin is individual killings of survivors of the

Sobibor and Belzec camps. It is important too to remember that Lublin was the political base of the new communist government, and many Jews were collaborating with them. A lot of Jews who had escaped were communists and worked with the new regime. Some worked for the secret police." The word "collaborating" is telling.

"This period in Lublin is not well documented because the situation was extremely chaotic after the war, but we have found out a lot of little details and they shed new light," Jeremcz adds. "The most important thing that had to be done was to make a list of survivors and this was done at Rybna Street. You had to register with the Central Committee if you wanted help, but it is important to remember that many people did not. They had false papers or were simply too frightened to identify themselves as Jews." Local groups in the liberated areas also sent lists to the committee in Lublin, which consolidated them into one list of survivors. The first of these lists had 2,393 names and was printed as a 15-page booklet by the World Jewish Congress. This would then expand into the 58,000-name *Register of Jewish Survivors II*, which was published in Jerusalem in August 1945. I will spend many hours hunting through it, looking for the people who sailed on the *Wedgwood*.

The new Polish authorities also permitted Yiddish broadcasts on the radio. They were the first of their type in Poland and their main purpose was to help survivors find their loved ones. The radio broadcast from Lublin railway station at 9 pm every evening until early 1945, when it moved to Lodz and then on to Warsaw until the programmes were stopped in 1949. They lasted fifteen minutes. I can imagine the *Wedgwood* survivors crouched over radio sets in Jewish safe houses across the country. "It was run by Diana Blumenfeld and Jonas Turkow, a husband and wife team," Jeremcz tells me. "She was a famous actress and a singer from Warsaw who had played a prominent role in the ghetto. The couple organised a concert of ghetto music in December 1944. The community also produced a daily paper, a simple typed page, again mostly made up of the names of survivors." This is the first time I have heard of ghetto songs and will discover that they were a popular genre among the survivors.

The threesome have also found the earliest existing Holocaust testimony that was taken down on 29 July 1944 in Rybna Street, where the Central Committee set up a Historical Committee. This body created a methodology and questionnaire for testimonies and began to train people, who were paid by the committee, to record them. Early in 1945, the committee also moved to Lodz and then to Warsaw, where it became the

Jewish Historical Institute. "There was no paper," Teresa tells me. "They wrote on the other side of German documents, even on the back of a board game. These testimonies were important because the survivors were looking for justice and wanted to provide material for possible trials. In the first three years after the liberation, 4,000 testimonies were given."

After the war, Lublin was but a temporary stop for most Jews. Numbers peaked at 4,000 but quickly dropped to 200. "There is no Jewish life here now," she says. "In the 1980s a few plaques were put up, but they moved the ghetto monument that had been erected in 1963 to make way for a new shopping centre. It's now next to a school," Teresa says with a sigh. "Lublin once again became provincial and poor. For the Jews there was no point in staying here." She shrugs and the conversation comes to an end.

Yet perhaps more than Lublin, Krakow, Auschwitz, Belzec and Treblinka, Muranow in Warsaw offers the most haunting reminder of what the Holocaust really was. The reality of what had happened to Jewish life in Poland was summed up in the rubble of the ghetto; an abyss out of which many of the survivors on the beach had had to climb. The stark reality of their journey was more clearly illustrated in Muranow when I first visited Warsaw in the 1970s. Around the memorial set up here was a vast empty park bordered by Zamenhofa and Anielewicza streets. This was the heart of the ghetto, which had been totally destroyed in war. A number of the people on the *Wedgwood* were in the Warsaw Ghetto and fought in the ghetto uprising of 1943. Immediately after the war the Jewish community set about raising money to build a monument in commemoration. This had already been designed by the sculptor Nathan Rapoport while he was in exile in the Soviet Union. It was officially unveiled in 1948, and when I first visited in the seventies, it towered over the newly planted trees. The empty, gaping space in front of it was like a vast wound. It was not just the Jews who were ostracised after the war, but also those who had helped them. The Jews were Polish citizens, even if many people did not think this was so, and the Holocaust wounded the society they left behind. Seven Jews from Jedwabne were saved by a local family, the Wyrzykowskis, who were forced to flee the town after the war. Account after account given by Holocaust survivors details how those Poles who saved them asked that their names be kept secret even into the 1990s. It is an unnerving aspect of the story and has much light to throw on what drove survivors to abandon their former homes and make the perilous journey to Palestine. In the 1970s that vast empty space in front of the Warsaw Ghetto monument summed up what the survivors had left behind.

The GPS takes me to a parking space on Anielewicza. I am disoriented and not sure where I am until I catch a glimpse of the ghetto memorial. It seems to have shrunk in size. The lonely square is now filled by a huge building that is home to the Polin Museum. Local residents, who were originally not from the city, were resentful that they lost their park when the museum was built, but since it opened its doors in 2013, Warsaw has gained a state-of-the-art museum that is attracting huge numbers of visitors. This desolate corner of Warsaw is now buzzing. Those who run the museum are keen to point out that Polin is not a Holocaust museum but celebrates the rich and vibrant Polish Jewish culture which played a central part in Polish life for a thousand years. As I walk in, kindergarten children are being ushered into the education centre to discover a world of dreidels (spinning tops) and Hanukkah candles. Outside, Japanese tourists are posing on a bench next to a statue of Jan Karski, who was a leading member of the Polish resistance and who warned the Polish government in exile of the worrying implications of the complicity with evil evident in wartime society. His comments were edited out of the translated version passed on to the Allied governments.

The Polin Museum runs an online programme that is designed to tackle head-on the issues that still surround the families of those who hid and supported Jews during the war. Those non-Jews who helped rescue Jews in the Holocaust are granted the accolade of Righteous Among Nations by Israel's Yad Vashem Holocaust Centre, and Poland has more Righteous than any other nation. Talking about them is an important educational tool which the programme's organiser, Klara Jackl, is keen to emphasise. She is young, pretty and deeply earnest. "The goal of the education department is to fill a gap in Polish education. The Jewish story is not really touched on in the curriculum and it is up to the teacher what they tell the children. There are just one or two sentences that need to be said by law and I must say the Jewish topic is treated far too fleetingly," she tells me as we sit in a chrome-and-glass meeting room. "Our mission is to fill that gap and invite as many schools as possible and teach the teachers, but there is still a lot of prejudice, especially in small towns and villages where teachers are nervous to raise this topic."

For Jackl, the Righteous programme is not just an educational tool but one for improving civic attitudes, as these deeds are potentially universal. "We connect the Righteous Among Nations stories with people who are acting in different worlds in different contexts. People today face the same challenges and dilemmas, so we have Righteous Without Borders.

Everyone can be a Righteous and we need these deeds every day, but to do so one needs to risk a lot. This comparison helps to prevent the exclusion of minorities in the contemporary world." In 2016 the Polish government refused to accept migrants from Syria and elsewhere into the country.

As I say goodbye to Jackl, she is asked by the woman selling tickets to help two elderly American men. I hover about, wondering who they are. The older of the two, Sal Bierenbaum, has come because he would like to give a testimony. Jackl ushers them to a side room and invites me to join them. He is thin and frail with liver spots on his face. Jackl takes brief notes about his life, but his story is difficult to follow as he assumes a familiarity with his life that we do not have. Bierenbaum was born and brought up in Radom, south of Warsaw. Jackl asks him if he feels Polish; she translates her question for me. "God damn it, we are talking in Polish," he says in English and then looks reflective. "Was I a Polish Jew or a Jewish Pole? I still don't know." He bangs the table with his fist and laughs. "I bought ham at the butcher's, you know the one on the main street?" Bierenbaum was in a labour camp before being transferred to Auschwitz with his younger brother, who was eight, and he says he "hit the gas" not long after arriving. He cracks one-liners, but his story rambles in the confusion of the memories that crowd out one story after another. He is travelling with his friend Matt, who tells me his family thinks he needs "looking after".

After the war, when 18-year-old Bierenbaum was liberated at a camp in Germany, he made his way back to Radom, but after finding no sign that his mother had survived, he decided that he would walk to Warsaw. "It was hot and a peasant woman gave me bread and water. Then God damn it, I found my mother. She was working in a children's home." Bierenbaum explains that he could think only of going to America where the family had relatives. He was desperate for an education and hated the Polish school he was sent to because his classmates and teachers were anti-Semitic. Like so many of the survivors on the *Wedgwood*, Sal Bierenbaum has left it to the last minute to tell his story. He is 91 and asks more than once why we are interested in his story, even though he has come here specifically to tell it. There is a nervousness in his demeanour, as if he thinks that here, of all places, he might not be taken seriously. At this point, just as he is opening up, Jackl, to my surprise, tells him that it takes a long time to organise the filming of testimony and suggests that he comes back to Poland next year. Bierenbaum is clearly disappointed but poses for photos showing his Auschwitz tattoo on his arm. He tells me he is going to Radom for a

Jewish "get-together". I assume he is off to the Jewish festival that is cele-
brating Traces of Jewish Radom, which I have come across on the Internet.
I am keen to trace the steps of Avraham Bornstein and Shmuel Glanczpigel,
who came from the city and ended up on the *Wedgwood*. We agree to meet
up in Radom. "I am your host," he tells me.

Radom is one of those eastern European towns that look as if they were
made from a nineteenth-century build-your-own SimCity kit. It has a
pretty pedestrianised street with elegant two-storey buildings with
wrought-iron balconies. Bierenbaum's mother ran a shop here that sold a
strange mixture of cosmetics and household paint. I book in at the
Europejski Hotel, where Bierenbaum is staying.

The local council has funded the publication in Polish of a Jewish
memorial book, *The Book of Radom*. There are about fifty people at the
book launch. Fifteen of them are from a group of survivors' relatives, who
I assume are here for the festival. There are no Jews left in Radom. The last
of the city's Jews erected a monument on the spot where the synagogue
once stood and then left for good. That is the official story, but Bierenbaum
has told me that he knew a number of Jews who stayed on and hid their
identity; he went to see them when he first came back for a visit in the
1960s. As the book launch draws to a close, I get a text message from him
telling me to join him and his friends for a Friday night dinner at the hotel.
I walk back through the park while clouds of crows caw and circle in the
evening sky. The meal has just started when I arrive. There is a large group
of about sixty people in the dining room but Bierenbaum is the only survivor among them. I wait by the door while the prayers are said.
Immediately a woman bustles up to me to ask what I want. I explain I am
Bierenbaum's guest, but she informs me that he does not have the right to
invite people to the dinner. She is clearly in charge and the kind of
American Jewish woman you do not argue with. I ask her before I retreat
if they are going to the concert being held at the site of the ghetto later
that evening, as it is the anniversary of its destruction. I am told sharply,
"Why ever would we go to that? The local people have organised that. We
are busy here." The inability to interact is a two-way process. I eat alone in
the nearby cafe.

The next day I drive back to Krakow and park in Kazimierz, the old
Jewish quarter. It is Saturday morning and Robert Gadek, who is one of
the organisers of Krakow's Jewish Festival, has time for a quick coffee
before he heads for a weekend in the mountains with his boyfriend. Gadek
is the trendy, alternative sort of character you would expect to find in the

arts scene, but this is a Jewish festival and he is not Jewish. He tells me over an Israeli coffee that he became fascinated with Jewish culture when he arrived in Krakow in 1989. "Kazimierz was abandoned and there was an amnesia about the past." The festival is one of Poland's biggest, and he puts its appeal down to two factors. "In the 1990s people were drawn to the event. Non-Jews were hungry for knowledge about this part of their past that had been stolen away, and then there were those Jews who had hidden their history and this gave them the opportunity to come out." Coming out as a Jew is a new concept for me.

In the Jewish Cultural Centre, I meet 31-year-old Olga Danek, a community youth leader who wears a t-shirt covered in pictures of the evil queens from Disney movies and has a nose piercing. She tells me that her story is typical. "I did not know I was Jewish until I was 12. It had always mystified me why my mother was so interested in Jewish culture and my parents had taken me to Auschwitz when I was five." When she confronted her mother, Danek discovered that her grandmother was Jewish. Then Danek felt that she was "the only person in this crazy situation. At this point I did not feel Jewish as I had to take a long journey before I could say 'I am a Polish Jew'." When Danek started wearing a Star of David necklace, her mother was afraid and asked her to take it off. "Deciding to be Jewish, even though I am by Jewish law a Jew, was a big decision for me." The cultural centre opened in 2007 and Danek tells me there are lots of young people in Krakow who come there to a "safe zone" where they can be Jewish in a secular environment. "Official statistics say that the Jewish congregation in Krakow is about fifty to a hundred people, but in reality the number of Jews is much much higher." She is angry that visitors only want to talk about the Holocaust and not the experience of being Jewish in Poland today, and says that there is a real Jewish life in the country. It is a bleak story on which she puts a positive spin. I try to look on the bright side, but it illustrates the harsh reality of post-war life in eastern Europe: it was one in which those who stayed felt that in future they should hide their Jewish identity.

Back in Warsaw, there is a rabbi who is capable of responding to this phenomenon. Joshua Ellis is small and thin and was born in Kansas. Ellis is not a man who thinks in terms of the numbers of the community in the synagogue but of the wider context. "The nineties was the breaking down of the walls," he tells me. "Today it is trendy to be Jewish. It is alternative. Jewishness comes up everywhere, but also young people want to be different and one way to realise this fantasy is to have Jewish roots. It gives you new ideas and a future. It is a revolt. It makes you part of a subculture and not the official mainstream." His office is a welcoming jumble of books, papers and piles of food and drink supplies. "Often people don't feel they want contact with the synagogue. They don't want people to tell them what it means to be Jewish," he says. "Jewish conversion is not regarded well by Jews because of stupid fights about stupid things. I see myself as a big Zionist, but it is our responsibility to look after the integrity of the nation not just in Israel. These people are sociologically not Jews but we have a responsibility to them. I am much more worried about giving people a home. Everyone needs a home. It is about anyone who is willing to buy in with us and believe in a God that is moral." Later in the day, I stand outside his Nozyk synagogue. The glass tower blocks of the new financial district that loom over it are a symbol of the new Poland, and I wonder if the Jews will have a place in it. It is a warm Friday evening and through the open windows I can hear the singing and the Friday night prayers. It is as if the ghosts of Poland's past are floating through the shadows. Alter Wiener is now one too: he was run over by a car one winter's evening on his way to the shops. Police said he should have worn brighter colours. I never had the chance to ask him what he thought of a Jewish revival in Poland.

5

BUCHAREST

AN EYE FOR AN EYE

Jewish life did survive the Holocaust and continued in Europe, but the Vilnius partisans who sailed on the *Wedgwood* might have rewritten that narrative had they been able to take revenge for the murder of six million Jews during the Holocaust.

Abba Kovner and his fellow partisans arrived in Bucharest in May 1945. Whereas most survivors say they had no desire to take revenge on the Germans, Kovner and his friends were different. Kovner was determined that he would not leave Europe until he exacted vengeance for what the Germans had done to the Jews. His ideas had begun to take shape in the forests during the war but seized hold of his imagination in Lublin. His story is interesting in itself, but in the wider context it shows how some survivors came out of the Holocaust feeling empowered.

On the outskirts of Lublin is the former Majdanek concentration camp. In August 1944, the headlines in Soviet papers were dominated by its discovery. Around 150,000 people were held prisoner here and 80,000 died during the war. When the Soviet secret police arrived in Lublin, they immediately saw the potential of the camp and incarcerated the members of the Polish Home Army whom they had captured, but they left alone the remains of the crematoria and the gas chamber. Within days it was a ghoulish attraction. Some sightseers came looking for relatives, but others came just to stare at the shocking reality of what had happened on their doorstep. There are pictures of parents with small children staring at heaps of ashes and old men peering into gas ovens. As early as 12 September 1944, the Polish–Soviet Commission for Investigating the German Crimes Committed at Majdanek turned part of the camp into a museum. The driving force behind the project came from the former Polish political and Soviet prisoners who had been held here by the Nazis. The museum opened in early November and was the first in the world to commemorate the atrocities of the Second World War. Kovner was one of the first visitors.

Today Majdanek is still deeply shocking, in part because so few people visit it. I stand alone, staring at the walls of the gas chambers that were stained blue by the Zyklon B gas. Later in a barracks I am the only person looking at 280,000 pairs of shoes brought from the nearby extermination camps of Belzec and Sobibor. Watchtowers and barbed wire fences line the walkway to the huge concrete dome that covers a mountain of ashes. Scraps of bone are clearly visible. Among those held in Majdanek was a young woman called Atara Borovsky, who had been in hiding with false papers. She was captured and imprisoned in Majdanek as a Pole. She would later sail on the *Wedgwood*. Her story, although important on an individual level, was incidental compared to the impact that his visit to the camp would have on Kovner. After having seen the camp, he was filled with a burning desire for revenge, which overtook his hope of leading the survivors to the Promised Land.

There were between 2,000 and 3,000 Jews living in Bucharest when Kovner arrived in May 1945. He quickly gathered around him a group of fifty partisans and underground fighters. Among them was his old friend Josef Harmatz, who had left Vilnius with his comrade Senka Nisanilevich on 17 January 1945. Harmatz, who had become a secret policeman, had lied to his Soviet bosses when he told them that his mother had been found alive in Bucharest and asked for the necessary travel passes so he could visit her. The men headed first to Lida, now in Belarus, and then to Lvov, now Lviv in Ukraine. There they met Nisanilevich's girlfriend, Zelda Treger. The Red Army was pushing further west and the railway stations were packed with soldiers. The partisans travelled mostly in freight trains until they reached Czernowitz, which had been part of Romania between the wars and which is now Chernivtsi in Ukraine. There their route was blocked by the Soviet authorities and they were forced to turn back to Lublin. Although the aim was to open an escape route for survivors, Harmatz said: "We knew relatively little about how many refugees there were altogether in Europe, where they were located, or how many more were yet to be liberated."

Harmatz set off again, leaving Nisanilevich and Treger in Lublin. Before he left, he tattooed concentration camp numbers in blue ink on his arm in case the papers he carried proved insufficient. Those who left the camps had no other form of identification, and it was enough to ensure a safe passage through a Soviet checkpoint if you said you were a survivor returning home. Unfortunately, in Uzhhorod, which had been in eastern Czechoslovakia before the war, and is now in Ukraine, Harmatz met a group of real camp survivors. They recognised him instantly as a fraud, as he had tattooed the numbers on his inner arm while the Germans mostly marked their prisoners with numbers on their outer arms so that they could be easily read by the guards. The camp survivors suspected he was a spy, and before he could be handed over to the authorities, he made a hasty move southwards.

Arriving in Bucharest, he found lodgings on Maria Rosetti Street, and eventually one night Nisanilevich and Treger knocked on the door. "Don't hug us," said Treger, "look who's right behind us." A lie turned into a reality. Harmatz's mother, Dvora, had indeed survived the concentration camp in Stutthof and had met the couple in Lublin. "Everyone in that room, all fighters hardened by years of battle, combat, and the struggle for survival, had tears streaming down their faces," because Harmatz says in his memoirs, "everyone in that room that evening cried, either with the emotion of the moment or with the thoughts and memories of their own mothers, or because of both."

In the weeks that followed, Kovner and Harmatz became increasingly obsessed with revenge and spent more and more time plotting how to settle scores with the Germans. After the war there were plenty of individual acts of revenge and dark murders in lonely back alleys, but the two had different ideas altogether.

In Bucharest, they had met Auschwitz survivors for the first time. Some were still wearing their concentration camp outfits. The stories they told of the camps seized the partisans' minds. Kovner's forest unit had been called Revenge—Nakam in Hebrew—but only now would it try to live up to its name. Harmatz says that, as they realised the true extent of what had happened, "we started to revolt inside ourselves … The more people that came out, the more stories we were told, strengthened our feeling that we should not leave the continent without having done something." As the partisans travelled around Lithuania and then Poland, they had seen written in blood on the walls of camps, abandoned ghettos and bunkers the demand: "Revenge". For Harmatz it was "the last will, the last legacy that these people wanted those of us who survived to do". He also wanted a sentence to be imposed for the crime committed: "If you say nothing, it is permitted, and should it then not be permitted today and tomorrow?"

Three of the Auschwitz survivors he met joined Nakam and as a result they would eventually sail on the *Wedgwood*. Zeev Shinar, Leopold Wasserman and Shimon Lustgarten were committed Zionists and had played a key role in the Krakow underground. Zeev Shinar was the son of a cobbler. He was 23 years old and the only member of his family to survive, the others had all been murdered at Belzec. Leopold Wasserman, known later as "Poldek" Maimon, had a steely gaze and piercing blue eyes, and had escaped from a death march in January 1945. The eldest of the trio, at 24, was Shimon Lustgarten. The three men had been betrayed and sent to Auschwitz after carrying out the Christmas 1942 grenade attack on Krakow's Cyganeria Cafe, which had killed seven German officers and wounded many more. Undeterred, in Auschwitz they joined the camp underground. So deep was the blow that had destroyed their world that Maimon says he contemplated suicide after the liberation. Revenge gave him a reason to carry on living, and it is clear that it would be wrong to think of those huddled refugees on the beach in Vado as downtrodden and broken.

The Nakam group also included 21-year-old Rachel Halperin, who had been a member of the underground in Vilnius but had been arrested as she fled the ghetto through the sewers. She was taken with her mother and her sister to the Kaiserwald camp in Riga, from where they were transported by boat to Stutthof. When the Soviet Army advanced, the camp guards fled in January 1945 and they found themselves suddenly free. They tried to return to Vilnius to discover what had happened to the rest of the family, but the journey proved too difficult. Halperin had then gone to Warsaw, where she searched the lists of survivors for her other sister and her father but could not find their names. In November 1945, her mother and sister sailed from Constanta for Palestine, but she was set on taking revenge and joined Kovner and Harmatz's group.

Speaking later of his state of mind as he drew up his bold and dramatic plans, Kovner said: "The destruction was not around us. It was within us ... We did not imagine that we could return to life, or that we had the right to do so, to come to the Land of Israel, to establish families, to get up in the morning and work as if accounts with the Germans had been settled." The young avenger himself admitted that the plan was not one that could have been thought up by any sensible person, but only by someone verging on madness. "We were all mad in those days," he reflected.

Kovner had a biblical world vision and retained a deeply religious way of thinking, even if he no longer believed in God. His thoughts were framed in Old Testament terms of vengeance and justice. He planned to inflict on Germany not the targeted killing of guilty men but the same fate the Nazis had inflicted on the Jews: indiscriminate killing on a massive scale. Key was the idea that Jewish blood could no longer be shed without reprisal. Kovner's goal was to carry out an operation that would cause a broad international response and give a warning to anyone who might consider trying to harm the Jews again. Kovner had two plans. Plan A was to murder six million Germans by poisoning water supplies, and Plan B was to murder a smaller number of high-ranking Nazis awaiting war crimes trials, again through poisoning. Plan A involved infiltrating the water systems of Munich, Berlin, Weimar, Nuremberg and Hamburg. The idea was that the partisans would shut off the valves that led to those neighbourhoods where foreigners lived, but elsewhere death would flow out of the taps, killing without discrimination both young and old, sick and healthy. Zeev Shinar had trained as a plumber and was to be sent to work at a water filtration plant to learn how it all worked. But the possibility of putting any plans for revenge into action was simply hot-headed talk until 8 May 1945, when the war in Europe came to an end. One day not long after, walking in the sunny streets of what was still elegant Bucharest, Vitka Kempfner stumbled across a group of British soldiers wearing the Star of David on their uniforms. They were members of the Jewish Brigade of the British Army who had flouted the order not to cross the Italian border. She rushed home to tell Kovner that she had seen the soldiers who could help them.

It is hardly surprising that Abba Kovner and Josef Harmatz thought that the Brigade would work with them, not just in leading the survivors out of Europe but in exacting revenge. "We were not terrorists," Harmatz says in his memoirs, "and we wanted a blessing." They were "bitter and tough" and they felt their plan was part of a war they had all been fighting against the Germans for years.

Kovner and his fellow partisans left Bucharest and headed for the northern Italian town of Tarvisio where the Brigade was based, confident that they would get help to exact revenge on the Germans. In a bright green alpine meadow Kovner addressed the Jewish Brigade in his deep, dramatic voice, setting out his plans. Some of the soldiers cheered. A photo shows them sitting on the grass listening as he stands in front of them, his hair wild, arms waving, describing the horrors he had lived through. He asked,

83

"If we do not take revenge, who will take it for us? ... I cannot promise you the Jews will be safe from another slaughter ... But I can promise you this: Never again will Jewish blood be spilled unavenged." The Brigade command, however, rejected his ideas. Kovner was shocked by the response but nevertheless, with their help, he set off alone for Palestine disguised as a Jewish Brigade soldier on leave. The commanders presumably left it to their seniors to decide what to do next.

In Tarvisio, Kovner's key group of activists, among them Zeev Shinar, Poldek Maimon, Shimon Lustgarten and Rachel Halperin, were joined by Leibke Distal. He, like Halperin, had been arrested as he was fleeing the Vilnius Ghetto. He had lost his fingers in the Holocaust but he did not let this deter him. The avengers set off for Nuremberg to prepare for Kovner's return. "Those who did support our plans helped in every way: with communications, transportation, information, directions," Harmatz recalled. The majority of the group left Italy on 7 September 1945. "We wore British uniforms, although if anyone had spoken to us in English we would have been stuck for words," Harmatz admitted. "Our targets were sites near concentration camps or which symbolised the Nazi regime." When they arrived in Germany they posed as former Polish slave labourers. Poldek Maimon remained in Italy and was responsible for the money supply in the run-up to the attack. He was also part of the team which was to organise the get-away afterwards, as were Zelda Treger and Senka Nisanilevich, who also stayed behind in Italy. They traded fake sterling printed on the old Nazi printing presses that the Germans had used to undermine the British currency. In Italy the team bought gold with the fake banknotes and then sold it in Germany.

While in Tarvisio, Maimon met and fell in love with Fedda Lieberman, who had just arrived from Sosnowiec.

> One day in the evening there was a storm, a heavy hail fell, and lightning lit the mountains. A rare sight in its beauty. It made a huge impression. In the corridor, next to the window, stood one of the girls from the Sosnowiec group, and looking at this wonderful sight of nature ... I thought it was a good moment to know the girl's soul,

he remembered.

> I was twenty-four years old. I went to the window and stood next to the girl .... We began to talk. It was an appropriate atmosphere, very romantic. I saw that the girl was serious, interesting, emotional, pleasant to talk to.

His former girlfriend had died in the Holocaust, and to open up his heart after such a loss was difficult, but he was not in a position to make any commitments as he was set on the task at hand. He left Lieberman in Tarvisio, not expecting to see her again. The plan was dangerous and he knew he might face a death sentence or years in prison if he was caught.

In Tel Aviv, Kovner's plans were received with cool scepticism. To most of those he met, he seemed a man still stuck in the recently ended war when the priority was now the establishment of a Jewish state. Many were suspicious of and hostile to Kovner, whose exploits were well known in Palestine but, after a month of frustrating meetings, he found his way to a biophysicist who provided him with the poison.

Disguised once more as a Jewish Brigade member, Kovner set sail for France with the poison hidden in two canisters of dried milk in his British Army duffle bag. It was unlikely that he had enough to kill six million people, but before the ship arrived in Toulon he was tipped off that he was about to be arrested and threw the poison overboard.

Kovner spent four months in a British prison. He always believed he had been betrayed by the Jewish Agency in Tel Aviv, but the experience changed him. He returned to Palestine and abandoned the idea of revenge as he too started to look to the future. It was a change of direction that his team in Europe would always resent.

It was now up to his second-in-command, Pasha Reichman, in Paris, to decide the next move. Reichman swiftly activated Plan B. Maimon was ordered to find Yitzhak Ratner, who had been a partisan in the Vilnius Ghetto and was a close friend of Kovner. He was already working for the Bricha in Italy, but the group needed his help as he was a chemical engineer. Ratner moved quickly to Paris and there he worked out that bread brushed with arsenic would be the best way of carrying out an attack. The target was a group of SS prisoners at Stalag 13 POW camp, not far from Nuremberg. The plan was to poison hundreds of loaves of bread meant for the SS. Distal and two others got a job at the bakery that supplied the prison with bread and spread white arsenic powder, which looked like flour, on the bottom of two thousand loaves.

On 23 April 1946, the *New York Times* reported that 2,283 German prisoners of war had fallen ill from poisoning, with 207 hospitalised and "seriously ill". Officially no one died, but Harmatz always maintained that a hundred did succumb but that this was covered up so as not to provoke panic in the other prison camps. Mission accomplished, it was decided that the group would split in two to escape. Maimon, Nisanilevich and Treger had to get the team out of Germany and into Italy, while the other half of the team was sent to France. This required the help of the Bricha organisation, which put Distal, Harmatz, Halperin, Lustgarten, Maimon, Ratner and Shinar on a fast track that eventually took them to Vado. It is possible that up to 25 or 30 of their colleagues sailed on the *Wedgwood*. Most of them never spoke about the plot, not only because they might be prosecuted, but also because the Israeli authorities disapproved of it. Kovner claimed that Shaul Avigur, the head of Aliyah Bet, knew of their plans, and though he had not actively supported them, he did not interfere, which explains why the Bricha jumped into action to save them. Maimon met his team at the Czech border and they stayed with Avigur's lieutenant, Levi Argov, in Prague. Harmatz remained unapologetic for his part in the plot. But the main plan had failed, and by focusing all his efforts on revenge Kovner had committed political suicide and left the survivors without a leader. Fortunately, the Jewish Brigade were stationed in the tiny Alpine town of Tarvisio, hard up against the Austrian border. They would take over the task of rescuing the survivors that Kovner had abandoned.

6

TARVISIO

THE GATEWAY TO ZION

There were fewer than 50,000 survivors on Polish territory, trapped as the war raged on until 8 May 1945, when the Germans finally capitulated. Among them was Alter Wiener, who, like many other young survivors, made his way to Sosnowiec in southern Poland, close to Katowice, where he had heard there was a group of Jews who were planning to go to Palestine. His stepmother, whom he adored, had dreamed of making *aliyah*, so it was natural that he was drawn to seek out others who came from Zionist families. Crammed into a tiny apartment with at least fifty young people, he found in the youth group a surrogate family. In another apartment was Fedda Lieberman and her best friend, Lea Diamant. The two women had joined the underground in Sosnowiec after they heard rumours of the murder of Jews in camps and, because of their Aryan looks, they had been sent to Germany as Polish underground agents. After the war they returned home. "We hoped we might meet survivors, friends or family, but received news that most of our dear ones were no longer among the living," Lieberman wrote later. The shock of discovering the extent of the catastrophe that had befallen them is difficult to comprehend. The survivors returned home to find their lives had been obliterated. The girls immediately joined a group that intended to emigrate to Palestine and eventually sailed on the *Wedgwood*. I asked Wiener if their names meant anything to him. They did not. There was no *Wedgwood* survivors' group, and many of them knew nothing about each other, not even their names.

The young survivors were thirsty for knowledge as they had missed so much education, and youth groups like the ones in Sosnowiec provided their first formal education for years. The lessons reinforced their Zionist feelings as they learned Hebrew, the geography of Palestine and basic life skills. The leaders of the youth groups had, like Lieberman and Diamant, been active in the underground. They had a natural authority and actively sought out survivors to join their groups and work towards the Zionist dream. But in the late spring of 1945, leaving for Palestine was for most survivors just a pipe dream. They were mostly lower-middle-class youngsters, they had no money and no idea how to get to Palestine without help. And even if they did, it was not safe to travel alone.

Like a miraculous apparition, Jewish soldiers with guns, army trucks, medicines and supplies came their rescue. Just as the survivors began to move southwards, the British Army's Jewish Brigade was moving north. Jewish battalions had been formed in Palestine when the war broke out in 1939. Over 120,000 Jews volunteered to fight with the British in the months that followed, and they saw action in the Balkans and North Africa. But London chose to give them mostly non-combat roles, keeping them on guard duty in Palestine, fearful of the reaction that arming Jewish units would provoke among Palestine's Arab population. Although the British had committed themselves to the establishment of "a national home for the Jewish people" in the Balfour Declaration in 1917, since they had taken control of Palestine after the First World War, attitudes in Whitehall had changed. Despite this, in the late summer of 1944, Churchill won a long-standing battle to allow a Jewish Brigade, which was to fight not under the Union Jack, but under the Zionist flag, and was to be deployed on the front line under the command of a Canadian-born Jew, Brigadier Ernest Benjamin. Most commentators dismissed the move as gesture politics. *The Times* dubbed it "symbolic recognition" and regarded the step as of little significance. How wrong they would prove to be. In the late autumn of 1944, the Jewish Brigade landed in Italy.

The journey to find the people on the beach takes me to Piangipane, just outside the Adriatic city of Ravenna, in north-eastern Italy. This is not picture-postcard country. The flat fields which produce abundant crops stretch as far as the eye can see and the road is lined with tatty-looking houses. Yet in 1945, this countryside was worth dying for and was a crucial battleground for some of those who would one day lead the Israeli Army. In the winter of 1944–5 the retreating German forces, which had occupied Italy when it dropped out of the war in 1943, dug in on the banks of the tiny Senio River. In the hamlet of Piangipane there is a small, and unusual, Commonwealth War Graves cemetery. A broad, neatly mown grass walkway leads to metal gates. Tall trees provide shade from the hot afternoon sun. Inside the small cemetery, rows of white headstones face a large stone cross. Slightly to the right, but still standing neatly to attention in front of it, are 33 graves marked with the Star of David; in front of each one is a small Israeli flag. The men who are buried here fought and died with the Jewish Brigade.

Set aside from the majority of the graves and facing in the other direction are the headstones of 120 Sikhs, Hindus and Muslims of Britain's Indian Army who fell in battle here. Standing in the graveyard is an important history lesson about something it is easy to forget. The Jews from Palestine, the Indians, the 6 Australians, 438 Canadians and 96 South Africans buried here were all part of the British fighting force. Palestine, the Promised Land which the survivors dreamed of, was part of a vast empire from which the British expected both loyalty and obedience and which was run for London's benefit. The 33 Jewish Brigade graves in Piangipane tell an important part of this story. It is vital to understand that the Jews in Palestine were not free to operate as they wished, and, numbering just 475,000 in 1945, they had to live within the rules set by their colonial masters. Plans were afoot in Palestine among the Jewish community to establish a state, and the experience men would gain by fighting in the Jewish Brigade was an important part of this objective. In any forthcoming battle for independence a fully trained fighting force would be crucial. It was the British reaction to the survivors' dreams of escaping to a new life in Palestine that was to set the Jews and the British on a head-on collision course. This would push the Yishuv, the Jewish population in Palestine, into desperate measures, and it is the reason that the *Wedgwood* would sail dangerously overloaded and in such secrecy.

The Jewish Brigade's khaki-coloured army jeeps were emblazoned with painted yellow Stars of David and the soldiers wore similar insignia and armbands. They had spent the previous months, while Kovner hatched his plot for revenge, in Fiuggi, a pretty spa town south-east of Rome. Thousands of Brigaders were billeted in the town's once elegant hotels. Army food was served under huge crystal chandeliers in grand dining rooms. Fiuggi was once a popular aristocratic resort famous for its *acqua di fiuggi* mineral water. Since the fourteenth century, this had been the medicinal tipple of Europe's nobility, its popes, kings and queens, and was renowned for its ability to cure kidney stones. Michelangelo was once a loyal customer. The water bottling plant was immediately taken over by the Jewish Brigade and became their headquarters. Every morning the officers made their way to their desks past crates of empty pale-green bottles. Outside, the sign identifying the building as the Fiuggi Bottling Works was replaced by one in large Hebrew script announcing that it was now the HQ of the "Jewish Fighting Brigade". Signs on every officers' mess, billet, dining room, washroom, latrine or storeroom were in Hebrew only. As many of the officers were British Jews, English was spoken by all HQ staff, but all the routine orders were posted in both English and Hebrew. On the parade ground all orders were given in Hebrew. Here, it was as if the British Army had morphed into a Jewish one. Times were tough in the spa world and the soldiers' arrival in town offered a good business opportunity for the locals. It was not long before Fiuggi's children greeted the Brigaders with a cheery "Shalom!" Every morning, in the main square, the blue-and-white flag with the Star of David was raised in a ceremony which clearly moved the soldiers. Soon Fiuggi was dotted with signs in Hebrew, and at Hanukkah a giant six-foot menorah was erected on a hill above the town, visible for miles around.

A sizeable number of the young Jewish volunteers were European-born: Polish, German, Austrian, Czech and Russian. Among the recruits was 25-year-old Leonard Sanitt, who had been born into a Yiddish-speaking family in London's Bethnal Green. Apprenticed to a diamond cutter, he was quick to join up when the war broke out and was one of the few Jews to reach warrant officer class in the British Army, having seen action at El Alamein and Monte Cassino. When he heard that the Jewish Brigade was in Italy, he quickly asked for a transfer. After years away from home serving in the regular British Army, he suddenly found himself "in a completely Jewish world where every action was determined by the effect we were making on Jewish history by being a Jewish fighting force." He wrote in his memoirs: "Every single soldier was aware that we were the beginning of a new era that would depend entirely on the courage and skill of Jewish fighting men for our very survival as a people." It is a key comment and is one reason why, when they arrived in Palestine, the people on the *Wedgwood* were willing to take up arms to fight for their dream of establishing a Jewish state.

Not only did the Brigade have a clear and striking Jewish identity, but it had its own agenda. In Fiuggi, the men began to hear eyewitness reports of the terrible and almost unbelievable things happening to the Jewish people in the various concentration and extermination camps in eastern Europe. Sanitt recalled that they "began to appreciate the horrors that our people had suffered. Our priority was to rescue those who had survived by any method we could devise to save Jewish lives." As more German-occupied territory fell under Allied control, various clandestine operations were set up by the Brigade to save as many Jews as possible once the war was over. The army chaplain, Rabbi Bernard Casper, who had been orphaned at a young age and who had won a scholarship to Cambridge, organised a voluntary cut in rations by all ranks to enable a store of food to be accumulated in anticipation of finding refugees. A Brigade Refugee Committee was set up to which members all contributed part of their pay. Sanitt was in command of military vehicles and would sign fictitious documents, authorising their use to build up a supply base and to assist local Italian Jews, who had been persecuted under the fascist regime.

As spring came, the Allied offensive redoubled. The Senio flows down from the Apennines to the sea and is the gateway to the Po Valley, but in spring it was, unlike many of Italy's other rivers, shallow and muddy and thus easy to cross. In early April 1945, the Jewish Brigade was assigned to the opposite bank of the narrow river facing the Nazi forces. The Germans had heavily mined the approach. Nevertheless, the Brigaders were hungry for battle and the men spontaneously danced a hora, the traditional circular Jewish dance, when they heard the news that they were to be deployed.

The battle to cross the Senio was vicious and the German prisoners taken were astonished when they saw the blue-and-white insignia and heard themselves addressed in their native tongue, and being asked if they knew that their captor's relatives had been gassed. Morris Beckmann reported that the morale of captured prisoners, which "was low as a result of their reverses on every front, became near panic when they learned that they were now facing a Jewish fighting force with a host of scores to settle". It only reinforced the Brigaders' determination to celebrate their Jewish identity, and in the midst of the battle, as the warm Italian sky sparkled with stars, Passover seders were held on the battlefield in whatever shelters could be found. The men knew that this night was unlike any other.

The assault across the Senio opened up the road to Bologna and, as the rout of German forces continued, the Brigade moved rapidly north through Ferrara and Padua, skirting Venice and on to Udine, now close to the border with Slovenia. As they advanced, the unit was kept out of the fighting, much to their annoyance, but they stopped to help local Jewish communities and reopened synagogues, clearing them of debris and rubble. Eventually, the high and menacing mountains that ring the plain of Friuli–Venezia Giulia beckoned the soldiers towards Italy's north-eastern border as the convoy of jeeps and lorries flying the Star of David began to wind its way up a steep road into the Alps.

Emotions were charged and British Army commanders were aware of the dangers of deploying this volatile group of young men across the border in Austria. It was decided that the Jews would halt their advance just before the frontier. On a clear spring evening, just as the light began to fade, the Brigade passed over a stone bridge into the little town of Tarvisio. They had orders to stand guard over the Val Canale in a remote mountainous corner of Europe, where sheer limestone peaks give way to deeply forested valleys dotted with Alpine lakes and bubbling light-blue rivers. But there was to be little time for basking in the spring sunshine. Brigade soldier Hanoch Bartov, who was just 19 and who was to go on to become one of Israel's most important writers, captured the scene in his novel *The Brigade*.

> Admiring the Alps was not our business, but who could not have been amazed at those awesome vistas suddenly thrust upon us. Certainly not us, from the lowlands of Palestine … Suddenly, around a bend, the mountains on the right fell away like gates flung open, and below us, in a broad valley, translucent water coursed over a smooth-stoned riverbed, bubbling, gushing, leaping with abandon over polished stones that seemed like the bottom layer of a mighty highway yet to be paved.

Tarvisio, however quaint, was a strange place. It had been mostly German- and Slovene-speaking and formed part of the Austro-Hungarian Empire until 1919. During the interwar period, a policy of Italianisation had turned the locals against the government in Rome. Under the terms of a 1939 treaty with Hitler, most of the German-speakers had left, and in 1943, when Italy capitulated, its border garrison resisted being disarmed by the Germans. For much of the war, an SS battalion had been garrisoned here. As the Brigade drew into town, Bartov writes that they saw on the outer wall of a two-storey house, above the doorway of a shop, a placard that "showed a hunchback Jew with a wispy beard, wearing a gabardine gown, hauling Uncle Sam on a leash, bent beneath a sack of dollars". In a school he was shocked to find a textbook with a picture of Hitler inside. "It was a beautiful book whose authors, editors, and printers had taken pains to see that a child would take it in hand." The Führer "seemed just like the rest of the book—very civil, bareheaded, double-chinned, beaming at a little girl in a peasant's dress with shining, yellow hair". Tarvisio had been an army convalescent centre and arms depot, and in the well-equipped hospital beds German soldiers lay recuperating. The new military

HQ was the abandoned SS barracks on the edge of town that had once belonged to the Italian Army. Howard Blum, who wrote a history of the Brigaders, says that they were billeted in houses where, weeks before, German soldiers had lived and pictures of Hitler had hung on the wall. Gestapo officers supervising the deportation of Italian Jews had worked at the local railway station, through which trains had passed to Auschwitz, and many locals had been employed by Hitler's Third Reich.

The town keeps little record of what happened in those vital weeks that followed the victory in Europe. In the tourist office there is a glut of leaflets detailing excursions to the ring of fortifications that were built across the Alps during the First World War. Tarvisio is just 50 km north of the site of the iconic First World War battlefield of Caporetto, now in Slovenia, and this is the kind of tourism that makes money here. In a local history picture-book on sale in the bookshop, there is a page that shows survivors in striped concentration camp outfits at the railway station taken in 1945, but it is the only reference to the Shoah in this story and is given without context. There is no mention of those who now passed in the opposite direction.

In 1945 Tarvisio was a microcosm of the bewildering turmoil that was to be found all across the continent. Hundreds of rootless people were wandering about, concerned with finding the basic necessities of life. Yugoslav partisans were crossing the high mountain passes; disarmed, disorientated German and Austrian soldiers milled about. Some were not Germans but had fought on the German side, and from across the Austrian border came Jewish refugees, emaciated and desperate to grab the lifeline offered by the Brigade. The British had handed the Brigade a trump card. Thanks to its unique geographical position, Tarvisio was the perfect place for the Jewish Brigade to set up its headquarters as it was just 7 km from the Austrian border and, with time on their hands, the Brigaders could follow their own agenda. As a result this tiny, inconsequential town became a staging post for thousands of desperate refugees who arrived in the valley, many still wearing their concentration camp uniforms. This is how the *Wedgwood* people made their way into Italy.

News quickly began to reach the Jewish Brigade about the dire situation in which fellow Jews had found themselves and the chaos of the post-war world across the Alps. Blum writes that, despite a strict non-fraternisation rule, not long after they had arrived a group of young Brigaders found themselves chatting with some Austrian girls in a cafe who asked them where they were from. When the girls discovered they were Jews, they laughed: "Don't pull our legs. There aren't any more Jews except in horror stories. They don't exist anymore. They're all gone."

It is no wonder that Abba Kovner and his partisan avengers thought that the Jewish Brigade would help them. Anger among its ranks was palpable. Despite instructions from high command, the Brigade had no intention of obeying orders; it was determined to cross the border and help the survivors. It would soon find a way to do this by joining forces with the chief advocate of one particular group of survivors who were still suffering in the former concentration camps: a young rabbi, Abraham Klausner, and his flock of survivors in US-occupied Germany. It was Klausner and a young doctor, Zalman Grinberg, a survivor of the Kovno Ghetto, who would realise Kovner's dream of giving the survivors a voice.

GERMANY

N

To
Stutthof

Theresienstadt

Prague

St Ottilien   Dachau   Mauthausen   Vienna
            Munich   Bratislava
Landsberg   Gunskirchen

Graz

Villach
Tarvisio

Tradate   Selvino
                    Mestre
Magenta   Milan

Turin

Modena   Bologna
Savona Genoa   Piangipane
        La Spezia
Vado   Florence   To   Adriatic
                    Fiuggi &   Sea
                    Santa Maria
                    di Bagni

© S.Ballard (2020)

7

DACHAU

HUMAN DEBRIS

The rain begins to fall as I drive out of Tarvisio. As I cross the border into Austria, the mountains disappear into the clouds and the car windscreen steams up. It takes over seven hours to reach Munich. The motorway skirts close to Hitler's retreat high above Berchtesgaden. Here, an odd kind of tourism keeps the tills ringing, and visitors tuck into hearty, meaty meals in the mountain hideaway where the vegetarian Führer liked to escape the pressures of war.

Twenty kilometres to the north-west of Munich is the town of Dachau, now part of the city's commuter belt. Here in this former concentration camp in southern Germany, the survivors of the Shoah found not only a spiritual leader in a small bespectacled army chaplain called Abraham Klausner, but a veritable Moses. Bavaria was to become the unlikely setting for a Jewish renaissance in the months after the end of the Second World War and at its heart was an unlikely leader, a 30-year-old rabbi from Denver. Klausner was the first outsider to draw up a plan to help the survivors and to directly impact on their lives. This was also a refugee crisis on a scale that had not been seen before, and the responses formulated in occupied Germany would lay the basis of an international response.

Klausner is a largely forgotten Jewish hero, a man who helped tens of thousands find their families, their route to Palestine and, most important, themselves, in the fetid and shell-shocked Displaced Persons camps of Bavaria in what was soon to be the American sector of an occupied and divided Germany. In the summer of 1945, thanks to the work of Klausner, southern Germany became an unlikely Zionist hub where the survivors came together as a united group intent on settling in Palestine. Again, their Zionism was driven by the way they were treated in the weeks after their liberation. Nineteen-year-old private Bob Hilliard was among the American soldiers who occupied Germany. When a concentration camp survivor asked him: "What's the difference between you Americans and the Nazis except you don't have gas chambers!" it became clear to him that "the genocide that the Germans had begun did not end. The American Armed Forces who occupied Bavaria and part of Austria continued it for months after VE Day, May 7, 1945. Genocide by neglect, some called it. Deliberate neglect, others suggested." It was an attitude that alienated the survivors and reinforced the idea that they had no future in Europe.

On 29 April 1945, the American Army came into the concentration camp that has made Dachau infamous. Bodies lay in cattle trucks in the sidings and spilled out of the open railway cars onto the ground. The prisoners had died while being moved to Dachau from the east when the Germans fled in front of the Russian advance. Army reporter James Creasman was one of the first to enter the camp. "Seasoned as they were to stark reality, these trained observers gazed at the freight cars full of piled cadavers, no more than bones and skin, and they could not believe what they saw … Riflemen, accustomed to witnessing death, had no stomach for rooms stacked almost ceiling-high with tangled human bodies adjoining the cremation furnaces, looking like some maniac's woodpile."

Dachau was the second major camp liberated by the Americans. The war had not come to an end quickly. This was almost fifteen months after the liberation of Rivne and three months after Soviet forces stumbled across Auschwitz. The Americans arrived just days after 7,000 mostly Jewish prisoners had been dispatched on a forced death march to the complex from the killing fields of the east and Dachau's sub-camps. This development created a picture that was in fact not representative of the camp's twelve-year history, during which time it had been a prison and not a death camp. In the closing weeks of the war, the death rate in many concentration camps in Germany reached one thousand per day.

Besides the dead, the American troops found 30,000 starving and disease-ridden prisoners crammed into infested barracks. Three of them, all Polish Jews, would end up on the *Wedgwood*—17-year-old Rivka Levin, her future husband Mordechai Perlmutter and Yakov Tsukert, who had survived a death march. Doubtless there were others but I have yet to track them down.

DACHAU

Dachau is not a place that lends much help to the road-trip historian. My GPS takes me through a small industrial park, past car showrooms and shops selling construction materials. In 1945 Dachau was surrounded by wealthy farms and lush fields. The visitor's carpark is full. There is a chill in the air and I put my coat on even though it is July. Uninteresting scrubby woods sit alongside the wide path that leads to the famous white gatehouse with its red roof and sinister black wooden watchtower. Tourists enter through a small gateway in the larger main gate, in which, worked into the metal, are the words "Arbeit Macht Frei", Work sets you free. It takes a while to walk through the small gate, as it seems nearly everyone wants their picture taken next to it. It is an odd place for a holiday snap.

Despite the number of visitors, the parade ground seems empty and the former barracks are full of a vast display of noticeboards that provide an information overload. What they tell is sanitised and empty. Few people read them all, even me. I gaze at latrines, wooden bunks and crematoria. It is oddly sterile. I walk back to the visitors' centre bookshop. It is not very busy. Everyone is in the canteen; there is a strong smell of chips frying. I scan the shelves. There is a vast choice of titles that cover the horrors of the Holocaust, but nothing about the years after the liberation.

So it is back to my computer and hours of searching. I eventually find the testimony of Abraham Klausner, the first American army rabbi to enter the camp. I then discover that he wrote a book about his experiences. I order it on Amazon. It is only available through third-party sellers. The book, *A Letter to My Children from the Edge of the Holocaust*, turns out to be a treasure trove. The copy that I buy has a sticker on it saying it once belonged to the Palm Beach County Library System, but inside it is stamped "Discarded: Outdated, Redundant Material". It has an address sticker inside the back cover showing that it had passed through the hands of a Mr Philip Aronson of Delray Beach in Florida before arriving in west London. The book is like a magic key and opens the door to the story of what happened to the survivors in southern Germany once the war was over. I am stunned as I read and reread the account.

Yet this young rabbi did not feel like Moses entering Dachau, but more like a fool as he walked in nervously fingering cellophane envelopes, filled with miniature mezuzahs, which the Jewish Welfare Board had given to him to hand out. He had no brief, and nothing summed up better how clueless the US Army and American Jewry were when it came to helping the Holocaust survivors than the mezuzahs in plastic bags. Surrounded by degradation, he watched an American GI deliberately flick a cigarette butt at three survivors in loose, hanging camp garb, who, darting under a fence like dogs, flung themselves to retrieve it. Klausner was appalled, shattered by the indignity of the scene. Aware that he must walk through the gates to their side of the fence, the young rabbi kept his eyes on the medical staff, who were starting the morning shift and were on their way into the camp. Visitors were doused with a blast of DDT by a nozzle placed into their sleeves. Klausner joined the queue and "felt the baptism of the powder".

Klausner steeled himself and entered one of the low-lying grey barracks. He was assaulted by the stench, "telling, by churning and cleaving to the gut, of the ethos of human degradation". To most he was nearly invisible, just "an apparition". The rabbi looked different from those the survivors knew. He was young, round-faced, and in American military uniform. Born in Memphis, Tennessee, he had been raised in Denver, Colorado, and had volunteered to serve with the US Army's Chaplain Corps, hoping he would be sent to the Far East where he felt his services were needed, not to Germany, where the war was over. On arrival in Europe, he was attached to the 116th Evacuation Hospital Unit and sent to Dachau on what, until then, he had considered a dull assignment. Yet he did have something to offer and would, in a matter of days, find himself the leader and father figure to some 32,000 liberated Jews in and around Dachau. Klausner was to be the survivors' rabbi.

This is how his work began. "I had nothing to offer. I had nothing to give," he recalled years later. "But nevertheless, there I was in Dachau and I felt I had to do something, and so I entered the barracks and stood there, terribly disturbed." Inside the barracks he saw "three rows of shelves, nothing other than the shelves. There wasn't … a piece of linen of any kind. There wasn't a bar of soap. There wasn't a chair, a place to sit down. It was just a dirty situation and here were the people either stretched out on the shelves or moving about listlessly. They paid no attention to me as if I didn't exist." He felt lost, hopeless and aghast as he faced the survivors. Could he ever do anything to help them? But then one weak voice pierced the silence begging—"Do you know my brother?" No name was given, but the voice that came from one of the shelves explained that his brother, who had emigrated to America, was also serving as an army chaplain. Klausner recalled: "I was attracted by the timbre of the voice, the weeping in the voice and I said, 'Yes, I know your brother,' and the voice said don't just say that to console me." To which Klausner replied, "I am not consoling you. I am going to bring your brother to you." At which point the rabbi rushed out of the barracks—afraid.

In the clear air outside he knew immediately he had found his role in Dachau. Once Kaddish, the prayer for the dead, was said and the bodies were buried, Klausner vowed he would reunite the survivors with what families and friends they had left. "I heard in them a cry for identity," Klausner later wrote. "Are we not, each of us, defined by our relationships with parents, clan, and country. Bereft of relationships, reduced to a number tattooed on the arm, they sought to discover through me a thread which would weave them back into a reality they once knew." It was to be his first battle with the military authorities. The survivors had just found their leader. Klausner had large ears and a crop of bushy hair, and his bookish looks were enhanced by his horn-rimmed glasses; Hollywood would never have cast him in the role. Fortunately, the dynamic Klausner was a man of determination and capable of ignoring red tape.

Dachau had opened in 1933 and was the first of a major system of concentration camps that would eventually spread out across Europe. It was a vast site with massive warehouses and storerooms. It was the perfect place for Klausner to set up operations. The rabbi rummaged through the stores, appropriating paper, pens, envelopes and typewriters. Driven by a desire to give back the survivors their identities, he asked the prisoners to list their names, ages, and places of birth. He believed that no sooner had these lists been seen in America than help and assistance would flood in.

In retrospect, if one reads survivors' statements and memoirs, it becomes clear that they were deeply affected by their loss of identity in the camps, when their name became a number, their hair was shaven off and their clothes taken away. Their first thoughts on liberation were of their families and finding those who might have survived. Klausner knew this instinctively. In the months and years that followed, he was consistently praised by the survivors, who came to regard him as their most trusted advocate, and called him "our chaplain".

Germany was divided by the victorious Allies into American, British, French and Soviet zones. The western zones, especially the American one, became the focal point for Jewish refugees, and many of those who would sail on the *Wedgwood* would not only be liberated in Klausner's patch but pass through it on the way to Italy. Klausner oversaw a vast area that stretched from Munich to the Brenner Pass and from Eggenfelden in the east to Türkheim in the west. It contained thousands of Jewish survivors and very soon Klausner realised that there were far more than he had initially thought. In Dachau and its vast network of sub-camps there were 67,665 registered prisoners, of whom 22,000 were Jews, and therefore came under his watch. But before he could set off to make a census of who was alive and find out who was dead, Klausner heard that the 116th would soon be leaving Dachau for a rest period and that he would accompany them. At first he followed orders but no sooner had he arrived at the resort where they were destined to stay than the intrepid rabbi jumped back aboard the final truck as it left heading back to Dachau. He was not in need of a holiday. It would be some time, and a number of court martials, before Klausner squared his absence without leave with the army authorities.

What Klausner saw as he toured his domain horrified him. Unable to cope with the situation on the ground, the army had resorted to military discipline and kept the survivors in the camps, where those now arriving in the American zone were also housed. They were surrounded by barbed wire and watchtowers. Klausner's first stop was Feldafing, south-west of Munich, where a former Nazi school was crowded with an assortment of displaced persons, referred to as DPs in the post-war jargon. The camp, which was made up of stone and wooden barracks and individual houses that had been requisitioned, was on the elegant Starnberger See, a popular holiday spot. In the complex was the house where Thomas Mann had written *The Magic Mountain*.

In Feldafing today there is little evidence that the camp was ever there, but in the early summer of 1945 Klausner was struck by the suffering that confronted him and the army's inability to cope with the people they had just liberated. Above all it was clear that there was little or no food. Then at Mittenwald, Klausner heard the unbelievable. He wrote: "American forces had surrounded the camp and threatened the liberated with live ammunition, all because they had protested the lack of food." He then travelled north to Buchberg, where he realised that, hemmed into camps with no shops and no provisions, the survivors had little choice but to resort to black-marketeering.

The survivors were not free but trapped. This was the experience of the people on the *Wedgwood*. If they tried to go home, they soon found nothing for them but a hostile reception. They were denied entry to America and Palestine, where strict immigration quotas were in place. They were an afterthought, at the bottom of the list of the Allies' priorities; they were powerless, homeless and unwanted, and mattered little to any future peace plans. This is the attitude the survivors' rabbi rebelled against. Klausner wrote endless letters to Jewish agencies in the United States asking for help but, because of military concerns about civilian personnel in a war zone, the NGOs, like the American Jewish Joint Distribution Committee, were kept well away by the army. The first Joint Distribution Committee team did not arrive in Munich until 4 August and then without supplies. When no help came, Klausner broke every rule in the book to provide it himself.

To Klausner's fury, "the people", as he always called them, were not even recognised as Jews but sorted as Poles, Romanians, Lithuanians and so on, and thus often forced into barracks with some of the very people who had persecuted them. The main body tasked with assisting the military was the United Nations Relief and Rehabilitation Administration, UNRRA. Its aim was to get home the destitute—Jews and non-Jewish survivors of the concentration camps, slave and forced labourers, prisoners of war, volunteer workers and refugees—as soon as was possible, in accordance with agreements made at the Yalta Conference in February 1945. If little had prepared the soldiers who liberated Dachau for their duties, the situation was little better among those whose designated job it was to care for the survivors. Francesca Wilson, an aid worker with UNRRA, who arrived at Feldafing in mid-May, wrote: "As for inmates of the camp, at first it was hard to look on them without repulsion ... all that was human had been taken away from them." Ignorance and misunderstanding hampered efforts to help. Allied relief workers struggled to understand the psychological experiences that the Jews had been through and had little knowledge of the complicated nature of European Jewry. They complained that they were divided into factions, that they argued about how things should be done. The aid workers were baffled to find that, after years of hard labour and little assistance from their new masters, the Jews refused to work. It mystified them that their charges were more than reluctant to enter the showers. Rabbi Klausner, however, treated the people differently. Unlike others who came in contact with them, the rabbi did not regard them as scum, malleable fools, raw material or pitiful sheep. Klausner saw them not only as equals but as tough Jews whose very souls had been reshaped by what they had experienced. Soon all Jewish life in the shattered landscape of Dachau and its sub-camps began to revolve around him.

The confusion and lack of understanding were made worse by the fact that accounts of what had happened in Auschwitz and the camps liberated by the Red Army were dismissed as Soviet propaganda and received little attention in the Western media as a result. The reluctance in Great Britain and the United States to believe the worst of the atrocity stories concerning the fate of Europe's Jews meant that the press tended to shy away from such accounts, leaving the public ignorant. Once the camps in the western zone were liberated, journalists tended to write about national groups and, as a result, the specific nature of what had happened to the Jews disappeared from view.

On returning to Dachau after his whirlwind tour of Bavaria, Klausner was greeted by a "cluster of figures" from a former prison complex in Neu Freimann, who had been told that they were to be moved east towards the Russian zone. Klausner immediately went to the camp and countermanded the soldiers' orders to move the Jews. The following morning two colonels arrived in Dachau and escorted Klausner into a side room. An argument ensued in which Klausner demanded to know why the Jews were being moved. General George Patton had just been assigned the command of the area. In Klausner's memoirs he says that he was told: "He doesn't want DPs in his area if he can help it. The camp is to be used as a motor pool." Flabbergasted, the rabbi set off immediately for the Neu Freimann HQ, where the commanding officer refused to see him and he was "shunted" into the repatriation office. Here he began to make his case, stating: "There are twelve hundred Jews …" but got no further as the officer in charge retorted: "There are no Jews in the camp!" He pointed the rabbi's attention to a population chart that listed Poles, Ukrainians, Yugoslavs and Greeks. Klausner, unable to believe what he was hearing, was then quickly ordered out of his office. The rabbi became more determined than ever to protect his people. "I, the little boy with his finger in the dike, was all the more determined after my dismissal by the repatriation officer to join forces with the liberated and stand fast against the Army's efforts."

There were, however, also more sinister forces at play. General Patton's dislike of the DPs was no secret. In his diary on 15 September 1945, Patton wrote that the reason the DPs had to be kept under lock and key was that, if they were free, they would "spread over the country like locusts" and his fear was that Germans would be murdered. Displaced persons were, he believed, not human beings, "and this applies particularly to the Jews who are lower than animals". On Yom Kippur in October 1945, Patton visited the camp at Feldafing with General Dwight D. Eisenhower. He recorded in his diary: "This happened to be the feast of Yom Kippur, so they were all collected in a large wooden building which they called a synagogue … which was packed with the greatest stinking bunch of humanity I have ever seen. When we got about halfway up, the head rabbi, who was dressed in a fur hat similar to that worn by Henry VIII of England and in a surplice heavily embroidered and very filthy, came down and met the General." What he failed to see was the intensity of that first Yom Kippur service after the liberation. It was attended by almost five thousand people, each mourning for a child, a parent, a loved one, brother or sister or everyone they had ever known. For Klausner, "looking back on the scene I see myself as a naïve apparition moving against the dark hatred of an American general whose heroic dimensions were matched by his iniquitousness. It is stupefying to see that a military officer who was so filled with anti-Semitic contempt could be assigned to command an area containing the largest number of liberated Jews, as well as those in flight from the inhospitality of their East European homes."

On 24 June 1945, desperate for help, Klausner wrote to all the leaders of the plethora of American Jewish organisations, informing them that "the camps are substandard. At Türkheim, four hundred and fifty Jews live in a double-wire enclosure, formerly a prisoner-of-war installation with its deadly electrical apparatus intact. The camp is a cesspool which should be condemned. At Buchberg, 1,000 Jews live in a once-active factory. The dilapidated structures are overcrowded. Items such as soap, toothbrushes, linen, laundry facilities are unknown. Plumbing, where found, is inadequate." As far as food was concerned, he reported that many inmates said that more was given to them in the concentration camps, and added that the majority of the former inmates still wore their camp uniforms. "Jews singled out for destruction are now caught up in a strange situation. They do not want to return to the scene of their destruction, yet want to make certain they have explored every avenue which might lead to surviving family members. They are not recognised as Jews by the military, but are counted among their persecutors." He concluded: "Liberated, but not free—that is the paradox. In the concentration camp his being was consumed with a hope of salvation. Saved, his hope dissipates. Suffering is his badge." Max Braude, the 7th Army's senior chaplain, decked out in riding breeches, boots and crop, came down from Heidelberg to reprimand Klausner for having written such a report. Years later Klausner would discover that his letter had been seen by Abba Hillel Silver, who later represented world Jewish interests before the UN in respect of the partition of Palestine and the establishment of a Jewish homeland. He noted that Klausner's report should be disregarded. Such was the lack of understanding.

8

ST OTTILIEN

THE DOCTOR AND HIS PATIENTS

The monastery of St Ottilien rises above ploughed fields and the green Bavarian pastures of southern Germany. This was the unlikely hub of the extraordinary Jewish renaissance that took place in Bavaria in the summer of 1945. In the weeks that followed VE Day, the building was a focal point for survivors in the US-occupied zone.

It is a bright but chilly late-winter Saturday afternoon when I arrive in the monastery carpark. The large complex is packed with visitors enjoying a drink in the beer garden, after a hike in the surrounding countryside, before visiting the vast collection of stuffed animals from Africa collected by the Benedictines while on missionary work. As he tucks into a large plate of Wiener schnitzel and downs a lager inside the restaurant, Father Cyrill expresses his sadness that most of the people who come to St Ottilien have no idea of the extraordinary events that took place here in the months that followed the end of the Second World War.

Father Cyrill's day job is running the monastery's Benedictine publishing house, but in his spare time he is busy collating and gathering information about a key but forgotten moment in both the monastery's and Jewish history. He wants to record not just the facts about what happened here and what the survivors endured, but hopes that by reminding people how Holocaust survivors found shelter in the monastery, he will help Germans care about the thousands of refugees who have arrived in their country in recent years.

In late April 1945, as the American Army advanced deep into Germany, a trainload of 3,500 mostly Jewish prisoners was being moved from Kaufering concentration camp, a satellite of Dachau. The prisoners were heading for the South Tyrol on the Italian–Austrian border where they were to build defences for the Nazis' last stand. In the village of Schwabhausen, nor far from St Ottilien, the train was strafed by US fighter planes. Ammunition in the sidings blew up, and in the confusion the SS who were guarding the prisoners fled.

Uri Chanoch, the older brother of Dani, who as a small boy worked on the ramp at Auschwitz and returned years later with his family and ate pizza in his former barracks, was one of the prisoners who suddenly found themselves free. He was 17 years old. Uri spent the night under the starry skies hiding in the forest with three other boys whom he knew from the Kaufering camp. He simply felt relief as he lay down to sleep on the cold earth of the forest floor. Weak, barefoot, hungry and crowded into the train at Kaufering, Uri had believed that death was near; the survivors had few illusions about their fate at this point. But, after four days in the woods and hiding in the basement of a deserted military camp, Chanoch and his friends encountered an American tank on a country lane. The soldiers, one of whom spoke Yiddish, handed the teenager a can of tinned beef, warning him to eat only a little at a time. It was sound advice that kept him alive. After years of starvation, death stalked the food that the survivors craved. If they ate too much, their bodies could simply not cope and many died, sometimes instantly.

In the morning after the air attack, some of the prisoners who had stayed close to the train regrouped in the bushes and trees alongside the railway tracks. Only 800 were left and they found themselves alone in the deserted station. For some hours they sat motionless by the tracks, inexplicably free, until, as the afternoon lengthened, they began to debate their next move. One by one they began to venture into the surrounding streets.

Among the survivors was a man more confident than the others, who, although he looked as if he was in his mid-to-late forties, was in fact just 33. Dr Zalman Grinberg was a physician who had specialised in radiology in Kovno, 1,500 km away in Lithuania. Grinberg knew that, alone, they had little chance of survival, so he quickly gathered the survivors together and, like a shepherd, drew his motley flock in, organising them so that they could forage for food in groups and sleep together in the freight cars while they waited for the Americans to arrive.

In every village that the survivors visited to beg for food, they were beaten and cursed. There were few men of fighting age in the villages and Grinberg felt they were the luckier for it because, if there had been, they would most likely have been lynched or shot. The young doctor set about trying to care for the sick and wounded, many of whom were women and children, but every day, despite his efforts, more of the survivors died. After some days while he was searching for food and help, Grinberg came across one of the first American officers in the area, Captain Otto B. Raymond, a gentile from St Louis, who, as luck would have it, had a sympathetic ear. Dr Grinberg set out a plan that Raymond was willing to help with. Grinberg would pretend to be a representative of the International Committee of the Red Cross and take over part of a nearby military hospital in the monastery of St Ottilien. Grinberg had studied in Basel and spoke fluent German.

Captain Raymond found the appropriate clothes and a false ID, and the two men drove to the monastery and demanded that the commandant in charge move some of his wounded German and Hungarian soldiers to make way for the Jews. At first the commandant refused, saying his men were too sick. Most of the patients, however, seemed, in Captain Raymond's and Dr Grinberg's eyes, in good health and hiding out rather than in need of nursing. With a clear conscience Grinberg in his "role" as a Red Cross official threatened the commandant with severe consequences if he did not do as they requested. Two weeks after VE Day, US Army ambulances moved 420 of the former camp inmates into the monastery. In modern-day St Ottilien, Father Cyrill tells me more details of the story, as further generous plates of food are placed in front of us. "The monastery had been closed down by the Nazis and the young monks sent to the Eastern Front," he says. "The older monks were sent to work as slave labourers on the monastery farm and in the military hospital that was set up here." When Grinberg arrived, it became the first Jewish hospital in Bavaria.

Grinberg was to become a close friend and ally of Rabbi Klausner. The young doctor had a daredevil reputation among the survivors, and his family thinks he was involved in smuggling children out of the Kovno Ghetto in potato sacks, including his own son. In July 1944, as the Red Army approached, the Germans razed the ghetto and transferred the remaining 6,000 Jews out of the city. The destruction was total and the survivors who witnessed it knew there was nothing to go back for. Even if they did feel a desire to return, they also knew that Soviet forces had reoccupied the area and they sensed they had no future under communism. Grinberg had managed to stay together with his wife until 1944, when they arrived at the train depot near Stutthof, in northern Poland, where she was ordered off the train. When Grinberg came to St Ottilien, he had no idea if his family was alive or dead. He was not unique; all of the survivors were in the same situation.

Some of the people on the *Wedgwood* were Grinberg's patients, whom he nursed back to health. One of the first of the passengers to make their way to St Ottilien was Harry Linser, who was just 17. He had been born in Vienna and was deported in 1942 to the Theresienstadt Ghetto and from there in 1944 to Auschwitz and on to Kaufering, the Dachau sub-camp. Linser had, like Chanoch, escaped into the woods when the train was attacked, and hid out with a Christian Ukrainian friend. As Linser had learned Czech in Theresienstadt, the two youngsters managed to communicate enough to make a supportive attachment. Linser had been wounded in the attack, so the two men hid in a barn until the German farmer to whom it belonged stumbled across them. Linser was quick-witted enough to tell him that the Americans had already arrived and the man, keen to be seen as a helpful German, quickly invited the two into his home for breakfast. The Ukrainian declined the offer, as he wanted to set off home immediately. Later Linser would learn that he was executed by the Russians because he had worked for the Germans as a slave labourer. The farmer, noticing Linser's wounds, took him to St Ottilien. Linser, who weighed less than 42 kg, would spend two months there convalescing before leaving for Vienna and then Italy.

After lunch, Father Cyrill takes me into the heart of the nineteenth-century complex, and we stand in the shadow of the cathedral with its solid grey steeple. The setting is idyllic. Orchards lead down the hill to the pastures. Father Cyrill points out a large pre-war building that is now used as a guesthouse. It was here that Dr Grinberg was allocated two floors in one wing of the large monastery complex, both with large open rooms full of cots and mattresses on the floor in every conceivable space. Chairs placed together with planks across them also served as beds. Conditions were dire; there were no blankets but, as it was summer, this was not a priority. What mattered was that there was no medicine and no food. Dr Grinberg was the only doctor capable of working although the survivors were lucky to have among them five doctors whom he would eventually nurse back to health. But, says Father Cyrill, "the young doctor was not just setting out to heal his patients' bodies but their minds as well". As he talks, his cassock is blown about in the February breeze. "He wanted to instil in them a desire to move forward and rebuild their lives. One of the most unusual things he did was to hold a concert on the monastery lawn where they played music that the Nazis had banned."

Nineteen-year-old Private Bob Hilliard from Brooklyn attended the concert, thinking it would make an interesting feature for a US army newspaper, the *2nd Wind Eagle*, which he edited. He took a jeep and set off in search of the story. This event would change his life. It was a cool spring day on 27 May 1945 as the young New Yorker turned onto the narrow dirt road off the highway from Munich to Augsburg. The track wound around farm buildings and fields full of wild flowers until the monastery rose majestically above the trees. The moment he arrived, Hilliard parked his jeep at the edge of the garden and stared at what he saw before him.

At the far end of the lawn was a stage several feet off the ground, made of nondescript, unmatching wooden boards and covered with a loosely stretched canopy of patched and sewn sheets and discarded parachute cloth. Rows of wooden chairs were set in front of the stage.

> In the aisles, on the chairs and on the grass, standing, sitting, walking, leaning, lying, were hundreds of stick figures, emaciated, pale, skeletal, expressionless, all dressed in the black and white striped uniforms of the concentration camps. They barely moved and when they did it was in the flickering slow motion of early silent films.

He pictured himself sitting in his college dormitory room reading Dante's *Inferno*. For several minutes the young man simply stared, unable to comprehend what lay in front of him. On the other side of a low wall he saw dozens of men wearing German army uniforms walking about in the careless manner of the privileged, some smoking cigarettes, some with bandaged limbs, some leaning on the uniformed female nurses in their crisp white uniforms. They were "able to look directly at the concentration camp survivors" but, as Hilliard noted, "there was no indication on their faces that they saw them".

Men and women soon appeared on stage carrying instruments that had been saved or provided by the Germans. The majority were surviving members of the former Kovno Ghetto Orchestra, among them the noted conductor and gifted violinist Michael Leo Hofmekler. He walked to the front of the stage and told the audience: "This is our liberation concert." At this point the young private left his jeep and sat down among the survivors while the musicians played Mahler and Mendelssohn and other music that had been forbidden for years. The movements of the musicians, Hilliard observed, were "cramped, tight, fearful, as if they could not believe there was room to move a bow or air in which to blow a note". He wrote later that it was a "liberation concert at which most of the people could not believe that they were free".

That was all about to change, and a major revival of Jewish identity and Zionism was about burst forth. Grinberg, who was tall and thin, stepped onto the stage to deliver a remarkable speech in which he described the odyssey he had undertaken. It was a chronicle of tragedy that cleverly linked all the survivors together; each had taken a different "road of torture" that formed "one common red thread of blood, torture, torment, humiliation—and violent death". His speech moulded his listeners into a community and restored to the survivors their self-confidence. "He gave the people a will to live. It was important and should not be forgotten," says Father Cyrill, his enthusiasm for the story evident. "It was an extraordinary event." Dr Grinberg spoke in German, the monk tells me, quoting Grinberg's exact words, "because we have here people from many countries and with many languages. German has become for us a common tongue." He spoke softly and slowly. He introduced himself as the "head doctor at this hospital for political ex-prisoners", as not all the inmates of St Ottilien were Jews. They included some communists and clergy. Grinberg said:

> We act as delegates of millions of victims to tell all mankind, to proclaim all over the world how cruel people may become, what brutal hellishness is concealed within a human being, and what a triumphant record of crime and murder has been achieved by the nation of Hegel and Kant, Schiller and Goethe, Beethoven and Schopenhauer,

he told his audience. There was no talk of revenge. Grinberg was no Abba Kovner. "If we took vengeance, we would fall to the depths of ethics and morals the German nation has been in for the last ten years." He concluded: "We are free but we do not yet grasp what it means to be free, perhaps because we still stand in the shadow of death." Grinberg's speech established an important theme among survivors—the significance of remembrance.

When Dr Grinberg finished speaking, some of the survivors moved slowly back to the buildings while others sat motionless in the chairs or on the grass. Among them may well have been two brothers who sailed on the *Wedgwood*, Shimon and Yitzhak Brindt, who are listed among the first patients to be cared for at St Ottilien. A third brother who travelled with them was at this point in Dachau. A few of the survivors talked quietly. This small, seemingly insignificant gathering represented a turning point. It was the first stirring of Jewish self-confidence on German soil. The event was an indication that the DPs had clearly defined interests and would lobby on their own behalf. In eastern Europe you could be as organised as you wanted but the authorities had no desire to listen, but in Germany there was one person who would make sure they would—Abraham Klausner.

Father Cyrill explains:

> The orchestra became a symbol of the renaissance that happened in St Ottilien and they played all over Bavaria in the months to come. They even played for the world's media at the Nuremberg Trials. I met the family of a survivor, Dr Chaim Ipp, who came to visit the monastery and I was deeply moved by their story and have been busy finding out everything that I can, and our community would like to set up an information centre. People think that the war ended, and everything was over, but it was not the case. It is the will to build a new life that we see here, and it is our obligation and our mission to commemorate what happened. This is not just a story of cruelty but one of hope.

When the concert ended, Bob Hilliard took the opportunity to seek out the doctor, whose confident manner he found was "reinforced by his clear straightforward tone and excellent English". Grinberg's harrowed face was set off by his dark hair and clipped moustache. Hilliard followed him to his room. There was a desk and a chair against the wall opposite the door. An old couch and another chair made up the main part of the room and, to the right, partially hidden by a curtain hanging on a rod across the ceiling, was a small area with a bed, a night table and a dresser. Hilliard told him he intended to write about the hospital and hoped it would result in some help from the United States. Dr Grinberg's words were cynical, even if the tone was gentle. "The world forgot about us for the past ten years. Why would they care about us now?" The young man asked him about his family. Grinberg had sent news to Kovno that he was alive, he told the army reporter, but no one had tried to contact him. At this point the doctor took a handkerchief from his pocket, opened it completely and held it over his entire face, then crumpled it up against his eyes. "So what can I do but cry? It was a hope." I think of the lists on which I have hunted for the names of those on the *Wedgwood* and wonder if, for some of those people, I am the only person who has ever searched for their names.

As the summer of 1945 progressed, there was a brief moment of hope when the hospital was officially listed as a DP camp. The news was met with the expectation of at least a minimum of supplies being provided, but no sooner was it announced than American military police arrived at the monastery and put up a barbed wire fence around the part of the compound where the survivors lived. Grinberg was told that it was to protect them from outside agitators, but the doctor was sure it was to stop the survivors from going into the local towns to seek food and clothing and infecting the population with diseases. "So they are erecting a barbed wire fence around us," Dr Grinberg told Hilliard. "Another concentration camp. An American one." The next time Hilliard and his friends visited St Ottilien they were stopped and the food they were bringing was confiscated. Orders had been issued that no unapproved goods were to be allowed into DP camps.

The true horror of their situation was made clear early one late-August morning when Hilliard was called by Grinberg. He urgently needed help. One of the survivors had been shot. Hilliard and his friend Ed Herman asked a senior officer for help; he requisitioned a jeep and the trio set off for St Ottilien. They were shocked by what awaited them. A hundred yards to the right of the gate, outside the barbed wire fence, a man was lying on the ground. Dr Grinberg and some of the other doctors were huddled around him. The man was under a blanket, his right leg partially propped up on a pillow covered with a piece of torn sheet. His trousers were cut all the way up his leg. He was bleeding badly. At least a hundred survivors stood behind the fence muttering. Armed American military policemen stood between the crowd and the man on the ground. When asked what had happened, one policeman explained coldly: "He was shot trying to get through the barbed wire." DPs were officially confined to the camp.

Grinberg looked up at the three young soldiers and said: "He was not leaving the camp without permission. He was trying to get back in. He had sneaked out last night to go to Buchloe to see if he could find some food. We don't have any food. He was trying to get back in with food for us. They saw him trying to get under the wire and shot him. Without any warning." The police had refused to let the doctors take the wounded man into the hospital. "He's bleeding badly," Grinberg told Hilliard's commanding officer. "If we don't get him inside, I am frightened he will bleed to death." At this point, the officer turned to the captain of the police and demanded an explanation. The captain answered: "We have our orders and they have their orders." In disbelief the officer retorted: "That man was in a concentration camp. He survived the concentration camps." Flabbergasted, he asked: "How the hell could you let him be shot?" Without blinking, the policeman replied: "He's only a fucking Jew. That's what all Jews deserve!" As the three soldiers turned to walk into the hospital, he muttered "fucking Jew bastards" behind their backs. The man who was shot did not die but his leg was amputated. The three soldiers concluded that there was nothing they could do, as the police were indeed carrying out orders.

The shooting at St Ottilien prompted Bob Hilliard and Ed Herman to take action. The two privates decided to write hundreds of letters which they sent through the military post in packages to friends in the United States, who then forwarded the individual letters to their friends, clubs, synagogues, youth groups and indeed anyone who might send a package of food, clothes or medicine. A month passed and not a single parcel arrived although the two young men had been assured by their friends in America that many had been posted. Then one night Rabbi Klausner had a tip-off that an important official, Dean Earl G. Harrison of the University of Pennsylvania Law School, a representative on the Intergovernmental Committee on Refugees, who had been sent to Germany to assess the situation, was staying at Munich's Excelsior Hotel. Klausner immediately "swung by". He was on a mission and took the dean under his wing, changing the itinerary that had been drawn up for him by the military. As he escorted him across Bavaria, Harrison made it clear to Klausner that he had not been sent by President Truman but was on a mission for the State Department alone.

Klausner later retold this story at a commemorative event in the US and was received with "uninhibited derision", as there were many who wanted to cast Truman as the survivors' saviour and present America as the protector of the Jews. It was a story that became part of the myth of the founding of the State of Israel. In his memoirs, Klausner laid bare his dislike of Truman and the falsity of the role in which history had cast him. This was to become a bone of contention between him and his vast array of critics in high circles in American politics. It is odd that this was to be such a wound, as in Truman's own memoir, *Year of Decisions 1945*, published in 1955, he himself states clearly that he did not send Harrison to Europe, and the question of the survivors takes up less than half a page in the book. He had many other things on his mind that summer, which fill the pages, like the decision to drop the atomic bombs on Hiroshima and Nagasaki. Klausner's people were not on the top of his list of priorities. Stoically, the rabbi said: "They wanted it to have been different. They wanted Truman to have sent Harrison to Germany." Nevertheless, when Harrison returned to Washington, Truman met him for fifteen minutes and the fifteen minutes made a huge impact. The rabbi's message had got through to the Oval Office.

In October, the packages that Hilliard and Herman had campaigned for finally arrived, and the privates drove the boxes full of clothes, food and yarmulkes to St Ottilien. Not long after, the two men learned that their letters had not just summoned up this bounty but, along with Harrison's report, had had a profound effect on US policy. Letters from home contained a newspaper cutting from the 30 September edition of the *New York Times*. Hilliard and Herman read the article aloud to their comrades in its entirety. Harrison's report stated: "As matters now stand, we appear to be treating the Jews as the Nazis treated them except that we do not exterminate them." The Israeli historian Yehuda Bauer noted: "Reading the report, one encounters phrases and turns of language that are so typically Klausnerian that one wonders how they got into the report of an American law professor". President Truman sent a sizzling letter to Eisenhower, military governor of the US Occupation Zone, demanding that he take steps to resolve the situation. Press coverage of the Harrison report now meant that the American public were made aware of the situation, and there was growing sympathy for the survivors' plight.

In a letter from his mother Hilliard discovered that, as part of his investigations prior to his departure for Germany, Dean Harrison had visited her to find out what sort of man her son was. Luckily, Hilliard's mother had kept all his letters, where he had described the conditions at St Ottilien. She presented Harrison with the pile, and he sat in the sitting room and read them. After twenty minutes he simply said: "I believe it." In Germany all that mattered was that, after the Harrison report, most of the DPs received their 1,200 calories a day.

What really excites Father Cyrill is that the monastery became home to a maternity hospital, just across the lawn, in which 427 babies were born. He points enthusiastically at a small cream-coloured building. "It was a symbol of hope for the Jewish people and some of those children who were born here visit us." Children represented the hope and continuity of generations after the murder of 1.5 million Jewish children, and, above all, babies symbolised the final victory over Hitler. Pregnancy was a major challenge for the female DPs suffering from malnutrition, typhus, tuberculosis and other ailments, and this made a maternity hospital all the more vital. The survivors were fearful of German doctors and rumours abounded of German doctors and midwives wilfully murdering Jewish babies.

It upsets Father Cyrill that some survivors and their descendants visit the monastery and do not see that their families are remembered here. "I try to help the survivors and the families of the survivors who come here in search of their stories. At the moment, people who spent time here as

Fig. 1: Yitzhak Kaplan, one of the *Wedgwood*'s youngest passengers, at home in Haifa.

Fig. 2: Moshe Ha Elion, a Greek Sephardi and Auschwitz survivor, at home in BatYam.

Fig. 3: Abba Kovner's bunker in the Rudniki Forest, where Jewish partisans fought the Nazis after fleeing the Vilnius ghetto.

Fig. 4: Abba Kovner testifying at Adolf Eichmann's trial in Jerusalem, 4 May 1961. After the war Kovner organised the Zionist exodus from Eastern Europe.

Fig. 5: Josef Harmatz, Kovner's friend and fellow partisan, who sailed on the *Wedgwood*; this is his military ID card photo, 1 November 1947 from his period of military service.

Fig. 6: Fania Brantsovskaya, another of Kovner's partisans, at the Ghetto Survivors' Office in Vilnius.

Fig. 7: Yehuda "Poldek" Maimon, a key member of the Krakow underground, who joined Harmatz in Kovner's postwar "revenge" unit before sailing on the *Wedgwood*.

Fig. 8: The ghetto memorial in Kielce, Poland. Many of Kielce's Holocaust survivors perished in a brutal postwar pogrom after returning home.

Fig 9: The Jewish Brigade section of the British Army cemetery in Piangipane, north-eastern Italy. The Brigade more or less went rogue after liberation in order to help organise survivors' emigration.

Fig. 10: The memorial stone at Kaufering, a satellite of Dachau concentration camp.

Fig. 11: The US Army chaplain Rabbi Abraham Klausner (sixth from left) at one of Bavaria's American-run DP camps, where he became the champion of survivors. 1945.

Fig. 12: Dr Zalman Grinberg, who would survive Lithuania's Kovno ghetto, set up the Holocaust survivors' camp at St Ottilien, and rally many there to the Zionist cause.

displaced persons come and have no idea that we care, but we do and St Ottilien is the home of any survivor and their children as much as it is mine." Grinberg gave the survivors a sense of pride and self-worth, and Father Cyrill would like to see that this is a key part in the way they are remembered. "They must be remembered with dignity and respect," he says determinedly.

In the sunshine Father Cyrill and I swap notes and regret that so many eyewitnesses have died. "This is why the evidence must be drawn together now as we are coming to the moment when this story really will be forgotten history, as there will be no one left alive who remembers it," says the monk wisely. In 2017 the monastery buried the last of the fathers who remembered the post-war years. "An information centre here is important for Germany. When I was young growing up in Freiburg, I remember that my father believed that an international Jewish conspiracy existed. Keeping these memories alive is important educationally."

We walk down through the gardens to the cemetery, although in fact there are two, one Catholic and one Jewish. The latter has small metal gates with a Star of David on them. It is a Jewish tradition that one puts a pebble on a gravestone when it is visited. I hunt in the neat flowerbed for one. Father Cyrill looks perplexed and I explain what I am doing. Here there are fewer graves than there once were, as some families have disinterred their relatives' remains and moved them, the monk explains. Many of the dead were children who died simply because they did not have the food and the medicines that were needed.

Father Cyrill poses for a picture by the new information board outside the cemetery, which explains to bemused passers-by why the monastery has a neatly tended Jewish graveyard. "It is a start, but I have a long way to go. This is not something that the Church must do alone. We must do it together, Catholics and Jews." Eighteen months later Father Cyrill will finally open a small exhibition dedicated to the survivors' story in the monastery gift shop.

9

LANDSBERG

THE TOWN WHERE NOTHING HAPPENED

It is dark and frosty when I arrive at the main square of Landsberg, a short drive away from St Ottilien. It was not by chance that Grinberg was a survivor of the Kovno Ghetto. This ghetto was one of the last to be liquidated, in July 1944, and the surviving men were brought to a sub-camp of Dachau. Their presence in Bavaria was to prove crucial to the survivors' story.

The city seems deserted and there is nothing to distract me from admiring the baroque Rathaus (town hall) in the triangular main square but the cold wind. Once in the hotel, I start reading. I am soon engrossed by films on YouTube of torch-lit parades of the Hitler Youth marching through the lonely square outside. It was a rite of passage to make a pilgrimage to Landsberg, where the Führer had written *Mein Kampf* while in prison here in 1923. This was the ideological hub of the Third Reich, but few people in the town choose to remember what happened here.

In the morning, I begin to realise that there is no trace of the Nazi past in the perfectly preserved medieval streets of this picture-postcard town, which sits on banks of the River Lech. In the tourist office I pick up a leaflet with the fairy-tale castle of Neuschwanstein on the front. It details a road trip along the "Romantic Road" from Würzburg to Füssen. Landsberg is one of the stops. The scant summary of the town's history reads: "Founded by Henry the Lion, Landsberg am Lech can look back over a history of more than 850 years. The heart of the old town on the banks of the River Lech is the spacious market place with its proud patrician houses, the town hall by Dominikus Zimmermann has an attractive stucco facade and the dominant 'Schmalz Tower'." I rummage through leaflets hoping to find something about the Kaufering camp just outside the town. It is where the *Wedgwood*'s Chanoch and Linser spent months in hellish conditions alongside a number of the other future passengers. There is nothing. I ask the assistant if anyone can help me and she disappears into a back room and reappears with a sheet of paper on which is a photocopy of a visitor's card. "This man, Manfried Deiler, will help," she says.

Half an hour later I am in the kitchen of a small suburban house on the other side of the River Lech and Herr Deiler is making coffee. He is the vice president of a local historical society, which is trying to set up a documentation centre and museum that will commemorate the Nazi years and their aftermath. It is a struggle and the project has been going on for almost thirty years. "I would love to put on an exhibition about people like Abraham Klausner," he tells me. I try to contain my excitement on finding someone who has heard of the rabbi and ask the retired civil servant how he became so interested in this forgotten part of Landsberg's history.

As he stirs his coffee animatedly, he tells me about a visit he made to Dachau in 1988, when he was 36. He did not suffer an information overload as I had, but read everything in detail. "I was astonished when I saw a picture of prisoners and below it said 'Kaufering'. I thought, wait a minute, that is right here next to Landsberg! Kaufering is moments' drive from here. There was a camp right here! I could not believe it." Deiler had always been interested in history and had asked his parents what happened in Landsberg during the war, but they said: "Nothing! Nothing ever happened here—look, the town is perfectly preserved." After his visit to Dachau, Deiler began asking questions. "But the elderly people said nothing." He waves his hand in the air, implying "nothing" means everything. I follow him into the sitting room. The table is covered in files and books. "Imagine my astonishment when I discovered there were 23,000 Jewish slave workers here," he says, placing the coffee cups on the table.

The day trip to Dachau changed his life and set him on a quest to document the real history of his home town of Landsberg. "Our teachers had been trained in the Nazi period so they did not tell us what really happened. We were naive. We believed what was said and did not ask." He remembers the Eichmann trial of 1961 and, as a child, watching it on television with his parents. "They talked about Auschwitz but never about what happened here. My father was in Russia, so maybe he didn't know, but my mother was here throughout the war." He places a large file of his research next to the coffee pot on the table. "You have to understand that if you know nothing, you cannot ask the right questions. You don't know what people are hiding." He is right. I am beginning that see that if I had not made this journey before I met the survivors who sailed on the *Wedgwood*, I might have missed what this story was all about.

It is, however, inconceivable that the elderly people in the town were ignorant of the camp. Uri Chanoch and Samuel Sadinsky, also on the *Wedgwood*, were sent to stay with German families in the town by the Americans after the liberation. Chanoch stayed for three months. Sadinsky was surprised to find that the father of the family with whom he was placed by the Americans had worked in the prison and met Hitler when he visited there. Sadinsky described them as courteous but uninterested in his plight.

Deiler is very proud of the historical society's recent find in the town archive. "We discovered the prison cards of the 23,000 prisoners who were in Landsberg. Now we can name each one of them. The Nazis used the IBM system, which was very efficient, but I thought, until the archive was opened four years ago, that all of this information had been destroyed, but no, it was simply hidden away." He looks exasperated. "So this is why I have done all this research. I was not told the truth. If you don't know the truth about the past, you don't know the dangers ahead!" He taps the file defiantly. "Now the people have their names back." Names are one thing and identities another, I point out. That much I have learned.

"There is so much history here, we have to talk about events one at a time," he says, opening one of his vast files. Deiler explains that, in the summer of 1944, the Nazis brought almost 4,000 survivors of the Kovno Ghetto to Landsberg to build gigantic underground factories where they were going to produce the revolutionary Messerschmitt Me 262 aircraft. The world's first jet fighter, it was Hitler's secret weapon with which he hoped to sweep the American and British planes out of German skies. But they were developed too late in the war to save him.

One of the men who arrived here in 1944 was 16-year-old Solly Ganor. He had been born in a small town called Heydekrug, in Lithuania, close to the German border, where everyone was German-speaking. (In Lithuanian it is called Silute.) At this point in his life, he was Solly Genkind. The atmosphere in his part of Lithuania changed overnight when Hitler came to power and his family moved to Kovno. At school there he met Uri Chanoch. The war brought them together and they remained close friends, even neighbours in Tel Aviv, until Chanoch died in 2015. Ganor did not sail on the *Wedgwood* but Chanoch did, and his story is an extraordinary example of how many of the passengers, including his younger brother Dani who survived Auschwitz, fought not only for their own lives but for the people around them. In his memoir, Ganor relates how Chanoch, who had a job working as an errand boy for the German Labour Office in the Kovno Ghetto, stole passes that enabled Jews to escape and join the underground. Uri Chanoch was always a committed Zionist, he writes.

When the Kovno Ghetto was destroyed, the people were herded onto trains. The women were ordered off at Stutthof and the sealed railway carriages travelled for days until the men reached southern Germany. When they arrived at a station called Kaufering, they were told to disembark. Once off the train, stiff, weak and filthy, Ganor could not believe his eyes. "The countryside spread around us like a vision. Everywhere there were beautiful stretches of cultivated land dotted with small woods. There wasn't a piece of paper or other refuse to be seen anywhere. How could so much evil dwell amidst so much beauty?" he wondered. "There were neat green fields everywhere, and lining the road were trees laden with ripening apples." The teenager, who was an avid reader, thought it looked like one of the towns in Grimms' *Fairy Tales*. "How could we come to harm in a place like this?" It seems that even in their darkest hours Landsberg and Kaufering looked, on the surface at least, picture-perfect. Yet a dystopian parallel universe existed here. Ganor then adds: "The entire transport was made up of Lithuanian Jews, which was a great advantage because we were all supportive of one another." This throw-away line helps to explain how those who were older, like Grinberg, would become leaders of a vocal Jewish pressure group in the American sector after the war ended.

One day Ganor was sent to deliver potatoes to one of the construction sites where the aircraft were to be built. It was known as Moll after Leonhard Moll, a Munich firm specialising in concrete, which exists to this day. As he entered the building, he heard "inhuman screams" coming from above. The men who were manoeuvring a huge hose spewing concrete had lost control of it and it knocked them one after the other onto the metal spikes that were to support the building. "It was like an enormous, evil hive," he wrote later. "I saw men fall into the concrete and they were entombed," as the hose poured concrete on top of them. The *Wedgwood*'s Harry Linser worked here. It was his job to carry 50 kg bags of cement from a collection point 50 metres away from the mixer. In his testimony he wrote: "I worked every day from five o'clock in the morning until six or seven in the evening. For breakfast, we got coffee, which was just water. For lunch, they gave us a quarter of a loaf of bread and a piece of cheese, a ration that I ate straight away as I saw no point in saving it for later because someone would have stolen it from me."

Deiler's historical society has bought the only surviving part of the camp at Kaufering, where the Nazis' prisoners were housed. He drives me in his small red car-cum-van to the site past the dense woods and flat, wide-open fields, which are moments from his house and which are exactly as Ganor describes them. He points out places where different camp buildings once stood. To the untrained eye it is impossible to spot the way the trees in the forest have been cut back into rectangular clearings where once there were prison compounds, but nothing now remains. "It's disappearing and soon there will be no evidence. That's why we made the effort to buy the surviving buildings and the land around them." We turn into an unmarked dirt track that is barred by a metal gate. He parks at the edge of the wood in a field with snowy patches. He unlocks the gate and takes me into the newly renovated women's quarters, which were camouflaged and dug into the ground. The buildings have curved roofs that remind me of pigsties. It is threateningly eerie and seems miles from anywhere.

Outside the fence that protects what is left of Kaufering camp from vandals is a large field. Deiler points to the area next to the road. "Here we are going to build our documentation centre," he says determinedly before marching off across the snow to the ruined foundations of a small building. My fingers are so cold that I have difficulty writing down what he has to say. "We must preserve this place now. We cannot wait. This is the most important building for the survivors and their families." I am bewildered. A small tree has started to grow in the middle of the ruin. "Here the dead were stacked prior to burial in the mass graves that are situated deep in the woods." He indicates a small path that leads to them. "Why do I spend all my time on getting the money to preserve this fallen-down building?" he asks me. He is a man clearly used to having to justify his actions. "I do it because I met a man called Zvi Kratz, who was in Kaufering with his father. They fought over religion. His father was a believer and he was not. When the father died, he somehow persuaded a guard to let him bury him on the edge of the forest. He marked the tree next to where he was buried, so he could one day place a headstone on the grave." After the war, Deiler continues, Kratz went back to Kovno and discovered that all of his family had been murdered. So he came back to Kaufering to mark the grave of his father—it was all he had left in the world. "But the trees had been chopped down and the grave was lost. All he had was this, the foundations of the building where his father's body had once lain," says Deiler, his desperation evident. He met Kratz in 1990 when the latter returned to Landsberg with his thirteen children and grandchildren, but he has still not managed to save the foundations of this building. "Everything needs to be marked and recorded. That way each individual is remembered and has their dignity." Before we get back in the car, he poses proudly by the metal poles that will soon hold up an information board telling the story of what happened in these now deserted fields. There will soon be a signpost on the roadside as well.

We drive back into Landsberg, taking a road that arrives at the edge of town on the top of a hill. Deiler turns quickly into a residential area of what looks like pre-war apartment blocks. "How would you ever know what this was?" he asks rhetorically, stopping the car next to the grey buildings. "Look carefully. You can see it was the barracks. This is where the soldiers who ran the camp lived. After the war the Americans housed the survivors here. This was the Landsberg DP camp." I understand Deiler's excitement. He knows the importance of this place in Jewish history.

Before the liberation there was an organised underground movement in the Kaufering camp led by Dr Grinberg, who would later become head of the hospital in St Ottilien, and the former district appeal judge of Memel, Samuel Gringauz. There was even an underground handwritten Hebrew newspaper. Kovno had been a world where Jews were confident to be Jewish. The city had a Jewish population of 30,000 before the war and there was a Jewish hospital, and Hebrew and Yiddish schools, and Jewish theatre thrived. It had an educated and sophisticated elite of which Uri Chanoch's family were a part. His father had had a match factory. Uri had been to the Hebrew school but the family were not religious. That said, Kovno had a strong religious community as well as a vibrant Zionist movement and a lively cultural life. In his testimony Chanoch said that in Kovno the Jews "did not live as they did in Germany. It was a Jewish society and they did not mingle other than in business." Well over 90 per cent of Lithuanian Jewry was wiped out in the Holocaust, but that a significant group survived in Bavaria was to be a key factor in the Jewish renaissance that happened here. The Kovno Jews were endowed with a unique sense of self and independence.

In the months before the liberation, they began to discuss what they would do if they survived. In Kaufering they listened to the BBC and were aware that in April 1945 the Allies had invited representatives of the World Jewish Conference and the World Zionist Organisation to the founding conference of the United Nations in San Francisco. In their eyes it meant that the Jews were to be recognised as a nation rather than as adherents of a particular religion. The men, who were all Zionists, decided that they had to act as a unified group and that the factional nature of Jewish life before the war had been a weakness. As a result, after the war Landsberg and St Ottilien became the hubs of this self-assertion and were of crucial importance because they were in the patch of Rabbi Klausner, who was to fight to have Landsberg made an all-Jewish camp. This was to give the Jews a separate, recognised identity among the DPs, who were till then divided by nationality. Now Jews were a nation just like others, and this sense of Jewish nationhood among survivors was nurtured in Bavaria. Also in the Landsberg camp was a significant group of partisans that included the *Wedgwood*'s Pesach Abramovicz, who had fought with the Bielski brothers. They had their own section of the camp known as Kibbutz Negev and their dynamism, the legacy of Abba Kovner, fed into the revival.

As we drive around the former DP camp, Deiler points to the former office of Colonel Irving Heymont, who was in charge of the camp from September to November 1945. He set out to turn the camp into a residential space rather than a detention centre when it became exclusively Jewish. He wanted Landsberg to be self-governing. He was just 27 and from Brooklyn but he hid the fact that he was Jewish. He and Klausner detested each other. Klausner's dislike was rooted not only in the fact that Heymont arrived in September 1945 when most of the groundwork to achieve his plans had already been laid, but in the way Heymont was ashamed of his faith in front of Klausner's people. It was an animosity that was still clear in exchanges of letters decades later. Still, Heymont was to write, "the few months at Landsberg taught me to be a Jew again and that the human spirit can be virtually indomitable—particularly the Jewish spirit".

In the past twenty years Deiler and his small band of volunteers have managed to set up a study programme in the local schools where teenagers learn about the Nazi past and investigate projects further. The group has invited survivors to come to talk to the students. "This is why we need a documentation centre where they can go to study and dig out the history themselves using original documents," he tells me. Heymont was involved with Deiler's project before he died in 2009 and sponsored an essay contest for local students on the town's history as it relates to the rise of Nazism and its role in the Second World War. In 1998, Landsberg's town council named a street after him in recognition of his activities at the DP camp. As we drive away, Deiler says that "after the war people regarded the Jews as privileged and it led to animosity. They didn't want the DPs and they didn't share." It is the reason they chose to forget, he adds. Deiler hopes that soon one of the information boards for which he has been campaigning will mark the former German barracks that became the Landsberg DP camp. "Nobody told me anything when I was a child. You need to tell people. There is no overload point for information, believe me."

For a town where Deiler's mother claimed nothing had happened, I cannot believe how steeped it is in history. We drive across the river to the prison where Hitler wrote *Mein Kampf* after the failed 1923 Munich Beer Hall Putsch. Deiler points to a small graveyard in which there are wooden crosses. They mark the graves of some of the 300 or so Nazi war criminals tried and executed in Landsberg after the war. After the liberation Solly Ganor, who spoke Lithuanian, German, Russian, English and Yiddish, worked as a US Army interpreter at the trials and witnessed the hangings. "The story of Nazi Germany both began and ended here," says Deiler in exasperation. "It has to be documented and explained. People want and need to see this, but there is no information for people. I need help from outside. I need the Jewish community to show that they're interested." He says more than once that he wants to see his documentation centre built before he dies.

Before we part, I ask Deiler about a story I have heard about Rabbi Klausner. As he toured his domain, he made a list of the survivors. His plan was to print the list and distribute it across Germany and send it to Jewish groups throughout the world. It was the reverse of the usual post-war ritual of publishing lists of casualties and those who had fallen in battle. The idea was not as simple as it first seemed, as printing by the army for anything other than military purposes was forbidden. The rabbi was undeterred and decided that he would do it illegally. As Landsberg was a frequent point of call, he decided to print it there, no doubt well aware of the symbolism. Klausner relates in his memoirs how he "rummaged" through the old lanes of the town until he found a printing shop to produce the first list of the survivors, which he had started to draw up once the dead were buried. He asked if the proprietor would print a thousand copies of the list, making it an attractive proposition "by spilling out an assortment of coffee, cigarettes, teas and sundry items" all stolen from the army stores. Even with this bounty in front of him, the printer, fearful of breaking the American occupation rules, claimed he had no paper. This, Klausner assured him, was no problem either, as there was plenty in the

Dachau storerooms. Deiler has not heard this story before and his eyes light up; he will research it and find the name of the shop, he assures me.

Klausner now faced a conundrum. What would he call his publication? In his seminary he had been fascinated by the prophets who agonised over the behaviour of their people and foresaw both their ruin and that God would never let them be totally destroyed. "There would always be a *sharit ha-platah*, a saving remnant, to treasure the call of the Lord," he recalled. He wrote on the cover of the list *Sharit Ha-Platah*, and left it with the printer. Klausner must have heard Jews from Kovno, who had survived the camp in Kaufering, use the term to describe themselves. There is also no doubt that Klausner relished the fact that it was being produced in the town where Hitler wrote *Mein Kampf*. On 26 June, the first edition of the *Sharit Ha-Platah* was ready and, as Klausner picked up the copies from the Landsberg printers, he left a new edition for printing. I will hunt through these lists looking for the people on the *Wedgwood*. The edition contained an article entitled "Regarding Your Status" in which Klausner informed his readership that "no Jew need return to his native land", which was contrary to military policy. I bid Deiler farewell and drive to Munich.

10

MUNICH

THE SURVIVORS' PASSOVER

When Rabbi Klausner drove into Munich, much of the city consisted of mere skeletons of buildings and through their broken windows the sky could be seen. Munich's once elegant shops were rubble. Not that the city was dead; it was only physically destroyed. Life carried on punctually in the basements where schools and the university continued to function. A bridge led across the green murky-coloured River Isar to the Deutsches Museum, Germany's principal science museum. The rabbi swung his jeep into its cobbled courtyard. To his left was the library, where just a few years before the Nazi propaganda exhibition *The Eternal Jew* had been held. It was early July and Klausner had just taken over an exhibition hall in the main part of the museum for the offices of his new Information Bureau. He walked up the steps to the colonnaded entrance and pushed open the heavy metal doors. During the Allied offensive, incendiary and high explosive bombs had fallen on the museum. Inside it was a surreal sight. The ceilings were gone, and rubble was scattered over the trains and boats on display, which were too big to be moved to a safer place and which were now exposed to the blue summer sky above.

Klausner's Information Bureau was divided into an open lobby and four enclosures. The first was a search office, the second a medical centre, but the third was a point of disagreement between Klausner and Yitzhak Rathner, a veteran Zionist from the Kovno Ghetto, who wanted to turn it into a Zionist office. For Klausner, to mark a difference between Zionist and non-Zionist did not help the situation, as he believed there was only one solution to the "problem of the liberated, and that was to win the right to emigrate to Palestine". It was a kind of Zionism, but he did not see it that way. The fourth was Klausner's office. In the lobby the newly printed edition of the *Sharit Ha-Platah* was placed on a table. It had 25,000 names in it.

Over the phone to San Francisco, I ask Amos Klausner, the rabbi's youngest son, why this extraordinary document has been overlooked by historians. "My father was a great storyteller and he preferred to tell his story from the stage. Facts and figures were not his thing. It was all about personal relations for him," he explains. "It is one of the most important documents of the period, but because it's not tied up with facts and figures, just people, just a list of names, it has never got the attention it should have done." But in 1945, news of the list travelled like wildfire along the Bricha network, and within hours the office was buzzing and Munich had become the unlikely new centre of Jewish life in Europe. The museum office was also involved in looking for children in eastern Europe. People who had left their offspring either with Christian friends or others wanted to find out if they had survived, so the rabbi set up a programme to search for Jewish children, "which was haphazard but in many cases it was very effective," he recalled.

One day Klausner was busy working in his office at the museum when a man carrying a child walked in and sat the child on his desk. He drew a piece of paper from his pocket, a page from one of the editions of the *Sharit Ha-Platah*. He unfolded the page and pointed at a name entered on the list: Grinberg, Zalman, Dr, Kaunas, 1912. The man pointed at the child, indicating he was the doctor's, and then disappeared, leaving the little boy behind. Klausner's heart was "filled with joy and anticipation" as he drove Emmanuel to St Ottilien, as "the child was my metaphor for survival. He was life, our tomorrows, bright and beautiful." As if to reinforce this ray of hope, Masha, Grinberg's wife, soon also made her way to St Ottilien. But this is a story with a sad ending. Although the Grinberg family moved to Palestine in 1946, where Grinberg became director of the Beilinson Hospital, little Emmanuel died of leukaemia. Grinberg suffered a serious mental collapse and was forced to leave for America, as war-torn Israel was not the best place to recover. Mental illness dogged him for the rest of his life.

The first two copies of the *Sharit Ha-Platah* list, which was printed in a small booklet, disappeared from the Information Bureau, so the third was nailed to the table by one of Klausner's assistants. But, he recalled, while the book remained there, its pages were torn out "one by one". But he said: "I was satisfied. I could tolerate losing a book a day." One man spent a long time looking at the list. He had failed to find a single member of his family in it, so he walked over to the long white wall in the exhibition hall and wrote a note for anyone who might see it, saying that he had survived. Klausner remembered, "if a person came and found no name in the book, they would go over to the wall—it was a very large wall—and they'd write a note on the wall saying, for example, 'I was here'—addressing it to a parent or to a child—'I've been looking for you, and I will be here or going there', so that there'd be some point at which they might be able to connect." In time, over one hundred feet of wall became Klausner's own Wailing Wall inscribed with hundreds of messages from "those who criss-crossed the devastation of Europe in search of a thread of life".

One day two junior officers arrived at Klausner's private cubicle in the exhibition hall and ordered him to close his operation immediately as it was against army rules. Before leaving, one pointed at the wall and ordered: "And clean up the goddamn wall." Klausner ignored them. "A lot of people like to say that my father was a Zionist," says Amos Klausner, the rabbi's son. "He wasn't. If the people said that they wanted to go to Palestine, he would help them. He did not engage in Zionism politically. He helped the people who came to him to do what they wanted to do. If it was going to Palestine, he would find a way to help them."

Klausner had his first meeting with the Jewish Brigade on 26 June 1945 when a reconnaissance group arrived in Munich. Although every eyewitness calls them the Jewish Brigade, the unit was no longer a part of the British Army, but a unit of soldiers who had effectively gone AWOL and adopted a set of orders that went against Whitehall policy—to help the survivors escape Europe for Palestine. Klausner leapt at this chance to help the survivors and so became a key conduit in their illegal immigration to Palestine. It was partnership that would take the people to the beach in Vado. They were Klausner's people. "My father was a realist and he did not care about red tape. He stamped a lot of false papers helping to make them look official," says Amos. His father remembered that, "first we collected every known seal, or 'staple' as we called them, and had them reproduced. A document, we discovered, took its importance not so much from its content as from its stamps: the more the better." The passes and papers that the rabbi stamped in his office were a crucial part of the Bricha operation. Even though the American military made every effort to keep the Jewish refugees from crossing the border into Germany, 300,000 Jewish survivors arrived, with the helping hand of Rabbi Klausner's colleagues, rabbi chaplains, who moved them across borders into Bavaria, bribing guards with cigarettes, which changed hands for up to $15 a packet—they were the currency of the time. Some nights the men of the book traded $45,000 worth of cigarettes to let their people cross into the American sector. Klausner also "borrowed" a fleet of six-by-six trucks that travelled from Munich to Prague, where survivors were sorted according to their wishes, and those who wanted to travel to Palestine were handed over to the Jewish Brigade. It was the operation that Abba Kovner had dreamed of but, thirsty for revenge, had not been able to create.

I have to see the office where Klausner worked his magic. When I arrive at the Deutsches Museum, the courtyard is busy with children and parents. It is the school holidays. I ask at the information booth in the main hall if they know where Klausner's office was. The two middle-aged women look blank but try to help and point me in the direction of an exhibition about the history of the museum. There is no mention of the *Sharit Ha-Platah*. I go back to the desk and ask them for more help, so they send me to the library where a librarian rummages through the books on the history of the museum, to no avail. He has never heard of the *Sharit Ha-Platah* list. He could not be more helpful. He then calls the director of the museum who is writing a history of the collection and its buildings, but he too has never heard of an American rabbi and Jewish refugees coming here. He has no knowledge of the Jewish history made in the museum in the days after the war and is too busy in a meeting to discuss it further. The librarian looks at me as if I am slightly strange, researching a historical event that no one has ever heard of in the huge building crammed with artefacts and knowledge.

Fellow chaplain rabbi Eli Bohnen described Klausner in a letter to the National Jewish Welfare Board as "the one bright gleam of hope in the whole mess," and went on to say: "He has done more for the thousands of Jews in Munich and in the surrounding camps than all the agencies combined and then some more. That's a mis-statement. The agencies have done practically nothing and he has, by himself, moved mountains. I cannot exaggerate the wonderful job he has done. That boy deserves the thanks of thousands upon thousands of Jews. He has literally saved hundreds of lives. How he manages to avoid a breakdown I don't know. I confess I was lost in admiration for him and his achievements." If he had the resources of the Jewish Distribution Committee at his disposal, he said, "he would have performed super miracles." Amos Klausner sounds almost as exasperated as his father must have been, when he tells me: "My father simply could not understand why organisations like the JDC did not drop everything to help." What mattered was not that the organisations were overwhelmed and did not at first understand the scale of the problem or that what they tried to do to help was blocked by the US military authorities; what mattered was how the survivors perceived their failure to help.

Klausner realised that if the situation was to improve, the survivors would have to organise themselves into an effective lobby group. On 1 July 1945, Klausner called on Lt Irving Smith, the commanding officer of the Feldafing DP camp, to inform him of his plans to hold a meeting with the leaders of the Jewish DPs and to ask for the use of his office. Smith's response was to shout: "I take good care of my people. We don't need your goddamn organisation!" Undeterred, Klausner went ahead with the meeting, which convened on a balcony in one of the apartments in the camp. At this point the commandant appeared and in "a raw mixture of English and German" broke up the meeting, telling the survivors to go and clean up the camp. The meeting reconvened in a room next to the kitchen, where the Central Committee of the Liberated Jews of Germany was born. Grinberg was elected chairman.

The Central Committee held its first conference at St Ottilien on 25 July despite the fact that it was not easy for the delegates to communicate. There was no post, as the military postal service was out of bounds to DPs, and the delegates who attended the conference had to be shuttled through military checkpoints by sympathetic army personnel. The July conference was significant: it gave the survivors a strong sense of unity as it brought together representatives from a large number of DP camps that were suffering the same privations.

The conference organised committees and boards which spent hours arguing over rules of procedure and governance. The hours of debate produced a ground-breaking document that outlined the hope for the future of those Jews left in this part of Europe. It called for reparations and war trials and for an end to military rule in the DP camps but, more significantly, it demanded the immediate establishment of a Jewish state, recognised by the United Nations, and the right for Jews to emigrate to Palestine. The document is evidence that the Zionism of the survivors was instinctive and not imported from outside. According to Samuel Gringauz, the former judge from Memel and one of the leaders of the Lithuanian Jews, the survivors had an ideology of their own because the fact that Jewishness had been the centre of their experiences meant it defined who they were, thereby creating a "Jewish universalism". He wrote: "This is why they see themselves prophets of a national rebirth" and that for them

Palestine had to be "a Jewish refuge". Zionism had become for survivors the assertion of a right, not a form of rescue.

For the people who would board the *Wedgwood* this conference was a key development as it created the momentum that would help them reach Palestine, and, in the meantime, it provided them with an organisation that could support them and speak for them. The establishment of the committee was a highly significant event. It transformed the survivors into a political body that the authorities had to deal with, especially after the American Army recognised them as official representatives in mid-1946. It meant that, as Jews began flooding into the American zone from the summer of 1945, there was a body that could organise, represent them and liaise with the Bricha commanders. In Bavaria, emissaries from Palestine began to arrive and started to train survivors for their new life in Palestine. Zionism infused everyday life. Schools, including agricultural schools called *hakhsharot*, were set up along with vocational training centres, youth groups and newspapers. For the survivors they became a lifeline and their only hope for a future. In late 1945, the UNRRA conducted several surveys among Jewish refugees, asking them to list their preferred destination for emigration. Among one group of 19,000 respondents, 18,700 named Palestine as their first choice, and then again almost every single one of them named it as their second choice too. At the camp in Fürth, respondents were asked not to list Palestine as both, so 25 per cent of the respondents then wrote "crematorium" as their second choice.

Yet, despite their hopes and aspirations, within weeks of the conference the newly elected Labour government in London sided with the Arabs in Palestine and refused to lift the monthly quota of Jews allowed to enter the country. This had been limited to 1,500 a month as a result of the 1939 White Paper, even though the party had been committed to open emigration while in opposition. The government's decision meant that helping those people in excess of the monthly quota who wanted to start a new life in Palestine remained an illegal activity. It is the reason that the *Wedgwood* sailed in secrecy in the middle of the night from a remote little fishing village.

The Second Congress of the Liberated Jews was held in Munich's city hall on 27 January 1946 and the key guest was David Ben-Gurion, then on his second post-war trip to Germany. His presence did not improve Klausner's mood, as at "the conclusion of the meeting, while touring our centres, he made it evident to me that it was not in the interest of the larger perspective, namely the state, to improve the lot of the liberated. To the contrary, he pointed out, keeping the situation as it was, threatening and screaming in the world's headlines, serves our battle." Keeping the people in the headlines served Ben-Gurion's goals, but he was also so confident of the survivors' Zionism that he was prepared to make the people wait. Indeed, there was little he could do. The Bricha had stretched the Jewish Agency's resources to the limit. The picture also looked different when seen from Palestine. Ben-Gurion's top priority was securing and protecting the Yishuv—the pre-existing Jewish population in Palestine—and not immediate Jewish immigration. By establishing a unified body in Bavaria, Grinberg and Klausner had in fact created a political tool that Ben-Gurion could manipulate. His visit showed that although the Central Committee had established themselves as a political voice, their power was limited and their demands could be ignored. This accounts for Klausner's frustrated anger, which was felt by nearly all survivors, and the *Wedgwood*'s passengers were no exception. It was an anger that fuelled their desperation to go to Palestine, a place they regarded as a safe haven, where they could organise to protect themselves.

Thousands of survivors, and many of the people on the *Wedgwood*, were thus left to rebuild their lives in the DP camps. Here again Klausner took the lead. He knew the survivors needed much more than food and clothes to move forward. They needed psychological strength as well. Passover 1946 was approaching and the Seder presented an opportunity to turn the festival into one uniquely tailored for the survivors by breaking religious orthodoxy to strengthen the Remnant. This was to be the Survivors' Passover. On the evenings of 15 and 16 April 1946, 200 survivors and GIs gathered in Munich's Deutsches Theater restaurant. This elegant spot had been popular with Nazi grandees and was one of the few restaurants still open in the city. This was to be a night different from all other Seder nights, before or since, as Klausner had discovered a radical revision of the Haggadah itself, written in Hebrew and Yiddish by Yosef Sheinson, a Hebrew teacher and survivor of the Kovno Ghetto, who had been in Kaufering camp. It took the traditional story of the exodus from Egypt and retold it through the experience of the Holocaust, a Survivors' Haggadah. It was to play a key role, because the rabbi knew that only a Haggadah written by and for Holocaust survivors could make Judaism meaningful for those who had seen the death marches. The opening page starkly rewrote the text's most echoing words as "We were slaves to Hitler in Germany". It reflected the feelings among survivors that their experiences in the camps were a calamity darker than slavery in Egypt. The rabbi, who saw survivors casting off a Judaism all around him that did not respond to the Holocaust, determined to publish this radical text, which some rabbis might even call sacrilegious. Klausner had a flair for the dramatic and could not resist.

General Patton had been replaced as military governor of Bavaria by the more considerate General Lucian K. Truscott, and Klausner was able to publish the Haggadah with help of the occupying American Third Army at the former Nazi printing house, Bruckmann KAG. The white front cover was decorated with the emblem of the US Third Army, with a white letter 'A' in a red circle on a blue circular background. The Seder would also build on the new-found sympathy from the occupying forces. In the English introduction Klausner wrote: "And the khaki-clad sons of Israel commanded by Lt. General Truscott gathered together as was the custom in Israel, to celebrate the Passover Festival." He was cleverly binding the liberator and the liberated together in one community. Sheinson was a committed Zionist, his text expressed this, and he hoped it would reinforce the survivors' feeling that the future lay in Palestine.

On the nights of the Seder, the dining room was as elegant as a Viennese restaurant. Everything had been done to make the survivors feel they were no different from anyone else. The long tables were covered with white tablecloths, silver cutlery and neatly folded white napkins, each set with flowers and bottles of sweet kosher wine. For the survivors the symbolism and luxury were breathtaking. Yet each agonised as to why they had survived and their loved ones had not. Klausner understood this, and when he rose to begin the Seder with a speech, he made a point to address all the hundreds of absent families and fellow Jews who had perished during the war, blessing their memory. That is why that night the text they read was both bitter and ironic: "When the righteous among the nations of the world saw that Hitler had decided to exterminate Israel, their great assembly came together and out of their great sorrow decided to keep silent. And the children of Israel groaned and cried out but were not heard. And they cried out to the Lord, the G-d of their fathers, who saw their suffering and oppression, and their cry went up." The Survivors' Haggadah spoke directly of the experiences of those assembled: "When peace came down on earth, the people of Israel were gathering. The surviving remnants were coming out of the caves, out of forests, and out of death camps, returning to the land of their exile. The people of those lands greeted them and said: We thought you were no longer alive, and here you are, so many of you. And they sent the survivors all sorts of messages, telling them to leave the land, even killing them."

The Survivors' Haggadah was given further terrifying majesty by seven haunting woodcuts by the artist Miklos Adler, a survivor from Debrecen in Hungary. One image showed a hard-faced Nazi officer separating a boy from his mother as Jews trudged off towards the smokestacks.

To the child's simple question of why this night was different from other nights, the Haggadah had the answer. The passage about the Four Sons was retold in Zionist terms. In the Survivors' Haggadah the Wise Son is told: "Who knows how long their charity and their protective arm shall be extended to us? A home and a country should not come out of charity but by right." One of those present was the lifelong friend of Uri Chanoch, Solly Ganor, who resolved immediately to go to Palestine.

To this day there is still something shocking about the Survivors' Haggadah, its simplicity and its terrifying woodcuts. Klausner's son Amos feels that his father's background was important in the way he shaped the Seder. "My father was the oldest of five children and his father was a religious Jew from Europe. He wanted his son to be a rabbi but my father studied education and wanted to be a teacher. He found it difficult to get a job because he was Jewish, so he decided to go back to school and the only way to find a way back to school that was possible, because the family had very little money, was to go to rabbinical school. He became a reform rabbi out of convenience and in his dealings he was always concentrating on bringing people together. A lot of the religious leaders and individuals in the DP camps did not respect him as a religious leader. That Passover was a show with political motives reflected in the guest list. Two hundred people were invited, mostly survivors, but also included were senior army officers and members of the [Jewish Distribution Committee] and other relief organisations. It was a calculated event. My father was a talented writer and speaker, and he used this to his advantage to get what he wanted."

The more I discover the more I am amazed about the story of Klausner and baffled as to why he is forgotten. To find an answer to this, I turn to the historian Avi Patt, who specialises in the history of the DP camps. He has studied Klausner's life because his parents retired to Santa Fe, like Klausner, and there was a family connection. "You could make a movie about him, he is so interesting," he says. "In terms of the setting up of the Central Committee he is the central figure. He was a young guy. He ends up there by accident and he spoke of divine providence. It is basically the Wild West and he is getting everything done. If he turns up at every critical juncture it is no coincidence. For the survivors he was almost an honorary DP." Patt adds: "But he was a difficult character and people didn't like him. He could be a real pain, especially when he wanted something done. He felt uniquely driven and that put some people off. He made a lot of enemies." He was engaged in a running fight with the American Joint Jewish Distribution Committee, whom he despised as johnny-come-late-lies and because of their inability to help "the people". In July 1946, the head of the Committee, Leo Schwarz, made it his mission to have the troublesome Klausner removed from the American zone. He described Klausner as "a sick young man, afflicted with a form of hypomania". Klausner was forced to leave Germany that month. Ben-Gurion asked Klausner to come and work in Israel, but he spent most of his working life at the Temple Emanu-El in Yonkers in New York. He stayed a positive and open-minded man. He continued to work to help survivors and to unite families, and was the author of a controversial guide to inter-faith weddings. He also hosted Martin Luther King at the synagogue.

After his departure the baton was handed on to three equally dynamic characters in Italy. Klausner had reinforced people's Zionism, but the people could go nowhere without a ticket out of Italy. Just as Kovner had played his part, so had Klausner, and now the story of the people on the beach would move across the Alps to Italy, the "Gateway to Zion".

ITALY

11

MILAN

PEDDLING HISTORY

Between 1945 and 1948 over 70,000 Holocaust survivors crossed into Italy. Many were cared for in displaced persons' camps dotted all over the country. Of the 56 boats that, between the end of the Second World War and the birth of the State of Israel in May 1948, smuggled Jewish refugees into Palestine, 34 set sail from the Italian coast. The sailing of many of the others, including the *Exodus*, was masterminded in Milan and the ships were equipped in the ports of the north-westerly region of Liguria.

Until recently, little was known of the help the Italian people gave the Jews in these crucial years. It is the reason why when I first asked about the *Wedgwood* I found so few people who remembered the ship and the survivors who had sailed on her. My travels thus took me south over the Alps on a quest to understand why the Italians were suffering from a national amnesia. But then I found that across the country small groups of activists were campaigning to commemorate the Jews' epic journey to Palestine.

Their motives differ. Some campaigners seek recognition of the role that the Italian state and Italians themselves played during the Holocaust. Others want simply to make sure that the facts are remembered and that history is correctly recorded. There are also those who hope that the story of the Jewish refugees and how they were helped by the Italian people will have a positive impact on contemporary politics. In recent years thousands of migrants have arrived in Italy. There has been an upsurge of populist politics, racism and anti-Semitism, and many of the activists I met hope that reviving the story of the Holocaust survivors who found refuge in Italy will bolster democratic values and highlight the importance of defending human rights.

It is an overcast evening and there are large spots of rain falling on the pavement as I wait outside Milan's Shoah Memorial. It is tucked away in a side street underneath the city's splendid Central Station. Eventually, the lycra-clad Giovanni Bloisi appears, beaming as he cycles up to the entrance. The desolate feeling of the place is immediately dissipated. Bloisi, a wiry man in his early sixties from Varano Borghi, hard on the Italian side of the border with Switzerland, is about to bed down for the night inside the Shoah Memorial-cum-museum.

Bloisi, known in Italy as the *ciclista della memoria*, the memory biker, is a lifelong left-wing activist and has just completed the second day of an epic 2,360 km bike ride to raise awareness of the Holocaust in Italy. The trip will take him through places of Jewish historical significance and several ferries via Greece to Yad Vashem, Israel's official memorial to the victims of the Holocaust in Jerusalem.

I follow Bloisi into the museum, which is hidden below the railway tracks. In this unassuming side entrance, over 2,000 Jews and political prisoners were gathered before being dispatched to their deaths from the infamous Platform 21, *Binario 21*. The platform was underground and had been designed as a novel way of loading mail and other goods onto trains. Away from the bustle of the elegant station, the parcels and letters were brought in by a side entrance. They were loaded onto wagons, which were then raised by an elevator to be coupled to the trains about to depart. It was the perfect place to deport Jews away from the public gaze. The deportations began after Benito Mussolini had been overthrown in September 1943, when the Nazis invaded and took control of northern Italy and made him a figurehead leader. Unlike in eastern Europe, the Nazis preferred to carry out the extermination of Italian Jewry out of sight. This was not the place for marching Jews to open death pits.

Bloisi intends to camp out at every significant place he visits along the journey to Yad Vashem. As trains rumble noisily overhead, shaking the ground, Bloisi spreads out his sleeping bag close to the memorial's cattle trucks, similar to the ones that transported the victims to their deaths between 1943 and 1945. From December 1943 trains left for Mauthausen, Bergen-Belsen, Italian transit camps in Fossoli and Bolzano, and Auschwitz. When the Jews were brought here, they would have heard the same noise of the trains overhead that I hear. There were snarling dogs to make sure they obeyed, as they were hastily pushed into the awaiting wagons.

Alongside the platform the names of 774 of the Jews who were deported on two of the trains that ended up in Auschwitz are projected onto the wall. Twenty-seven of the names are highlighted and belong to those who were the only ones to return home. Work only began on the memorial in 2010 and is still in progress. The names of those on the other twelve trains that left have yet to be added to this part of the exhibition. As Bloisi unpacks his bags, he tells me it is important to remember that it was not just Jews who were deported from here but political prisoners too. Before arriving at the station they would have been tortured at the Hotel Regina on Via Santa Margherita, now a bank, where the SS had their headquarters, before being transferred to the notorious San Vittore prison. I watch Bloisi walk thoughtfully along the platform. He is clearly deeply moved by this haunting place. He bends down to touch the plaques commemorating the trains that departed from here while today's trains rumble above.

At this moment, one of the organisers of the memorial, Daniela Tedeschi, the vice president of the Association of the Children of the Shoah, a thin and intense woman, arrives to greet Bloisi. Standing by the cattle trucks, she tells me: "The Jews and political prisoners were awaiting deportation here but, above, people were catching trains, getting on with their ordinary lives. There were two levels of life in Italy; the hidden and the ordinary." I feel that an equivalent can be found today in what is forgotten and what is remembered.

Tedeschi points at the lift. "Look, it still carries its original notice stating that it is 'Forbidden to Carry People'." Bubbling over with enthusiasm, she tells me: "The potential of this place is enormous. We have sessions here to train teachers on how to talk about what happened in Italy and they are packed out!" She adds excitedly that until recently this part of the building had been used to shelter over fifty refugees from Eritrea, "but sadly, we have become so busy with school visits that we can no longer house the Africans here."

This is a book about what happened after the fighting in the Second World War stopped, and the memorial is all about the horrors that took place during that war, but watching a lifelong left-wing activist camping out alone in the Shoah Memorial is as much about the present as it is about the past. It is a story of a country coming to terms with immigration. It is also a tale that has much to tell us about why Italy became the "Gateway to Zion" for the survivors, and explains why the *Wedgwood* passengers felt only admiration for and gratitude towards the Italians.

Italy's Jews were, and are, unusual. The core of the community is made up of the "Italkim" or Jews who have resided in Italy since Roman times.

They have been joined by both Sephardi and Ashkenazi Jews over the centuries. The community was small when it was emancipated in 1870, but what was significant was that the Jews saw the founding of the state of Italy as the key to their emancipation and gave it their wholehearted support. The debate over just how anti-Semitic Italy was is not one for these pages, but what matters here is that the community was largely well off and well educated, and the Italian state born out of the Risorgimento in the nineteenth century was happy to reward the community for its support. Italian Jews prospered in the new country and were Italians first and Jews second. The community was engaged and politically active. Giuseppe Ottolenghi became a minister of war and both Luigi Luzzatti and Alessandro Fortis served as prime ministers. As a result, the 1938 Racial Laws came like a bolt out of the blue for Italian Jewry. More draconian than the Nuremberg Laws, although implemented with some leniency, they forbade Jews to work at or attend Italian schools and universities, and excluded them from public office.

Italy emerged into the post-war world with an immense baggage of unresolved questions about itself, its responsibilities and its future. The Holocaust was mixed into this tangled web, but the Jewish community, which had one of the highest survival rates after those of Denmark and Bulgaria, saw this as an opportunity to reinstate the values of the Risorgimento, as did those who had opposed the fascist regime and who were now in power. The National Liberation Committee was made up of anti-fascist parties and was set up in Rome on 9 September 1943. It immediately took control of the rest of the country as the Germans retreated and was to rule Italy until 1946, when Italians voted in a general election and for a republic in a referendum. It is important to remember that resistance in Italy was not just a resistance against Nazi occupation but a broader social movement against fascism.

Raffaele Cantoni, a Jewish anti-fascist and socialist, was a prominent member of the National Liberation Committee and, although he is little known outside Italy, he was one of the most important Italian Jews of the twentieth century. Like Kovner, Grinberg and Klausner, he was to be a key player in making the dreams of the *Wedgwood* people a reality. He was a courageous character with a spirit of adventure, and in 1945 he was the man of the moment. He had both the energy and a vast array of contacts that he could activate to help not only his community and his country but also the survivors flooding in across the Alps. Born in Venice in 1896, Cantoni was brought up in Padua but always spoke with a Venetian accent.

A patriot, he spent his school days reading Dante and was quick to join up when Italy entered the First World War in 1915. He was briefly a supporter of Gabriele D'Annunzio, the poet and proto-fascist, but soon became deeply concerned about the dangers posed by fascism, and was drawn to socialism. But Cantoni is a difficult man to pigeonhole. He was also a Freemason with friends in the Catholic clergy. He was neither intellectual nor religious, but a man of action. An accountant by profession, he had excellent management and negotiating skills and an astonishing capacity for fundraising. He was appointed director of the Committee to Assist Jewish Refugees from Germany, which was set up in Milan in 1933. As director, he found himself working with the international organisations that were trying to help German Jews, among them the American Jewish Joint Distribution Committee and the World Jewish Congress. He became friends with Saly Meyer, a Swiss industrialist who ran the Joint Distribution Committee's office in Switzerland and was the organiser of the Swiss Union of Jewish Communities. Through his work he also developed links with Italian Zionists.

Cantoni was tireless and worked all hours of the day. He used summer camps to house refugees and was able to organise basic agricultural training for many of them before they left for Palestine. He knew many landowners who were willing to let their properties be used for this. There were forty such camps in northern Italy in 1938. During the early years of the fascist regime Mussolini presented himself as a friend of the Jews. Italian universities were open to foreign students and many Jews came to study there. Among those families Cantoni helped was that of the *Wedgwood*'s Anna Kohn. Her father was a doctor and had been one of a number of Czech Jews who moved to Italy before the Second World War. After the Racial Laws took effect, the family moved from Merano to Milan and there her father continued to work despite the ban on Jewish doctors. Anna was one of the pupils at the Jewish school on Via Eupili until it closed in 1942.

Cantoni was a member of Giustizia e Libertà (Justice and Liberty), one of the leading anti-fascist movements. As a result he was under constant surveillance and resigned as the director of the National Liberation Committee in 1936, though he continued his work unofficially. Cantoni was also a leading figure in the Delegation for the Assistance of Jewish Emigrants (DELASEM), which was set up in 1939 after the Racial Laws took effect. Under fascism it was actually a legal organisation until 1943, when it went underground. It received funds from the Joint Distribution

Committee and the Hebrew Immigrant Aid Society. As a result of his experience and contacts he was in a position to swing into action the moment the war came to an end. Like many other leading Jews and anti-fascists, Cantoni had fled to Switzerland but only after he had been arrested and escaped by jumping from a train heading for Auschwitz.

Milan was liberated on 25 April, now a national holiday in Italy. Every year in Milan the end of the war is commemorated by a big parade in which surviving Jewish members of the 745th Company of the Royal Engineers, the first soldiers to enter the city, take part. The company included men who worked for the Solel Boneh construction firm from Palestine, which had been founded in 1921 by the Histadrut, the Jewish labour federation, in order to build roads and erect buildings there. During the war it worked for the British Army in Syria, Cyprus and elsewhere, and in 1942 the army had recruited the 745th Company from among its men.

Cantoni returned to a city in chaos. There was no electricity. Bridges and railway tracks had been blown up and the roof of the Central Station was peppered with holes. Yet the fact that Rome had been liberated for almost a year helped Milan to get back on its feet. It was a bombed and wounded city but it rapidly sprang back to life. Five days after the liberation, Cantoni spoke on the radio, recalling the active role of the Jews in the partisan struggle.

The Jewish community was, however, in disarray and the synagogue on Via della Guastalla had been bombed by Allied planes in 1943. But Cantoni was just what Milan's Jews needed to help them rebuild their lives. Described by those who knew him as dynamic, outspoken and impetuous, he was ready to shout out loud if his ideas were not immediately accepted and was not averse to hurling furniture around the room. Using his role on the National Liberation Committee, Cantoni took over the grand sixteenth-century Palazzo Erba Odescalchi, at Via dell'Unione 5, a few minutes' walk from the city's magnificent cathedral. The palazzo had been a billet for fascist militias and was now standing empty. The reception centre he set up here was originally intended to help the Milanese Jewish community put their lives back together, but it was soon to become the pulsating heart of the Bricha in Italy. Its address travelled like wildfire along the Bricha bush telegraph. As Cantoni opened the doors there were streams of survivors walking across Alpine passes knee-deep in snow. They had little luggage, often just a knapsack and the odd suitcase. They stumbled and fell, dressed in clothes suited for city life, not for winter in the Alps.

The palazzo is in one of Milan's tiny, elegant streets. It is a large, imposing building with four wings surrounding a central courtyard with an arched loggia. In the two years after Cantoni opened the centre, 35,000 people would pass through its doors, and its kitchen served over a thousand meals a day. In 1945, its courtyard was always full of Jewish Brigade military vehicles dropping off refugees. Once settled back into a routine in their home city, Milan's Jews were soon to be found working alongside the soldiers, whose enthusiasm with which they rounded up the survivors the Milanese admired. The Jewish soldiers, who had by now broken away from the British Army, and had their headquarters in nearby Via Cesare Cantu, tried to bring order to the chaos. The rooms at Palazzo Odescalchi were filled with bunk beds, and people even slept on the beautiful spiral staircase.

On his return to Italy Primo Levi, the young chemist who had been in Auschwitz, was a frequent visitor, as he had a friend who worked at Via dell'Unione 5. He described it in his novel *If Not Now, When?* "The Assistance Centre was teeming with refugees, Poles, Russians, Czechs, Hungarians; almost all of them spoke Yiddish; all of them needed everything and the confusion was extreme. There were men, women, and children encamped in the corridors, families that had built themselves shelters with sheets of plywood or strung-up blankets ... The air was torrid, with odours of latrine and kitchen. An arrow and a sign, written in Yiddish, indicated the window the newcomers should report to; they got in line and waited patiently." It is more than likely that here Levi found people who were willing to listen to what he had been through and that this was a factor in drawing him to the palazzo. "At that time, people had other things to do," he wrote. "People did not want to listen to this; they wanted something else, they wanted to dance, for example, to have parties, to have children." Ordinary Italians may not have had time to listen to him, but Levi nevertheless felt a compulsion to tell people what he had lived through and even told his story to strangers on the train on the way home to Turin, after days in Milan.

Yitzhak Kaplan, the first of the *Wedgwood* survivors I tracked down, and his family, who had fled from Rivne to the Soviet Union, spent two weeks at Via dell'Unione 5 sleeping on the floor. Many of the people on the *Wedgwood* passed through here. A few of the volunteers spoke German but many of the soldiers were fluent in Yiddish. Outside on the street and in the adjacent alleyways people traded goods and currencies and sold cigarettes, watches and cameras. It is difficult to imagine the bustle of activity today in this smart part of the city. The building is marked with an information board that describes in detail the architecture, but of its place in Jewish history it mentions only that after the war it was the temporary home of the synagogue until 1951. The palazzo is now a police headquarters, but it is still possible to see the small window at the entrance where newcomers were told to report.

Twenty-two-year-old Atara Borovsky arrived in Milan in the summer of 1945. She had joined the youth group Dror at the age of nine and always dreamt of going to Palestine. She had survived the war hiding as a Pole with false papers, but had still been a prisoner at Majdanek. She spent her first night in Milan sleeping on the floor in a crowded room in the Palazzo Odescalchi. A Brigade soldier, whom she regarded as "a saving angel", told her where to go to join a group preparing to travel to Palestine. "I went to the office to which I had been sent, but they refused to accept me, perhaps because I looked like a gentile," she recalled later. "At that moment I became very despondent and did not know what I could do to prove that I was a Jew." She had no money and nothing to eat. She and another girl discovered that the Jewish soldiers' headquarters was on Via Cesare Cantu and made their way there. "It was a very hot day. I had not eaten properly for some time and felt dizzy and on the verge of collapse. I saw a command car nearby, opened the door and lay down inside until help came." The soldiers who found her, she says, "took care of me, called a doctor and I think actually saved my life!" Four days later Borovsky was recruited and was to spend a year working with the Bricha before sailing on the *Wedgwood*.

Like Borovsky, the people surging into Italy had no inclination to stay. They were filled with a burning desire to start a new life in Palestine. But how were they to get there? The two mysterious Jewish agents on the beach in Vado, the pretty aristocratic Ada Sereni and the dashing emissary code-named Alon, would provide the answer and complete the work begun by Kovner, Grinberg and Klausner.

Alon was the cover used by Yehuda Arazi, a leading member of the Jewish underground. He was the son of a prosperous Jewish family, the Tenenbaums, from Lodz. He had emigrated to Palestine with his parents in 1923. Although he went to live on a kibbutz and became a founding member of the Haganah, he was never a real Galilee man and had the looks and manners of a society dandy. He always dressed with care and neatly combed back his gleaming hair, but he was also a daredevil adventurer who in the pre-war years had worked as an arms trader and had even set up his own small munitions factory in Poland.

Arazi was almost 44 in the autumn of 1944, when he was smuggled into Bari, in the south of Italy, by a Polish aircrew. Arazi quickly moved north through Italy and was in Milan days after it was liberated. He immediately made contact with the men who were part of the 745th Company that had liberated Milan and who were settled in barracks on the southern out-skirts of the city. Like the men of the Jewish Brigade, its troops felt their duty was first and foremost to support fellow Jews. From now on they would respond to Arazi's orders.

Arazi was something of an aristocrat in taste and manners, and felt more at home in the country houses of Italian nobles than the communal dining rooms of a kibbutz. He was soon well known in Milanese Jewish society and quickly got to know the elegant and sophisticated Raffaele Cantoni. Arazi, however, went immediately to the Jewish Brigade's base in Tarvisio to organise illegal emigration to Palestine, expecting no more than 5,000 people would ever make the trip. It was this visit that prompted the Jewish Brigade to make their first sortie into Austria. This took them to Munich on 26 June 1945, where they met with Rabbi Klausner.

Arazi worked hand in hand with Ada Sereni. She was both an unlikely Zionist and, in what was a man's world of clandestine activity, an unlikely leader of a secret underground movement. She had grown up in one of the richest Italian Jewish families in Rome, the Ascarellis. As a young woman she had never carried money and had her own bathroom, something that even in aristocratic circles of the time was considered extravagant. She was distantly related to another important family in the capital, the Serenis. The father of the family was the doctor at the Quirinal Palace, the official royal residence in Rome, and they lived on Via Cavour, close to the Colosseum. As a child she had played with the youngest of the Serenis' five children, Enzo. Eventually, at the age of 14, Ada and Enzo found them-selves in the same class at school; they were the only Jews and it brought them together. The couple married in 1927. Ada was short, with a sweet moon face and large brown eyes. She was neat and always restrained. Enzo Sereni was short and wore round spectacles, but behind them his grey eyes gleamed, giving him a hard look that sat uneasily with his charming man-ners. He had a magnetic personality and was a promising scientist.

Enzo, like Cantoni, was, after the First World War, a fan of the national-ist poet Gabriele D'Annunzio, but at the age of 17 he became a Zionist, which was unusual in the Jewish community in Rome, where the Risorgimento had left the community with a deep commitment to the Italian state. It was as if his politics were a reaction to those of his parents' generation. He was soon driven by the ideals of the Kibbutz movement at a time when Italian Zionists were convinced that Eretz Israel was destined for the poor persecuted Jews of eastern Europe while their duty consisted in helping those unfortunates. Ada had never expressed an interest in Zionism, but nevertheless she followed her husband and moved to Palestine in 1927, where they became founding members of Kibbutz Givat Brenner near Rehovot. For Ada, life on the kibbutz was hard and lonely, she kept to herself and was regarded as haughty. There was no indication of the crucial role she was to play in the Bricha movement and beyond. Ada had always held her own opinions and was impressively articulate and soon she joined the secretariat and was put in charge of the kibbutz industry, which made jam for the British Army.

The dynamic Enzo moved in top political circles and was a close associate of Avigur, the elusive brains behind the Bricha. In 1942, Avigur sent Enzo as an agent to Iraq to liaise with the Jewish community, which he did under the cover of working for Solel Boneh, which had labour battalions there working for the British. Next he was put in charge of the team of agents who were parachuted into occupied Europe. Enzo was supposed to be running things rather than actively taking part but, against everyone's wishes, even Ada's, he decided to join the team that were to be sent into Italy. His brother was a Marxist and had been captured by the fascists, and Enzo wanted to discover what had become of him. Before he left, Ada served him coffee with tears in her eyes. Enzo's intention was to infiltrate the north of Italy, organise the remaining Jews and bring them to Palestine. On 10 March 1944, he and nine others destined for Hungary, Romania and Yugoslavia left for southern Italy. He carried papers identifying him as a Captain Barda. He had chosen a spot on a tourist map near Florence called Campi di Annibale and guessed that if Hannibal had pitched his tents around there, then it must be flat. Moments after he parachuted onto the field, he was captured and held as a British POW. On 9 October 1944 Shmuel Barda prisoner 113,160, born 22 June 1895, arrived at Dachau. On 20 October he was moved to Mühldorf, where he spoke with a survivor from the Vilnius Ghetto, who, when Sereni told him he was from Palestine, said that it was as if an angel had come from a long-forgotten world.

Ada Sereni welcomed an invitation to join the Jewish underground in the hope that she might discover what had happened to her husband, but she herself needed no recommendation. In a community as small as the Jews of Palestine, everybody knew everybody else. Certainly among the closed circles of the elite of this community, being the wife of Enzo was good enough. Now approaching 40, she had two grown daughters, Hannah and Hagar, who also joined the underground in 1946. She was immediately sent to Italy. Sereni knew that her husband had been taken to Dachau but still clung to the hope that he had survived. However, Jewish Brigade brought her a list of the names of some of those who had been killed in Dachau, and her worst fears were confirmed. Enzo had died on 18 November 1944. Sereni was now determined to carry on his work.

Arazi and Sereni were the final pair in a series of crucial personalities who had, in an almost Moses-like fashion, opened the way for the people on the *Wedgwood* to travel to Palestine. Under Arazi's and Sereni's guiding hands, more ships departed from Italy than from any other European country. Sereni provided Arazi with contacts and an understanding of the Italian way of thinking, the Italian character, and Italian manners. She was the perfect partner, sophisticated and aristocratic. At first she assisted Arazi in putting together a web of deals with merchants, ship and shipyard owners, banks and Italian Jews whose help he needed. She was his trusted lieutenant with regard to financial dealings and purchases necessary for their work. She also made and handled contacts with the Italian authorities, opening every door as she went.

While Ada Sereni had the connections and the inside knowledge, it was Arazi who was the mastermind of the black-marketeering that funded the illegal immigration organisation Aliyah Bet in Italy, as the Jews in Palestine were not a rich community and, although the Joint Distribution Committee settled the payment for much of the work, the organisation was always short of money. The chaos of post-war Italy provided the perfect backdrop for Arazi. Jewish Brigade soldiers gave up their weekly ration of a bottle of whisky or rum, which Arazi turned into valuable cash for his operations. When the Brigade was moved out of Italy in August 1945, Arazi lost a crucial military presence, but he reacted with audacity by inventing his own military unit which many of the former Jewish Brigade soldiers joined. At first the Haganah leadership dismissed him as mad, before giving him the green light to create a phantom platoon. Arazi immediately took over a large courtyard and garage in the centre of Milan. Here he set in place every detail of an authentic army unit, complete with workshop, regimental police, MP signboards, guards, and all the documents necessary to validate them.

The team who worked under Arazi and Sereni was known as Ha'Chavura, 'the Gang'. They consisted of Jewish Brigade soldiers and Haganah agents like Sereni from the Yishuv, many of whom had been in the Palmach, the naval wing of the Haganah, and selected survivors like Atara Borovsky. When Borovsky had fainted in Milan, the three soldiers who helped her were actually key members of the Gang. Among Arazi's lieutenants were Yisrael Libertovsky, who was later manager of Israel Shipyards; Moti Hod, and would go on to become the chief of the Israeli Air Force; Shalhevet Freier, who became head of the Israeli Committee for Atomic Energy; and Zorik Dayan, brother of Moshe Dayan, the Israeli defence minister. When the Jewish Brigade was ordered back to Palestine, over a hundred of the men selected survivors who looked like them. They gave them their uniforms and their military IDs. The lucky impostors sailed on British military vessels to Haifa, and the Brigaders who stayed went to work for Arazi and joined his brigade of sham troops.

Arazi and Sereni's gang ran three operations from their Milan HQ. One group was sent to work moving the survivors of the Holocaust from central and eastern Europe to the Italian ports. Another was sent to schools in the hills around Turin where they gave the survivors weapons training and cared for young survivors in children's homes like that of Selvino. The third group dealt with all the logistics inside Italy and was under the command of Eliyahu Cohen, later General Ben Chur. In the Gang's office one wall was covered by a large map of Italy, which marked every British and American army base, where the Gang could stop off to pick up "supplies" as part of this elaborate subterfuge. All the paperwork, the truck identifications and the transport orders were forgeries. No one was deployed twice to the same base in case somebody recognised them, but nevertheless there were many in the British Army who chose to turn a blind eye to their activities. The drivers, disguised as British, South African or Australian soldiers, covered vast distances and often had to drive 2,000 km from Milan to Apulia, in the heel of Italy, and back in just 48 hours. Although the DPs were housed in Apulia or close to Milan, many of the ships organised by Aliyah Bet, like the *Wedgwood*, left from the mountainous coastal region of Liguria where life in its ports and hilltop villages was hard and there had been a big partisan movement during the war. Sereni and Arazi were the saviours that the *Wedgwood* survivors and thousands of others had been waiting for.

12

SELVINO

THE MOST VULNERABLE PEOPLE IN THE WORLD

It is a cold March morning in the holiday resort of Selvino high up in the mountains behind the northern Italian city of Bergamo, 70 km from Milan. The ski slopes are dotted with patches of snow and sweep down into the centre of town, as they did in 1934 when the Italian Touring Club's *Guida Pratica ai Luoghi di Soggiorno e di Cura d'Italia* described it as boasting six hotels and as "open, sunny and panoramic", which is still true. It also says that the people are happy and laugh a lot. The season is now over and the town is deserted so, as regards the local temperament, I am left in the dark. I have arranged to meet the mayor in the lobby of the Harmony Suite Hotel at eight o'clock in the morning but he does not turn up. I am left to find my way to the venue where the memory biker Giovanni Bloisi is visiting a school on his marathon bicycle journey to Jerusalem.

The focus of Bloisi's epic bike ride is the forgotten tale of 800 Jewish children who survived the Holocaust and who were brought here to Selvino for recuperation by Raffaele Cantoni. Bloisi is not Jewish but was inspired to make this extraordinary trip when he met the survivors Avraham Aviel and his wife Ayala Lieberman, when they returned to the now ruined orphanage in Selvino for first time in 2015. Aviel had survived by hiding in the forests of what is now northern Belarus after his family were all murdered.

I ask the girl behind the hotel bar if she knows where the cyclist is talking to local children. She has no idea and has never heard of the former children's home. Three women in their fifties gossiping over espressos know there is a cyclist in town but are not sure why he is here. I walk

153

along to the town hall where the woman at the reception is equally vague, but she calls the mayor on his mobile and then takes me over to the secondary school and knocks on a classroom door. The mayor, Diego Bertocchi, sticks his head out. I am surprised how young he is. He is baffled as to why I want to come in and see Bloisi talk to the students. I have been warned that Bertocchi sits firmly on the right of the Italian political spectrum. Bloisi has also told me that he had been working hard "bending his ears" and that Bertocchi is coming round to the realisation that the story of Selvino orphanage is one that needs commemorating. As I walk into the classroom, Bertocchi is taken aback when Bloisi greets me as a long-lost friend and immediately tells the children: "Look how important this story is. This lady has come all the way from London to find out what happened in your village and how you helped the most vulnerable people in the world!" I feel I have done my bit bending ears.

At the heart of Cantoni's work was his commitment to the children who had survived the horrors of the Holocaust, and the children's home in Selvino was one of his most important projects. Immediately after the liberation Cantoni and his assistant, Matilde Cassin, the daughter of a Florentine lawyer, set out to find the dozens of children who had been hidden in Italian monasteries and convents, and resettle them in the Jewish community. They were old hands at this sort of thing because they had rescued Yugoslav Jewish children during the war. Cassin, who was active in the Zionist youth movement in Florence, had helped to hide many of the Italian children in the first place and had tried to keep in touch with as many as she could, until she was forced to flee the country. Cantoni believed that the youngsters, who had been cut off from their families and their Jewish roots, needed to be re-educated by placing the emphasis on Zionism rather than preaching about a return to old customs and traditions. His views were to prove crucial and have a life-changing impact on thousands of young survivors who passed through Italy and well over a hundred of those who sailed on the *Wedgwood*.

In June 1945, he opened a children's home on Via Eupili, in the former Jewish school in Milan. Many of the first children to arrive wore the black clothes they had been given in the convents, and crosses hung around their necks. If the staff tried to take them off, the children would fall to the floor sobbing. The youngest remembered nothing of their childhood upbringing and the older ones were heavily influenced by the time they had spent with the nuns. In the evenings they would kneel and recite their Catholic prayers. The summer heat of Milan was not good for the children, so

Cantoni began to look for a place in the country. First, he took them to a solitary house in the wooded valleys of Piazzatorre, between the lakes of Como and Iseo. From there the Italian children were quickly found by their families or were adopted. The nature of the challenge faced by the staff changed as the Jewish Brigade brought the first of the children from eastern Europe to the village. The team who cared for them grew and a doctor, dentist and other professionals were added. Soon the house at Piazzatorre was not big enough, but Cantoni knew of a former fascist holiday camp near the village of Selvino, south of Piazzatorre, that had been given to the Socialist Party of which he was a member. He begged the National Liberation Committee, who held the keys to the hilltop house, to hand them over to him. They did not hesitate.

The children's new home in Selvino was an ugly four-storey, fascist-era building with many wings and outbuildings. The name "Sciesopoli" was emblazoned in large letters under the top-floor windows. The house was named after Amatore Sciesa, a revolutionary executed in 1851 for participating in the struggle against Austrian rule. Fascist leaders used to review parades of fascist youth who spent their summers here, from the rounded balcony. Slogans were emblazoned on the walls, and drums, bugles and fascist insignia decorated the library. In the large entrance hall the walls were covered with marble plaques that listed the names of those who had made donations to the school, among them Benito Mussolini himself. Two flagpoles stood before a broad curving staircase that rose up from the marble hall while on either side gleaming corridors led off from the entrance. In all, over 800 children would pass through Sciesopoli under its new management and, as summer faded, the Jewish Brigade brought more and more children from all over Europe, including the *Wedgwood*'s Menachem Kriegel, then aged 16. Most of them were sole survivors.

The story of the "most vulnerable people in the world" was completely forgotten in the village until 2012 when Miriam Bisk from Ithaca in New York state, the daughter of two youth workers who spent time at Selvino, decided to retrace her mother's personal Bricha. Armed with her mother's diary, Bisk arrived in Selvino with the Milanese historian Marco Cavallarin. She was so horrified that the building was about to be demolished and the land redeveloped that she tracked down surviving "Children of Selvino", as they are known, and started a campaign to restore the building and to commemorate what had happened in this tiny mountain community. It is the first time on my long journey that I have heard of a group of Israelis and foreign Jews involved in commemorating

155

what happened during the Bricha in Europe. Although the building has only a preservation order on it, there are hopes that the Italian National Trust might buy the building. Cavallarin hopes that, if this happens, "it could be used by the university in Bergamo for peacekeeping classes or something fitting with the story of the children of Selvino, like a museum of Aliyah Bet, but this is far in the future. Our first goal is a small museum in the town hall." Also involved in the campaign is film-maker Enrico Grisanti, who has a holiday house in Selvino. His wife's uncle was Jewish and worked as an engineer equipping the *Rondine*, another illegal immigrant ship, whose story I will discover later.

Step one has been getting the people in Selvino interested in the story and to raise awareness across Italy. That is why Bloisi is in his biking gear standing next to his bike and talking to children in the school in Selvino. When it comes to questions, one boy in the front asks Bloisi why he is not travelling by car. He tells the children how the bike was a symbol of the resistance and used by the underground to carry secret messages. Afterwards he tells me that "the bike speaks to people and it makes them listen to my story. A car would never do that." Before I bid farewell, the 29-year-old mayor draws me a small map showing how to find the former children's home. Later in the day, I see he has asked to become my friend on Facebook.

It is difficult to find Sciesopoli despite the mayor's directions, and the GPS has no idea where Via Cardo 64 is. Children who spent time at the house have described it as a fairy-tale palace with dormitories, classrooms, a cinema, gymnasium, heated swimming pool, spacious kitchen with the most modern equipment, living rooms, craft rooms, clinics and bath-rooms. There were luxuries here that children had not seen for years— white sheets, blankets and plenty of food. Some of the children took the sheets off their beds, too frightened to sleep on them lest they slide off. In front of the house and extending down the slope of the mountain was a large garden with trees, shrubs and flowers. A path led to a glade of pine, fir, cedar and cypress where there was a pergola as well as pavilion.

When I eventually arrive at the house, it is a moving moment to stand in front of the padlocked gates and to turn around and look down the steep driveway that leads to the main road from which the children left for Palestine in the Brigaders' trucks. The house is a sorry sight. It has a dirty peach-and-red colour and the rickety green shutters are closed on all but one window. On the gate there is a new notice in both Italian and Hebrew briefly detailing what took place here between 1945 and 1948. It notes that the director of Sciesopoli was Moshe Zeiri. Zeiri, who was from the Kibbutz Kvutzat Shiller in the heart of Palestine, ran a tight ship. He had no formal qualifications as a teacher but had attended a teacher's seminar in Poland and was a youth leader in his kibbutz. He had come to Italy as a soldier as part of the Solel Boneh company, the Jewish engineering unit attached to the British Army.

Life at Sciesopoli was highly ordered, and a sense of community and working together lay at the core of the institution. The children had to carry out daily tasks to keep the house clean and running. They worked in squads scrubbing the stairs, hoeing the gardens, chopping vegetables in the kitchen and doing the laundry. The scurry of children's feet on the stairs and, after a time, laughter and chatter filled the house. The majority found friendship and entertainment in the jobs they were allotted, but not all. Some found it hard to adjust to the rules. Others cried themselves to sleep and woke screaming from nightmares. After years of near starvation, most of the children hid pieces of bread under their mattresses, which they were prepared to fight for if they thought others might steal their stale slice.

Zeiri had a flock of charges who spoke Polish, Yiddish, Ukrainian, Romanian and Lithuanian and many a garbled mixture of more than two of them. He used song, mime and dance to bring the children out of themselves, to teach them how to express their feelings, to help them learn Hebrew and connect with Jewish culture. In tandem with communal singing and folk dancing, the children celebrated Jewish holidays. On Friday night tables were laid with white tablecloths and decorated with greenery. For many of the children these Friday night Shabbat meals stirred deep memories—but Zeiri had no time for them. Moreover, the children were forbidden to speak anything but Hebrew and were told not to talk about the past. I am a little unnerved when I read this. I cannot imagine this would have happened in Bavaria under the watch of Grinberg and Klausner. Indeed, something had shifted in the way the survivors were being treated. In Italy the Jews who had survived the catastrophe met the Yishuv Zionists, and nothing encapsulated this more than life at Selvino. Zionism was a movement of fervent disciples, who had left behind families and traditions in an age when the chance of seeing them again was remote.

Zionism was not just a desire to live in Palestine, it was a political idea, one that was to change its adherents into New Jews who tilled the land, and many of them wanted to live in a communal, socialist fashion. It was one of the great ideological beliefs of the twentieth century. The Palestinian Jewish community were looking to the future and not the past, and the children were being trained for *aliyah*. The Yishuv wanted the best immigrants and these children were the perfect people to make quality candidates for *aliyah*. In Selvino they were connected to life in Palestine by newspapers, news from the former breakaway Jewish Brigade, and even emissaries who visited the home—it had a growing reputation in Palestine for bringing the lost children back to life. Zeiri's moving stories about Eretz Israel, the traditional name for the Jewish homeland, and his graphic descriptions of Galilee made Palestine the focus of their dreams. Zeiri had been a Zionist pioneer in Poland and the movement emphasised a collective preparatory programme of studying and working before making *aliyah*. He was one of the thousands of Polish Jews who had left their families behind and travelled to Palestine. He had committed his whole life to the Zionist dream.

According to the Israel writer Aharon Megged, who has chronicled the story of the Selvino children, the Organisation of Selvino, the survivors' club in Israel, sent a questionnaire to those children, now grown up and many themselves parents and grandparents, asking them what they took from Selvino. The replies included the following: "Faith in mankind", "It gave me back my self-confidence and youth … a framework for normal living … released me from fear" and "I discovered there was a ray of sunshine in my life." Zeiri and his youth workers certainly did the best they could, but things were far from perfect. Avraham Aviel, the Selvino veteran who inspired Bloisi to make his trip, who had hidden alone in the forests and then joined a partisan unit, has said that the children were unhappy. "They carried with them the burden of their sufferings, which they were unable to unload, and from which they were unable to release themselves. Sympathetic ears and comforting arms were lacking. Their sufferings were to remain deep inside for many years, until time had blurred these fearsome memories, and the right person was found to whom they could reach out for comfort and sympathy." Aviel says that Zeiri was preoccupied with the running of the house and was "incapable of helping the children psychologically. 'We do not talk about the past; it is gone, it has to be forgotten. We have to plan for the future,' he told the children." The children were plagued with guilt, often believing that they could have done something to save their families, and self-harm was common. Zeiri was later to make a public apology for his mistakes in an impassioned speech at his seventieth birthday party, but these were days when few had any idea of how to deal with post-traumatic stress disorder in everyday life, let alone after the Holocaust.

The children who spent time in Selvino stuck together for the rest of their lives and had regular reunions in Israel. Their children have been helping Bloisi to organise his trip, and when I ask his support team in Israel if anyone knows what became of 16-year-old Menachem Kriegel, the bush telegraph is instantly activated. Within days I am chatting to him over the phone in Haifa, where he now lives. He has a frail voice, which I soon learn hides a determination to tell his story. We start chatting every Tuesday at 2 pm Haifa time. He begins by saying: "Every one of us on the *Wedgwood* had a different story. It wasn't all the same experience. One had been in the forest, another in a camp. We had little in common. Nor were we all from the same sort of family background. Most of the Jews in Poland were very, very poor and did not come from a cultured background. What did I have in common with them? Not everyone was as lucky as me to have an education and a cultured family." He repeats this a number of times, not because he is an old man and cannot remember what he has said, but because he wants to make sure I understand. It is the same with the fact that he is from Buchach, where S. Y. Agnon, the Israeli Nobel Prize-winning Hebrew writer, was also born. Agnon's work captured the magic and traditions of his home town but also has at its heart the theme of being trapped between two worlds and belonging to neither. Kriegel is well read and went to university after he retired to get a degree in history and politics. It is no coincidence that he mentions his books. Many of Buchach's 10,000 Jews perished in Belzec, but of the 100 who survived one was the Nazi hunter Simon Wiesenthal. I mention this but he does not pick up on it. I have begun to understand that survivors know exactly what they want to tell you, but some of them choose almost to tease you to see if you can understand. They drop tantalising titbits of information and see if you know enough to pick them up. If you do, they open up and start to tell their story at a deeper level.

Our first call lasts over an hour. Kriegel tells me how his father had hoped to take the family to Palestine in the 1930s but his mother was reluctant to go, as she knew that life there was hard. All the same his father was busy getting the paperwork organised when he fell ill in 1939. He had already sold land and property to gather up the small fortune of £1,000 in cash which the British required in every Jewish immigrant's bank account. Kriegel's brother and sister were in the right-wing Zionist youth movement Beitar and were part of a group that was due to leave for Palestine when the war broke out. His father died just before the 1941 German invasion, "but even though I was a small child," Kriegel says, "I listened to the conversations and I knew what was going on. It was something that stayed with me and influenced me after the war."

Kriegel's brother was a bright young man and was shot by the Nazis within days of their arrival. His 19-year-old sister Sophie, whose looks meant she could pass for a Pole, was a nurse and went to Lvov, where she hid with false papers. Kriegel and his mother were left alone but were hidden by the Ukrainian Schcerbata family in a tiny village about 15 km from Buchach. The Kriegels were well off and owned land, and they had done business with the family.

It is only on our second conversation that he tells me this. He says it is because he now knows that I have been to Ukraine. "I don't tell everyone this as people say I am stupid and this could not have happened." To my surprise the woman who hid the Kriegels turns out to have been a fervent supporter of the Ukrainian nationalist Stepan Bandera. It is his followers that both the rabbi in Rivne and Yitzhak Kaplan told me murdered Jews and Poles before and after the liberation. Buchach is less than three hours' drive south of Rivne and Kriegel's story is an important one, as there are people who find it all too easy to jump to conclusions about how people behaved in the Holocaust. Mrs Schcerbata's husband and eldest son were sent to Siberia when the Russians arrived in 1939 after the Molotov–Ribbentrop Pact. The Soviet authorities disliked all forms of nationalism, not just Zionism. Mrs Schcerbata hid Kriegel and his mother behind a false wall in the woodstore of her tiny house, filling half of the space with logs so that if someone tapped on it, it would not sound empty. As a result, the hideout was extremely cramped and, Kriegel says, "a year there was a lifetime." He spent fourteen months behind the false wall. "I don't hate nations," he says. "I hate people who are bad. People were saved for all sorts of reasons, but in the end it was Ukrainians and Poles who saved people." In 2000 Kriegel finally returned to Ukraine "with thousands of dollars to give the family to say thank you", only to discover that Mrs Schcerbata had been killed by the Soviet secret police, the NKVD, in a shootout after the war, as her home had become the local hub for the Bandera movement. None of the neighbours knew what had happened to the rest of the family.

When I arrive in Israel, I take a taxi up to the top of Haifa's Mount Carmel. Kriegel lives not far from Haifa Zoo. He is a small, round man with an enormous smile. He greets me on the doorstep of his house.

Before we go in, he points to a car parked in the driveway: "That's my car. I can't drive it any more but that's my car." I will later get a tour of his house. He is rightly proud of what he has achieved. He trained as an engineer and joined the Israeli merchant navy. The boy who was hidden in a cupboard has been all over the world and is forthcoming and friendly. He waited until he retired to tell his story. "After the war, when we came here, Israelis were not very polite to the survivors," he says. "They say 'this would not happen to us'. It meant I did not talk and the memory was squeezed somewhere inside me."

He bustles about in the kitchen. There are lots of appliances and gadgets on the worktop. He is cheerful and friendly. I can see that living with the Holocaust does not stop him being a fulfilled and happy person. "I was 14 years old but looked like I was 10 when I came out of hiding. I had long hair like a girl," he says as he makes coffee, although he thinks that as a British person I should really be drinking tea. We settle down on the sofa and he shows me snaps of his trip to Ukraine. The house where he was hidden was destroyed in the shootout, but he has a picture of an identical one, which is more of a hovel than a house. In winter the woodstore, which was between the main room and the stable, was not heated and temperatures plummeted to minus twenty. "We could only speak in whispers and in Ukrainian in case we were heard," Kriegel tells me.

As soon as the Red Army liberated Buchach, Mrs Schcerbata took the Kriegels back home even though there was thick snow and she had to use her sleigh. She was fearful in case anyone found out what she had done. The Kriegels' trials were not over. "We found our flat but it was empty and we slept on the floor. After a day, because we had not walked for over a year, our feet started to swell and we could only crawl around."

Talking to him, I realise that it is far too simple to say he was liberated in March 1944, as "after five days there was a German offensive and the Soviets evacuated the town. We had to drag ourselves after them." About a thousand Jews who had come out of hiding were killed by the Germans when they arrived. The road east was crowded with soldiers and civilians. "It was 5 am and bombs were falling. It was the front line but a farmer stopped his cart to catch a Red Army officer's horse that was galloping through the crowd. It was frightened and the officer must have been killed." When the cart stopped, Kriegel's mother pushed him onto the back of it. "It was high up and I did not have the time nor the strength to pull her up after me. The farmer was quick and caught the horse in seconds and, as soon as she put me on the cart, it moved off." Kriegel never saw his mother again. "Nobody ever saw her again and I don't know any-thing about what happened to her. This was for me my moment of trauma." He shows me a picture of himself standing on the bridge during his trip. "I can never get this out of my mind," he says.

The farmer was a kind man and took Kriegel to the Soviet field hospi-tal, but there he was told he was not ill and should go away. "I was aban-doned and sick and nobody cared for me. I wanted somebody to look after me but there was nobody," he says. Eventually Kriegel met the first of two Soviet officers, both Jewish, who would help him. The officer listened to his story. "I was crying and crying all the time." He ushers me to the kitchen table. He has cakes and an orange cut carefully into segments on the table. The perfect host, he offers me whisky and vodka.

Kriegel spent weeks wandering from place to place and eventually got a job translating Gestapo documents, as the boy who spent a year hidden in a woodstore could speak six languages. "To remain alive you don't *do* a thing. It is not an accomplishment. One was killed; the other was not. It was by chance you survived." He wags his finger back and forth. "After you are liberated you start the fight for life. This is on you. Here what matters is how you were raised and what your abilities are as a man. That is what determines if you are clever enough to survive, to get an education and to make your life." Back in the spring of 1944, the fighting raged around him. It was a dangerous situation for a young teenager. Eventually, another Jewish officer took pity on him and he was adopted by her unit in line with an initiative to keep feral orphans off the street. He was now about to begin a life in Soviet Russia when one day he heard someone call his name. His sister had heard that he had been spotted and had come to rescue him. Kriegel and his sister then found a cousin, Menachem Hirschorn, who had also survived, and the threesome left for Krakow in January 1945.

"I was always wandering around the city. I was curious and wanted to see everything. Then one day, I met a group of people who wanted to go to Palestine and I knew it was difficult for my sister to look after us, so I thought 'we will go with them'." Kriegel and Hirschorn joined a group of thirty orphans. They were taken to Lodz, which was a Bricha hub. Youth groups were housed at Zadocnia 66. Kriegel remembers that con-ditions were tough with survivors sleeping on the floor, lucky to get a blanket. They were fed potatoes and bread but little else. Kriegel spent his time wandering around the old ghetto and exploring it. He has a 20 mark note that was only used in the ghetto, which he shows me. His group were then moved out of the country by the Bricha, posing as Greek

DPs. Many of the survivors on the *Wedgwood* tell a similar story of travelling out of Poland with papers saying they were Greek Jews returning home. It was a bluff that was surprisingly successful. Those who had only a smattering of Hebrew had learned to sing "Hatikva" (Hope), a nineteenth-century song that expressed the Jews' desire to return to the Land of Israel, which is now the Israeli national anthem. They were told that in case they needed to sound Greek they should chat to one another using its lines. As the Bricha organisation grew, it became more and more sophisticated, and it eventually hired its own train in October 1945 to transport children out of Poland.

"We were always in groups. You had to belong to a group of 20 to 30 people of the same age led by an instructor." In Vienna he was taken to see *Madame Butterfly* and fell in love with opera. While in Italy he would also be taken to La Scala in Milan. A trip to Herzl's grave in Vienna was also on the Bricha agenda. Here he was given a small bag of earth, which he revealingly tells me "got lost or I threw it out somewhere along the way".

In Graz, in southern Austria, the group were picked up by the Jewish Brigade, who took the younger members, including Kriegel and his cousin, to Selvino. "Italians are not for fighting. They don't hate people but we didn't have much to do with the people of Selvino. When you have been in hiding or in a concentration camp, you are on another planet." Kriegel says: "I ate, I slept and I relaxed. That was it. And we sang. I sang in a choir. My wife and children can't believe this, I am tone deaf, but I did and I have a photograph to prove it!" One thing all the teenage survivors did was to visit the local photographer. They were given pocket money and they spent it having their picture taken. It is easy to understand why. The pictures would be mementos of their new life, something to look back on, when all other physical reminders had been lost and erased.

Kriegel has a picture of himself at Selvino ready to show me and I immediately recognise him. He taps it. "That's me but I am Emmanuel here. When I came to Palestine I thought I had better change my name, as it didn't seem very Jewish, as it was the name of the King of Italy. I wanted to be Mendel like my grandfather but was told I was going to be Menachem."

At Selvino he and his cousin did not stay to become part of the group who emigrated together to Palestine, but in the spring of 1946 they were moved elsewhere and joined another group who would sail on the *Wedgwood*. The guiding hand behind this was another relative of his who had survived. He was a doctor who clearly had some influence in Bricha circles. "That is when I became an enemy of the British Empire," says

Kriegel. "I was an enemy of the British people—me—a child—I am laughing at this!" He has a smile like an emoji. It looks like it has been drawn by a child and curves right up his face. It is very engaging. But it is time to leave.

We have been talking for four hours and I am sure he is tired even though he assures me that he never sleeps. We arrange to meet again on the following Sunday. His other days are taken up by bridge and lectures he is attending. He walks me to Wedgwood Avenue—named like the ship after Josiah Wedgwood, the British politician—where he puts me on a bus heading downtown. In a fatherly moment he tries to pay my bus fare.

13

FIESOLE

THE LOST BOYS OF THE BENCISTA

One day while searching for the names of passengers I stumble across the website of the University of Southern California's Shoah Foundation, which has an unparalleled archive of audiovisual testimonies of both survivors and witnesses of the Holocaust. There are 65 interviews that mention the *Wedgwood*, although in the archive it is spelled Wedgewood. In order to watch the films I have to go Royal Holloway College, part of the University of London, surrounded by damp woods in Surrey not far from Windsor Castle.

In the brand-new library surrounded by twenty-year-olds snacking on crisps and chocolate while they work, I click on the face of Jack Bursztain and begin to watch his story, which takes hours to tell. The tapes were recorded in 1995 when he was 68. He is an engaging speaker and I am quickly drawn in. He laughs and wipes away tears as he tells his tale. It is a lesson in the importance of oral history because, although Bursztain died in 2015, you feel as if you are actually meeting him. His account reveals the story of friendship and survival among a tight-knit group of teenage boys who travelled on the *Wedgwood*. I watch his account twice. It is an intimate experience that takes up the best part of the day.

Bursztain was born in the Polish industrial city of Lodz in 1927 in a poor area known as Baluty, which was almost 99 per cent Jewish. Before the war a third of Lodz's 670,000 inhabitants were Jews and it was the second-largest Jewish city in Poland. Jews in Lodz came in all shapes and sizes and so did their wallets. They owned over half the businesses in the city, and not everyone was as poor as the Bursztains. Some were manufacturing tycoons who lived in lavish palaces.

Bursztain had an older sister, called Hava, and the family lived in one room and slept in one bed, head-to-toe like sardines in a tin. There was no running water in the tenement and only outside toilets. Bursztain's father, Alter, was a kind, gentle man and made his living as a tailor. In the 1930s he went to Canada in the hope he would make enough money to bring his wife and children over to start a new life thousands of miles from the polluted chimneystacks of Lodz. The distance and the desperation of such a move are brought home in Bursztain's account of the momentous occasion when a postman arrived in the tenement courtyard with a letter from his father. Despite their dreams, the Bursztains' new life was not to be. Alter failed to make enough money and was forced to return home. Hardship aside, the Bursztains were a happy family and soon there was a new baby called Mordechai.

When the Germans invaded in September 1939, Lodz was incorporated into the Third Reich and given a brand-new name: Litzmannstadt. The Nazis originally had plans to ship the Jews to the Baltic states or the General Government area and to Aryanise the city, but instead they interned the Jews in a ghetto, part of which included Baluty. It functioned like a huge labour camp, which furnished the Reich with elegant clothes, shoes and uniforms. Tailors were in high demand. Jack Bursztain, now 12 years old, was sent to work alongside his father, who sang while he sewed from early morning to late into the night. Bursztain tells us that he always sings in the shower. I am drawn in by his warmth and smiles, but within seconds he has moved on to describing ghetto life and a daily routine of "hunger, starvation, sickness and suicide". Life in Litzmannstadt was a strange existence of parallel worlds. The ghetto was surrounded by barbed wire and was close to the park and the city zoo. Tram 41 continued to function as normal and ran through the ghetto so that outsiders could see what was happening. The Lodz Ghetto was the second largest in Europe and had a controversial Jewish leader, Chaim Rumkowski, who believed that by cooperating with the Germans and working for them lives would be spared. It is not my place to judge him, but it is a fact that the Lodz Ghetto was one of the last to be destroyed and Bursztain only arrived in Auschwitz in July 1944.

If Bursztain's parents knew what awaited them when they arrived in Auschwitz, they did not tell their children, who had no idea where they were going and what was about to happen. On the ramp at Birkenau stood Dr Mengele, one of the medical team who decided who would live and who would die. When Bursztain's little brother was condemned as unfit for work with the flick of a finger, his mother chose to stay with him even though she had been deemed fit to live. Bursztain's father and sister Hava disappeared into the crowd, while he was marched away with a group of other boys from Lodz to the red brick buildings of Auschwitz II. There they were set to work as apprentices in the building trade, in the Maurerschule. By August 1944, there were 220 boys in this group, nearly all from the Lodz Ghetto; other youngsters would join the group and it eventually numbered 251.

It is at this point that Bursztain begins to talk about his friends and how they "looked after each other and would stick together", always sharing what food they had and looking out for each other. It feels as if he is talking directly to me, although for a journalist the frustration is immense as I cannot stop and ask a question to clarify this extraordinary story of friendship and solidarity that I am hearing. It is obvious that many of these boys were not strangers and must have known each before and had probably even gone to school together, as they were roughly the same age. Nor did any of them have any illusions about what had happened to their families. Bursztain says that "you smelt the stench of flesh the whole day". At one point he talks about how he and his group of friends were lined up outside the gas chamber and waited for hours, but there were simply too many people and they were sent away again. The fact that they remained together as friends clearly transcended the horror of the moment in Bursztain's mind.

In November 1944, roughly half of the boys were forced to march from Auschwitz to Sachsenhausen, not far from Berlin, a distance of over 600 km, which takes almost six hours by car along Europe's modern highways. The march was one of the worst moments in Bursztain's life. "You had no food. We had no clothing. If you could not continue, they just plain shot you in the head straight," and "at night they would say just lie down in the snow. People would lie down and sleep in the snow, and in the morning hundreds would not wake up." The prisoners' clogs clattered on the cobbles of the streets in Potsdam as they walked through the city during the freezing night. "We did not know where we were going and why," he says. "We" is the crucial word in the sentence, for when Bursztain collapsed and could not walk, he was carried by his friends, one of whom he says was a redhead. I note down this one key identifying fact as I begin to sense that this friendship is a key to his survival. Bursztain was unconscious and only discovered how he made it to Sachsenhausen years later when he was told by his friends how they had saved his life. The group have stayed close friends and meet up every five years in Israel. It is clear this is an event of tremendous importance in Bursztain's life, for he repeats it several times.

The horrors continue as Bursztain is brought back to the story by the interviewer, who is not interested in the reunions. At Sachsenhausen, the boys were forced to sleep naked on the floor in the middle of winter before their senseless odyssey continued. They were made to march to Mauthausen in Austria, more than 650 km to the south. At one point Bursztain recalls a moment of respite when they were allowed to sit on a riverbank. "We found snails crawling out from the river. I remember eating them alive. I remember tearing out leaves from a tree and eating the leaves." His voice wavers as if he is unsure if he really lived through this nightmare, but he soon regains his focus in his entertaining English, which I wonder if he learned from watching John Wayne cowboy films. He describes Mauthausen as "A son of gun camp … It was crowded. It was bad. It was terrible. No food. Nothing!" Luck was on the side of the boys, however, and their lives were saved when someone tipped them off that soup they were given was poisoned and that they should not drink it.

The friends were then death-marched to Gunskirchen, near Wels, 50 km to the west, although at the time Bursztain says they had no idea where they were. Here they still stuck together and helped each other pull themselves up onto the rafters of the barracks. Here they spent their days and nights on the beams in the ceiling because "The floors were full of dead people. Literally dead people by the thousands." Bursztain starts to cry when the interviewer asks him if he witnessed cannibalism, which he did. Then late on a Friday afternoon in May, the American Army arrived. Not that this brought a happy ending. "People by the thousands ran to the kitchen for some food. And those who were strong enough did get some food … there was killing … there was robbery," Bursztain tells us. One of his friends saw a man drop dead holding a can of meat in his hand. "I walked like a 96-year-old. I was filthy and dirty and it was cold, bitter cold," he says. He weighed no more than a "large turkey" and soon, when he started to eat, he "swelled up like a pig". Some of the boys in the group died after eating for the first time in weeks. Bursztain concludes: "It was a different world all of a sudden. It was something new. It was something to be fearful of. I did not know what tomorrow would bring. I didn't know where to sleep, where to eat. I didn't know nothing at all and I was 17½ years old."

It is not surprising that when Bursztain talks about his new life with his band of friends, it involves theft and black-marketeering. It is a tale of what today we would call utter delinquency. They stole everything they needed and dressed in German uniforms which they found in a storehouse though they ripped off the Nazi insignia. In the ravages of post-war Austria the boys seemed condemned to a life of crime until one day they were found by soldiers from the Jewish Brigade. One Brigader, Yehuda Tobin, wrote home from Austria in June 1945: "Have you seen ... the faces of the survivors of the death camps? I have seen them with my own eyes ... The hair of the young boys has started to grow; the heads full of stubble look so odd. The special look that I don't have the power to describe, the facial expression. These boys ... they were 10, 11, 12 when the war broke out. They 'spent' most of the [last] 5–6 years in ghettos, concentration camps, forests, on the run ... Fear grips me when I think about those young boys. What have they not endured? How did they manage to evade death? What kind of youth did they have?" He could be describing Bursztain and his pals, who, perhaps surprisingly, immediately accepted the authority of the Brigade soldiers and agreed to be taken to a DP camp in Graz and from there on trucks to Italy. Such was their experience that they would only listen to Jewish soldiers.

Bursztain's face lights up as he tells the story. "I remember one beautiful night, the first night in Italy, and we got off the trucks and it was the first time in my life I have ever eaten a cherry tomato. First time in my life I have seen white bread that the Anglo-Saxon world eats. We lined up and they gave us soup and some sandwiches. Being concentration camp kids we started putting sandwiches in our pockets, being fearful that tomorrow we might not have any, and one soldier notices and says, 'What are you doing?' and we said naturally, 'For tomorrow'." The surprise and wonder of the moment show on his face decades later. Bursztain is wide-eyed as he tells the story. "He couldn't understand us and we in turn could not understand him."

The arrival of Jewish refugees like Bursztain was also a lifeline for the soldiers of the Brigade. Hanoch Bartov recorded his experiences in his 1969 novel *Growing Up Pains*, in which he described how the stories that the soldiers heard stoked the Brigaders' hatred for the Germans and those who had collaborated with them to such an extent that there were fears that this would spill over into violence, retribution and murder. Bartov remembers the rage but, more than anything else, he recalls that he and his comrades were young men who needed a purpose. Once that purpose was provided, all their energies were directed into helping the Jews who had survived. Rage, anger and frustration were replaced by hope. The

Brigade's quest to save the survivors channelled their emotions in a positive direction.

Bursztain and his friends were taken to Modena where they spent two months as the survivors were sorted into groups. The youngest were taken to Selvino, and the teenage survivors of Auschwitz and the death marches were dispatched to a villa near Florence with a group of about forty girls and a small number of other teenage survivors who had been in Bavaria. In Florence they were cared for by a Jewish soldier called Arie Avisar. Like Zeiri, who ran the children's home in Selvino, he had been born in Jerusalem and arrived in Italy with the British Army's Water Transport Company 148, which had landed on the Italian coast at Salerno in 1943. The stories told by the teenage survivors paint a cameo of Avisar, who first helped the Florentine Jews put their lives back together and cared for the children who had been hidden in villages and convents. He reopened the Jewish school and served as its principal while other members of the unit worked as teachers. Avisar's importance is shown by the fact that there is a memorial to him in the grounds of the Jewish nursery school in Florence. When he heard of Bursztain's group, he travelled to Modena to meet them.

At this point Bursztain shows more emotion than in any other part of his testimony. When he talks about Avisar, he wipes the tears from his eyes. "He gave his life for us ... He taught us to be *menschen*, to be honest, to be good ... We had a beautiful life. We were kids. We were happy. We had enough food. We had a *madrich*, a teacher." He says Avisar taught them to dance. "He taught us geography, arithmetic, everything. And when we had problems we could talk to him. He was like a father. He was always with us." Bursztain also recalls that they "had doctors and I remember they gave us peanut butter but only to those who needed it, who were not strong enough." Above all, he stresses that "we became *menschen* and all of us, all of our boys and girls that I meet today, turned out *menschen*." The group spent almost a year in Florence before sailing on the *Wedgwood*.

It is dark outside by the time I have finished listening to Bursztain tell his story and the library is emptying out, as it is early in the academic year, but I am hooked and move on to listen to the other interviews on the USC Shoah website. In this strange, virtual world of Holocaust testimonies, I meet Meyer Swartz, the son of a Lodz furrier, who arrived in Auschwitz on his 17th birthday on 25 August 1944. He was an only child and lost all his family apart from a distant cousin. Significantly, he lists Bursztain among his friends and had red hair, so he could have been the boy who saved Bursztain's life. The interviewer, however, does not ask who he is referring to when he says: "We all had partners. We watched one another and looked out for each other." He has a deadpan delivery, which reinforces the horrors of the ghetto and the violence and degradation to which the boys were subjected. Swartz was also in Florence. He talks about how their lives were turned around by the Jewish soldiers and that not one of them was ever arrested by the police or committed a crime in later life. "We grew up to be pretty productive people. None of the people I knew in the camps ever had any trouble with the law" and most were "pretty sane", he says.

When I listen to the story of Akiva Kohane, the son of an importer of Swiss watches from Katowice, I learn that the group that ended up in Florence was actually consisted of boys who were taken on a number of different death marches, the second of which left Auschwitz for Mauthausen on 18 January 1945. It is the same death march that Dani Chanoch, the pizza-eating survivor, had endured. Again, in the English of American Westerns, Kohane describes his first encounter with the Jewish Brigade. "At some point we heard a rumour that there were some Palestinian soldiers that had arrived in town. I couldn't believe it and then I will never forget when they came in with their truck. They had a Star of David marked on the truck. I got a shock when I looked inside the driver's cabin as there were two Tommy guns with the Star of David on. It just killed me to see a weapon with a Jewish sign on it!" Again he mentions the name Avisar. I find his son on Facebook. He lives in New York, where Kohane lived and died. He has a thick New York accent and is on the subway when we talk. He is more interested in what I can tell him than what he can tell me.

I begin to wonder about the girls in the group. I listen to Hayah Yomshtik, who had escaped from a death march and hid in the forest until she made her way to Rivne after the Soviet Army arrived. She is more precise in her testimony than the men, but less engaging. Listening to her speak, I learn that the villa they lived in was called the Bencista and was actually in Fiesole, which sits on a hill overlooking Florence. I am taken aback and cannot believe that these traumatised teenagers ended up in this iconic little town immortalised in E.M Forster's *A Room with a View*. None of the survivors who mention Fiesole blink, and I wonder if they ever realised that thousands of tourists have dreamt of spending a night there gazing over the rooftops of Florence.

It is after midnight when I leave the now deserted library. I am determined to find the names of the other people on the *Wedgwood* who were at the Bencista. Such was the German obsession for paperwork that there were lists of everyone held in the Lodz Ghetto and of those who arrived in Auschwitz and were lucky enough to be tattooed with a number. There are also records of those who marched to Sachsenhausen on 27 November 1944, and then to Mauthausen. I start ticking off the names on my list against those who survived the death march. There is also a list of those who left Auschwitz on 18 January. Slowly, I begin to identify names, but the problem is that the boys' dates of birth vary considerably within a roughly three-year period; this adds confusion and at first slows me down. Hours spent searching deliver few leads and I turn my attention to tracking down the family of Jack Bursztain, who eventually settled in Montreal, where he died in 2015. His testimony lodged at the USC Shoah Foundation includes the names of his children, and I find someone I think is his daughter, who has left comments under articles on various Canadian news sites. I find an address associated with a family funeral and the shiva that followed and decide to write to her. I put the letter in a brown envelope and head for the post office.

I search for the names of Bursztain's friends in Hebrew. I have identified Yechiel Aleksander as one of the group, but know nothing about him. I put his name into the search engine in Hebrew. To my surprise it throws up a series of articles in German. Aleksander is a Holocaust education campaigner and has just completed the Walk of Life, which retraced part of the death march from Gleiwitz to Mauthausen. I cannot believe it—he is alive! I discover that Aleksander did not speak about what had happened to him until 1994, when he made a trip back to Poland with his wife, Bella, and felt that past come bursting out. He realised he had a duty to ensure that the next generation understood what happened in the Holocaust when he met teenagers who had never heard of the Spanish Inquisition and the expulsion of the Jews from Spain. He now escorts groups of school children and Israeli soldiers on trips to Auschwitz. When he arrived in Auschwitz on 24 August 1944, aged 17, he was selected with the women and children to go to the gas chambers, but a Sonderkommando member from Lodz warned him and told him to slip away and join the men. He too became an apprentice bricklayer. One of the first and most bizarre jobs that he was given was to convert a water reservoir into a swimming pool for camp guards. The day after he arrived in Auschwitz, the Germans had surrendered in Paris and meanwhile the Russians were moving towards Warsaw, but it seems the SS just wanted to cool off. I am so excited not only that he is he alive but that he is happy to talk about what happened. My only challenge is to track him down.

Dropping his name into the search engine in Hebrew eventually pro-
vides me with an address in Israel. Google Maps tells me it is in an industrial estate in the town of Pardes Hanna. It does not seem very likely but I
have nothing to lose, so I write a letter in English and use Google Translate
to turn it into Hebrew, explaining that this is my only option. I put the two
pages in another brown envelope and walk to the post office. A few days
later the letter from Canada is returned, saying the daughter of Jack
Bursztain is not known at the address I had. There is no reply from Israel.
I feel disheartened until one afternoon a few weeks later, my Messenger
app pings. I have a message from someone called Nimrod Fishbein. I click
on it and discover he is Yechiel Aleksander's grandson.

A month later I am standing outside the station in Binyamina in central
Israel waiting for Nimrod to pick me up. He is in his mid-twenties and is
a farmer on the local moshav, a collective farm without communal living
arrangements. The back of the car is full of boxes of passion fruit. I apologise for bursting in on the family, but he tells me his grandfather has talked
of little else since he received my letter and has been counting the days to
my arrival. So have I.

Mr Aleksander lives in a bungalow in a pleasant area that does not look
anything like an industrial estate. As Nimrod opens the door, his grandfather comes up to greet me waving the brown envelope in his hand, pointing at the stamp with the Queen's head on it. He is smaller than me with
a tiny amount of wispy white hair.

We settle down at his little kitchen table and, over tea and cakes, he
starts answering my questions. We do not talk for long about Auschwitz,
but he is keen to show me a picture of his father in the uniform of a Polish
officer. He was in Pilsudski's army that fought off the Russian invasion in
1921. I ask him about the liberation and he tells me that when it happened, he and fifteen other boys had immediately left the camp at
Gunskirchen and taken refuge in Wels train station. "I was just 27 kg but
we were bad, very bad," he says in Hebrew as Nimrod translates. "We stole
and swore and were very, very violent and went out in groups of eight to
ten. We were out of control." Aleksander's mother had died in 1941 and
his father had been shot. Aleksander says that even in the ghetto he and his
friends ran wild, stealing and finding any way to survive. "We did not listen
to anyone until one day soldiers from the Jewish Brigade came and saved
us." He beams and ticks me off for not drinking my tea before he recounts
that they were taken to Graz and then to Italy. He says the British offered
him the chance of coming to the UK. I wonder if this would have been

part of an initiative sponsored by a Jewish organisation, the Central British Fund, which persuaded the government to grant immigration visas for 1,000 youngsters. He does not know but says: "We said no. We only wanted to live among Jews." Many others must have felt the same, as only 732 teenagers took up the offer.

When I ask him if he was in Tarvisio, his mouth falls open and he taps his head with his fingers. "*Ken! Ken!*" he shouts out in Hebrew. "Yes! Yes!" and quickly adds, mystified: "How do you know this? It was just one night in my life." When I tell him that I have been there, he begins to describe the valley and the mountains, now breaking into Italian. He is even more astounded that I know he was in Modena and confirms that the group was taken to the former military academy buildings. While he was there, a Christian family offered to adopt him but he only wanted to stay with his friends. I ask Nimrod to ask him if he was at Fiesole. This time he raises both hands to his head in disbelief and, when I say the word "Bencista", he reaches both arms out across the table. Nimrod turns to me and says: "I have no idea what you are talking about, but you are clearly scoring points with my grandfather." Aleksander is too astounded to say much and sits shaking his head. I can only imagine how I would feel if a total stranger arrived in my house and started to ask me questions about things I have never discussed with anyone else who was not there.

I ask him what Italy meant to him. He does not hesitate and replies "*Amore! Civilizzazione!*" Nimrod is taken aback by his enthusiasm. I then ask his grandfather if he knew Arie Avisar. He does not need a translation. He jumps up from his chair in amazement. When he regains his composure, he tells me that Avisar was an extremely kind person and took time to learn Yiddish and find out what had happened to the young people in his care. "He taught us to be people." When I ask him if the stories that I have heard about trips to the opera in Florence are correct, he confirms that he saw *La Bohème*. Nimrod is somewhat surprised as he had clearly never seen his grandfather as an opera-goer. Aleksander obviously takes some pride in the revelation.

Nimrod wants me to know that his grandfather has an impressive military record and that in 1948 he fought to secure the area around what is now Ben-Gurion airport. I get the impression that Aleksander does not want to talk about this, so I let it go, but he changes his mind and tells me that he served with nine of the boys in the Palmach, which was to become the core of the Israeli Army, and that Menachem Gutterman, Lajzar Blumsztajn and Shmuel Cohen were killed. I have pictures of some of the boys who were in the same group as Aleksander, which I have found on the website of the Atlit detention camp. When I open up the screen, he is understandably baffled and cannot believe that I have pictures of his best friends on my computer. He finds it amusing but is not distracted from being a good host and presses a slice of raisin cake on me as he promises to tell me a funny story. He says that the pictures I have were taken for safekeeping by one of the soldiers who cared for them before they sailed on the *Wedgwood* in case the British discovered them and used them to try and work out names and places along the Bricha trail. They were then posted through the British Army postbag to an uncle of Moshe Malineski, one of the boys, who lived in Tel Aviv. He kept them safe until they were able to collect them. Aleksander is rightly tickled by the ruse.

The soldiers also told the boys to say that they were three years younger than they were if the authorities asked them, in the hope that the British would take less interest in them. It explains some of the problems and discrepancies that have hampered my attempts to identify them. When I say this to Aleksander, he tells me that he actually had no idea how old he was until he made his first trip back to Poland in 1994. It turns out that his grandfather had told the German authorities that he was three years younger than he was, and Aleksander had assumed that this was his correct age. He was surprised to find out that he was three years older and was actually born in 1927, not 1930. This may seem unbelievable but Alter Wiener has told me that he had never celebrated his birthday until he was 19 years old.

In his excitement he wanders off to his large bookcase without telling Nimrod and me what he is looking for. A few minutes later, he comes back with a list of his friends' names and details of their regular get-togethers. "To have friends was to live," he says. "If you had friends you were not alone in the struggle to survive. This I tell you from my heart." It is clear that the friends became surrogate family. Nimrod reminds him that I have a list of names of people who sailed on the boat and he animatedly waves his hands at me to speed me up in opening my laptop again. He spots a name immediately. "Ronski. Yes, the Ronski brothers Avraham and Aryeh. They live in Haifa but they don't talk. I will get their numbers." He goes back to the bookshelf and returns with an address book. He dictates their numbers. I wonder how he knows that they do not talk about the Holocaust. Do they sit down at the regular get-togethers and discuss who has said what? Indeed, they do. "They said I was mad to start talking and they will never go there," Aleksander says, "but they might talk to you." I have no intention of harassing old men who have made their intentions clear. Guided by Nimrod, he comes back to my list and identifies a cousin, Ada Katz, who was by coincidence also on the *Wedgwood*. He spots one person who is entered under two names, as he changed his name on arrival in Palestine, as did many survivors. Then he sees the name of Yosef Hardstark and takes a step back. "He was my close friend. Each of us had someone we paired up with and we watched each other's back. He was my double. We even slept next to each other." His story is just like Burzstain's.

It is a cold January evening and Aleksander takes a break to stoke up a Heath Robinson-looking stove, which he tells me proudly he built himself. He is getting tired and it is time to leave. In the cool air outside he turns the tables on me and starts to ask questions. When he discovers I have twins, we all bond as Nimrod is a twin.

A few days later I meet with Dani Chanoch. I am surprised when he mentions that he was at the Bencista, as was his elder brother, Uri. After Uri was liberated from Landsberg, he searched through the lists of survivors in Munich. The last person he expected to find alive was Dani, but to his amazement he saw his name listed in a DP camp in Austria. There was no sign of the rest of the family. When their mother was taken off the train at Stutthof, Dani was hidden so he could not say goodbye to her, but she managed to give Uri a picture of herself, which he hid in his clog during the months of hard labour that followed. Eventually, the sweat rubbed the picture away and much later he was to work out that his mother's face finally disappeared from the photograph on the day she died.

In the weeks after the liberation, Dani, who had survived Auschwitz, distanced himself from the other survivors and started trading on the black market with another boy, whose name he cannot remember. They stole a horse and cart and traded clogs until one day some soldiers from the Jewish Brigade found them. The Brigaders were like brothers, he says, and reunited Dani and Uri in Bologna. Of the reunion Uri said: "I found him but we didn't hug, we didn't kiss. Something happened inside us, something had been uprooted." The boys were detailed to join Avisar's group. I can see from the picture that Dani shows me of the two boys at the Bencista that they must have learned to show emotions there. Uri has his arm around his brother. When I ask Dani what he remembers about Italy, he replies: "Love! Incredible love. I made my recovery in Italy. I made a quick recovery. I did not let life slip away."

Like Moshe Zeiri in Selvino, Avisar used songs and music as an educational tool, but whereas Zeiri forbade Yiddish, Avisar was keen to learn it.

Uri was multilingual and spoke good Hebrew. Soon he became Avisar's right-hand man. Dani points him out in the picture I have of the children saluting the flag. He is next to Avisar. But communicating with the children in their mother tongue was not the only striking difference between Zeiri and Avisar. Zeiri did not talk about the past but only of the future, while Avisar spent time with his young charges talking about what had happened to them and developing strategies to deal with their problems. Samuel Sadinsky, who had been in the Kaufering camp with Chanoch, was also in Florence and talks in his recorded testimony about how the group were given some of the first personal possessions they had owned in years: a rucksack, a watch and a comb. He says that at the Bencista he was in a little group of Lithuanians, presumably with the Chanoch brothers, and one Austrian, who must be Harry Linser, who had been in St Ottilien.

Linser had returned home to Vienna as soon as he recovered but found himself all alone. His brother had been sent to England on a Kinder-transport before the war and, at this point, he had no idea that his mother was also alive. There was no welcome homecoming and he found his neighbours as anti-Semitic as ever. The experience of Linser was no differ-ent from that of other survivors in Poland and Lithuania. The city's Rothschild Hospital was a well-known stop-off on the Bricha route and there were plenty of Bricha activists and Jewish agents based there. In charge of operations from November 1945 until 1947 was Asher Ben-Natan. He was 25 years old, personable and elegant, and worked under-cover posing as a journalist for news agencies in Palestine. He persuaded Harry Linser to leave for Palestine. He would make his home there while his mother would join his brother in England.

Avisar clearly filled his charges with a love of Palestine and a deep Zionist commitment. At Yom Kippur the teenagers were taken to the huge Moorish-style synagogue in Florence. When Kohane, the watch-importer's son, finally managed to make contact with his relatives in America, even though they invited him to come and live with them, he was "set on Palestine" and turned down their invitation. He would later change his mind, however.

* * *

I have been charmed by the story of the children's home in the mountain village of Selvino in the foothills of the Alps. Those who are campaigning to preserve the building and the memory of the vulnerable children who were cared for there run a slick operation. Until now I have believed, as I think they do, that the story of the children of the Sciesopoli home is unique, but there was a parallel in Florence.

Today, the Villa Bencista is a hotel, but on the website, even on the page that explains in detail the history of the building, there is no mention of Holocaust survivors. On the website of the United States Holocaust Museum, however, I find a picture of some teenagers on the terrace of a villa near Florence. The large terrace looks identical to that of the Bencista. More than one of the survivors has stated that the Bencista belonged to a fascist youth organisation, and as I ring the bell next to hotel's imposing gates, I wonder if that is why the owners have glossed over the story.

A long twisting driveway leads down the hill through woodlands and olive groves to the dusky yellow mansion. Walking through the door is like stepping back in time. The house has a dark terracotta-tiled floor and is full of heavy wooden furniture and faded rugs. A large mahogany dining table serves as a reception desk. I am here to see the owner, Simone Simoni, who is 88. His family bought the villa in 1925 and have been hoteliers here ever since. Signor Simoni has slept late and is still dressing, so I am invited to take a look around. French windows lead from the reception out onto the terrace. Below, silver-green olive trees cover the steep slopes and in the valley below sits Florence, its rooftops dominated by the vast dome of its cathedral. Behind lie the Chianti Hills.

The Bencista is a rambling house with numerous sitting rooms and a vast dining room that was once used as a studio by the Swiss painter Arnold Böcklin. He painted mythical, surreal scenes and was a favourite of Adolf Hitler. A version of one of his best-known works, *Isle of the Dead*, hung in the Reich Chancellery and there were copies in homes all over Berlin. The picture was inspired by Florence's English cemetery where his baby daughter was buried.

Simoni and his wife, Carla, are having coffee in the small sitting room in their private apartment when I am ushered in. They are smiling and welcoming. Signor Simoni is slightly deaf so I am told to sit close to him and he holds my arm throughout the conversation. Until the war broke out, the Bencista was an elegant place, he tells me, where dinner was served by waiters wearing white gloves and the ladies changed into long dresses before pre-dinner drinks on the terrace. But in 1942 the family were told that they must move all of the furniture out of the hotel as it was to be requisitioned by the authorities, who wanted to move Florence's Meyer children's hospital into the villa. The hospital was in

178

danger of being bombed as it was situated close to the railway lines in central Florence. But it turned out that Fiesole was not the safest place to move the children to. The battle for Florence was fierce. In their retreat the Germans blew up all the city's bridges, sparing only the Ponte Vecchio, before holding out at Fiesole. The Bencista is just below the town and was directly in the firing line.

Carla Simoni has a copy of the picture of the survivors on the terrace that I have seen online. She points out the shell damage clearly visible in the corner of the terrace and is impressed when I tell her it was taken by Zoltan Kluger, one of the most famous photographers from Palestine at the time. The Bencista was badly damaged in the fighting and the windows were riddled with bullet holes. Although Jack Bursztain was impressed by the sheets and could not sleep on the bed, feeling more comfortable on the floor, the Bencista was far from the luxurious place of the survivors' memories. After the Allies had secured control of the area, the hospital was moved back to its original building and the Bencista was used as a billet for British and American soldiers, who Signora Simoni says left the place in a terrible mess.

Her husband was 16 in 1945 when the survivors arrived at the Bencista. Signor Simoni does not know why his father was asked to take them in but remembers that he was paid 90,000 lira in rent. "It was not much, but enough for us to start some repairs," he says. He tells me he made friends with a girl from Poland, whose parents had been murdered in Auschwitz. She spoke English, as did Simoni. When I press him, he cannot remember her name and I wonder if he is being diplomatic, as his wife is sitting alongside him. I ask what they talked about and how much he knew about what had happened in the Holocaust. His wife answers for him. "We knew. The Racial Laws of 1938 had been the big shock and my parents helped their Jewish friends, but no one wanted to talk about what had happened afterwards. It was a time to get on with the next thing, the past was over." Her husband adds, "We talked only of the present. They never spoke about what had happened to them and were quite normal kids."

He tells me that, as soon as they arrived, the group were asked to cut a large cypress tree and clean it to make a flagpole. "They placed it into an empty well on the lawn and secured it with stones. Every morning they raised the flag and sang a patriotic song." He hums some bars of "Hatikva", but does not know its name, only the tune. On the Atlit detention centre website there are pictures of teenagers saluting the Star of David flag taken by the well-known Florentine photographic company, Foto Levi. He laughs when I show him the picture and carries on with his story. "They studied hard. In good weather they had lessons on the terrace which had been damaged during the shelling and in bad weather in the dining room. They learned Hebrew all day and about the land of Israel." He was clearly impressed that the soldiers who looked after them had a Dodge truck, as he tells me this twice. They used it to drive down to Florence and load up with meat, milk and vegetables.

It all seems as if it was an idyllic life, but I have read the Israeli novelist Aharon Appelfeld's *The Man Who Never Stopped Sleeping*. It is the story of a group of boys who are prepared for *aliyah* by an emissary from Palestine. The characters in his book are haunted by what it means to give up their mother tongues and to change their names, to reject the names that their parents had given them and the surnames of their ancestors. The exercise routine and basic weapons training are turning them into new Jews, but part of them longs for home, even if it no longer exists.

Also having coffee with us is a pretty, delicate old lady in a pale blue dress who does not speak English and who has been quietly reading the newspaper. At this point Simoni introduces her as his sister-in-law and tells me that her family helped hide the famous anti-fascist Jewish writer Carlo Levi, who was released from prison in Florence after the fall of Mussolini. During the Nazi occupation, under their protection, he wrote his famous novel *Christ Stopped at Eboli*. She and her sister, who had a baby, were resistance couriers who hid messages and packages under the mattress of the pram. The Simoni family were clearly well-connected with the socialists and the Jewish community, so it's no surprise that the Bencista was chosen as a home for the teenage survivors. The atmosphere in their house is warm and caring, and I am sorry I ever doubted them.

Fig. 13: Yehuda Arazi, one half of the Jewish agent duo from Palestine smuggled into postwar Italy to oversee Europe's biggest clandestine emigration operation.

Fig. 14: Arazi with David and Paula Ben-Gurion in Israel.

Fig. 15: Ada Sereni, Arazi's counterpart. An Italian Jewish aristocrat, she used her connections to organise the operation, while Arazi handled the black-market fundraising and the "army unit" running the ops.

Fig. 16: Ada and Enzo Sereni with their daughter Hana in 1927. Ada returned to Italy after the liberation partly to find Enzo, but learned he had been killed in Dachau.

Fig. 17: Moshe Zeiri, director of the Sciesopoli child survivors' home near Milan, presiding over the Passover Seder, 1946. Zeiri wanted the children to reconnect with Jewish culture.

Fig. 18: Menachem Kriegel in Haifa. From a wealthy Zionist family, he and his mother were hidden in a tiny annexe by a Ukrainian villager for over a year, before being separated. His wanderings eventually took him to Italy under the care of the Jewish Brigade.

Fig. 19: Menachem Kriegel (centre) aged 16 with the Red Army not long after liberation.

Fig. 20: Survivor children at Sciesopoli. Kriegel is on the far right in the second row from the back.

Fig. 21: The dining room of the Villa Bencista, a home for teenage survivors outside Florence.

Fig. 22: The orphaned Yechiel Aleksander after liberation. Death-marched from Auschwitz to Sachsenhausen, he ultimately made it to the Villa Bencista and sailed on the *Wedgwood*.

Fig. 23: Yechiel Aleksander and his grandson Nimrod at home in Pardes Hanna. Today Aleksander helps to educate the next generation about the Holocaust.

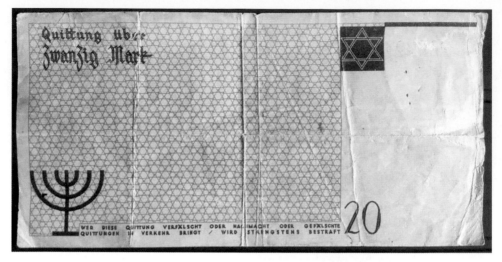

Fig. 24: A 20 mark note from the Jewish ghetto in Lodz, picked up by Menachem Kriegel as he passed through after liberation.

Fig. 25: The Chanoch brothers, Dani (left) and Uri, who were reunited in Bologna after liberation and spent time at the Villa Bencista before boarding the *Wedgwood*.

Fig. 26: Uri Chanoch just after the *Wedgwood* docked in Haifa.

Fig. 27: Dani Chanoch, now living in Karmei Yosef.

Fig. 28: Yehuda Erlich, who crossed Europe after liberation to leave on the *Wedgwood*, at home in Tel Aviv.

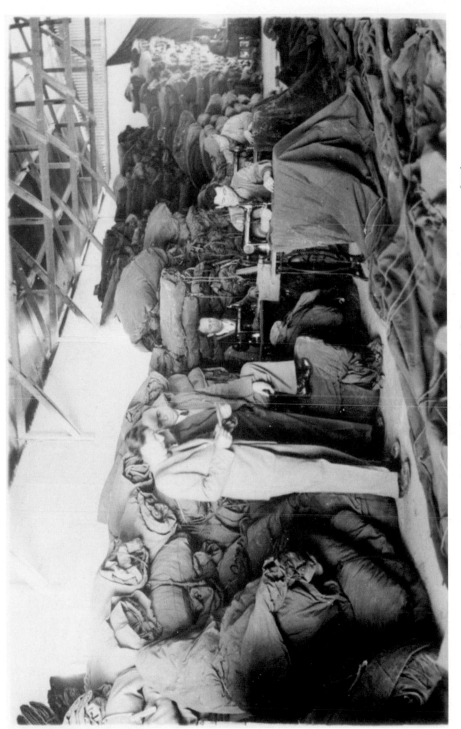

Fig. 29: *Yehuda Arazi (left) and Aliyah Bet head Shaul Avigur in Magenta, west of Milan, where everything was readied for Jewish emigration ships to run the British blockade. 1946.*

Fig. 30: "The Sons Will Return to Their Home": one of the silver medals Arazi gave to those who helped his and Sereni's operations, from the ships' crews to Italian police.

Fig. 31: The *Wedgwood* arriving in Haifa on 1 July 1946.

14

SANTA MARIA DI BAGNI

TIME TO BREATHE

As I travel around, I continue my conversations on email with the Waldenburg survivor Alter Wiener, who now lives in Oregon. Wiener had experienced an icy reception when he returned to his Polish home town of Chrzanow, but it's a photograph he has on his Facebook page that intrigues me. It was taken a year later and shows him with a group of friends standing in front of the gate of a villa. They are dressed in uniform. It suggests how the Bricha organisers drew the youngsters in, creating unity among a disparate group of people. Wiener says it was taken in Genoa. "I am in the back row on the left, at the end. In front of me is my best friend Yehuda Erlich. He was on the *Wedgwood*." I check my list. He is one of the people I know nothing about. I just have his name and the fact that he was born in Poland in 1925. Wiener sends me his email but does not offer any more information nor does he seem to remember any of the other people in the picture.

Erlich lives in a bungalow in Ramat Gan in Tel Aviv. Shabbat has just finished when I ring on the doorbell. Erlich is a tiny man with a round face. He is at home with his family. Before he tells me his story, he is interested to hear why I am here, who I am and what my interest is in the story. He points out that Whitehouse is not a Jewish name. This is not the first time I have been asked this by the survivors. As before, I explain that I am married to a Jew and we have brought up our five children to be Jewish. It is an explanation that puts the survivors at their ease. It is telling that they feel more comfortable talking to a Jew or to someone who feels Jewish.

His son David and his nine-year-old twin grandchildren, a girl and a boy, gather round the dining room table to hear their grandfather's story.

David runs the well-known Jerusalem literary cafe Tmol Shilshom, where many of the country's famous chroniclers of the Holocaust have spoken. "Alter is my father's closest friend," David tells me. I quickly see that Erlich is far more down to earth than the Wiener I have got to know and wonder if that is why they are friends. Erlich is a practical man who takes things step by step and is possessed of a dogged determination. He is also phenomenally sharp for his 93 years. A former school principal he has trained scores of Israel's teachers. He gives me a detailed account of his journey, where he went and who paid for his food and accommodation. He speaks good English and used to read *The Times* every day.

He was born in the small village of Kanczuga now in the south-eastern corner of Poland mid-way between Rzeszow and Przemysl on the Krakow–Lviv road. "It was a real shtetl," he says. "There were 2,400 people of whom about 1,000 were Jews. In 1944, when the Red Army arrived, about twenty came back, and during the night of the first Passover after the war six were murdered by Poles. We all left." Erlich is the last-known living survivor and was hidden by a Polish family called Wiglusz.

Erlich went to Rzeszow, where he found somewhere safe to stay. He says he had a good eye for spotting who was Jewish and whom he could ask for help. "I would approach them and say, 'Shalom!' It was in Rzeszow that I heard about the Bricha and that it was possible to get false papers saying you were Greek and wanted to return home." Armed with a new identity, he and a group of others jumped on a freight train heading for Slovakia. They travelled on to Romania. "There was always someone from the Bricha who paid our way," he says.

Survivors who joined an official Bricha trip usually left what money they had behind as it was too dangerous to carry it over borders illegally, and they were given receipts in Hebrew which were honoured by the Bricha organisers when they connected with them in Bratislava, Bucharest or Prague. The money left behind was used to finance more escapes. The Bricha was a strange mixture of organisation and disorganisation, and those involved in it knew very little about its structure so as to prevent infiltration. Bricha workers were not paid but given food and shelter. The principle was that no one wishing to use their services needed to pay either.

In Oradea, in north-western Romania, Erlich received money directly from the American Jewish Joint Distribution Committee. "Here I had to wait for some weeks and they gave me somewhere to live with a woman who was half-Jewish, half-Hungarian. I could not go alone. I had to wait to be taken in a group to Budapest." There they waited to be transferred to Austria. "We were a group of about forty men and women but there were no children. There were no children anywhere and no old people." The group travelled at night to Graz. Here they were put up in a hotel that had seen better days and where they slept on the floor. Erlich laughs and tells me he has taken his wife there and it is now a luxury five-star hotel. The Joint Distribution Committee paid for the food and lodging. They were then taken to a DP camp, which was where he met Alter Wiener. "Food was short and we used to cut trees for the British Army. For one day's work you got a tin of sardines."

Erlich was a studious young man and as a young teenager had helped coach children in his village. "I used to read history books, Hebrew books—everything. They were looking for people who could teach the younger teenagers and I was recruited to teach Jewish history by the local Bricha organisers. Among them were people from Palestine who talked about Zionism." The group were then told that they were to be moved to Italy. "We arrived at Mestre and that gave me a chance to see [nearby] Venice. It was the first time I had seen the sea! It was very interesting." At this point his son interjects: "That must have been fun!" But his father reiterates: "No, it was very interesting." Erlich's group had now organised, as did many youth groups, into a "kibbutz", creating a unit that would settle together in Palestine. It had about 160 members. After Mestre they moved to Genoa, which was another city he found "interesting" to explore. It was here that the picture I have seen on Alter Wiener's Facebook page was taken.

His son David has told me not to ask too much about Pola, the young girl who stands on his right, who was at this point his girlfriend, but Erlich quickly identifies the others. This Pola is, I am sure, the only person by that name on the *Wedgwood*, Pola Klogir. The girl who stands next to Pola is Rivkale, who was at the time romantically involved with Wiener. When her family was burned alive in the synagogue of her home town, she fled. Wiener wrote in his autobiography that Rivkale "strove to survive because she loved life, and she knew the pleasures that life had to offer. She wished to survive as the remnant of her family. Despite her traumatic past Rivkale was full of life and hope." Rivkale was 20, and she and Wiener "swapped our tragic war experiences". What is fascinating is that after the hellish world of the camps, Wiener was shocked by her story, of how she survived after her escape to the forest. He says: "She was short, stout and had radiant brown eyes that grew bigger when we spent time together." In the photograph the girls in particular look as if they are recovering from extreme starvation, as they are very rounded and slightly swollen. Wiener says: "I was still in poor health. My digestive system was unable to absorb all kinds of food. I was lethargic and could not participate in many physical activities that the Brigade soldiers initiated."

By this point Erlich had become the secretary and leader of the group. He is keen to tell me again that he taught Jewish history. Teaching in Italy had a profound impact on him. Not only did it give him a role and a job, it showed him that there was something that he was good at; it gave him a future. Erlich was asked to stay in Italy by the Bricha but he was determined to get to Palestine as soon as he could. "I decided not to stay in Italy as I had a girl and wanted to be with her. But I was also a committed Zionist. I wanted only to come to Palestine," he says. "I only wanted to be here. I trained as a locksmith on the kibbutz. When the war of 1948 broke out, I joined the Haganah and I had no regrets ever about coming here." Then he moved to Tel Aviv where he could study at night, as his dream was to become a teacher. "I was 39 when I went to university and I had a wife and two children." The twins have lost interest in the story and are playing Monopoly on the carpet. It is time to go. As Erlich gets me my coat, he says: "I wasn't wanted in Poland, and when I came here I was told by the Arabs and many others that it was not my home either. I fought for everything I have."

Italy was the place where the survivors recovered and learned to live again like normal people, but it was also something of a pressure cooker. Not everyone who arrived there was a committed Zionist, but with few or no other options and little desire to stay in Italy, they had no choice but to go to Palestine and believed it was there that they could build a new life. The people on the *Wedgwood* were unwanted refugees with nowhere else to go. Every day, every passing month that the survivors spent in Italy reinforced the idea that Palestine was the only future they had. Yehuda Erlich was recruited to reinforce these ideas. The survivors had to be taught Hebrew and Jewish history; their Zionist feelings were fed and watered.

It was not just the eastern European survivors who fell under the spell of the Jewish Brigade. Elena Morpurgo was an Italian who sailed on the *Wedgwood*. She found that her allegiances changed during the war. In 1945, when she was 21 years old, she told a Jewish newsletter that she was frightened to bring up her children in Italy. The Jewish Brigade's first job was to help the Jews in Italy put their lives back together. Both of its chaplains, Efraim Urbach and Bernard Casper, were keen Zionists. Every meal that was served in the food kitchens they set up came with a spoonful of Zionism. In Florence, the Brigade's soup kitchen's walls were covered with pictures of Palestine. Morpurgo, who had spent the war in hiding, said that her parents had too many ties to be able to leave. It is also important to say that after the war Jewish lives in Italy were not in danger. It was not a land of pogroms, and people had a real choice as to what they could do. Morpurgo had been 14 when the Racial Laws were introduced and had no adult memory of better times. She was drawn into the Zionist dream and sailed on the *Wedgwood*.

The day after talking to Erlich, I find myself having tea with Moshe Ha-Elion, the Greek survivor of Auschwitz, and poet. He was one of the 180 Greeks in his DP camp in Austria, both Christians and Jews, who were set on returning home. "We were in lorries moving through the beautiful Austrian countryside when I suddenly spotted a convoy of trucks with the Star of David on," he tells me in his quiet, confidential way. "The soldiers had little signs on their arms that had the same Star of David on. I realised they were Jews and it was a wonder." He still looks surprised as he tells the story. "When we arrived in Villach near the border with Italy, we seized the chance to speak to them. I had studied Hebrew at school, so was able to talk to them. I told them we were going back to Greece. Then, when we got to Mestre in Italy, a couple of them we had met came to see us in the big villa where we were staying. 'What are you doing going back to Greece?' they asked us. 'You have no family there and there is a civil war going on. If you go back, you will be called up into the army.'" The officer came three days running and on the last night he asked the group which of them wanted to go to Palestine. "We talked about it," Ha-Elion tells me. "There was a big debate and in the end about forty of us said that we would like to go, and after that things moved quite quickly." The group was taken by train to Bari in southern Italy. The journey lasted almost five days as the railways were badly damaged. There they were registered with UNRRA and then moved to a small fishing village in the heel of Italy, called Santa Maria di Bagni, not far from the town of Nardo in Apulia. "We were the first group to arrive," says Ha-Elion. "It was late June 1945. They put us in a big villa that was from the Mussolini era. In time thousands of survivors came from all over Europe, from Poland, Romania, from all over eastern Europe, and they all wanted to go to Palestine."

Santa Maria di Bagni was one of five DP camps spread along the coast. It had a population of about 7,000 people in 1945 but at its peak, when Ha-Elion and the other Greeks who sailed on the *Wedgwood* were there, it was home to 2,300 Jewish DPs. In Santa Maria di Bagni there were no guards and no barbed wire. The survivors were housed in large villas with elegant gardens. They were crammed with people, and some of the refugees even slept on the floor. Food and clothing in the camp was supplied by UNRRA and the American Jewish Joint Distribution Committee, but, as was the norm, many survivors turned to black-marketeering to make a living. The clothes the Joint Distribution Committee supplied were American second-hand fashion wear and were in high demand. Even today there are Joint Distribution Committee blankets that are still in use in the town.

Relations between the survivors and the locals were close. The Greek Jews spoke Ladino, the language of medieval Spain, which they had brought with them when they were driven out of Spain during the Inquisition. Ha-Elion says: "As Ladino is a Latin language, we could speak to the people. The Italians are *brava gente*, good people, and it was such a small place that we soon fitted in. They were not against us. We never saw any anti-Semitism there." The refugees helped with the harvest for no pay and were rewarded with bottles of wine. The survivors fell in love, and there were plenty of marriages among the group. One young woman lent her wedding dress to all the other young brides. It was in Santa Maria di Bagni that Ha-Elion met and fell in love with Hanna Waldman, a young Romanian survivor. "We were put in the same kibbutz and at first we spoke with our hands. Then I taught her some Hebrew and she taught me some Yiddish. That was how it began. Soon we adopted her into our group and she became an honorary Greek," he laughs.

In Santa Maria di Bagni, as elsewhere, the emphasis was on preparing for life in Palestine. There were workshops to teach the DPs trades, and sport was an important part of the routine, as preparing the young men to join a potential fighting force was high on the agenda. Organised group singing of the epic songs of Aliyah Bet drew the survivors together. Each of the songs told, in either rousing verses or melancholy tunes, the story of the Bricha. Among the most popular were 'The Brigade Song', 'To the Captain of the Hannah Szenes' and 'Hora in a Foreign Land'. Getting out of Italy was the fairy-tale ending towards which the survivors worked. They often marched through the town demonstrating against the British policy of restricting immigration, and in April 1946 they went on a hunger strike. But no one, it seems, was angrier than the forty Greeks. "They told us all about Palestine and I got very excited, but with time we realised that people who arrived after us had already left," Ha-Elion says. "Most of these people were Poles and they were moved quickly, but we Greeks just sat there." He opens his arms and looks heavenwards and then flicks one hand. "They were members of political parties, you see. They were in the right youth movements, but us, we were not involved in any of that." As soon as Ha-Elion and the rest of the Greeks realised what was going on, they were furious. "We were so angry, we made a real fuss. Some of us went to Bari and met with one of the organisers. We threw tables and chairs until they agreed to take us to Palestine." Ha-Elion is such a tiny man that I cannot imagine him hurling tables, but he is so excited by the recollection that he has stood up and is miming the act of hurling a chair. The group were quickly moved to Rome and told they would be taken to Genoa to be put on the next ship. Many of the non-Greek passengers on the *Wedgwood* had been in Santa Maria di Bagni and the other DP camps in Apulia. Many of them travelled as couples.

Unlike everywhere else in Italy, the people of Santa Maria di Bagni have not forgotten this period in the village's history. Many of the buildings in Santa Maria di Bagni still have Hebrew names and slogans written on them. There is also a small museum that is home to some extraordinary murals painted by the Romanian Holocaust survivor and artist Zvi Miller. His pictures have a sort of mythical quality to them, with images of menorahs, camps and the Jewish Brigade all mixed together, but the style is also reminiscent of Soviet propaganda posters. It is thanks to the staff at the museum that I am taking tea with Moshe Ha-Elion, as they put me in contact with his daughter, Rachel.

When the survivors arrived, the locals were struck that there were no families, no small children and no elderly. Those that remember them recall the DPs as taciturn, sad and thoughtful, but photographs of the survivors show young people in bathing suits smiling at the camera. Survivors write about how they changed physically in the time they spent in Italy, how their hair grew back. As they began to eat properly and to exercise, they rounded out and looked years younger. Many children were born in Santa Maria di Bagni, but Ha-Elion says that among the Greeks there were no children. "That all came later when we finally got to Palestine."

Ha-Elion's and Erlich's dreams of building a new life in Palestine were to depend on dynamics beyond their control. They, and the other survivors who made the journey to the beach, relied on the help they would get from the Italian Jewish community and their links to the country's socialist politicians and partisans. In Italy Aliyah Bet often worked alongside the authorities. London sought to put pressure on the Italian government, but British threats and sanctions had little impact on the National Liberation Committee. Italy was still occupied by the Allies and would be until December 1947, and hampering British strategy in the Mediterranean was a way to reaffirm Italy's partial autonomy. The Italians knew that the debate over Jewish immigration into Palestine was being closely followed in the United States, and goodwill and aid from America were vital to the Italians.

15

MAGENTA

THE SECRET CAMP

In late 1945, Arazi, the leader of Aliyah Bet, the secret underground organisation for illegal immigration, made contact with a businessman in the port of Savona in Liguria, north-western Italy. He had been told that the man could help him find ships to take the survivors to Palestine. This was Giuseppe Musso, who had been a partisan in the war and was a local bigwig, with offices in a high-rise tower on the harbourside. Savona and the mountains behind it were partisan country, and this gritty city had a left-wing tradition. Sandro Pertini, the socialist president of Italy from 1978–1985, was born in the village of Stella in the steep valleys behind Savona. Musso was a safe contact and was happy to take on this kind of brokering job. The first ship located by Musso had been built in the tiny fishing village of Arenzano, to the east along the coast in the direction of the regional capital of Genoa. Ada Sereni, Arazi's partner, made a trip there to secure the deal.

I follow the Bricha route to Arenzano, now a small holiday resort a stone's throw from the headquarters of "starchitect" Renzo Piano. Arenzano has grown considerably since 1945 and its fields, once famous for their strawberries, have been covered in 1970s apartment blocks. The team behind the epic cyclist Bloisi have given me the name of Lorenzo Giacchero, who they say knows more about the ships that left from Liguria than anyone else. In a small cafe near the seafront, we settle down for a coffee and he immediately erupts with information about the first ship that Sereni brought, the *Rondine*, which means swallow. He scarcely takes a breath while his wife sits patiently at his side, as does his friend, Franco Caviglia. Giacchero has written two books crammed with information

189

about the *Rondine*, which he has found online and in archives he has visited across the globe.

Giacchero explains that during the Second World War, Arenzano had an important little shipyard that specialised in making wooden-hulled boats. As the Germans wanted to get rid of the mines off the coast, they commissioned a new ship to be built, the *Rondine*. Wooden boats are perfect for minesweeping, he tells me. The *Rondine* was a huge ship that dominated the seafront, its prow almost reaching the road. Today, the spot where it was built is home to a beach concession, the Bagni Miramare. "No one is interested so there is nothing to tell you what happened here," says Giacchero in exasperation, waving in the direction of the busy seafront, which is dotted with colourful children's rides and vending machines selling trinkets. "I am the only person, alongside my friend Franco, who is interested in this topic here." The two men worked together on the railway that runs along the Ligurian coast and now spend their time delving into local history.

In 1945, Arenzano was a tough little fishing village and the workers who came from the surrounding coastal towns and villages to build the ship, while happy for the money, had no desire to help the German war effort. So, as Giacchero explains, they worked as slowly as they could. As a result the *Rondine* was only finished in September 1945. It was an important moment, as it was the first big ship to be built in Italy after the war. After it was launched, it sailed off to Savona to have its engines fitted, right in front of Musso's office. Sereni, happy with the deal she had pulled off, returned to Milan where she was to find out that her husband, Enzo, had been killed in Dachau. Each of the boats that sailed in the Aliyah Bet fleet was renamed at sea, Giacchero explains, and this was the reason why the *Rondine* was renamed the *Enzo Sereni* when she sailed from Savona. In the small local history museum which he runs with Caviglia in the back room of a local church, he has the neck of the champagne bottle that launched the *Rondine*. "There has always been a link between Liguria and the Holy Land," he tells me proudly. "The Crusaders sailed from here," he says pointing at the deep blue sea that can just be seen behind the beach concessions. "It's just across the sea. We are linked."

Giacchero is 68 and is not Jewish. I wonder why the story of this ship had caught his imagination. He has been talking over two espressos for over an hour and does not stop to answer my question. His wife prompts him to answer it. He suddenly becomes quiet and reflective. "Something lit up in me when I realised my home town of Arenzano had something to do with the Jews." He speaks slowly all of a sudden. "I have always found the story of the Shoah incomprehensible. It is like looking at the sky at night. It is full of stars and you don't understand why it is there. You cannot understand why they killed all these people. My interest is philosophical. I am interested in the migrants coming to our country today, but I find the story of the Jews different. It was a biblical moment when they sailed from here, returning to the Promised Land." His words remind me of the memorial to the children murdered during the Holocaust at Yad Vashem, where you walk through a room of seemingly endless stars.

On 9 September 1946, the *Rondine* set sail with 908 passengers crammed on board, although the boat was meant to carry no more than 90 people. On the ship were 40 orphans who had come from Selvino, heading for a new life on a kibbutz in Palestine that they would help build with their own hands. The ship also left from the tiny port of Vado. An electric shock shoots through me—this was the other boat that was mentioned by the fisherman on the beach. But the story of the *Rondine* did not end there. One of the bizarre facts that Giacchero tells me before we part is that the *Rondine* ended its life as an Egyptian galleon in the 1963 epic movie *Cleopatra* which starred Elizabeth Taylor and Richard Burton. It was burned in a dramatic scene at the film studios in Rome.

I wish Giacchero farewell, get into my car and take the motorway north, leaving the mountains of Liguria behind as they give way to the flat, fertile plains of Piedmont and then Lombardy. The most important place in Arazi and Sereni's operation lay just outside the upmarket little town of Magenta, west of Milan. A dirt track leads off the SP11, just before a bridge over the River Ticino, to an area known as Boffalora sopra Ticino. I am going to meet Elisabetta Bozzi, an enthusiastic ANPI activist and friend of the cyclist Bloisi. ANPI, the Associazione Nazionale Partigiani d'Italia, is the national partisans' association, which campaigns to highlight their role in the Second World War and the founding of the republic. Bozzi, who has only recently discovered the story of this place, is very excited to show it to me. She stops the car on the Fagiana estate outside a somewhat run-down piece of land surrounded by a barbed wire fence within which sits a large turreted villa. It was once a *tenuta*, the Italian word for an agricultural estate, and is now the headquarters of the Ticino Park. For three years this building was Camp A, where everything that was needed to equip the ships was prepared. "This place was the most top-secret place in the Aliyah Bet," she tells me as the breeze rustles the leaves on the trees. "It was here that they prepared the voyages, which tried to run the then British naval blockade of Palestine." I stare at the deserted garden and try to imagine it back in 1946, covered in military tents and teeming with people. This was the nerve centre of the operation run by Arazi and the Gang.

In Primo Levi's novel *If Not Now, When?*, the band of partisans who are the protagonists are given the address of the camp by the Jewish Brigade when they arrive at Via dell'Unione 5. They are soon moved to a farm in the Lombardy countryside where they are greeted by a brisk young man from Tel Aviv. No doubt describing La Fagiana, Levi writes: "This was a strange farm, where farm work counted little, instead there was a great traffic of merchandise. There were crates of food and medicines, but some were too heavy for you to believe what was printed on them, in English. The young man said everybody had to lend a hand to load the crates onto the trucks." I wonder if the group he is describing are actually the Nakam members on the *Wedgwood*, Kovner's unit, which had just carried out the poison attack in Germany. They were rushed along the Bricha and spent some time at Magenta before being moved for the final leg of their journey to nearby Tradate.

The *Wedgwood*'s Fedda Lieberman and Lea Diamant, the girls who had worked in the underground in Sosnowiec, spent some months in a DP camp at Mestre, outside Venice, until one day they were told to prepare to leave for Palestine. They were instructed to take the minimum of clothing with them and they travelled by night on a train from Milan to Magenta. They were to sail on the *Rondine*. On arrival Lieberman wrote that they were given health checks and divided into groups. "They asked us questions about our past, requested that we keep everything secret, and suggested that we go to work for Aliyah Bet. It was a bit hard to decide because our group had consolidated itself, we wanted to go and build a kibbutz, and here we were on the verge of *aliyah* to Palestine. Nevertheless, we were thrilled by the suggestion. We understood the importance of being able to take part in the actual work of *aliyah* and felt an obligation and privilege." The two women were part of a group of twelve who stayed behind at La Fagiana and joined Arazi and Sereni's gang, working alongside Atara Borovsky. Their first job was to guard the camp, armed with kitchen knives. Lieberman recalled that there were "storerooms for food and clothing, and all sorts of things," and that the organisers "would 'get' material of all kinds from British warehouses and bring them to us for storage. I was put in charge of storage." The food had to be sorted and a menu drawn up. Lea Diamant was the manager of the clothing store. "The boys in our camp had plenty to do in unloading stuff that arrived at the camp, which included fuel; later, weapons were also brought and they could board the ship." In "A" camp, she writes, "we had everything we needed to outfit a vessel. We had canvas and we had a lot of rope with which hammocks could be made. There were also barrels of fuel buried in the fields to look like ordinary fields of cabbage." The villa is still surrounded by fields of freshly dug clods of earth.

It was not just people who were being shipped to Palestine. "A small road led to the town and at the entrance to the town stood a small villa with a large courtyard. The courtyard was surrounded by buildings and one of them had two storeys. This is where those who accompanied the vessels lived. Opposite the tall building was a little one, and this was where weapons were hidden. When the weapons had been cleaned and packed, the door of the hideaway was sealed with cement. Big vases were placed in front to hide the entrance." When Yechiel Aleksander was moved from the Bencista, he was assigned to the weapons squad where he cleaned and inspected the arms. Yehuda Erlich was also here and it was his job to teach the survivors Hebrew when their tasks were done. The work was hard and the team received no pay, but they were given pocket money for a day trip to Milan. Nevertheless, Lieberman remembers her time at Magenta as "one of the most beautiful periods of my life after a period of deep sadness from the loss of my dearest ones in the Holocaust. This was a period of action, or doing what had to be done for a very good cause—bringing the survivors of the Holocaust to Palestine, and at the same time, meeting and working with the young Israelis who were 'the cream of the crop'. This served to ease my pain." Lieberman had met the Nakam avenger Poldek Maimon in Tarvisio, and when he arrived at Magenta their romance took off.

The Milanese Jewish leader, Cantoni, was instrumental in getting use of the house for Arazi and Sereni. It had been a partisan hideout during the war. "There were lots of partisans in the area," Bozzi tells me. "The Jewish Brigade worked with them, but without the help of the Italian partisans none of this would have been possible." Nor would it have been possible without the help of many others either, she explains. "It was a completely isolated spot hidden by the trees, but importantly it was right next to the railway line that runs west from Milan to Novara. They brought the Jews at night secretly by train, which went very slowly as it passed by here, and they jumped off the train, which did not stop. The train drivers knew what was going on, as they were socialist activists too and happy to help. The

Jews then walked down the twisting dirt track to the villa." I can see Lieberman and Diamant, if I close my eyes, walking down the pathway from the railway line.

Today, even though the house is still known as La Casetta di Ebrei, the Little Jewish House, most of the locals have no idea why. Bozzi says that is because the camp was so secret. Others I have spoken to claim that the political left's links with the Palestinians since the declaration of the State of Israel in 1948 meant that they chose to turn their back on their connection with the Bricha story. Bozzi does not choose to elaborate on why the left forgot the 70,000 Jews who passed through Italy after the Second World War, but she bubbles over with the excitement at the newly found story. The left see themselves as guardians of the history of the liberation from fascism. The number of migrants who have arrived in Italy in recent years has become an issue, and this story is suddenly politically useful, as the Italian right campaigns against the number of illegal migrants who have arrived in the country. "Resistance was a complicated thing," Bozzi says as we drive back to town to have supper at a local pizzeria. "It was not just the partisans who fought in the hills and mountains, but the workers went on strike and Italian soldiers also refused to fight after 1943."

The next morning I link up again with Bloisi. Dressed in his cycling gear, he is meeting teenagers in the wood-panelled hall of the symbolic Casa Giacobbe, whose facade is still pock-marked with cannon and bullet holes that date from the 1859 Battle of Magenta, a key moment in the unification of Italy. Bloisi has an earthy sense of humour. He cracks some jokes to put the children at their ease, but once the kids have engaged with him he gets to the point and tells them why he has decided to stop in Magenta on the way to Jerusalem. "Resistance", Bloisi tells the children, "was a way of building a just society and it is vital in this difficult moment in Europe, with nationalism and anti-Semitism on the rise, that we remember what happened." Referring to the orphans from the Selvino home, he says: "These kids had seen unimaginable horrors but were welcomed in Italy, cared for and brought back to life." The message is then rammed home by Marco Cavallarin, the authoritative academic, who is a good friend of the cyclist. Bloisi's quest to keep memory alive is not for the sake of memory alone, he explains to the attentive audience. In the last few years, hundreds of thousands of refugees and migrants have flooded into Italy, and he contrasts the friendly reception Jews received in the country after the war with what is happening today. The disgust is discernible in his voice. Cavallarin then tells them about a village near

Brescia, just over 100 km away, which has just held an unofficial referendum to reject giving shelter to six refugees. "How can a human being not put a hand out to help another human being?" he asks. The teenagers are clearly taken aback; some glance down at their laps and others shuffle in their seats.

Bloisi then begins to explain that remembering is an act of justice that gives back dignity to the victims. "This story must be told and retold now. It must be written down before it is completely forgotten," he tells me later as he straps on his helmet. "Those who experienced injustice are dying and the moment that the story can be told by word of mouth is passing." Above all, Bloisi says that he is frightened that if history is forgotten or rewritten it will have a negative impact on the future. He wants to defend democracy and the rule of law. It is a reason that I have heard given again and again by those Jews and gentiles who are struggling to have the events of the Holocaust and its aftermath remembered.

TO PALESTINE

16

NEW YORK

F***B SHIPPING

When the Copacabana, on East 60th Street in Manhattan, opened in November 1940, the Latin-themed nightclub oozed Hollywood glamour and sophistication. Above it was the Hotel Fourteen, which catered to rich widows and society types. It had been bought in 1944 by Fanny and Ruby Bennet, who was once the secretary of Chaim Weizmann, the first president of Israel. While the party never stopped in the club, life in the hotel was a far more serious affair. It was a world of intrigue and spies of which the prim society guests were oblivious. Hotel Fourteen was known as Kibbutz Fourteen and was the unofficial American headquarters of the underground Jewish paramilitary organisation, the Haganah. Every Friday night its agents met for a Shabbat dinner. One of the guests who checked in during the winter of 1945 was Zeev Shind, a 36-year-old redhead who went by the name of Dani. Shind had been born in Vilnius but had left eastern Europe for Palestine when he was 20. Sixteen years later, he was a senior Haganah official and had worked on a number of important projects during the war. He had also played a key role in bringing illegal immigrants into Palestine before the war.

Shind met with Ben-Gurion in October 1945 to discuss the possibility of buying larger ships on the other side of the Atlantic where there were a lot for sale, unlike in Europe. In the closing months of 1945 only one ship with more than 200 refugees had left European shores bound for Palestine. The war over, Ben-Gurion was keen on sending small, armed boats to break the British blockade, because he believed the British would not fire on small ships. But his advisers pointed out that actually the British public would have no stomach for images of large ships being fired on, emblazoned across the front pages of the newspaper on the breakfast table next to their tea and marmalade made from Jaffa oranges. He was thus persuaded by his colleagues in the Jewish Agency to buy and equip two of the vast number of former naval ships that were now being sold as scrap and going for a song along the American coast. The plan was plotted and put together in a haze of cigarette smoke in the Hotel Fourteen.

The money to buy and refit the ships was raised across the US under the guise of the Sonneborn Institute. On 1 July 1945, Ben-Gurion had attended a gathering at the New York apartment of Rudolf Sonneborn, who headed a small group of activists that wanted to send arms and supplies to the Jews in Palestine. The group was clandestine but had a nationwide reach. Sonnenborn was an influential oil executive and businessman and was also, as luck would have it, the fourth husband of Dorothy Schiff, owner and publisher of the *New York Post*. The official line was that the Sonneborn Institute raised money for agricultural and medical supplies for Palestine, but in reality it was busy buying ships, planes, jeeps and arms. Every Thursday people arrived at the hotel with money and jewellery to fund the project.

The purchase and equipping of the ships was a business that had to be carried out completely legally, and Aliyah Bet set up a number of front companies. One was known as FB Shipping, either named after Fanny Bennet or, more likely, a play on the name of the British foreign secretary, Ernest Bevin: hence F***Bevin Shipping.

In mid-June 1945, the Royal Canadian Navy decided to put three hundred corvettes out of service, one being the *Beauharnois*, which was just nine months old. In October, she was purchased by the United Shipping Corporation of New York and in late December the company brought the *Beauharnois* and 29 other corvettes to City Island in New York. In January 1946 the *Beauharnois* and one of her sister ships were bought by a Panamanian company called the Caribbean Atlantic Corporation, a front that had just been registered by Zeev Shind and that had for its cover a respectable office in New York's shipping district. The *Beauharnois* had seen action in the Battle of the Atlantic it was this ship that was to become the *Wedgwood*. The vessels were 650-ton class and could do up to 20 knots, they were big enough to carry significant numbers of refugees. It was a major upgrade for the Bricha compared to the ships that had sailed before.

At City Island the gun turrets were removed and the two ships were then taken to Staten Island for provisioning and refurbishment. The ship that was to become the *Wedgwood* was now renamed the *Colon*. Ada Sereni's husband Enzo had spent time in the United States before the war and learned that the best way to get support from American Jews was not to go cap in hand asking for help, but with an offer to get involved in a joint venture. Although many in the Haganah were opposed to American involvement beyond American Jews financing the project, the decision was made that the ships would be crewed by American volunteers. Until now local crews had been hired in ports on the Black Sea and the Mediterranean, but in America things had to be done by the book. So another front organisation was born, Palestine Vocational Services, which sought to attract young men to train on farms in preparation for a future life in Palestine. Under this guise Shind spoke to youth groups across the country. In December 1945, he addressed a youth group in Detroit and inspired Moshe Kogan, Moshe Katz and 17-year-old Eli Cohen. Cohen had already tried to get into Palestine illegally and was desperate to emigrate. He said later that his motives for volunteering were more selfish in nature than altruistic. It was self-interest that also motivated David Gottlieb, who was another Detroit boy from the wrong side of the tracks, the son of Jewish immigrants from the Russian Empire. In April 1945, at the age of 16 he had joined a Jewish youth training centre in Cream Ridge, New Jersey. On the farm he heard about the ships and was "grabbed" by the idea of volunteering. "Some of my motivation to be involved in transporting refugees was the whole idea of adventure. I didn't think carefully of consequences. But I wasn't really prepared for what I saw," he admitted years later.

These youngsters had never been to sea, and so sailors in the American Merchant Marine were tracked down. Land and Labour for Palestine was another front that was used to recruit sailors. Ten per cent of American merchant navy sailors were Jewish, so finding recruits with experience to man the ships was not difficult. Marvin Bacaner, who was the first engineer on the *Wedgwood*, was on shore leave in Belgium when he met a member of the Jewish Brigade who told him about Aliyah Bet. When he got home, there was a letter waiting for him from his Zionist youth leader, asking him to drop by for a chat. Bacaner signed up and was part of the team who sailed the *Beauharnois* to City Island. He was in charge of refitting the boat and training the new recruits. While the ship was being refurbished, the crew lived in a special house in Coney Island. The volunteers served without pay but were given pocket money and cigarettes. During this period Gottlieb worried that he was in over his head. "Clearly, we were an assembly of odd and diverse characters who would never have qualified for duty on any military or licensed commercial cargo or passenger ship."

The crew were given the briefest of training and sent home for Passover to say goodbye to their families. On 18 April 1946 the *Beauharnois* set sail under the Panamanian flag as the *Colon* with her sister ship the *Balboa*, which was later renamed the *Haganah*. The commander was a hard-drinking 28-year old captain Jacob Jerome Lichtman. With blue eyes, brown hair and a boxer's physique, he did not look like the son of Brooklyn Yiddish-speaking immigrants. He was a tough American seaman who chewed tobacco. He was also an anarchist keen not just to help Aliyah Bet, but to fight the imperialist British. He had dodged German U-boats and sailed to Murmansk, and he scared the young volunteers. Unsurprisingly, Lichtman spent most of the journey across the Atlantic wound up and tense, worn down by the responsibility of heading a ship crewed by amateurs. He was right to be anxious. Corvettes are infamous for their roll and pitch, and although the sea was calm and the weather good, on board it felt like the ship was in a major storm and the inexperienced volunteers were all soon violently sick. After one week on the high seas, the *Colon* broke down, as the rookie crew were too ill to carry out their duties. The ship nevertheless made it to Ponta Delgada in the Portuguese Atlantic islands of the Azores, where she put in for repairs. Here the boat picked up its first refugee, a Lithuanian rabbi from the local synagogue, who, when he met the crew and discovered their mission, begged to be taken along. He had fled Europe and ended up in the Azores. He was put to work in the galley with the fiery redhead cook, Yaacov Pleet.

Although the Bricha was a secret underground movement, Tel Aviv took a gamble, and as the ships prepared to sail, Ben-Gurion decided that he was going splash the survivors' story on the front pages of the newspapers. I.F. Stone, the well-known American correspondent, who had grown up in a Yiddish-speaking Jewish household in Philadelphia, was invited to travel with the survivors on the *Wedgwood* from Italy to Palestine. The hope was that the publicity that his story received in the US would put pressure on the British to abandon their immigration restrictions. Once Stone arrived in Europe, he was hoping to board the illegal boat immediately, but his Haganah contact joked that Aliyah Bet was "far from being as well organised as a Cook's tour". He suggested giving Stone unparalleled access to refugees along the Bricha trail, but he warned him not to go to Poland as "conditions are very unsettled and Jews are often shot at by bandits or anti-Semitic gangs on their way out".

Stone set out in search of the story and was immediately struck by the dangerous situation in Germany, where he thought that the mutual hatred of the Germans and the Jews was a tinderbox waiting to ignite. He stopped at Landsberg, where he found "a lot of ill-dressed Jews walking around in a rather dispirited and desultory way" and thought them "an unattractive lot". He followed a group of teenagers through Bohemia to Bratislava and on to the Rothschild Hospital in Vienna. He wrote how he handed "caramels" he had brought from America to what were in his eyes "youngsters" with a sweet tooth like any others.

As Stone sat among the survivors, he felt that he could easily have been one of them had his parents stayed on in Europe. He told his readers that "the big news about the Jews of Eastern Europe is not that they have suffered. That is an old story, grown weary in the retelling. The real news is that so many of these people came across the border with tremendous vitality, with spirits unbroken. These Jews ... who returned to find themselves without home or family, have a will to live and a will to build that are wonderful to see." He was moved by their spontaneous singing. "I have never heard singing that touched me so much. The songs I heard were songs that had sprung from the Nazi-created ghettos, the concentration camps, and the forest hideouts of the Jewish Partisan bands." He sat next to a 16-year-old who had been in Buchenwald, who sang a song called "Es Brent" about a shtetl being burned during a pogrom. "For these children, on their way out of Europe, the songs they sang said farewell to vanished homes and parents," Stone told readers.

Once the survivors arrived in Bratislava, many of them were taken to the dormitory town of Devinska Nova Ves. It was separated from Austria by the pretty little Morava River, spanned by a wooden bridge. In 1946 thousands of Jews were among the 100,000 who walked across the border here. Following the Bricha route I set out to find it but, as I drove up and down the town's residential streets, I was beginning to think that the story was a fairy-tale. All of a sudden I passed a street of old houses that led directly to an impressive modern bridge. A rush of adrenalin sped me out of the car and onto my feet.

The street was full of old-world Austro-Hungarian charm and was clearly a popular spot for day-trippers: mothers with small children were busy lifting bikes out of the boots of their cars in the carpark. I walked down to the river in the warm sunshine and up onto the bridge, which is a splendid cycle highway that stretches over the meadows and the meandering Morava. There were families picnicking on the riverbank. It is an idyllic and peaceful spot, and lovers' padlocks are collecting on the metal-work in the middle of the bridge. The original bridge over which the survivors streamed was small and impassable when the water was high. It was wrecked by ice floes in the harsh winter of 1946, but the American Jewish Joint Distribution Committee paid the authorities to build a new one. They also paid for a hostel in town that could put up 300 survivors a night. The new bridge did not last long as Devinska Nova Ves was on the front line of the Cold War and the Morava River was to become part of the Iron Curtain. As the Russians took control of eastern Europe it became a no-go area with watchtowers and barbed wire, which is one reason why the banks of the Morava have such an old-world charm about them and are home to rare wild flowers: the area was inaccessible for a generation. Now there is a monument next to the bridge that says it is called the Most Slobody, the Freedom Bridge. It was built in 2012 to celebrate the new-found liberty of the post-Soviet world. There is no mention of the Jewish refugees who passed this way after the war and the leaflets in the tourist office make no mention of them either.

It was the emerging Cold War that was to push the survivors' needs off the political agenda. They were part of yesterday's story. Fears of Soviet expansion dominated thinking in Whitehall. A common description of the British foreign secretary Ernest Bevin is that he was an anti-Semite. Two American army rabbis, close associates of Abraham Klausner, made a journey to London to meet with Bevin to put their case. Rabbis Herbert Friedmann and Philip Bernstein found him, Friedmann recalled, "sitting at his desk all wrapped up in a fur coat, scarf around his neck, hat on his head and a little electric heater by his feet. This was the Foreign Minister of the Empire of Great Britain." His mood was "lousy" and Friedmann said the conversation "was one of the most profane. It was an incessant barrage." He reported that Bevin said to him in his West Country accent: "You Jews are the cause of all the troubles in the world; no wonder everybody hates you." The fact that MI5 had warned him in the spring of 1946 that Jewish terrorists planned to assassinate him and launch a terror campaign in mainland Britain similar to that run by the IRA in 1939–40 must have tested his sympathies. He regarded Zionists as a dangerous religious clique.

A solution might have been reached had it been at the top of Bevin's agenda, but Palestine was not the most pressing problem facing the Empire. Besides the emerging Soviet threat, Bevin was preoccupied with the situation in India. Added to that was the fact that the Labour government's priority was its social reform agenda at home. Nevertheless, as the *Wedgwood* was being fitted out, diplomats and politicians were trying to find some compromise in Palestine. In February 1946, the Anglo-American Committee's fact-finding mission began investigating the situation. The committee had been set up in the wake of the Harrison report, in which Rabbi Klausner had played such a crucial role; it had recommended that the British should admit 100,000 Jewish refugees into Palestine. The committee was to assess if this was possible but also to examine the problems faced by Jews both inside and outside Palestine. Bevin had jumped at the opportunity as it delayed any decisions that had to be made.

The Labour MP Richard Crossman, a pro-Zionist and one of the most dazzling Labour intellectuals of his day, was a member of the committee, and his account of its investigation, published in 1947, gives an insight into the views and thoughts of the politicians involved in London, Washington and Jerusalem. The committee first heard evidence in Washington, where Crossman wrote that its British members disliked "the self-righteousness of American support for a cause for which America was not prepared to assume responsibility". Bartley Crum, a liberal San Francisco lawyer, became one of the best-known members of the committee after he warned that there would be mass suicides if the DPs were not allowed into Palestine. His comments were widely reported in the American press. Crossman was left in no doubt of either the strength of the Zionist lobby or the difference it would have made if some of the British cabinet members had 20,000 Jews in their constituencies. That lobby had its limitations, however: the American administration maintained its own strict immigration quotas, and did not throw open the doors of America to the survivors.

Crossman's observations of the Bricha are also worthy of note. The committee realised that although thousands of Jews were arriving in Germany every month, the number of Jews registered in the DP camps stayed the same. "Obviously the zone was a funnel through which the Jews were passing. Where were they going?" If this was a mystifying revelation to a committee devoted to studying the problem, it highlights just how little was actually understood in Whitehall of what was happening on the ground in Europe. The committee considered what were to them new questions about the possibility of rebuilding Jewish life in Europe and how the position of Jews in the rest of Europe differed from those in the United Kingdom. Again, their thinking shows how out of touch they were with men like Zalman Grinberg and Abraham Klausner. In Cairo, the committee heard British officials explain that the 1939 White Paper was the cornerstone of British foreign policy and that "it could not be rescinded without throwing the Arabs into the arms of Russia. Britain was already committed up to the hilt and a change of policy would be disastrous." Significantly, Crossman found that in private American officials held the same view. "Everyone in Cairo was obsessed by the fear of Russian expansion, and frantically trying to build up something, however makeshift, as a bulwark against it." If the Arabs were to be that bulwark, Zionists would pay the price. The need to protect the oil fields and air routes was of paramount importance.

In Jerusalem the committee met with the leaders of the Jewish Agency. Above all, Crossman was struck by the fact that the Jewish Agency was a "state within a state" and that the strength of the Haganah meant that a conflict between Britain and the Jews was inevitable as they almost had a state to fight for already. At his home in Tel Aviv, Ben-Gurion was found by Crossman surrounded by Greek texts, studying Plato. He had wind that the committee was to recommend that the Haganah be disarmed and the Jewish Agency reorganised, as it was in fact to do. He warned Crossman: "In deciding our destiny, don't make the mistake of thinking of us as Jews like the Jews you have in London. Imagine we're Englishmen fighting for our national existence, and calculate that we shall behave as you would behave if you were in our situation." As he got in the car to drive back to Jerusalem, Ben-Gurion overheard Crossman's bodyguard make a comment about the safety of the road. Ben-Gurion poked his head in the car window and said jokingly: "It's OK. I've telephoned the terrorists all along the route. Goodbye."

17

LA SPEZIA

MOVE OVER, PAUL NEWMAN

As the engines of the *Colon* were repaired in the Azores, in April 1946, the port city of La Spezia, not far from the Tuscan border with Liguria, was abuzz with rumours that Italian fascist and German Nazi bigwigs were going to try to flee the country in secret on the 650-ton *Fede*. The ratlines that were used by former Nazis and fascists led through La Spezia and Genoa, so it was highly possible that this story was true. When the police went to the dock to check if the *Fede* was in fact about to take on a shipment of salt destined for Sardinia, as its papers stated, they discovered that it was equipped to accommodate hundreds of passengers for a long journey. As the news spread, workers laid down tools and took to the streets in protest.

The stage was set for a drama that was to inspire the Leon Uris novel and Hollywood blockbuster *Exodus*, which starred Paul Newman as the Haganah secret agent who led the refugees to British Mandatory Palestine. Yet 56-year-old local historian and novelist Alberto Cavanna only discovered recently that illegal immigrant ships had been fitted out in the dockyards where he worked for many years. One of the ships refurbished in nearby Porto Venere was the real-life ship *Exodus*, which made its own voyage from the south of France in 1947. "In the novel the action takes place in Cyprus and until recently I had no idea that in reality it happened here and had little to do with the *Exodus* at all," he says, the surprise still evident on his face. In the fictional story Ari Ben Canaan, played by Paul Newman in the film, calls a hunger strike when the Royal Navy blockade the harbour of Famagusta in Cyprus when he attempts to lead the illegal voyage of a ship full of Holocaust survivors. In reality the drama unfolded on the *Fede* in the harbour in La Spezia.

The *Fede*, which the local police assumed was about to transport Nazis to South America, actually belonged to Ada Sereni and Aliyah Bet. The real-life Paul Newman was her colleague, Yehuda Arazi. Their plan was for the ships to sail on 2 April, which was the first day of the month of Nisan, the first month in the Jewish calendar and the day that God told Moses to leave Egypt. The survivors were to say farewell to Europe when the first thin sliver of the new moon appeared in the sky. It was a plan full of symbolism. Not expecting any complications, Sereni had taken her first leave for eight months and returned to Palestine to see her son and daughters.

As the police arrived at the dock, trucks were moving through central Italy. On them were survivors from Santa Maria di Bagni, among them Moshe Ha-Elion, his future wife and the other Greeks in their group. Another convoy headed by Arazi was preparing to leave from Tradate, close to the present-day Milan-Malpensa airport. There the survivors were loaded onto 37 British Army Dodge trucks to begin their journey to La Spezia.

One of those on the trucks was 16-year old Yitzhak Kaplan with his sister Leah, who had hidden out in the Soviet Union during the war before returning to Rivne. "We had to leave behind our mother, our sister Pola and her husband, the partisan Iser. Pola had a brand-new baby and was not ready to make the journey," Kaplan recalls as we chat in his sitting room in Haifa. Not only were families being separated but close friendships were formed in the DP camps, and amid the excitement of the departure there would also have been an undercurrent of apprehension. Some of those who left on the trucks had only been in Tradate for a matter of days, and such was the secrecy involved that testimonies reveal that they did not know where they were. Some believed they were in the south of Italy; others say that Tradate was close to Genoa. "We set off in a convoy. They were covered with tarpaulins and we could not see out. We were told not to say a word. There were two motorcycles in front and two behind. They had sirens so that nobody stopped us," Kaplan tells me.

Eventually, the convoy arrived in Sarzana on the plain below the Carrara marble mines, where Michelangelo picked out the stone that was to become *David*. As it pulled into the town's large main square, it was halted by an armed group of former partisans. Arazi tried to turn around but it was too late. Shots were fired and the situation became tense; the police soon arrived. Thinking that they had intercepted fleeing fascists on the way to Franco's Spain, they informed the local police commander in La Spezia and he duly reported the operation to the Allied Control Committee. The

British had been reluctant to try to capture a ship in an Italian port, fearing the bad publicity that would result, but now the Italians had done it for them, as the Italian police refused to let the *Fede* set sail. Immediately, Arazi issued orders to stop trucks moving up from the south. The whole operation of the Bricha was in danger of discovery.

Once the police who had stopped the convoy realised that it was made up of Jewish survivors, who showed them their concentration camp tattoos, apologetically they finally agreed that it could move to the port but only under police escort. It was late at night when the convoy arrived at the dock. The communist paper *L'Unità* sent its reporters to find out what was going on and the headline on Thursday, 4 April, read: "900 ebrei tentato l'espatrio clandestino" (900 Jews attempted illegal emigration). The journalists reported that far from finding fascists, they had discovered something else: "Crouching on the ground on the Pirelli dock in an indescribable confusion of luggage, about 900 melancholic and defeated Jews were surrounded by a strong police cordon."

No sooner had the Spezini read the story than the mood in the city changed. Crowds appeared at the Pirelli dock to show their support for the Jews and to bring them food. It was a spontaneous action that was all the more impressive as La Spezia was in ruins. The magnificent broad bay that Napoleon had declared the world's most perfect harbour was peppered with sunken ships. After the unification of Italy, the town and the crescent shoreline, which had inspired Shelley and Byron, became an important naval base. As a result it was a prize possession and had been fiercely fought over during the war. Allied bombing raids had left only a few streets intact. There were mounds of rubble everywhere.

Despite being thwarted, the Kaplan siblings were overjoyed to see the sea for the first time in their lives. But no sooner were they aboard the *Fede* than a jeep full of British soldiers showed up and boarded. There was no panic, just undaunted resistance. The survivors shouted that they would never leave the ship and that Palestine was their national home and threatened to throw the British soldiers overboard if they did not leave the boat. Outnumbered and subdued, the British left, rushing to their jeeps. Triumphant and boisterous, the refugees pursued them down the pier, where they quickly formed a circle around the jeeps, dancing a wild hora, using the dance as a weapon.

It was the perfect set for an actor like Arazi. A wanted man, Arazi assumed a new identity, that of Holocaust survivor Dr Yosef de Paz. Dr de Paz stepped forward as the spokesman of the refugees. Arazi was an improviser with an aura of authority and a unique charisma that made him the perfect leader. Kaplan watched him from afar with admiration. The following day Arazi summoned some of the refugees who had suffered the most to tell their stories to the head of police and to show their greenish-blue camp tattoo numbers. The *carabinieri* were sympathetic and offered help, while the survivors began to settle themselves into the ship. Local support was largely spontaneous and there was by now a large crowd of locals at the gate to the pier offering moral support. La Spezia was also a city with a left-wing tradition and was in the control of the partisans. Once proud of its navy, the townsfolk resented British control of their coastal waters. The large crowds that arrived at the port unnerved the British, who were frightened that they would riot. Aldo Rastani, a young Genoese journalist, volunteered to become the intermediary between the ship and the outside world. As a result of his actions it was not long before members of the anti-fascist resistance in Liguria and other underground fighters were offering their assistance.

On the third day the British again arrived at the portside in jeeps and the commander proposed moving the refugees to a DP camp near Genoa. Arazi answered that he would rather set fire to the ships with everyone on board. The British officer then asked Arazi what he should tell his commander if he did. The answer was swift—that they should not give inhumane orders. Arazi observed with satisfaction that the officer seemed somewhat perplexed and the British left, unsure what to do next.

Arazi did not hesitate. At dawn on 7 April, as the sun rose twinkling on the sea, Arazi called all the refugees onto the pier and explained that the fight would be hard and those who wished could leave then. He explained that their best tactic was to frighten the British and he called for a hunger strike. Not one person moved away. All that could be heard was the noise of the waves crashing against the quay. All the survivors were prepared to starve themselves to death. The fight had begun.

Kaplan says that he will never forget the hunger. In the bowels of the ship, people lay in their bunks, motionless, staring into space, quietly contemplating what was going to become of them. The mood was subdued and depressed. The placard at the gate read "Seventy-two hours of hunger strike". Passers-by stopped to stare and shake their heads in astonishment. The British, however, were no pushover and a Royal Navy ship sailed into the bay across which Byron had once famously swum. From the deck the British demanded that the survivors disembark immediately. Arazi shouted back that he would blow the ship sky-high if the British tried to forcibly remove them. Kaplan was nervous when the British arrived but says that "more than anything I was angry. But I was never frightened, even when Arazi said he might blow up the ship." The British officers at the end of the jetty withdrew to plan their next move, though they also moved the warship alongside the *Fede*. I can still sense Kaplan's anger, a sure sign of the survivors' focus and determination that they would make that journey to a new life in Palestine.

As the British sealed the port off with tanks, the news of the Holocaust survivors' plight made headlines around the world. Arazi sent radio messages to world leaders, including President Truman and Prime Minister Attlee, informing them that a thousand survivors of Hitler's camps were crowded into a small ship in an Allied port, being besieged by the greatest navy in the world. He talked about the sick, the handicapped, the hundred and fifty pregnant women, and the dozens of small children trapped in the ship. It was not long before reporters arrived, not just from Italian papers but from the international press, and most importantly the American papers. Arazi gave daily briefings at the port gates explaining the refugees' position. Soon refugees in DP camps across Italy were also threatening to go on a hunger strike. A stagnant, rancid air inside the ship forced people out, and they began sleeping on the pier.

The survivors were told little about developments though there were regular lectures on Zionism. Many of the refugees were sick and scabies was spreading. Tensions were rising when, with the agreement of the port, Arazi hung up a sign on the gateway proclaiming it was "The Gateway to Zion" and flew the Zionist and Italian flags side by side. The British were compelled to move their troops back as the demonstrations at the port gates grew and the windows at the British commander's residence in La Spezia were smashed.

Arazi's actions were to have a profound impact on American foreign policy in the Middle East. On 20 April the Anglo-American Committee submitted its findings and Truman quickly endorsed the recommendations that 100,000 Jewish refugees should be immediately admitted into Palestine and Jews be permitted to buy land, a right which had been suspended in 1939. Whitehall was furious. The cabinet agreed that the report should be rejected unless the US administration was willing to provide financial and military assistance. However, the Americans, like the British, eager to demobilise rapidly, rejected the request. The British government was in no mood to offer the survivors a helping hand. Arazi had had several heart attacks since arriving in Italy and the strain was pushing him to the limit, but the daredevil in him was carried along with the fight and he knew that this was the culmination of his life's work.

In Palestine itself, the Jewish Agency faced a dilemma and, to avoid sanctions, distanced themselves from Arazi, but crowds demonstrating their support in La Spezia continued to grow and in Genoa port workers went on strike. The weak and faint were carried onto the deck and the quayside for the press to see, and an eerie silence hung over the ship. Italian politicians now began to send messages of support. Arazi held a press conference in which he reiterated that his people would rather die than give in. The Italian authorities, fearful that the situation among their own citizens would get out of control, rebuffed British demands to interrogate the refugees in an effort to expose who was in charge.

On the fifth day, two British cars drew up, one carrying Harold Laski, a high-ranking member of the British Labour Party and scion of an influential Jewish family. Raffaele Cantoni, who was in Florence where both men were attending a socialist conference, had asked him to intervene. Laski urged Arazi to return the Jews to DP camps while he interceded on their behalf, but Arazi refused. He then upped the ante and informed Laski that next morning ten of the refugees would commit suicide and every dawn ten more would do the same again until they were allowed to sail. Laski was convinced that Arazi was a lunatic but agreed to discuss the situation with Bevin and Attlee. The suicide threat was then lifted, as was the hunger strike, and an uneasy truce ensued.

It was just in time for Passover on 16 April 1946, a festival full of significance and perfect for Arazi to use its symbolism to reinvigorate the refugees with determination. The matzo and wine were brought in from Palestine, but the rest of the food was given to the refugees by the people of La Spezia. On the pier a roll of white paper was laid on the ground as a makeshift tablecloth and the survivors sat squatting in long rows on either side. They ate the Seder meal and recited the traditional verses of the story of the exodus from Egypt. Arazi was in charge of the Seder and, after the meal, handed out silver medals to three of the crew on which was an image of a ship on a stormy sea and the inscription "The Sons Will Return to Their Home". The medals had been made by the famous Italian Jewish sculptor Arrigo Minerbi and were to be given to the police officers, sailors and officials who had helped Arazi and Sereni in their work.

While Laski talked to people in London, Arazi again raised the stakes, announcing that if the *Fede* sailed for Palestine it could bring back Italian POWs whose return had long been delayed while the British procrastinated. Arazi was now the toast of Italy. Laski returned with a deal. The British government offered 679 entry certificates, a number that would be deducted from the regular monthly quota. Not surprisingly, Arazi refused. Finally, on 8 May Kaplan remembers watching Laski, a tall, distinguished man, return with news that permission had been obtained for them to proceed. Arazi had won his battle though he was on the verge of another heart attack. The British had given in and agreed to the immediate admission of all the passengers without any effect on the quotas.

The ship was dangerously overloaded, and it was decided to use an extra ship, the *Felice*, to transport the refugees in better conditions. Kaplan tells me: "The leaders came to ask for volunteers to give up their places to pregnant women and old people so they could get to Palestine as soon as possible. Thirteen of us young guys volunteered to get off. Leah my sister decided to stay. When I got off the boat, I suddenly thought of my mother and asked if she could go in my place. The organisers agreed and sent a car to bring her from Tradate." By the time his mother arrived on the quayside, Kaplan was on his way back to Tradate. It was a good choice as from now on "the Gang rewarded us with American chocolate and cigarettes and treated us as if we were one of them". Despite the hardships, I have the feeling that for a teenage boy this was a great adventure.

After 45 days in port, a whistle announced their departure to a huge crowd of local well-wishers, and the *Fede* and the *Felice* finally set out to sea. They left singing and waving — not sneaking away in secret, in fear.

Though the story may have been altered, Uris's novel captures this crucial moment. The events in La Spezia represented a point where the story of the Jews changed. They took a stand and they won. It was an act of empowerment. The book was a blockbuster success and devoured by millions. While in the book myth replaced reality, the essence of the novel caught this moment of self-assertion. The atmosphere of empowered determination would be a characteristic of the new Israel. It was a key moment in the founding of that state.

Over time, however, the people of La Spezia forgot the role they had played in the story. That was until 1996, when journalist Marco Ferrari came across a report on the news wires of a concert in New York and Tel Aviv to commemorate the event. "I'm the son of a partisan and I've lived all my life on the left, but I had never heard people talk about the aid the partisans gave the Jews," Ferrari says. Does it matter? I wonder. Yes is the answer. For Ferrari it is a matter of historical record. He says that "the partisans did not want to remember the part they had played in the conflict with the Palestinians". When Ferrari was the cultural director of the local council, he set up the Exodus prize for intercultural cooperation, but he says that in recent years interest in the story has waned. "Local people are apathetic, but it's important to remember what happened here. Historical facts are in danger of being forgotten and that leads to historical revisionism," he says. "The partisans helped well over 20,000 Jewish refugees leave for Palestine in the run-up to 1948, and they also trafficked arms that were used in the battles against the Arabs. Not to remember the true facts is to leave history open to distortion." Alberto Cavanna, the historian, notes that "the agents of the Haganah swore the locals to secrecy. They were fearful to speak out afterwards. There was a lot of gun-running too and this was certainly something people didn't want to talk about."

An €11m redevelopment scheme has all but destroyed the pier where the story of the *Fede* and the *Fenice* was played out. When I arrive in La Spezia on a hot sunny May morning, I stumble unexpectedly into the heart of a campaign to erect a memorial on the site where the hunger strike took place and which is now being turned into a marina. One of the leaders of the campaign, Maria Luisa Eguez, a local school teacher, tells me, referring to the number of migrants who have arrived in Italy in recent years, "the people of La Spezia are by nature not open and friendly, but they opened their arms to help the Jews even though the city had been very badly destroyed in the war. If it happened once, it can happen again, and that hope drives me forward."

In his large office with commanding views across the Gulf of La Spezia, Mayor Pierluigi Peracchini, head of the first centre-right coalition to run the city since 1945, explains that until two years ago the Pagliari Pier had been a military zone and is now owned by the port authority. "My mother-in-law was one of those who helped the Jews and brought them food," he tells me, adding: "You're right to ask why this story isn't being remembered here, and it's close to my heart." He then slips into his back office to make a call to the port authorities, emerging minutes later to announce that a competition will be held for a suitable memorial to be put up at the new marina.

By chance and an odd twist of fate, I discover that Orli Bach, the granddaughter of Arazi, is visiting the city on holiday with her husband. I catch up with her by the building site on the old Pagliari Pier. She is busy telling a group of local reporters: "The people here have a lot to be proud of, and pride in this story can feed into the commercial sector and attract lots of tourists. Solidarity between Italy and Israel is important. I grew up with stories of my grandfather all my life. He was a real hero. He was very courageous and committed to helping the survivors." A year later the pier is still a building site—but a building site with a monument.

Back in 1946, once the ships had sailed out of the harbour, her grandfather left them to sail to Palestine and returned to the Italian coast. Arazi then called all of the Gang together at the Magenta camp. Fedda Lieberman remembers being ordered with the other women to prepare a celebration and wrote later that the "Old Man", as they all called Arazi, said triumphantly: "This is the first thousand but there will be many thousands more". Arazi handed out more medals to everyone who had worked on the operation, including several local police chiefs.

Shortly after the party, the agents from Palestine who would sail on the *Wedgwood* arrived in Magenta and preparations for its departure began. Lieberman recalls that they even practised walking up a rope gangplank. Yisrael Rotem and Benjamin Nativ were both Palmach-trained naval men and they went to join Yisrael Auerbach, who was already at Magenta. Dov Berchik, who was to take over as the captain, also arrived from Palestine. At this point he claimed later that relations between the agents and the Gang were tense. "Arazi was brave and tough and knew how to do things, only in his own way," he wrote. "He did not want to depend on men of the Palmach who had been educated differently. Ada Sereni ignored us and believed only in the Italian admirals. They were a different kind of people with different backgrounds and this led to poor relations and lack of mutual respect." In Tradate and Genoa, where many of the *Wedgwood*'s passengers were gathered for departure, there was considerable apprehension as to what awaited them when their turn came, but also a determination that they would get to Palestine at any cost.

18

HAIFA

THE PEOPLE'S TRAFALGAR

After three weeks in the Azores while the La Spezia affair was being resolved, the *Wedgwood*, or *Colon* as it was still called at this point, was given the order to sail. It was the first week of May 1946 and its destination was the socialist and partisan stronghold of Savona.

Not long after it docked, a luxurious private car with Swiss number plates appeared on the pier. Yehuda Arazi had arrived to take charge. But Arazi was not a happy man. He was not pleased that the crew was made up of American Jews. Until now, he and Sereni had manned their boats with regular Italian crews. As far as he was concerned, this was a one-off, and it would be a year before another American-crewed ship docked in Italy. Arazi later wrote: "On the day that the ship arrived in Savona, we already saw the difference between work with a Jewish crew and work with a regular, hired crew. The captain was an old drunkard (he was Jewish); a man who did not succumb to any authority; the crew was a varied mix of a kind that I had never seen in my life." The first day the ship arrived in the port of Savona, the market was flooded with fresh American cigarettes, smuggled in by the crew. In a city where people picked up cigarette butts off the pavement, this was a giveaway that there were foreigners in town. The *Colon* was to spend seven weeks there, during which bunks and hammocks were installed for the refugees to sleep on. The official story was that the ship was a banana boat. Anyone who knew anything about bananas would have known that they are transported hanging on hooks.

While the *Colon* was in Savona, the crew's inexperience almost ruined the venture for a second time, when one of them, who had connected a

217

pipe to the water hydrant on the quayside, forgot to turn it off. The ship was saved when two female passers-by alerted the captain. There was little for the crew to do and they spent their time swimming and sightseeing, even making a trip to La Scala in Milan. David Gottlieb, who had been recruited to Aliyah Bet at the Cream Ridge farm in New Jersey and who wrote about his experiences in his memoirs, recalled that the poverty shocked him. "Elderly women would gather around the docked ships pleading for the leftovers. Children begged for food, cigarettes, and money. Other kids served as pimps, assuring all takers they could provide young virgins. Older men would follow behind us in hopes of picking up discarded cigarette butts."

The crew were keen to meet their passengers and asked if they could visit the survivors. It was arranged that they would go in groups of five to a camp in Genoa, where a couple of hundred of their passengers were living. They were given strict orders not to say who they were and what they were doing in Italy. Gottlieb's memoirs describe the DP camp. He recalls that in the barracks "there were few, if any, amenities. Windows were bare of curtains; overhead lighting came from a bare bulb attached to a socket hanging from the ceiling." He talks of families and young children and says: "The first person I spoke with was a 38-year-old man born in Poland. His name was Avram, and he had a wife, Lisa, and a daughter Golda, aged two."

On the list I have seen that was published in the Hebrew newspaper *Lakkarow W'Larahok* when the boat finally docked in Haifa, and in the names registered in Atlit, there are no children. I had found this odd as I have read many times that the DPs quickly paired off and had children; birth rates were high among them. Gottlieb tells us: "Avram was born and lived for many years in Warsaw. After completing high school he had enrolled in a technical college where he wished to study civil engineering." His family had been sent to a concentration camp, but Avram survived as he was hidden by a non-Jewish friend on a farm. "When he returned to Warsaw, he learned that his entire family—parents, brothers, uncles, and aunts— had all been murdered. Avram was the sole survivor." He travelled to Italy with a Jewish youth group and there he met Lisa. Lisa had a child that Avram told Gottlieb was not his, and when Gottlieb congratulated him on having fallen in love with Lisa, "Avram looked at me as if I had completely missed the point." He told Gottlieb that love had nothing to do with it. "Rather than love, it was the unbearable pain of loneliness that brought them together."

The crew drove back to Savona in silence. Gottlieb said, "Each of us needed our own quiet time to deal with what we had experienced." He noted that what "impressed and surprised me was that despite all they had endured, despite the meagreness of their surroundings, these people were neither sombre nor defeated. It was as if being a survivor had left them with an attitude of 'no matter what comes, I will not be broken'."

Just before the boat was due to leave, the American journalist I.F. Stone arrived in Savona. He had been sent to the south of France where Aliyah Bet planned to let him sail on the *Wedgwood*'s sister ship, the *Haganah*, but the sailing had been delayed and so he was sent to Italy to join the *Wedgwood*. He arrived in Savona wearing a Basque beret that he had been given by a French Jew and headed down to the dockside to meet the crew. Stone had small round gold-rimmed glasses and tiny ears that stuck out from the side of his head and a mop of bushy brown hair. Although he looked unassuming, he was a veteran correspondent. He noted that partisans kept a watch on the harbour from the "waterfront saloons".

Nevertheless, even Savona was too open to the prying eyes of British spies for the refugees to board here, and so in mid-June the *Colon* set sail empty at eight o'clock in the evening, as if it was going elsewhere for its bananas. She sailed to La Spezia to test the engines and then put into harbour for a few days to take on supplies. Gottlieb says that morale was low. "We were hot, tired, anxious, and getting to a point where it was too easy to find fault with others. Most frustrating was the belief that our leaders had the answers to all of our questions but chose not to share the information with us." Yet, when they set sail back along the rocky coast, they were filled with excitement as they received instructions on how to greet the survivors. Each passenger was to be given a piece of paper detailing where they would bunk down, and men and women were to have separate sleeping arrangements. Each person was to be issued with their own bowl and cutlery.

As the survivors prepared for the trip, Alter Wiener, who was at this point in Tradate, says they "were ordered to destroy any personal documents and anything that might reveal our refugee status. We were not told why." In fact it is clear that the survivors were told very little about what was going to happen, but, according to Samuel Sadinsky, the teenage veteran of the Kovno Ghetto, "we were all anxious and eager to move on … We got up early in the morning and got onto the trucks." A fleet of former British Army trucks which had been taken over by the Gang arrived in Tradate during the early hours of 18 June. The survivors quickly clambered inside them. They were covered in tarpaulins so they could not see where they were being taken. Later they would learn that they sailed from near Savona, but at the time they had no idea the port was called Vado. They were ordered not to speak and at daybreak the convoy of 850 people set off from Tradate. A second convoy set off from Genoa later in the day. I asked Menachem Kriegel how he felt at what must have been a momentous occasion, but to my surprise he told me: "We had been moved to so many places, it was just one more move. They did not tell us where we were going." It was, he said, just another step in the long exodus.

In order not to arouse suspicion, Sereni and Arazi spent the day sightseeing in Genoa with Stone, checking constantly that they were not being followed by British agents. They then had a leisurely dinner and drove along the coast road to Vado, which the journalist found "narrow and precipitous". It was midnight and he recalled: "Behind us rising cliff-like from the narrow mountain road along the beach were the mountains of the Riviera, huge dark shapes against the sky. There were no lights along the road. All we had to see by was the faint glow of a cloudless, starry sky." In 1946, the coast between Savona and Vado looked dramatically different from today's suburban stretch. There were orchards of apricot trees, and a long pebbly beach curved around the bay until it reached Vado. The plan was that the ship would collect the refugees at just after midnight. Out of the darkness the headlights of the first convoy from Genoa came into view. The mayor of Savona had ordered all traffic on the narrow road to Vado to be stopped so that the convoy could move as fast as possible. The people jumped out quickly and stood quietly on the beach. The moon lit up the bay like a stage.

Shortly before one o'clock in the morning, far out at sea, a tiny triangle of light began to move towards them. It was made up of three lights, one red, one green and one white. Stone said that the boat looked like a ghost ship as it hovered off the coast. The agents were mystified by the delay, and later Arazi would claim the captain was drunk, which may or may not have been a story he made up to prove that he had been right all along that volunteer American Jews could not crew refugee ships. Other crew members mention that the current took them by surprise, and there is indeed a dangerous current at this point on the coast.

The second convoy of refugees from Tradate then arrived, having been delayed on its journey through the mountains to the coast when the vehicles proved too large to cross a Bailey bridge and had been forced to make a 20 km diversion. The trucks drove off the moment they disgorged their passengers. As they walked onto the beach, there was silence, and, according to Stone, "There was no noise but the crunch of gravel under hurrying feet." Beaches in this part of the world are mostly pebbly, and when there is sand it is grainy and rough. When Stone tried to talk to the survivors, they gave him angry stares. At this point several small fishing boats appeared and became visible as they turned on their bright searchlights to attract the fish. Arazi and Sereni, whom Stone refers to as "Mrs A", became more and more nervous as sooner or later the fishermen would not help noticing that something odd was going on.

The *Colon* finally sailed up to the jetty at three in the morning and a hail of expletives from the crew could be heard. The crowds, or the frantic ship-to-shore signalling that had been going on, had by now attracted the *carabinieri*, who, unknown to Arazi and Sereni, were driving along the coast road. Suddenly six sprang out of the darkness. According to Stone, they shouted: "*Ragazzi, Ebrei!*" (Hey, fellas, Jews!) Kriegel and the others I have spoken to all mention this moment. Kriegel says: "We were anxious and nervous that the British would stop us." It looked as if the whole plan was scuppered, and Stone feared that the scenes at La Spezia were about to be repeated or that the refugees would rush to board and the *carabinieri* would start shooting. "We were scared. We thought the boat was lost, that all the hard work of getting it over from America and finally clearing it out of port had gone for nothing," wrote Stone. Sereni tried to reason with the police, at which point Stone intervened. "With Mrs A as interpreter, I went over to the leader of the *carabinieri*, pulled out my most impressive reporter's card, a red State Department card with a gold eagle on it, and said 'I want your name and rank'. This request took him by surprise." Stone then began to hand out Camel cigarettes and the *carabinieri* "visibly softened", but Stone would not give up and pressed the officers: "Let these people go! What are they to you?" The police chief then ordered two of his younger officers to escort Arazi, Sereni and Stone to an awaiting police car, and they were driven off at speed to their HQ in Savona.

On the beach Akiva Kohane says that the remaining policemen had no idea what to do and stood around looking confused. At this point, the Palmach captain, Dov Berchik, took charge and handed out more American cigarettes to bribe the police. They did not need much persuading to let the people board the ship. The women began to climb up the rope gangplank, but it was so unsteady that it looked as if they might tip into the water at any moment. Among the first on board were Fedda Lieberman and Lea Diamant. They had been detailed to tie up hammocks as there were not enough bunks and some of the survivors would even have to sleep on the deck. Gottlieb recalled that as he greeted them on board, "some carried boxes; others had pillowcases containing all their belongings in the world. Many wore clothing they had been given by Jewish aid groups once they had been emancipated from the German camps. Their faces were sombre, even frightened, as they once again confronted the unknown."

In the early morning the police chief came to question Arazi, Sereni and Stone, and reported the capture of the illegal ship to the British military in Genoa. Stone knew that the crew needed warning before the British dispatched a warship to prevent the boat from sailing, and claimed he could not answer any more questions until he had a new battery for his hearing aid, which was in his bags that he had left on the beach. It was agreed that Arazi would go with a policeman to collect them. He then told Berchik to move as quickly as he could, and so he immediately took an axe and cut the mooring ropes in order not to waste a second. The *Wedgwood* slipped into international waters shortly after 9 am on Wednesday, 19 June 1946. Yechiel Aleksander and Yitzhak Kaplan were both on the deck and saw Berchik cut the cord that tied them to Europe. It was a dramatic and emotional moment, and when he related to me what happened, Aleksander reinforced the story by whacking his hand like a karate chop on the kitchen table. "Then we simply left," he said, waving his hand to indicate that the boat sailed smoothly away. The passengers on the *Wedgwood* had had a lucky escape. The ship first stopped outside Italian territorial waters before heading for the open seas while some of the Palmach agents were dropped off by boat near La Spezia and made their way back to Magenta.

As they now drove home to Milan, Sereni and Arazi listened to Stone's endless complaints that he had lost his story. But he had no reason to fear as he was part of a wider plan and would eventually sail from Marseille on the *Wedgwood*'s sister ship, the *Haganah*. One of the survivors he would meet on deck was the Nakam partisan Vitka Kempfner, en route to a new married life with her fellow fighter, Abba Kovner. Kempfner was shocked by Stone, who after a few days on the ship was suffering as much as a man who had spent two years in Auschwitz. Of the people on the ship Stone wrote: "I was impressed, on my underground voyage, with the vitality I found among these, my brethren from the East. What is the source of this vitality and strength?" The answer was clear, he concluded, and "lies in the Zionist idea, in this romantic dream of a Viennese journalist in the late nineteenth century, the dream of a Return. This has given them a goal, their lives a purpose, their shattered selves a focal point around which to reintegrate their personalities and to recover their moral health." I am sure he would have said the same of the people on the *Wedgwood*. Later by complete coincidence Gottlieb would sit next to Stone on a train in America. He recognised him and got chatting. When it came for them to part, he asked for something to remember him by. Stone got out his notebook and wrote: "In remembrance of a night in Italy."

* * *

The *Wedgwood*'s journey took eight days, but was uneventful and the weather was good. All the same the passengers were ordered to spend as much time as possible below deck so they would not be spotted by any British patrol. Listening to the survivors, I realise that they had little idea how the story might have been different if they had run into storms. The *Wedgwood* had been designed for a crew of 50 but, as it sailed through the narrow Strait of Messina separating Sicily from the Italian mainland, it had 30 crew on board plus well over 1,250 passengers. The survivors were crammed into every crevice. If something had gone wrong with the ship, the passengers would have had little chance. The boat had only two motor launches with room for 25 people each and 168 life jackets. Yechiel Aleksander and his friends slept under a large tarpaulin cover on the deck, as did all those who had jobs to perform on the ship.

As Gottlieb walked around, he was amazed at the different languages being spoken. "On the port side of the ship, a group of Orthodox men wrapped in prayer shawls were swaying back and forth as they davened (prayed). Not far from them, a small group of Turkish men had removed their shirts and were performing a very fluid, sensual dance. Two men accompanied them—one played a balalaika, the other a wooden flute. A short distance down the deck, a group of Polish Jews was having a heated political debate about Communism and the future of Europe." When he says Turks, he must be referring to the Greeks on the ship. On Friday evening the aft deck was converted into a temporary synagogue. "The Sabbath was celebrated with the lighting of candles and a beautiful blessing was sung by a woman from Poland. On the other end of the ship, a group of youthful *Chalutzim* (pioneers) would celebrate their own *Oneg Shabbat* by dancing a hora and singing a Hebrew song. If America, because of its diversity, could be called a 'melting pot', then our ship, because of the limited space, could pass as a 'pressure cooker'," wrote Gottlieb. He testifies that the weather was wonderful and the sea calm, but he must have become used to the rolling of the ship. Below deck there was an overwhelming stench of vomit. Menachem Kriegel had never seen the sea before but did not take long to find his sea legs. He went on to become a sailor in the merchant marine.

Each person was issued with a sick bag but, when they ran out, the sanitation problems really began. The passengers were, according to the stories of the crew and Fedda Lieberman, quick to show their anger. They called the crew and fellow survivors who worked alongside them "Kapos", after those coerced to work for the Nazis in the camps, and said they were even worse than the Nazis. Wiener and his friend Yehuda Erlich were stuck below deck. Erlich put his palm up to his face when he described the conditions. "I lay on my bunk and the next person was right here on top of me, right in front of my nose!" Wiener remembered: "Our hopes for a better future were marred by the poor conditions on the ship. It was very crowded. We had no hot meals, just crackers and cheese. Even our water was rationed. Many of the passengers got seasick … There was no ventilation and the sanitary facilities were very primitive. The atmosphere was quite tense." He then said something that surprised me. "A mixture of families with small children (born to partisans in the forests of Europe) and many young adults of diverse political affiliations sometimes caused heated debates and friction. I felt drained."

This is the first reference I have seen, other than Gottlieb's account, to children. Gottlieb says, "The children were the first to adjust to being on a ship and were soon running around the deck." He also describes mothers breastfeeding infants and of meeting the couple he had encountered in the DP camp in Genoa and their toddler called Golda. Neither men has any reason to make up such stories. Gottlieb went on to become a respected professor of sociology. Yet, in the archives at Atlit, no children's names are listed and every survivor I have met, besides Wiener, says that there were no children on the boat, even Erlich. The only answer I can assume is that the children were registered under their parents' names. Moreover, the survivors I have found may simply not have been part of the group who had children, and people travelled in tightly knit groups. It is possible that those with children formed one such group. The groups stuck together on the boat, and as there was no space to move around, it was possible to be on the boat and never see the children. Kriegel has told me he spent all his time alone with his cousin because they were not part of a group. Dani Chanoch says he was the youngest person on the boat and was adopted by the captain, who let him sleep in the crew's bunks. "The captain took me upstairs. I did not see the suffering of the people. Where there is suffering, and you cannot help, you stay away." Sadly, Wiener died before I could ask him about this in a follow-up email, and who the children were remains a mystery.

Dov Berchik, Israel Averbuch, Zvi Katznelson and the radio operator Moshe Yerusalami were in charge of daily life on the ship. The partisans, and those who had joined the Gang, like Lea Diamant and Fedda Lieberman, were also part of the team that organised life below deck. Lieberman's future husband, Poldek Maimon of the Nakam group, who had plotted to poison the drinking water in Germany, was ironically in charge of the water supply. Distributing food was complicated as some people were too sick to get up on deck to collect their rations, and carrying buckets of hot soup in the cramped conditions below deck was a hazard. Despite these conditions, Gottlieb says there was plenty of food and it was kosher. But he recalls there was a lot of seasickness and much cleaning up to be done. "That's when I noticed many of the passengers had numbers that had been tattooed on their arms." There was a strict cleaning rota and a survivor, who was a doctor, had a sick bay where some women passengers worked as nurses. According to Gottlieb, "During the course of the voyage, there were two births, two weddings, one bar mitzvah, and, fortunately, no deaths." Because he could speak Yiddish and Polish, he was often called upon to be a translator.

Now on the high seas, the *Colon* changed its name, as did all the Aliyah Bet ships. The *Colon* was renamed after a member of the British House of Lords, Josiah Wedgwood. Colonel Josiah Wedgwood was a veteran of the Anglo-Boer War and the Gallipoli campaign, and his great-grandfather had established the famous china factory in Staffordshire which still produces classical Greek-style china for elegant English tea tables. A committed Christian, he was also a Zionist and a friend of the right-wing Zionist Zeev Jabotinsky. In domestic politics he was an MP for the Labour Party until he was elevated to the Lords in 1941. He had been a fiery critic of the 1939 White Paper and had died in 1943. He was one of the last remnants of Christian Zionist forces in British politics. That the ship was named after a British politician surprises many people in Israel, who do not know of Wedgwood's unflinching support for Zionism; certainly it surprised many of the survivors, who had probably never heard of him. Their anger at Britain's refusal to recognise their plight was one of the common threads that united them. As the *Wedgwood* sailed across the Mediterranean, the gulf of misunderstanding between Britain and the Palestinian Jews was proving impossible for the diplomats to resolve.

On the final day at sea an announcement was made that the ship would soon arrive in Haifa. Cheers erupted and Yechiel Aleksander told me that he began to pray, but, as the shouts of "Eretz, Eretz, Eretz, Israel!" died down, the passengers on the deck were told that they would most likely be taken to an internment camp. I have asked each of the survivors I have found if this had ever been mentioned before. Not one of them knew that this would happen. The passengers were then given a blue entry card issued by the Jewish Agency with Hebrew written on one side and English on the other. They were told to fill in their name, place of birth and nationality, and then ordered below deck and the lights were turned off. Kriegel was detailed to work in the engine room. The British were the enemy.

On 25 June, south-west of Cyprus, the *Wedgwood* was spotted by a British reconnaissance plane and three warships were dispatched to intercept her, the *Venus*, the *Talybont* and the *Haydon*. The fear was that the immigrants would transfer to smaller vessels outside territorial waters and make a dash for the shore. Two of the ships on either side, at half a mile's distance, tracked her course. The *Venus* fired warning shots across the *Wedgwood*'s bow. The *Venus* was a V-class destroyer launched in 1943 and had taken part in the Battle of the Malacca Strait in May 1945 against the Japanese; now she was at war with refugees and had successfully intercepted the *Rondine* earlier in the year. "When our ship tried to evade the British blockade, the marines fired above our heads as a warning. My stomach twisted and churned; it was a terrible trauma for all of us. We were gritting our teeth and clinging grimly to the battered hope for a peaceful landing," says Wiener. The *Venus* fired for seven minutes over the bridge and ordered it to stop. The *Wedgwood*'s captain took a megaphone and yelled and harangued them, his anarchist hatred at boiling point. Interestingly, Jack Bursztain, who had been at the Bencista, says that no instructions were given to the passengers as to what might happen or what they should do. Akiva Kohane and Jack Bursztain both say in their testimonies that there were illegal weapons on board the *Wedgwood* and that the crew stalled for time and did not react to the British demands until they had been thrown into the sea. Kohane and his friends were ordered to help throw the weapons overboard.

The plan had been for the *Wedgwood* to get as close as possible to the beach in Tel Aviv and for the people to try to make it to the shore, but at this point the Yishuv commanders radioed instructions to the crew that the passengers would be taken to the Atlit detention camp and they should not resist capture. The Panamanian flag was taken down and replaced by the Magen David. Then, after fourteen hours the crew signalled that their food stocks were exhausted and that there were sick people on board. The *Venus* advised her to enter Haifa but that Palestine regulations applied at the three-mile limit. The crew disabled the engines so that the British Navy was forced to tow the boat into Haifa. Across the bridge a banner was unfurled that read: "We survived Hitler. Death is no stranger to us, nothing will keep us from our Jewish homeland. The blood is on your head if you fire upon this unarmed ship." As the British prepared to board the *Wedgwood*, they stood in ranks on the deck of the destroyer, but the survivors on the *Wedgwood* were not intimidated, and all the passengers came out and stood there in a solid wall. Then spontaneously they began to sing "Hatikva". As the song died away, the British boarded the ship. The crew had been told to mingle with the passengers and pretend they were Polish immigrants to avoid arrest. Despite the fact that they were under escort, when the survivors saw Mount Carmel in the distance they began to cheer and there was singing and laughter.

In Haifa, thousands of people lined the dockside waving and offering food and blankets as the boat came into port. As the *Wedgwood* dropped anchor, the passengers burst into the iconic Yiddish "Zog Nit Keynmol", a song written in Vilnius Ghetto in 1943, which had become a partisan anthem. The first line translates as "Never say there is only death for you," and the song ends with the words "the hour we have hungered for is near … we are here!" The well-known American war photographer Emil Reynolds caught the scene in images that were printed in papers around the world. The boat docked alongside the Haifa port authority office, a squat three-storey building which flew the Union Jack.

The festive mood did not last long. As they stepped onto Palestinian soil, the survivors were escorted to a row of desks manned by representatives of the Jewish Agency, who took the blue cards from the passengers and directed them to 35 buses lined up on the dockside and 15 trucks into which their meagre belongings were to be loaded. Gottlieb was shocked. "You could see it on the faces of the people—the utter devastation." There was anger and confusion. Some people tried to run away, but there was no way out. Yitzhak Kaplan realised that because he had given up his place on the boat in La Spezia, his family would know he would be on the *Wedgwood*. He went up to one of the porters and asked him if he knew his sister.

Incredibly he did and he told Kaplan that she was standing by the gate but was not being allowed in.

Josef Harmatz was struck that "on the quay were dozens of women eagerly offering out drinks to the new immigrants, and more important, seeking news of relatives who might have survived in Europe. They would shout out the names of the towns and villages: 'Warsaw, Krakow, Lublin'." As they were put into the bus, Harmatz was among those who made a huge commotion in order that the Palmach members could slip away. "In a flash I gave my sunglasses to Berchik, so he would not be recognised, and years later, when I saw him lunching on the Champs-Elysées, I reminded him that he still owed me a pair of sunglasses."

The passengers were driven to the Atlit detention centre, 20 km south of Haifa. On the bus, Harmatz stood next to an old friend from the Rudniki Forest, Grisha Gurevich, whom he had met up with in Milan. Gurevich was working with the Bricha and Harmatz had talked him into travelling with his old comrades-in-arms. "There he had at his disposal a beautiful shiny Lancia car to which he was very attached, and he needed a lot of convincing to leave the car behind for a new country and a new life." As the bus drew out, the two men watched an elderly Arab riding a donkey. Gurevich turned to Harmatz and let out a profoundly explicit Russian curse. 'You took me away from my trusty Lancia to a place with this kind of transportation."

* * *

From the train window the old watchtower is clearly visible as Atlit station draws near. Not far from the camp are the ruins of a Crusader castle. The countryside is scruffy and it is clear why Kriegel was a little disappointed with his first view of the Promised Land. "I could see nothing. Only stones everywhere." In 1946 the Atlit camp was much larger than it is today and the perimeter fence was patrolled by soldiers with dogs. On their arrival the men and women were separated, sprayed with DDT and told to undress and enter the showers, which some of them were too frightened to do. Many of the testimonies of the passengers express their surprise at being taken to what they call "a British concentration camp". It is telling that despite the hours of Hebrew lessons and the classes on the geography of Palestine they had attended in Italy, the *Wedgwood*'s passengers had very little idea of what was in store for them and of the actual politics on the ground. It is all the more surprising, as Atlit was not new and had opened its doors in 1934 when illegal immigration had begun in a serious way after Hitler came to power in 1933 and illegal immigrant ships started arriving in Palestine. British policy was to arrest any illegal immigrants, take them to Atlit and let the Jewish Agency in effect choose when to release them by insisting that those freed had to be given visas from the quota. According to Samuel Sadinsky, there was "a lot of hatred and disappointment", and Yechiel Aleksander has told me that in Atlit "we were frightened by the fences that greeted us. Our associations were traumatic. Our spirits, however, calmed when we were told we would only be in the camp a few days." He added: "We had a great deal of energy and we made as much trouble as we could for the guards."

Before it was turned into a museum, Atlit had almost entirely fallen to pieces. In 1956 and 1967, it was used to house Arab prisoners of war, and much of it was dismantled in the 1970s. The dusty grounds are pleasant enough in the January sunshine, but I can imagine the July heat and the scorpions. The Austrian Harry Linser was stung by one and had to be sent to hospital in Haifa. One of the huts is now a research centre. The small team have taken testimonies of some of the inmates. They have interviewed ten of the *Wedgwood* passengers and happily give me their names. They are in Hebrew, but I am told that the tapes are private and not for public access. On their list are some familiar names, but others I do not recognise at all and cannot find on my list. Whenever I have found people's names on Nazi lists or those put together after the war, I have noted down the names of parents. For survivors it was a key way of identifying if someone was actually your loved one. I look up Avraham Doron, who is one of the people interviewed by the Atlit team. Fifteen minutes of searching identifies him as a leading academic, an expert in social policy and the welfare state, with a PhD from the London School of Economics. He was born in Radom, Poland, in 1929. His parents were Israel and Rachel. I search my list for a man born in Radom in 1929 and find Avraham Bornstein with parents Israel and Rachel. He had been in the Kielce Ghetto and eventually ended up in Mauthausen. I wonder at his ability to persevere and rise to the top of academia. When he arrived at Atlit, he was alone in the world and just 17 years old.

The survivors' shock at arriving in Atlit was short-lived. The camp may have been guarded by the British but it was run by the Jewish Agency, and there were Hebrew lessons and talks on life in Palestine. The men and the women lived in separate barracks, but the women in the camp danced the hora and the men would come and watch. The drinking tap, which was in the women's barracks, was a meeting place where romances started. Jack Bursztain laughs when he talks about his time in Atlit and describes it as "joyful". He remembers that he was happy, as there was no work and no regimentation. For many it was the first time they had eaten watermelon, pomegranates and bananas.

The atmosphere in Palestine was, however, tense. Jewish terrorism was a regular occurrence, and on 16 June, eight roads and railway bridges had been blown up, and the following day railway workshops in Haifa were attacked. Six British officers had also been kidnapped by the Stern Gang. On 29 June, the British cracked down in an operation that has come to be known as Black Saturday and arrested 2,700 people in raids across the country. Among them was Yitzhak Kaplan's sister Chaya, who left for Palestine before the war. She had attacked a British soldier when the troops came to search her kibbutz. Like many of those arrested, she ended up in Atlit, which was thus seriously overcrowded, and many of the *Wedgwood* veterans were forced to sleep in tents. "I had no idea that she was there," Kaplan tells me. "Until one day I saw a British soldier holding a box of grapes walking up to the fence. A woman was next to him and he started calling my name, and after ten years I was face to face with my sister. If you were arrested, you could receive food parcels, and she had demanded the right to see me, and he was a gentleman and carried the box."

* * *

The number of refugees who arrived on the *Wedgwood* and the *Haganah* shocked the British authorities, and it was decided that, from then on, illegal immigrants would be shipped to Cyprus, where conditions were appalling. Although most people in the UK are totally unaware of this snippet of British Imperial history, a small group of Christians have made it their mission to apologise for the then government's behaviour. The group is led by Rosie Ross, a Jerusalem-based activist. She has often said that she is concerned that if Britain does not face up to the anti-Semitism prevalent in British society during the Mandate period, history could repeat itself. Until this point, I had put the Royal Navy blockade down to a simple game of Whitehall defending national interests, but it seems I was wrong. There was serious anti-Semitism in Britain, and in the Ridley Road in London's East End the fascist Black Shirts were on their soapboxes ranting against the Jews.

I wonder why I have never heard this piece of history discussed in Britain. Seeking an answer, I take a tube train to Hendon in north London. In the basement of a Costa coffee house I meet with Dave Rich, an expert on anti-Semitism. The last post-war years in Mandate Palestine were a dark moment in the history of the British Empire, but Rich says that is not why this story is ignored in the UK, and not often discussed here, even in Jewish circles. Rich says that this is because the left are incapable of dealing with the Jewish experience and the memory of genocide. "If you look at the standard left-wing narrative, it sees Jews before the Second World War as anti-fascists, during the war they are the victims of the worst of fascism, but after the war those Zionists who went to Palestine are seen as fascist oppressors." Holocaust education has not helped, he claims, because "as knowledge of the Holocaust has grown, so has increased public discussion about it and, as a result, the hard left began to compare Israel's actions to those of Nazi Germany and to lament the failure of the Jews to learn the lessons of their own genocide. The left has a long tradition of opposing anti-Semitism and fighting for equality, but it also has other traditions and trends that encourage or incubate anti-Semitism."

The topic is too uncomfortable even for the Jewish community, he says: "The situation was akin to the issue of home-grown Isis terrorists today. British Jews were going to Palestine to fight. The situation was very tense and there were serious anti-Jewish riots. It's something that nobody wants to talk about here." As a result, the story of the survivors between 1945 and 1948 has been forgotten. The conversation answers something that has perplexed me for years on a personal level. When I was a child, my mother was sympathetic towards Israel, but after years of reading *The Guardian* she developed a passionate hatred of Israelis. I found it difficult to fathom, as my Catholic grandfather had fought in the British Army in Palestine in the First World War and was with General Allenby when he entered the Old City of Jerusalem in 1917. He had even trained some of the first battalions of the Jewish Legion who fought with the British.

I feel that Rich's answer is insufficient and sense that there is more to the British angle of this story. In a scruffy common room in Westminster College in Cambridge, an enthusiastic evangelist, the Rev. Alex Jacob, one of Ross's fellow campaigners, muses on the importance of the Balfour Declaration and how Britain turned from supporting a Jewish homeland in the 1917 statement to rounding up would-be Jewish immigrants into a detention centre. He is the sort of man that Lloyd George would have recognised. The prime minister apparently knew the map of Palestine like the back of his hand but had no idea where any of the main towns in eastern Europe were. Jacob tells me that when the Balfour Declaration was issued in 1917, most people in high places felt, like him, that they had a Christian mission to encourage Jews to return to the Promised Land.

"Christian Zionism predates Jewish Zionism," he says, leaning forward, a religious book in hand. "What it is important to see is that by the time we get to 1946, the generation of 1917 had lost their influence and the role of the church in politics had faded in Britain. The Evangelical Sunday School influence waned." He adds: "We turned away from the Jews the moment they needed help, and this is one of the things we should say sorry for under the Mandate. But even out of something awful like the Holocaust some good things can come, as it made the Jews return home." I find his enthusiasm for Christian redemption somewhat unnerving. It also sounds as if the homecoming when they arrived in Palestine was simple. It was not.

As the Jewish Agency ran the Atlit camp, it was up to them to decide when to hand out the immigration certificates permitted in the British quota. The *Wedgwood*'s Leon Pesses, who had survived the Warsaw Ghetto, was watching Kovner's partisan colleagues argue with an Agency representative, insisting that they receive special treatment, when he got lucky. The official gave in to the partisans and issued them with immigration certificates. Pesses was mistaken for one of the partisans and received one of the first certificates to leave the camp. Although it meant leaving his wife behind, Pesses grabbed the opportunity, and with the £5 he had been given by the Agency set off for Tel Aviv to find somewhere to live. The first thing he did was to buy a large bunch of grapes from an Arab with a donkey as he made his way into the harsh reality of his new life. In his testimony he says that finding himself alone and penniless in Tel Aviv was one of the worst moments of his life. Both he and his wife had come from wealthy and successful families, and the shock of being penniless and alone was too much—even worse than life in the Warsaw Ghetto. He sat down and cried.

19

TEL AVIV

ONLY YESTERDAY

Moshe Ha-Elion is the last of the survivors that I meet in Israel. On the way back to the hotel after having had tea with him, the bus drops me on the waterfront. Tel Aviv's high-rise hotels stand, one after the other, facing the beach. It is early evening and despite the chill there are still some kids playing volleyball on the sand. The sky has cleared, and even though it is dusk, I can see the sea stretching out before me.

On the waterfront in nearby Jaffa there is a map of the Mediterranean on the harbourside. A plaque marks the distance to each of the major ports. It is 2,625 km to Genoa. I turn and walk up through the Aliyah Bet memorial, which was created when the London Garden was dug up and turned into a carpark. It had been opened in 1942 to mark the solidarity between the people of Tel Aviv and London during the Blitz. One layer of history hides another. There is a children's playground in the shape of a ship. You can play at storming the British blockade. The information board says that during the Mandate from 1920 to 1948, "After many failed attempts to disembark on Israel's other beaches, several ships came to Tel Aviv. Here they were welcomed on the beach by crowds that took them [the illegal immigrants] into their homes before the British patrols could arrest them." It is good myth-making material. Myths build nations but the welcome was not always warm. This is another truth about the journey of the survivors that is left untold. The people from the beach in Vado were to find out that when they arrived in Palestine, they did not simply land on a new shore but entered a new chapter in history. The Holocaust, and everything they had survived, was now yesterday's story.

Until they were released from Atlit, the *Wedgwood* survivors' only experience of the Yishuv was their encounters with the Jewish Brigade, whom they regarded as saviours and angels, but in Palestine the people they met were not always so sympathetic. Even before the war there had been a deep-seated negative attitude towards the Jews in the diaspora among those Jews who already lived in Palestine. Zionism had, after all, been a revolt against that diaspora and their habits and traditions, which the Jews who had left eastern Europe looked down on. The Zionists in Palestine wanted to create a new way of life and a new Jew. Rather than the Yishuv holding out a helping hand and lending a sympathetic ear, the survivors were expected to change and fit the vision of the new Jew. As a result a major mental and physical effort to adapt was demanded of them.

To succeed in their new life, the people of the *Wedgwood* had to assimilate, and like many immigrants they changed their names, taking on a new identity. Those who did not or could not change were looked down upon. It was an attitude that put the Yishuv first and Holocaust survivors second. As a result the survivors were, in this period, not respected and their experiences were downgraded. The Jews in Palestine frequently described the survivors as "human dust" and they were seen not just as weak and dependent but even as suspect. Many survivors say that the first question they were asked was "How did you survive?" and implicit in the question was the belief that they must have done some wrong in order to still be alive. It discouraged some from even admitting that they were Holocaust survivors. Wiener said in his typically measured tone: "Many people listened sympathetically to our horrific stories. After a while they got tired and were no longer moved. Some let up a sigh, and some shed tears, but eventually they forgot. Such is life." As regards the survivors, he felt they developed a sort of "collective amnesia".

What is surprising is how little Jews in Palestine actually knew of what had happened in the Holocaust, let alone the work of the Jewish Brigade. The popular culture of Holocaust memoirs and novels that surrounds us today had yet to be written: the survivors only began to put pen to paper in the 1950s. The first stories that received public attention were those of the partisans. A whirlwind of publicity had accompanied the arrival of Ruzka Korsczak and Avraham Lidovsky, as the ghetto fighters and partisans, and the myth that had built up around them, fitted the national narrative of the moment. It made those who had not taken up arms, or been unable to do so, ashamed of their experiences. Until this point I had naively assumed that it was simply good luck for me that so many partisans with their tales of derring-do had sailed on the *Wedgwood*, but the reason so many of them appear on the passenger list I have compiled is that they were given priority and pushed to the head of the queue. They were the sort of Jew that the Yishuv wanted. The new Jew faced his enemies with a gun in hand.

After ten days in Atlit, Wiener was interviewed by officials from the Jewish Agency. "Most of the refugees had prearranged locations where they could go to live with relatives and friends. I did not know the addresses of my uncles and aunts. I could hardly remember their first names and I had no idea if they were alive. Since I was not in a position to direct the officials where I would like to go to, they sent me away with several other lonely souls to a 'kibbutz'." There, he said, he was "put in a tent with three other new arrivals. Each occupant was furnished with an empty [fruit] box in which to keep our personal belongings. It was a year since the liberation. I had been wandering since then, but now I had my semi-private corner in a friendly environment." But he could not speak Hebrew, so could only talk to the people who spoke Yiddish. In his oral testimony Akiva Kohane still sounds angry that the group from the Villa Bencista with whom he had travelled since the liberation was split up and sent to two different kibbutzim. It is evidence that little attention was paid to loyalties built up in the time spent on the Bricha route.

The new society was based on working the land. The survivors of the *Wedgwood* were mostly urban and had grown up in the tenements of Lodz or the wealthy houses of Kovno, and the kibbutz life they found them-selves leading was a shock. A group of boys from the Bencista were sent to Kibbutz Alonim in northern Israel, but it did not suit Dani Chanoch, who ran away to Tel Aviv. Wiener was assigned to pick oranges, but despite the hard work he could not sleep at night because of the heat and the mosquitoes.

Life on the kibbutz was not just hard but also confusing. There were rules and regulations that the survivors did not understand. On arrival in a kibbutz, a person was given a bed, a table and a chair, but you had to stay a year before you received a bedspread. Kibbutz veterans alone had ward-robes and curtains. The uninitiated survivor might complain they did not have bedspreads like everyone else. To the kibbutz residents they looked spoiled and demanding while in the survivors' eyes they were being dis-criminated against. Life on a kibbutz was also dangerous, and they were often attacked by Arabs as Palestine descended into war.

After a year, Wiener went to Haifa where he got a part-time clerical job and went back to school. He would finally graduate with a high school diploma at the age of 35. Of those survivors who arrived in the years 1946 to 1947 and were sent to a kibbutz, at least half of them left it. Wiener was disorientated and confused by everything. "Whatever I saw bewildered me. Men and women were joyful. The beaches were full of sunbathers, and there was not one emaciated body among them." He window-shopped on "ritzy" Allenby Street in Tel Aviv and on "seeing Jews walking freely, I wondered if it was real".

Nakam member Rachel Halperin left Atlit on 15 July, and she and her mother Rosa went to live in a tiny shared apartment in Holon. She was soon employed helping new immigrants to settle. In May 1948 Rosa was killed in an Egyptian air attack on Tel Aviv bus station that claimed the lives of 42 just four days after the creation of the State of Israel. Halperin wanted to return to Germany with her husband, Symcha Glicksman, to seek revenge but was prevented by the Israeli secret services. She trained as a teacher and then became a housewife and mother of three. She has always believed that the Holocaust could happen again as no retribution was taken. Many other Nakam members felt the same.

When the Israeli state came into being in 1948, the people of Tel Aviv danced in the streets, but what was already a war between Palestine's Jews and Arabs now turned into a full-blown Arab–Israeli war. Partisan leader Abba Kovner picked up his gun again and joined the war effort, as did nearly all the men who had arrived on the *Wedgwood*. Some of them, including the friends of Bursztain and Aleksander, lost their lives. Others were injured. Not that the rights and wrongs of sending young boys who had just survived Auschwitz into the front line were ignored by the leadership in Tel Aviv. In the end, despite misgivings, they sent them to the front, as there was a desperate shortage of manpower.

Many of those who arrived on boats during the 1948 conflict were collected on the quayside and given a uniform and a gun. Within hours they were on the front line. Despite the stress of being so quickly plunged into another conflict, the war presented the *Wedgwood* survivors with an opportunity that those who arrived after 1949 did not have. The fact that they served in the armed forces during the war was a key factor in helping these survivors integrate into Israeli society. It gave them connections and made them part of the country's founding myth. The war also breathed new life into the *Wedgwood* itself when it joined the Israeli navy. The ship had been confiscated by the British and left tied up in Haifa port alongside the jetty. The corvette was given yet another name and was now the *K-18*. Its sister ship, the *Haganah*, became the *K-20*. More than anything, the

1948 war changed the dynamics of the lives of the survivors by moving the focus from their past to building a future in a new country. Protecting their families became a priority for the men, and many like Moshe Ha-Elion built a career in the army.

Getting a job, if you chose not to stay on a kibbutz, was a challenge as the majority of the *Wedgwood* survivors had not completed their education. But their determination to get one is striking. Many had a burning desire to study and get on in their new life. When Harry Linser was released from Atlit on 11 August, he was sent to Kibbutz Dorot. "There I met friends whom I last saw in Theresienstadt who were committed to the idea of kibbutz life," he wrote later, but by December 1947 he had decided the farming life was not for him. He wanted to join the air force and, in order to do that, he had to get a high school diploma. The boy who had been a slave labourer in Kaufering, building cutting-edge aircraft, studied to become an aeronautical engineer. The drive to learn led both Dani Chanoch and Menachem Kriegel to university long after they had retired. When I met Kriegel in Haifa he had just come back from a lecture on the functioning of the brain.

Life in the new state of Israel was hard, and there were few resources to help survivors. Leon Pesses finally got a job on a farm and his wife, Lisa, worked in the shoe department of a large store in Tel Aviv. Her father had been a wealthy tea importer in Warsaw, and she tried to claim back the money that the family had carefully put in an account in a Swiss bank but lost her case. The couple were dogged with bad luck. Lisa gave birth to a sickly child, who could not be cared for in Israel, and friends in America helped them relocate. Ill health was also to force Alter Wiener to leave Israel and settle in New York. Wiener's death in a traffic accident in 2018 seems to prove the point that survival is a random lottery.

For some survivors the pull of family was too strong. Bursztain discovered that his sister was alive and living in Canada. Although he said that he loved Israel and would never forget what the country had done for him, in 1951 he left for Toronto. He arrived with just a dollar in his pocket and, as he did not speak English, the only person he could talk to was an Italian man who ran the local coffee shop. After the months in Italy, Bursztain had learned Italian and the barista helped to teach him the basics of English.

Former partisan Josef Harmatz worked on a building site and in a petrol station. In Tarvisio he had met a soldier who made fun of his communist ideas and pointed out that when he reached Palestine he would be faced with the reality of building a new life. One day the same soldier stopped by to fill up his old car. "You see," he said, "what did I tell you back there in Italy? It's not exactly how it sounded there, is it?" At this point Harmatz and his mother were living in such a small apartment that he had to sleep on a board on top of the bathtub.

Ten years later Harmatz was working in Geneva for the Israeli government when Abba Kovner came to visit him. He told Harmatz how aggrieved he was that the Germans had never been punished for what they did and that he would like to try again to seek vengeance. Harmatz turned him down as he had heard rumours that the government had plans to hunt down and arrest former Nazi leaders. Harmatz says: "Abba left disappointed." A few years later Israeli secret agents captured Adolf Eichmann, a key figure of the Holocaust, and spirited him from Argentina to Israel where they put him on trial. "The fact that Abba himself was called as a witness at the trial—and his testimony was one of the most dramatic— compensated us in a certain way," Harmatz said. In an impassioned speech Kovner told the story of the girl who had crawled out of the death pits in the Paneriai Forest. The trial was front-page news and prompted a new openness in Israel. For the first time many survivors shared their stories, though many did not.

One of those who held his tongue was Harmatz. In his oral testimony he said: "You run away from it, you don't want to remember it." He was eventually to become the director general of ORT Israel. ORT is a global Jewish educational and vocational training organisation, which he also worked for in London, where he lived between 1980 and 1993. He says ORT took him into a positive world of training and helping people. He never showed any remorse for the Nakam plot and was sorry that it had not worked. When he and Leibke Distal spoke publicly in 1999 for the first time about what they had done, the German police began investigations but decided not to file charges because of the "extraordinary circumstances".

As I listened to the survivors' stories I was reminded again and again of Rabbi Klausner's observation that "The people I came to know, having been to and returned from the edge of annihilation, were not changed … They were as they were prior to the Holocaust, only more so." The survivors I have met, both in real life and in the virtual reality of emails and Holocaust testimonies, were above all dynamic, open-minded, friendly and optimistic. They must have always been like this, and it was, they all say, the key to their survival and their ability to build a future. As Nimrod Fishbein drove me to the station from his grandfather Yechiel Aleksander's house, he said: "The one thing that my grandfather taught us all is that to get on in life and to survive, you must be friendly and help others." It was not a lesson that I expected to learn from Auschwitz.

And what of those who had brought the people of the *Wedgwood* out of Europe? Not far from Tel Aviv University, swanky new blocks of flats are going up on the site of the old Ramat Aviv Hotel. It used to belong to Yehuda Arazi, who went into the hospitality trade and opened a modern hotel and bungalow complex. One of his partners was Ada Sereni. Sadly, Arazi died of a brain tumour in 1959 aged 51. After Arazi left Italy in 1947, Sereni took control of the operation until the last boat sailed from Italy on 14 May 1948. She then occupied herself with arms smuggling until she returned to Israel in 1950. There she joined Nativ, a branch of the Israeli secret service, which helped Soviet Jews make *aliyah*. Poldek Maimon, one of Abba Kovner's avengers, was also a member and worked at the Israeli Embassy in Warsaw in the 1960s during a new period of anti-Semitism. From 1958 to 1967 Sereni was based in Rome, helping Soviet Jews who had managed to leave the Soviet Union. She died in Israel in 1998, aged 92.

Just like Maimon and Sereni, many others who had worked in the Bricha moved on to help Jews who needed an escape route from other countries in the decades after the Holocaust, notably from the Arab world. It meant that the Bricha had to remain secret. The producers of the Israeli version of *This Is Your Life* asked Golda Meir, then prime minister, if they could make a programme about Shaike Dan, the daredevil emissary who had set up the Bricha in Romania in 1944. In his memoir written years later, he wrote: "It included the story of my former ties with security service people and their chiefs in the Iron Curtain countries; my ties with border jumpers; my work in getting weapons, ammunition, and planes for Israel … and other secret trips that resulted in Jews coming to Israel." As a result, Meir "took a look at the folder and said: 'A television programme about Shaike Dan? So long as there's a single Jew in exile, there can't be any programmes about him.'"

It was only in retirement that the survivors I have met were gripped with a fear that their story would be forgotten and that generations to come would not recall what had happened to them. In the 1990s Uri Chanoch became, like his brother Dani, a campaigner for Holocaust survivors' rights and a guardian of how the Holocaust is remembered. In retirement the two men began to accompany school groups to Germany and to Auschwitz. Yechiel Aleksander regrets that he took so long to tell his story.

As ever, Abba Kovner was one step ahead of his fellow survivors. He had a unique response to the fear of forgetting and wrote an account of the

Holocaust that could be read like a biblical story in a traditional Jewish scroll or *megillah*. The text is surrounded by commentaries in the margin as if it were the Talmud. It is frightening to read a text where, in the margins, there are explanations aimed at readers who have never heard of Hitler, the SS or Buchenwald. The *Scrolls of Testimony* is an epic poem with no hero. It is the story of his people, the people on the beach. Ironically the copy of *Scrolls of Testimony* that arrived in my letter box had been remaindered by Lake County Public Library in Indiana. This is why Moshe Ha-Elion's parting words were that we must never forget the Holocaust or what happened after it.

Walking along the Tel Aviv waterfront, I am drawn back to the list that I have made of the names of the people who sailed on the *Wedgwood*, to the names that have no story behind them. I open up the list when I get back to my room. I randomly look one more time for Moshe Becker, who was born somewhere in Poland in 1930. His is just one of hundreds of names that have not yet revealed to me who they were or maybe still are. As the clock ticks, time is taking away the hope that history will record what happened to them all. As I walk through Tel Aviv, I find myself looking at the elderly people around me and wonder who they are and what brought them here to Israel. Maybe I have just sat next to Moshe Becker on the bus or walked past him in the supermarket.

LIST OF THE PEOPLE ON THE BEACH

The names of the places and countries where people were born are listed as they were known in the interwar period.

Abarwanel, David *Greece*, 1922
Had been in Flossenbürg concentration camp.

Abramovich, Eliezer *Romania, 1919*

Abramovich, Emanuel *Piotrkow, Poland, 1924*
Father: Yehonatan. Had been in Buchenwald concentration camp.

Abramovich, Miriam *Kovno, Lithuania, 1923*

Abramovich, Rachel *Romania, 1921*

Abramovich, Sara *Bedzin, Poland, 1923*
Father: Salomon.

Abramovich, Scharlotte *Romania, 1922*

Abramovich, Yakov *Romania, 1925*

Abramovich, Yona *Lithuania, 1919*

Abramovici, Chaim *Romania, 1911*

Abramovicz, Pesach *Baranowicze, Poland (now Baranavichy, Belarus), 1924*
Father: Feivel. In the Novogrodek Ghetto but escaped and joined the Bielski brothers' partisan group in the Naliboki Forest, where he was wounded. Was in Landsberg DP camp. He joined the Palmach in 1948 and lived at Kibbutz Kinneret near the Sea of Galilee.

Abramovicz, Yevseievich Israel *Baranowicze, Poland (now Baranavichy, Belarus), 22.8.1919*
Fought as a partisan in the Naliboki Forest.

Adler, Nathan *Bialystok, Poland, 1927*
Parents: Moshe & Amelai. Father died before the war, and his mother and sister Raschka were murdered in Treblinka in 1943. Was in the Polish air force in the Soviet Union in the war with his brother Pinhas, and both became pilots in the Israeli air force.

Adler, Rachel *Czechoslovakia, 1925*

Adler, Shimon *Satu Mare, Romania, 1921*
Father: Hirsch.

Agber, Yodel *Latvia, 1901*

Aharon, Hedwig *Hungary, 1921*

Aharon, Hugo *Hungary, 1921*

Aharon, Sandor *Hungary, 1928*

Aibeshiz, Moshe *Poland, 1909*

Aisenberg, Isaac *Hungary, 1925*

Alallouf, Barzily *Greece, 1925*

Aleksander, Yechiel *Sulejow, Poland, 19.3.1927*
Parents: Avraham & Miriam. Born Heniek. The couple had ten children. Family moved to Lodz in 1938. Sulejow is close to Lodz. In the Lodz Ghetto. Father was shot. Mother starved to death. Youth groups: Hashomer Hatzair & Bnei Akiva. In Auschwitz. Survived death march to Mauthausen on 20.1.1945. Part of the group of boys who were at the Villa Bencista in Fiesole.

Alexandrovich, Moshe *Poland, 1925*
Parents: Ester & Moshe. Deported to Auschwitz in 1943. Survived a death march to Mauthausen. Liberated by the US Army in Gusen. In DP camps in Linz and Ebensee until taken by the Jewish Brigade to Santa Maria di Bagni. Married and had a son and a daughter.

Alfandari, Nachman *Thessaloniki, Greece, 1923*

Allaluf, Meir *Thessaloniki, Greece, 25.5.1920*
Born Marius. Brother of Yosef. In Auschwitz I, Auschwitz III-Monowitz, and Mauthausen. Liberated in Gusen by US Army. In DP camps in Linz and Santa Maria di Bagni. Married Esterala Bibas, who sailed on the *Wedgwood*. Had a daughter and two sons.

Allaluf, Yosef (Papo) *Thessaloniki, Greece, 25.7.1926*

Alperovich, Anatol *Kurenets, Poland (now Belarus), 1913*
Father: Moshe.

Alperovich, Rivka *Kozienice, Poland, 1923*
Parents: Moshe & Sonya.

Alter, Moshe *Poland, 1927*

Alter, Naftali *Ostrowiec, Poland, 1925*
Parents: Mordchau-Abram & Lea.

Alter, Yitzhak *Romania, 1927*
Father: Nali.

Alterman, Simcha *Poland, 1915*

Altman, Shraga *Poland, 1929*

Amar, Ugo *Thessaloniki, Greece, 1925*
Had been in Dachau.

Apter, Yona *Daugavpils, Latvia, 1924*
Father: Mordechai.

Arfa, Zvi *Sierpc, Poland, 7.1.1918*
Parents: Kalman & Tovah Leah Hersch.

Ashkenazi, Eli *Thessaloniki, Greece, 1928*
Father: Avraham.

Ass, Batya *Vilnius, Poland (now Lithuania), 15.7.1920*
Father: Israel Zangvil. Had been in Flossenbürg and Stutthof concentration camps.

Auspitz, George *Hungary, 1923*

Auspitz, Ilona *Tolcsva, Hungary, 19.7.1914*

Auspitz, Pinchas *Debrecen, Hungary, 1930*
Father: Yitzhak.

Auspitz, Uri *Hungary, 1929*

Auster, Chana *Poland, 1915*
Father: Raphael.

Auster, Selig *Stanislawow, Poland (now Ivano-Frankivsk, Ukraine), 29.6.1923*
Was in a DP camp in Germany.

Avred, Yakov *Poland, 1917*

Axel, Nathan *Romania, 1923*

Baer, Elchanan *Lithuania, 1917*

Bankier, Avraham *Poland, 1914*
Had been in the Lodz Ghetto and the Mauthausen concentration camp.

Banonisty, Yitzhak *Greece, 1914*

Bar Kochva, Simcha *Yugoslavia, 1921*

Bar Sade, Yoel *Rabka-Zdroj, Poland, 6.1.1924*
Parents: Dvorah & Yitzhak Braunfeld. Had two brothers. In the Krakow Ghetto before being taken to camps in Plaszow, then Auschwitz II and death marched to Mauthausen and Gusen. After the liberation the Jewish Brigade took him to Udine and he went from there to the Magenta Aliyah Bet camp in Italy.

Barbar, Avraham *Romania, 1928*

Barth, Avraham *Poland, 1923*

Barth, David Yishaya *Poland, 1914*

Barzili, Meir *Greece, 1920*
Father: Shabtai. Married Malkah Beleli, who was on the *Wedgwood*. Died 2013.

Bas, David *Poland, 1927*
Fled to the forest near Rafalowka with his father & sister. Accepted into the Bogdan partisan regiment. Member of a group of Jewish saboteurs that destroyed a train. After the war was in Kibbutz Ginosar but was killed in 1948.

Basser, Yitzhak *Poland, 1923*

Baum, Avraham Yosef *Poland, 1910*
Father: Yezekiel. Spent time at Villa Piacenza DP camp in Italy.

Baum, Leiser *Poland, 1925*
Father: Yezekiel.

Baum, Rivka *Tuczyn, Poland (now Tuchin, Ukraine), 1918*

Baumgarten, Bluma *Zdunska Wola, Poland, 1922*
Parents: Issak & Machze.

Bauminger, Stefa *Poland, 1918*

Bavli, Pinchas *Romania, 1916*

Beck, Chaim *Poland, 1925*

Beck, Osnat *Kovno, Lithuania, 1919*
Father: Haim.

Becker, Moshe *Poland, 1930*

Beleli, Malkah *Kerkyra, Corfu, Greece, 15.8.1925*
Parents: Nasu & Ester. Had three brothers and a sister. Was in Haidari concentration camp in Athens before deportation to Auschwitz II. Transferred to Bergen-Belsen, Gellenau, a sub-camp of the Gross-Rosen, and then Mauthausen. Survived a death march. Liberated at Mauthausen by the American Army. Was in DP camps in Italy near Bari, Villa Piacenza in Italy, and Grottaferrata (Villa Cavalletti). Married Barzili Meir, who was on the *Wedgwood*.

Beilis, Yehuda *Kovno, Lithuania, 9.2.1927*
Parents: Eliezer, a doctor, & Chana, a dentist. Father also owned a printing shop, apartments and warehouse. Had two older brothers, Chaim and Yosef. In October 1941, taken from the Kovno Ghetto to the Ninth Fort where his family were killed. He woke up when the burning lime was placed on the bodies and crawled out of the pit, but in the ghetto nobody believed his story. Fled the ghetto and hid on the farm of his uncle's friends the Premeneckas. Returned to the ghetto and joined the Beitar Zionist movement which trained him in sabotage. Smuggled children out of the ghetto in potato sacks. Transported to Landsberg in Germany. Joined the Irgun and was wounded in 1948. Worked in Haifa as a car mechanic.

Wrote his memoirs in Hebrew. Married with two daughters and a son.

Belijinski, Berek *Poland, 1919*

Ben Yehuda, Moshe *Piotrkow, Poland, 2.11.1913*
Parents: Faygah & Yehudah Yosef Horn. Had one sister and two brothers. Were an Orthodox family. In Piotrkow Ghetto and camps at Petrikau-Bugaj, Buchenwald, Schlieben (Germany). Liberated at Theresienstadt by the Red Army. Youth groups: Maccabee and Dror. Was in Bologna and Bari. Married and had two sons.

Benclowich, Pinchas *Poland, 1921*

Benclowich, Tova *Poland, 1918*

Benedykt, Dawid *Lodz, Poland, 18.4.1926*
Parents: Alter & Rachel. In Lodz Ghetto, where he worked as saddler. A friend of Shmuel Rozenzaft. Transfer to Sachsenhausen 27.11.1944. Arrived Mauthausen from Sachsenhausen 26.2.1945.

Berezin, Berl *Poland, 1916*

Berg, Andor *Hungary, 1929*

Berg, Mikalosch *Hungary, 1924*

Berger, Aharon *Poland, 1925*

Berger, Chaim *Czechoslovakia, 1921*

Berger, Gutte *Czechoslovakia, 1924*

Berger, Rachel *Czechoslovakia, 28.2.1928*
Parents: Wolf & Mirjam. Later became Rachel Muntz.

Bergman, Ester *Bielsko-Biala, Poland, 1927*
Father: Asher.

Bergman, Sheya *Poland, 1909*

Bergman, Solomon *Poland, 1905*

Berkovich, Avraham *Czechoslovakia, 1921*

Berkovich, Dora *Czechoslovakia, 1929*
Parents: Dawid & Perl.

Berkovich, Gittel *Czechoslovakia, 1926*

Berkovich, Mikscha *Hungary, 1920*

Berkovich, Moshe *Czechoslovakia, 1925*

Berkovich, Rosa *Bilky, Czechoslovakia (now Ukraine), 7.10.1925*
Parents: Yaakov & Rivka. Had three brothers. In Edeleny and Miskolc ghettos in Hungary. In 1944, taken to Auschwitz, then to Plaszow, Markkleeberg in Germany and Hertine in Czechoslovakia. Liberated in Teplice Sanov in Czechoslovakia by the Red Army. Went home and then to Hungary and Graz. The Jewish Brigade took her to Udine. Was in Bologna, Padua and Salerno DP camps. Married and had three daughters. Changed name to Rahel.

Berkovich, Simon *Barlad, Romania, 1926*
Father: Avraham.

Berkovich, Theresa *Czechoslovakia, 1923*

Berlinski, Leib *Poland, 1929*

Berlovich, Yitzhak *Memel (now Klaipeda), Lithuania, 1924*
Father: Eliezer.

Berman, Israel Fishel *Poland, 1910*

Berman, Yona *Poland, 1919*

Bern, Khat *Poland, 1927*

Bern, Mina *Poland, 1920*

Bern, Nathan *Poland, 1917*

Bernhaim, Dora *Poland, 1920*

Bernovich, Hersch *Poland*, *1922*

Berson, Ella *Lodz*, *Poland*, *5.12.1924*
Parents: Leibush & Ester Rosenstein.

Berzak, Pesach *Poland*, *1919*
Escaped the Novogrodek Ghetto and was a partisan with the Bielski brothers in the Naliboki forest. Was in Landsberg DP camp. Married Renia Berzak, who also escaped the Baranowicze Ghetto. She sailed on the *Dov Hoz* from La Spezia in May 1946 and gave birth to a daughter in July 1946. Had two children and moved to Houston. Died 14.12.1994.

Bicher, Herman *Romania*, *1911*

Biederman, Sara *Warsaw*, *Poland*, *1923*
Father: Binyamin. Youth Group: Dror. Was a Warsaw Ghetto fighter and part of Benjamin Wald's group. At the end of the uprising she left the ghetto through a sewer in Ogrodowa Street. Was shot in the stomach trying to escape and left for dead. Hidden by her university friend Helena Balicka who took her to hospital. She was later recognised as one of the Righteous Among the Nations, as was her father, Zygmunt Balicki, who was caught helping Biederman and others and sent to Auschwitz. He survived. Took part in the Warsaw Uprising of 1944. She joined Kibbutz Lohamei Hagetaot. Died 1972.

Bikel, Oskar *Vienna*, *Austria*, *30.5.1926*
In the Lodz Ghetto with his mother, who was murdered in an action in the ghetto hospital. Was in a camp in Czestochowa. Sister escaped to Palestine in 1940. After the war joined a *hachshara aliyah* training camp in Warsaw. Was in Landsberg DP camp. Settled in Kibbutz Lohamei Hagetaot. Changed name to Yeshayahu.

Bilizer, Chana *Hungary*, *1926*

Bimkah, Avraham *Kolberg*, *Germany (now Kolobrzeg, Poland)*, *18.3.1930*
Parents: Moshe & Hanah. Was in Auschwitz III Monowitz. Survived death march to Mauthausen, Melk and Gunskirchen. In Linz DP camp and Milan. Married and had a daughter and two sons.

Binke, Eliezer *Poland*, *1925*

Birenbaum, Feivel *Romania*, *1923*
Father: Benjamin.

Bisztricer, Meir *Czechoslovakia*, *1926*
Father: Mordechai. Had been in Auschwitz and Buchenwald concentration camps.

Bitkower, Rubin *Vama*, *Romania*, *1916*
Parents: David & Zizel. Transported to Transnistria.

Bivas, Estheria *Thessaloniki*, *Greece*, *1922*
In Auschwitz and Ravensbrück. Liberated in Germany by the Red Army. Married Meir Allaluf, who was on the *Wedgwood*.

Blanc, Sandar *Poland*, *1915*

Blau, Chava *Czechoslovakia*, *1924*

Blaustein, Chana *Poland*, *1925*

Blaustein, Yakov *Zloczow*, *Poland (now Ukraine)*, *15.3.1925*
Changed name to Jacob Avinatan.

Blumenstein, Kreindel *Poland*, *1925*
Parents: Eliezer & Lea.

Blumkin, Jakob *Poland*, *1926*
Father: Gabriel & Lea. Friend of Arie Seagalson, who was on the *Wedgwood*.

Blumsztajn, Lajzar *Lodz*, *Poland*, *7.7.1927*
Parents: Chaim & Chaya. Was part of the

group of boys who became friends in Auschwitz and were at the Villa Bencista near Fiesole. Survived the death march to Sachsenhausen and then Mauthausen. Killed 1948.

Bochor, Zili *Romania, 1920*

Bodinger, Nathan *Romania, 1929*

Bodo, Yosef Dov *Ozd, Hungary, 1928*
Parents: Imre & Mirijam.

Boim, Zili *Hamburg, Germany, 1918*
Father: Paliks.

Boimblit, Simcha *Poland, 1918*

Boimel, Moshe *Nowa Slupia, Poland, 3.3.1923*
In Opatow Ghetto, close to Kielce, and then in camps in Skarzysko-Kamienna and Czestochowa. Liberated by the Russians. Changed his name to Martin.

Boltansky, Baruch *Romania, 1928/1927*
Father: Yosef.

Bord, Yakov *Poland, 1928*

Bornstein, Avraham *Radom, Poland, 1929*
Parents: Israel & Rachel. Was in the Kielce Ghetto and camps at Pionki, Sosnowiec and Mauthausen. Parents and younger brother and sister were killed. Joined the Haganah on arrival in Palestine. Studied social work at Hebrew University and became a social worker. He was awarded a PhD from the London School of Economics and became a leading academic in the field of social policy and the welfare state. Wrote a memoir *My Universities, 1943–45*.

Bornstein, Chaya *Poland, 1929*

Borochovitz, Miriam *Taurage, Lithuania, 9.1.1927*

Parents: Shmuel & Sara. Youth group: Dror-Habonim.

Borovsky, Atara *Zyrardow, Poland, 16.12.1924*
Born Blumenstein. Parents had a large bakery. Youth group: Dror. When the Jews of Zyrardow were ordered to move to the Warsaw Ghetto, she and her older sister went to work on a German farm. Sister moved to Czestochowa in 1941. She was ill and was cared for by local Poles. Assumed the identity of a Polish orphan. Arrested as a Pole in 1943. Sent to Warsaw's Paviac Prison and transferred to Majdanek but released. Then met two Polish girls working in the underground and together they went to Germany as volunteer workers. Worked in a hospital until the end of the war. In Stuttgart she met two other survivors, both boys, and they acquired false papers. They joined a group and crossed into Italy from Austria. They went via Unione 5 and she was recruited to work for the Bricha in Magenta. Lived on Kibbutz Alonim, where she worked in the vegetable garden and vineyard. Married and had three children. Died 2016.

Boslik, Sandar *Poland, 1916*

Bovilsky, Chana *Poland, 1920*

Bovilsky, David *Poland, 1919*

Brainer, Rachel *Hungary, 1920*

Braitstein, Zlate *Poland, 1927*

Bratt, David Yeshayahu *Zembrzyce, Poland, 12.2.1914*
Parents: Chaim & Sprinze. Youth group: Beitar.

Bratt, Glezer Dvora *Przemysl, Poland, 11.2.1915*
Parents: Shimon & Chaya. Youth group: Beitar.

Braun, Moshe *Romania, 1927*

Braun, Rachmiel *Poland, 1921*

Brauner, Itzhak *Bedzin, Poland, 1923*
Parents: Zeev & Ester.

Braunstein, Chaya *Czechoslovakia, 1926*

Brenner, Lea *Latvia, 1923*
Father: Avraham.

Brenner, Yakov *Poland, 1928*
Was in Germany after liberation. Killed in action in 1948.

Brillant, Yosef *Poland, 1925*

Brindt, Shelomoh *Siauliai, Lithuania, 1925/6*
Was in the DP hospital in St Ottilien in Bavaria. Brother of Shimon & Yitzhak.

Brindt, Shimon *Siauliai, Lithuania, 27.1.1923*
With brothers Yitzhak & Shelomoh. Youth group: Beitar. In Shavli Ghetto. Member of the underground movement Massada, which put out a newspaper and carried out weapons training. Transported to Landsberg with his brothers. Parents murdered. Liberated after a death march by the Americans at Bad Tolz. Was at St Ottilien before the Jewish Brigade took him to Italy. In the DP camp at Santa Caterina near Bari. Moved to Genoa before embarking on the *Wedgwood*. Married Tanya Selinsky, whom he met in Italy and who was on the *Wedgwood*. Had three sons. Died 2009.

Brindt, Yitzhak *Siauliai, Lithuania, 1928*
Parents: Ben Tsion & Blumah. Brother of Shelomoh and Shimon. All three brothers are on the original list of the *Sharit Ha-Platah* drawn up by Rabbi Klausner of surviving Jews in Dachau.

Bronschter, Avraham *Romania, 1928*
With Nechamia Kurlander. Frida Weiss was his sister.

Bronschter, Fryma *Romania, 1930*
Sister of Avraham.

Bronstein, Chaim *Poland, 1925*

Bronstein, Yitzhak *Czechoslovakia, 1929*

Broyer, Sara *Latvia, 1919*

Brunner, Baruch *Lodz, Poland, 1927*
Father: Yerachmiel. Was in the Auschwitz bricklayers' school. Part of the group of boys who became friends in Auschwitz.

Budik, Moshe *Radauti, Romania, 1922*
Father: Mendel.

Budik, 'Zuza' Shoshana *Krakow, Poland, 29.12.1921*
Father: Hanoch Taubman, a journalist at a Jewish newspaper, was a socialist and the family were immersed in Polish culture. Attended a Polish school even though the Jewish school was closer to home. Boy-friend was killed by the Gestapo. Parents and brother deported. Hid on false papers in Jaroslaw with the family of her aunt's husband who was not Jewish until she was caught and taken back to the ghetto. Escaped again. Hid in a Czech village near the border. After the war she returned to Krakow. Lived in Azur, Israel. Had two children. Died 2016.

Buchman, Hadasa *Staszow, Poland, 1926*
Father: Shmuel.

Buchsbaum, Tova *Poland, 1919*

Buchsbaum, Yehudit *Poland, 1928*

Buchsenbaum, Yakov *Poland, 1924*

Bunes, Liber *Poland, 1915*
Father: Moshe.

Burg, Genya *Poland*
Youth Movement: Beitar.

Burger, Oskar *Poland, 1922*

Bursztain, Yankel 'Jack' *Lodz, Poland, 1.5.1927*
In Lodz Ghetto and the Auschwitz brick-layers' school. Survived death marches to Sachsenhausen and Mauthausen. Was liberated in Gunskirchen. Taken to Italy by the Jewish Brigade and was in the Villa Bencista near Fiesole. Died in Canada in 2015.

Candel, Eliezer *Poland, 1927*

Campner, Moshe *Poland, 1924*

Cepelsky, Moshe *Poland, 1917*

Cerni, Avraham *Romania, 1927*

Cerni, Sara *Lithuania, 1927*
Parents: Grisha & Polia.

Chanoch, Daniel *Kovno, Lithuania, 2.2.1933*
Brother of Uri. In the Kovno Ghetto, Landsberg, Dachau and Auschwitz. Death march to Mauthausen. Moved to *Zeltenlager* (tent camp), Sankt Florian. Liberated by the US Army at Gunskirchen. Found by the Jewish Brigade who took him to Tarvisio. Was in Mestre, Bologna, Modena, the Villa Bencista in Fiesole and Tradate. Hospitalised in Milan. Married. Had a son and a daughter.

Chanoch, Uri *Kovno, Lithuania, 1928*
Parents: Frida & Shraga. Father owned a match factory. Chanoch studied at the Hebrew school. Youth group: Beitar. Transported to Landsberg. Father and brother were taken from there to Auschwitz and his father was gassed. Reunited with brother Dani in the Villa Bencista in Fiesole. In Palestine, joined

the Palmach and became an officer in the IDF. Was an industrialist. Active public speaker on the Holocaust. He and his life-long friend Solly Ganor ran the Association of Survivors of Dachau, Landsberg and Kaufering. Member of the Claims Conference Board and of the World Jewish Restitution Organisation where he fought for compensation from Germany for Lithuanian Holocaust survivors. Married and had three children. Died 2015 in Tel Aviv.

Chasanowitz, Chaya *Czechoslovakia, 1926*
Married to Falek Chasanowitz. Born Bronstein.

Chasanowitz, Falek *Vilnius, Poland (now Lithuania), 1926*
Parents: Avraham & Chaja. In the Ichud Zionist pioneering training programme, and active in the Bricha. Was in an *aliyah* training camp in La Picciola, Italy with friend Elchanan Segalson and with wife Chaya, who both sailed on the *Wedgwood*.

Chaskal, Ruth *Poland, 1929*

Chayat, Ita *Poland, 1927*

Chefer, Sara *Poland, 1923*

Chermet, Rachel *Hungary, 1927*

Chidarski, Moshe *Poland, 1923*

Choronsizky, Feige *Lithuania, 1920*

Choronsizky, Meir *Lithuania, 1911*

Cohen, Aya *Oradea, Romania, 1924*
Father: Kalman.

Cohen, Dov *Lithuania, 1923*

Cohen, Eliezer *Janow Podlaski, Poland, 1911*
Father: Yehuda.

Cohen, Felix *Sroda Wielkopolska, Poland, 1927*
Father: Yaakov.

Cohen, Hersch *Poland, 1929*

Cohen, Reuven *Greece, 1918*

Cohen, Reuven *Riga, Latvia, 1912*

Cohen, Shmuel *Poland, 1930*
Part of the Auschwitz group of friends. Killed in 1948.

Cohen, Yehuda *Greece, 1929*

Colteck, Chana *Poland, 1928*

Colteck, Dvora *Poland, 1929*

Crohn, Hersch *Poland, 1925*

Crohn, Shlomo *Poland, 1917*

Cruparu, Barish *Romania, 1922*

Cruparu, Yanko *Romania, 1910*

Cukiert, Jacob *Poland, 1924*

Cyngler, Fella *Poland, 1925*
Wife Perec. Met in Tricase, Italy.

Cyngler, Hersch *Pabianice, Poland, 20.5.1925*
Parents: Chaim, a decorator, & Gittel. Younger sister Pearl was murdered in Treblinka in 1943, after which his father gave up hope and died four weeks later. Youth group: Hanoar Hatzioni. In Pabianice and Lodz ghettos. In Auschwitz. Transported to Braunschweig and Drütte in Germany. Liberated with his brother at Wöbbelin. Returned to Lodz, where they met Jews planning to go to Palestine. Travelled with this group to Budapest and Graz in Austria. Married a survivor he met in Atlit. Had three sons. Moved to Australia.

Cyngler, Perec *Poland, 1920*
Brother of Hersch.

Cwibel, Sheindel *Romania, 1925*
Possibly with daughter Chaya. Married to Shlomo. Changed name to Jaffa. Born Broide.

Cwibel, Shlomo *Romania, 1924*
Married to Sheindel.

Czentochowski, David *Poland, 1922*

Czipser, Yakov *Czechoslovakia, 1925*

Czudler, Chaim *Sarny, Poland, 1911*
Parents: Jakob & Malka.

Dagan, Eliezer *Skalat, Poland (now Ukraine), 1913*
Father: Yehuda.

Danziger, Eliezer *Hungary, 1924*

Dasaro, Ovadia *Greece, 1926*

Datner, Hanoch *Sosnowiec, Poland, 12.2.1917*
Father: David. Was in Bergen-Belsen.

Datner, Yakov *Poland, 1918*

Dattner, Yosef *Poland, 1924*

David, Yosef *Romania, 1928*

Davidovich, Baer Dov *Lithuania, 1929*
Parents: Mordechai & Soshana.

Davidovich, Shulem *Iasi, Romania, 1926*
Father: Moshe.

Davidovich, Zeev *Sighet, Romania, 1925*
Father: Yezekiel.

Delariche, Mikol *Florence, Italy, 1930*
Father: Fortunato.

Dembovich, Beisel *Poland, 1925*

Dembovich, Zundel *Poland, 1920*

Den, Naftali *Poland, 1914*

Den, Tova *Poland*, *1918*

Denon, Esther *Yugoslavia*, *1929*

Derash, Michael *Poland*, *1924*
Father: Eliezer.

Deutsch, Eliahu Miskolc *Borsod*, *Hungary*, *4.9.1922*
Father: Zvi.

Deutsch, Fritz *Austria*, *1925*
Was in Theresienstadt.

Diamant, Avraham *Poland*, *1930*

Diamant, Bard Lea *Sosnowiec*, *Poland*, *30.11.1925*
Youth Group: Hanoar Hatzioni. Active in the underground in the war. Sent to Germany with false papers as he had blond hair and blue eyes. Worked for the Bricha in northern Italy. Died 1953.

Diamant, Shoshana *Poland*, *1915*

Diamant, Zeev *Poland*, *1919*

Dimant, Ester *Poland*, *1922*

Distal, Arie Leibke *Vilnius*, *Poland (now Lithuania)*, *26.11.1922*
Father worked for a Zionist organisation. Youth Group: Hashomer Hatzair. Blue eyes, blond hair. Arrested when the Vilnius Ghetto was liquidated. Sent to Kurome in Estonia and then by boat to Stutthof. Escaped in transit to Dachau and travelled to Italy. Arrived in Tarvisio in June 1945. Joined Nakam. Arrived in Italy weeks before the *Wedgwood* sailed. Settled in Kibbutz Yakum.

Djalcka, Ketta *Poland*, *1927*

Djalcka, Reuven *Czestochowa*, *Poland*, *1923*
Father: Yosef.

Dobovich, Shoshana *Poland*, *5.5.1925*

Related to Zultak Dvora Kaplan & Hanna Kochman.

Dolinska, Lisa *Bialystok*, *Poland*, *1919*
Father: Avraham.

Dolinski, Pinchas *Poland*, *1914*
Father: Israel.

Dreifuss, Sami Berlin *Germany*, *1921*
Father: Rudolf.

Drezhner, Miriam *Poland*, *1916*

Drinbar, David *Poland*, *1923*

Druck, Reuven *Riga*, *Latvia*, *1917*
Father: Zalman.

Dunkelman, Carmela *Lodz*, *Poland*, *12.11.1925*
Born Mendelbaum.

Dworkowitz, Rafael *Kovno*, *Lithuania*, *1910*

Eden, Arnon *Nowy Targ*, *Poland*, *15.10.1923*
Changed name to Arnold Feller. Had been in a concentration camp.

Ehrlich, Yehuda *Poland*, *13.7.1925*
Youth group: Hashomer Hatzair. Hidden by a Polish family. Worked for the Bricha in Italy. Became a teacher. Married.

Eigelberg, Shoshana *Stopnica*, *Poland*, *1926*

Einrieder, Shoshana *Bedzin*, *Poland*, *1926*

Einstein, Rachel *Maniewicze*, *Poland (now Manevychi, Ukraine)*, *1927*
Father: Shimon. Youth Movement: Dror-Habonim. Nearly the entire population of Manevychi were killed in the Holocaust.

Eisenschmidt, Dafner Yehudit *Poland*, *20.05.1920*
Born Wolbrom. In Auschwitz. Wife of Eliezer. Met September 1945.

Eisenschmidt, Eliezer *Lunna, Poland (now Belarus), 27.1.1920*
Parents: Yehoshua & Yehudit. Was a Sonderkommando prisoner in Auschwitz. Escaped a death march to Mauthausen and was saved by a Polish family that lived near Auschwitz who cared for him. With wife Dafner. Died 11.12.2014.

Eisner, Yitzhak *Borszczow, Poland (now Borshchiv, Ukraine), 1928*
Father: Yakov.

Elbaum, Mordechai *Lodz, Poland, 1928*
Father: Yechiel.

Elentuch, Eliyahu *Poland, 1919*

Erkin, Herzel *Zhetel, Poland (now Belarus), 1927*
Youth Movement: Hashomer Hatzair.

Erlich, Dvora *Poland, 1916*

Erlich, Feige *Poland, 1924*

Erlich, Leiser *Poland, 1915*

Erlich, Mordechai *Poland, 1922*

Erlich, Yosef *Lodz, Poland, 1924*
Father: Beer.

Esterkin, Moshe *Poland, 1918*

Faber, Mina *Poland, 5.4.1924*
Youth Movement: Gordonia. Related to Zultak Dvora Kaplan and Hanna Kochman.

Fainer, Sela *Poland, 1928*

Faktorovski, Tuvia *Lithuania, 1914*

Faygenblat, Aba *Warsaw, Poland, 11.4.1930*
Parents: Genyah & Gershon. Hid in Lublin where liberated. Then went to Chorzow and Slask. In St Ottilien and Feldafing.

Feibish, Solomon *Romania, 1925*

Feiblson, Yaakov *Poland, 1916*

Feig, Hersch *Romania, 1926*

Feingold, David *Poland, 1926*
A friend of Moshe Reindorf, who was on the *Wedgwood*.

Feld, Avraham *Poland, 1911*

Feld, Chaim *Poland, 1919*

Feldman, Gavriel *Derecske, Hungary, 26.12.1924*
Parents: Yafah & Yezekiel. Orthodox couple who had three sons and two daughters. In Auschwitz and then Furstenstein in Germany. On death march to Buchenwald. After liberation he went to Prague, Budapest and Albiate in Italy. Married twice. Had two daughters.

Feldman, Idel *Poland, 1927*

Feldman, Refael *Poland, 29.9.1922*

Feldman, Shlomo *Poland, 1919*

Feller, Chana *Poland, 1927*

Feller, Israel *Poland, 1916*

Fetter, Avraham *Poland, 1928*

Fetter, Hinda *Poland, 1900*

Fetter, Israel *Poland, 1924*

Fetter, Sara *Poland, 1923*

Fidelholc, Menachem *Poland, 1924*
Born Mendel. Husband of Rivka.

Fidelholc, Rivka *Sighet, Romania, 27.1.1927*
Father: Yehuda Daskal. Wife of Menachem.

Figovaski, Yitzhak *Poland, 1924*

Figur, Perl *Poland, 1928*

Finkel, Irena *Poland, 1924*

Finkel, Rivka *Poland, 1925*

Finkel, Simcha *Poland, 1916*

Finkel, Yakov *Poland, 1927*

Finkelstein, Chaya *Poland, 1896*

Finkelstein, Eliezer *Kovno, Lithuania, 1928*
Parents: Dawid & Ester. One of the 131 young boys transported from Kovno to Kaufering. In Auschwitz. On death march to Mauthausen and Gunskirchen.

Finkelstein, Israel *Poland 1896*

Finkelstein, Zirl *Poland, 1926*

Finkovici, Efraim *Galati, Romania, [?].7.1922*

Fisch, Moshe *Romania, 1926*

Fisch, Shmuel *Romania, 1914*

Fischman, Avraham *Poland, 1918*

Fischman, Moshe *Romania, 1921*

Flamenbaum, Miriam *Poland, 1914*

Fleischer, Israel *Poland, 1906*

Fleischer, Mordechai *Poland, 1927*

Fleischer, Sonia *Poland, 1922*

Fogel, Perl *Poland, 1927*

Forman, Bertha *Poland, 1922*

Formanovich, Rachel *Poland, 1926*

Freid, Shmuel *Czechoslovakia, 1910*

Frenkel, Vaicman Dina *Baranowicze, Poland (now Baranavichy, Belarus), 17.2.1925*
Youth group: Bnei Akiva.

Frichman, Menashe *Romania, 1924*

Friedlander, George *Hungary, 1929*

Friedlander, Otto *Hungary, 1921*

Friedman, Avraham *Poland, 1916*

Friedman, Chaim *Czechoslovakia, 1912*

Friedman, Feige *Hungary, 1926*

Friedman, Fella *Poland, 1918*

Friedman, Frania *Sosnowiec, Poland, 21.12.1917*
Parents: Avraham & Endale. Travelled with husband-to-be, David Shahar.

Friedman, Israel *Poland, 1926*

Friedman, Meir *Hungary, 1916*

Friedman, Menachem *Poland, 1920*

Friedman, Paul *Romania, 1906*

Friedman, Rosa *Poland, 1918*

Friedman, Yakov *Hungary, 1928*

Friedman, Yente *Poland, 1910*

Friedman, Zacharia *Poland, 1902*

Friedman, Zelig *Radom, Poland, 1920*
Parents: Benjamin & Chaja.

Friedrich, Shmuel *Poland, 1919*

Friedrich, Yaffa *Poland, 1926*

Friedrich, Yosef *Poland, 1917*

Fries, Avraham *Lithuania, 1927*

Friesinger, Gershon *Poland, 1911*

Frimerman, Shelomoh *Lodz, Poland, 17.5.1925*
Parents: Belah & Hayim. Had four brothers. In Auschwitz and then to Gleiwitz. Survived death marches to Gross-Rosen and Blechhammer where he was liberated by the Russians. Went first to Czestochowa, then home to Lodz. Travelled to Romania where the Jewish Brigade took him to Mestre in Italy, then to Magenta and Tradate. Met Hanah Zilbergold in Tradate. Travelled together on the *Wedgwood*. Married and they later had two sons.

Frisch, Max *Poland, 1923*

Frohman, Rivka *Lodz, Poland, 1928*

Fromerman, Zisele *Poland, 1925*

Fromm, Rachel *Poland, 1925*

Fromm, Yakov *Poland, 1914*

Fruchtman, Israel *Romania, 1927*

Frymerman, Avraham *Poland, 1923*

Frymerman, Chaim *Poland, 1902*

Frymerman, Yitzhak *Poland, 1928*

Frymermann, Shlomo *Poland, 1925*

Fuchs, Andor *Hungary, 1924*

Fuchs, Avraham *Hungary, 1923*

Fuchs, Baruch *Romania, 1904*

Fuchs, Bracha *Hungary, 1916*

Fuchs, George *Hungary, 1919*

Fuchs, Miriam *Hungary*

Fuchs, Shlomo *Romania, 1906*

Fudalovich, Israel *Ciechanow, Poland, 18.3.1922*
Parents: Shifrah & Dov were Hassids. Had three brothers and a sister. Youth Movement: Beitar. Deported from Ciechanow Ghetto to Auschwitz. Survived a death march to Neu-Dachs and Blechhammer, where liberated by the Red Army. After the war he went to Czechoslovakia, then to Italy. Was in Tradate. With his wife Tovah. Had two sons.

Fudalovich, Tovah *Czechoslovakia, 16.11.1923*
Born Sajevitz. Youth Movement: Beitar. Husband Israel.

Fuksberg, Alexander *Boryslaw, Poland (now Boryslav, Ukraine), 1924*
Mother: Sara.

Furcajg, Laja *Poland, 1922*

Wife of Leon Pesses, who also sailed on the *Wedgwood*. In the Warsaw Ghetto.

Gabai, Silvia *France, 1924*
Father: Eliyahu Beeri.

Galferin, Meir *Romania, 1923*

Galkin, Avraham *Riga, Latvia, 1921*
Parents: Zalman & Sheina. Both died with his two sisters in the Holocaust. Died 1991.

Galkin, Yitzhak *Riga, Latvia, 1924*

Galper, Ben-Zion *Vilnius, Poland (now Lithuania), 1916*
Father: Benjamin.

Gammerman, Pinchas *Poland, 1910*

Gantz, Grishkan Miriam *Latvia, 1923*
Husband Israel.

Gantz, Israel *Krakow, Poland, 1912*
Father: Benjamin. Married Miriam.

Gartner, Feige *Poland, 1927*

Gasoschnick, Lea *Lithuania, 1928*

Gaz, Mendel *Maramures, Romania, 1921*
Father: Shlomo.

Gedalovich, Avraham *Czechoslovakia, 1923*
Father: Menachem.

Geisler, Frida *Czortkow, Poland, 1924*
Father: Fishel.

Geisler, Hersch *Poland, 1910*

Gelberg, Chaya *Poland, 1928*

Gelbort, Moni *Poland, 1919*

Geliebter, Chaim *Poland, 1926*

Gendelman, Isar *Poland, 1921*
Father: Yehuda. Died 2005.

Gendelman, Nathan *Poland, 1919*

Gerard, Elsa *France, 1928*

German, Aharon *Romania, 1925*

German, Harri *Romania, 1926*

German, Lupu *Bucharest, Romania, 1921*
Father: Moshe.

Gersht, Yerachmiel *Poland, 1913*

Gerstner, Hella *Poland, 1925*

Gerstner, Yanka *Poland, 1924*

Gevirz, Brunia *Ternopil, Poland (now Ukraine), 1928*
Father: Aharon.

Gewerz, Avraham *Poland, 1929*

Gilinska, Sara *Vilnius, Poland (now Lithuania), 1916*
Father: Beer. In the Vilnius Ghetto with her husband Leib.

Gilinski, Leib *Vilnius, Poland (now Lithuania), 1915*
Father: David. Wife Sara.

Ginsburg, Rachel *Poland, 1913*
Father: Yosef.

Glancszpigel, Sara *Karnitz, Poland, 1922*
Father: Gats.

Glick, Anschel *Hungary, 1918*

Glicksman, Symcha *Poland, 1927*
Husband of Rachel Halperin. Died 1994.

Gliksberg, Nachman Natan *Biala Podlaska, Poland, 29.4.1924*

Glucksman, David *Czestochowa, Poland, 23.11.1913*

Gold, Rivka *Poland, 1928*
Father: Yezekiel.

Gold, Shalom *Poland, 1922*
Father: Yosef.

Goldberg, Lotka *Poland, 1918*
Father: Moshe.

Goldberg, Shmuel Yona *Radom, Poland, 20.3.1929*
In Lodz Ghetto and Auschwitz. Survived death march to Mauthausen, Lieberose, Sachsenhausen and Gunskirchen where he was liberated. Only brother Zisman survived. His mother Sheindel was a member of the Bund and asked husband Chaim to leave Poland but refused. Mother gassed on arrival in Auschwitz. Father died in Dachau 6 January 1945. Part of the group of friends at the Villa Bencista in Fiesole.

Goldberg, Yakov *Lodz, Poland, 1930*
Listed among Jews in Mauthausen born in Litzmannstadt as 28.8.1928. Occupation apprentice. Arrival at Mauthausen 25.1.1945 from Auschwitz.

Goldberg, Yitzhak *Poland, 1914*
Father: Zvi.

Goldberg, Yitzhak *Poland, 1922*
Parents: Akiva & Chana.

Goldenberg, Anna *Romania, 1922*

Goldenberg, Isidor *Romania, 1921*

Goldferb, Avraham Zvi *Poland, 1909*

Goldferb, Rosa *Poland, 1917*

Goldin, Sara *Kovno, Lithuania, 1927*
Father: Pinchas.

Goldman, Moshe *Poland, 1924*

Goldrott, Tzila *Bedzin, Poland, 1925*
Father: Moshe.

Goldstein, Baruch *Poland, 14.12.1916*
Married to Gota Goldstein.

Goldstein, Gota *Warsaw, Poland, 24.2.1921*
Born Gitela Fridman.

Goldstein, Miriam *Poland, 1917*

Goldstein, Shmuel *Poland, 1916*

Goldstein, Wilmos *Hungary, 1928*

Goldstein, Yakov *Romania, 1925*

Gorman, Avraham *Poland, 1925*

Goterman, Mania *Poland, 1925*

Gottesman, Mordechai *Czechoslovakia, 1930*

Gottesman, Yetti *Romania, 1924*

Gotthelf, Dina *Poland, 1918*
Father: Aharon.

Gottlieb, Genia *Rokitno, Poland, 1925*
Father: Avraham.

Gottlieb, Vizia *Rokitno, Poland, 1927*
Father: Avraham.

Gottner, Liba *Lithuania, 1916*

Graiver, Michael *Poland, 1926*

Grauman, Moshe *Poland, 1920*

Greenbaum, Chaim *Poland, 1926*

Greenbaum, Chana *Vilnius, Poland (now Lithuania), 1918*

Greenbaum, Yosef *Poland, 1920*

Greenberg, David *Poland, 1924*

Greenberg, Moshe *Romania, 1918*

Greenberg, Paula *Romania, 1921*

Greenberg, Sofi *Romania, 1927*
Father: Yitzhak. Deported to Transnistria.

Greenfeld, Alexander *Poland, 1922*

Greenziger, Freidale *Poland, 1926*

Grinboim, Haym *Lodz, Poland, 22.12.1926*
Parents: Akiva & Malkah Grynbaum, who had two daughters and two sons. The family were in the Lodz Ghetto. In Auschwitz, then Sachsenhausen, Mauthausen, Amstetten and Gunskirchen, where he was lib-

erated by the Americans. Survived a death march. Was in Linz DP camp. Married. Had one son.

Groag, Miriam *Budapest, Hungary, 1916*

Grochowina, Yoel Zeev *Sosnowiec, Poland, 1912*
Father: Hanoch.

Grodzinska, Sonia *Poland, 1923*

Grolach, Breindel *Poland, 1925*

Gross, Avraham *Romania, 1927*

Grossman, Natan *Zgierz, Poland, 27.9.1927*
Parents: Abraham & Bluma. Father a cobbler. In the Lodz Ghetto. Older brother, Berek, died at Chelmno. He was sent by a youth organisation to discover what happened to the transports and help the people. Father beaten to death and mother starved as she gave him what food she had. Was in Auschwitz. Then taken to camps in Vechelde and Braunschweig in Germany. Returned to Lodz before leaving for Palestine. Now lives in Munich. Often speaks about his experiences. Subject of a film, *Line 41*.

Grossman, Shmuel *Poland, 1924*
Father: Shlomo.

Grottas, Avraham *Thessaloniki, Greece, 1916*
Parents: Josef & Miriam.

Grottas, Bela *Thessaloniki, Greece, 1920*
Parents: Avraham & Dodon Ergas.

Growas, Zyrech *Poland, 1914*
Had been in Warsaw during the war.

Gruber, Binyamin *Romania, 1928*

Gruenbaum, Shaul *Neustadt, Poland, 1914*
Father: Leib.

Gubinski, Chaim *Poland, 1926*

Gurevich, Fania *Baranowicze, Poland (now Baranavichy, Belarus), 1921*
Father: Shlomo. Registered in Radom after the war. Was in Feldafing.

Gurevich, Grisha *Vilnius, Poland (now Lithuania), 1920*
Father: Yosef Had been a partisan in the Rudniki forest. A friend of Josef Harmatz. Worked for the Bricha in Milan.

Gutman, Abraham *Lodz, Poland, 1927/6*
Father: Yosef.

Gutman, Mordechai *Plonsk, Poland, 1924*

Gutterman, Menachem *Lodz, Poland, 1930*
Parents: Moshe & Sarah. Was part of the group of boys who were in Auschwitz. Was in Kibbutz Alonim. Trained as a carpenter. Killed in 1948.

Guttman, Nachman *Proskurov, Soviet Union (now Khmelnytskyi, Ukraine), 1919*
Father: Gershon.

Guttman, Yezekiel *Lodz, Poland, 1923*
Father: Moshe.

Guttmark, Golda *Poland, 1918*

Guttreich, Yakov *Lodz, Poland, 10.10.1929*
In Lodz Ghetto and Auschwitz.

Gzimek, Aba *Poland, 1929*

Ha-Elion, Moshe *Thessaloniki, Greece, 26.2.1925*
Born Moritz Aelion. In Auschwitz, Mauthausen and Ebensee. Was in Santa Maria di Bagni after the war. He saw service in the 1948 War. Known as a writer and poet, he sat on the board of Yad Vashem. Married Hanna. Had two children.

Ha-Elion, Hanna *Targu Neamt, Romania, 19.5.1925*
Parents: David & Mina Waldman. Youth group: Dror-Habonim. In Auschwitz. Was in Santa Maria di Bagni DP camp where she met her husband Moshe. Died 2010.

Halle, Moshe *Lodz, Poland, 10.10.1920*
Parents: Fishel & Gittel.

Halle, Simon *Lodz, Poland, 29.9.1926*
Parents: Fishel & Gittel. Brother of Moshe. Brothers were in the Lodz Ghetto and Auschwitz. Survived a death march on 25.1.1945 from Auschwitz to Mauthausen. Part of the group of boys who became friends. In Kibbutz Alonim.

Halperin, Rachel *Vilnius, Poland (now Lithuania), 26.4.1924*
Parents: Rosa & Shmuel. Had one brother and two sisters. She was caught while a member of the Vilnius Ghetto underground and sent to Kaiserwald. In Stutthof and Thorn. Survived a death march. Liberated at Fordon in Poland. Then went to Warsaw and on to Lodz. In Romania, she joined Nakam group who tried to murder six million Germans. Married Symcha Glicksman, who was on the *Wedgwood*. After the war, had two sons and a daughter.

Halpern, Frida *Poland, 1920*

Halpern, Max *Poland, 1910*

Hamlisch, Miriam *Romania, 1926*

Hamlisch, Nathan *Hungary, 1924*

Hammer, Avraham *Poland, 1929*
Parents: Yechiel Meir & Riwka.

Hammerstein, Helina *Poland, 1923*
Youth group: Hashomer Hatzair.

Hanan, Avraham *Thessaloniki, Greece, 1928*
Born Albert Hanna.

Handel, Chanoch *Poland, 1928*

Hangeltoub, Sima *Poland, 1918*

Hardstark, Yosef *Lodz, Poland, 1929*
Parents: Herzel & Dwora. One of the boys in the Auschwitz group of friends. Survived death marches to Sachsenhausen, Mauthausen and Gunskirchen, where he was liberated.

Hardstein, Sabina *Poland, 1928*

Harmath, Eliyahu *Hungary, 1926*

Harmatz, Josef *Rokiskis, Lithuania, 23.1.1925*
Parents: Abrasha & Dora, who owned a warehouse in the main market square in Rokiskis and had three sons. The family moved to Vilnius in 1940. His elder brother Zvi fled to the Soviet Union and was killed in the Red Army. Father killed himself in 1942. Mother was sent to Kaiserwald in 1943. She survived Stutthof and was liberated by the Russians. Harmatz's other brother, Ephraim, died in Klooga. With the other FPO partisans, Harmatz fled the ghetto for the Rudniki forests in September 1943. After the liberation he worked for the NKVD until he left for Lublin in January 1945. He worked to secure the Bricha route from Poland to Romania. Shortly after reaching Bucharest, Harmatz was reunited with his mother, who left for Palestine. In Tarvisio with Abba Kovner and on 7 September 1945 he left for Nuremberg to carry out the group's plan to poison the water system. Married and built a career in the Jewish Agency and ORT Israel, a Jewish educational NGO. Died 2016.

Hass, Zeev Wolf *Poland, 25.12.1920*

Hatberg, Henech *Poland, 1917*

Heliszewicz, Yehudit *Poland 1915*

Henfeld, Ida *Poland, 1922*

Henner, Aharon *Poland, 1921*

Henner, Sara *Poland, 1923*

Heonig, Yafah *Vrbas, Yugoslavia (now Serbia), 5.12.1927*
In Auschwitz. Survived a death march to Bergen-Belsen where she was liberated by the British Army. Returned to Centa in Yugoslavia but then travelled to Modena. Youth Movement: Dror-Habonim. Married. Had a son and a daughter. Sister of Zvi.

Heonig, Zvi Diazi *Centa, Yugoslavia (now Serbia), 1.2.1926*
Parents: Moshe & Sara. Born George. Youth Movement: Beitar. In Auschwitz. Then sent to two different labour camps in Luxembourg and salt mines in France. A welder, he worked in the Volkswagen factory in Wolfsburg, Germany, and on the V-8 rockets. Mother died in Bergen-Belsen. Married Anna Khon, who sailed on the *Wedgwood*. With sister Yafah.

Herfa, Hersch *Poland, 1918*

Hershbein, Malka *Warsaw, Poland, 1915*
Father: Doyach.

Hershbein, Zvi *Warsaw, Poland, 1908*
Father: Eliezer.

Hershberg, Moshe *Poland, 1920*

Hershkowitz, Feivel *Galicia, Poland, 12.7.1927*
Father: Eliezer. Youth Movement: Hashomer Hatzair.

257

Hershkovitz, Isaac *Romania, 1924*

Herzfeld, Eliezer *Hungary, 1912*

Herzfeld, Rachel *Warsaw, Poland, 1928*

Herzfeld, Sara *Warsaw, Poland, 1926*

Hirschenboim, Fredi *Bucharest, Romania, 1923*
Father: Yitzhak.

Hirschorn, Menachem *Buczacz, Poland (now Buchach, Ukraine), 1929*
Parents: Isidor & Sara. Cousin of Menachem Kriegel, who sailed on the *Wedgwood*. Later Rishek. Both were in Selvino, Italy, after the war.

Hirsh, Shmuel *Transylvania, Romania, 17.4.1929*

Hochberg, Ania *Poland, 1917*
Registered in Lvov (now Lviv, Ukraine) after the war.

Hoffenberg, Olga *Warsaw, Poland, 1920*
Father: Shlomo.

Hoffman, David *Hungary, 1928*

Hoffman, Yakov *Drahov, Czechoslovakia, 1914*
Father: Efadim.

Honig, Yosef *Poland, 1921*

Horn, Leib *Poland, 1918*

Horn, Zerka *Poland, 1918*

Hornstein, Beni *Romania, 1922*

Horowitz, Avraham *Poland, 1919*

Horowitz, Naftali *Tarnow, Poland, 1929*
Father: Yitzhak. Youth Movement: Hashomer Hatzair.

Horowitz, Shmuel *Chrzanow, Poland, 1924*
Father: Shmuel Horowitz. The family moved to Oswiecim in 1936. Deported to the Chrzanow Ghetto in 1941. Married his cousin, who was the only member of her family who survived.

Housman, Hersch *Poland, 1927*

Huttman, Shmuel *Poland, 1929*

Hybner, Tuli *Romania, 1919*

Icht, Noah *Poland, 1918*

Ingerman, Alberta *Trento, Italy*
Born Marini. Was part of an anti-fascist family active in the underground. It was her connections that enabled Sereni and the Gang to take over the villa in Magenta in Italy.

Ingerman, Yaakov *Shepetivka, Russia (now Ukraine), 1919*
Studied mathematics at the University of Kiev. Became a teacher. When the Nazis invaded the Soviet Union, he was enlisted in the Red Army, underwent a combat intelligence course, and since he knew German he was sent as a spy to work behind enemy lines and recruit activists into the partisans. Became the interpreter of a German unit. In 1943, he was transferred to Italy. Worked with Italian and Yugoslav partisans near Trento, where he met his wife Alberta. In May 1945, the unit surrendered to the Americans, revealing to its amazed commander that he had always worked for the partisans. The couple worked for the Bricha and organised the renting of the villa in Magenta. Divorced. Alberta returned to Italy, with her daughter Miriam. Ingerman remarried and had another daughter. Wrote a memoir, *A Jew in the Service of the Reich*. Died 2007.

Isaac, Kathrina *Greece, 1928*

Israel, Israel *Thessaloniki, Greece, 20.10.1925*
Parents: Shalom & Dudan. Arrived Auschwitz 20.3.1943.

Jadbebinski, Yosef *Poland, 1920*

Jama, David *Lodz, Poland, 8.6.1925/6*

Janover, Mala *Sosnowiec, Poland, 1922*
Father: Yissachar.

Janover, Yosef *Poland, 1914*

Jochimek, Israel *Poland, 1912*

Jona, Yakov *Greece, 1925*

Jung, Baruch *Poland, 1926*
Registered in Sosnowiec.

Jung, Shmuel *Czechoslovakia, 1926*

Jungblat, Leon *Romania, 1922*
Father: Marcos.

Kac, Michael *Lodz, Poland, 8.3.1929*
In Lodz Ghetto. Arrived from Auschwitz
in Mauthausen on 30.1.1945.

Kaczala, Izion *Poland, 1921*

Kaczanowski, Avraham *Poland, 1915*

Kaiser, Helina *Poland, 1925*

Kajzer, Halina *Czestochowa, Poland,
15.8.1928/1929*
Parents: Adolf & Leosia.

Kalkstein, Grisha *Czechoslovakia, 1925*

Kalvaria, Chaim *Kovno, Lithuania, 1924*
Parents: Leib & Tsipi. On a *Sharit Ha-
Platah* list published by the Central Com-
mittee of Liberated Jews of Bavaria in
1946. He had three brothers. Married.
Died Bulawayo 1969.

Kalviski, Yitzhak *Poland, 1915*

Kamin, Yosef *Poland, 1926*

Kamelgaren, Rivka *Poland, 1925*

Kaminer, Yehudit *Poland, 1920*
Parents: Alechum & Lea.

Kaminska, Fella *Poland, 1923*

Kaminski, Yakov *Poland, 1929*

Kanielsky, Nachman *Kremenchug,
Ukrainian People's Republic (now Ukraine),
1919*
Parents: Mordechai & Sara.

Kapellner, Helena *Germany, 1920*

Kaplan, Dawid *Pruzhany, Poland,
20.6.1928*
In the Pruzhany Ghetto, Auschwitz and
Buchenwald. Endured a death march,
26.1.1945.

Kaplan, Yitzhak *Rovno, Poland (now
Rivne, Ukraine), 10.10.1930*
Fled with family to the Soviet Union.
Returned to Rivne after the war. Joined a
group and travelled the Bricha route to
Italy. As a truck driver, worked for Egged
until 1988. Served in the reserves for 35
years and participated in the Six-Day War
and the Yom Kippur War. Married. Had
five children. Lives in Haifa.

Kaplansky, Menachem *Poland, 1925*

Kaplonsky, Leon *Poland, 1918*

Kaplusch, Taivka *Siauliai, Lithuania,
8.12.1926*
Parents: Zalman & Cilla. Became Jona
Berkovitz. Had one brother and three sisters. It was an Orthodox family. In Siauliai
Ghetto and Stutthof. She and her sister,
Leah, escaped a death march. Hid in barns
until the Russians arrived. She was in a
Russian field hospital. Trained to be a
nurse. She joined a youth group and went
to Italy. Married but lost her first child due
to back injuries inflicted by the Nazis.
Worked as a nurse in the Beilinson Hospital. Went to the USA where she had a son.

Kaplush, Janina *Lithuania, 1919*
Father: Mordechai.

Kapulsky, Israel *Kovno, Lithuania, 1925*
Parents: Manasze & Chaja. On the *Sharit Ha-Platah* in Feldafing.

Kapulsky, Leib *Kovno, Lithuania, 1924 or 1928*
Father: Moshe. Was in Dachau. On the *Sharit Ha-Platah* list.

Kapulsky, Moshe *Vilnius, Poland (now Lithuania), 1902*
Was in Dachau.

Karolicka, Luba *Poland, 1930*

Karolicki, Meir *Poland, 1888*

Karpel, Chanan *Poland, 1927*

Karpilovich, Hersch *Russia, 1928*

Kashziber, Israel *Poland, 1919*

Kasner, Shmuel *Poland, 1918*

Katushevsky, Eliyahu *Poland, 1929*
In Lodz Ghetto and Auschwitz. One of the group of friends in Auschwitz.

Katz, Ada *Poland, 1926*
Parents: Hayim & Sarah. Had one sister and one brother. In Auschwitz II and Merzdorf in Germany, where she was liberated by the Red Army. Was in Graz before being transferred to Italy by the Jewish Brigade. Wife of Avraham Katz. Later had a daughter and two sons. Cousin of Yechiel Aleksander on the *Wedgwood*.

Katz, Avraham *Zarnow, Poland, 1925*
Parents: Jacob & Bejla. Was in Lodz Ghetto. Wife Ada.

Katz, Chana *Targu Mures, Romania, 1923*
Youth Movement: Hapoel Hamizrachi. Husband Simcha Katz.

Katz, Chana *Poland, 1926*

Katz, Chaya *Vilnius, Poland (now Lithuania), 1925*

Katz, Erwin Yosef *Hungary, 1924*

Katz, Herman *Hungary, 1912*

Katz, Hinda *Poland, 1901*

Katz, Miriam *Poland, 1915*

Katz, Miriam *Czechoslovakia, 1923*

Katz, Sara *Hungary, 1925*

Katz, Simcha *Czechoslovakia, 1918*
Father: Yitzhak. Married to Chana Katz.

Katz, Yitzhak *Czechoslovakia, 1921*

Kaufman, Isaac *Lodz, Poland, 1927*
Father: Menachem. In Lodz Ghetto and Auschwitz. Arrived in Mauthausen 16.2.1945 from Sachsenhausen.

Kaufman, Lea *Poland, 1925*

Kawiat, Tova *Poland, 1923*

Kazav, Yakov *Vilnius, Poland (now Lithuania), 1928*

Kedari, Shmuel *Hungary, 1920*

Kempner, Moshe *Poland, 1924*
Parents: Efraim & Chaja.

Kermayer, Rita *Romania, 1925*

Kermayer, Yetti *Romania, 1927*

Kidron, Brakha *Ternopil, Poland (now Ukraine), 3.9.1928*
Parents: Lizah & Aharon. Born Bronyah Gvirz but changed name on release. Had one sister. In Podhajce and Ternopil ghettos and camps in Brezowica and Ternopil from which she escaped. Lived under a false name in Ostalowice and Suszczyn until the Russians arrived. In DP camps in Munich, Landsberg and Leipheim. Was at Tradate DP camp. Youth Movement: Hashomer Hatzair. Married. Had a daughter and two sons.

Kien, Alexander *Hungary, 1911*

Kimchi, Eliezer *Greece, 1908*

Kimhi, Ishak *Thessaloniki, Greece, 9.2.1918*

Kinstler, Yakov *Poland, 1928*

Kirschenbaum, Maria *Radomysl, Poland, 1904*
The family had run a grocery store. Was saved by Dominik Glowacki, who hid her and her three daughters, Regina, Miriam and Rachel/Rysia. He was awarded the Righteous Among the Nations medal.

Kirschenbaum, Miriam *Radomysl, Poland, 1929*
Parents: Yechiel & Maria.

Kirschenbaum, Rachel *Radomysl, Poland, 1930*
Sister of Miriam.

Kiwasz, Yitzhak *Poland, 1912*

Klapholc, Mordechai *Poland, 1925*

Klapholc, Moshe *Poland, 1921*

Klayn, Iboya Yehudit *Hungary, 1921*

Klayn, Pinhas *Uzhhorod, Czechoslovakia (now Ukraine), 20.1.1926*
Parents: Nehah & Yosef. Had two brothers and a sister. In Uzhhorod Ghetto and Auschwitz. Transferred to Buchenwald, Mittelbau-Dora, Harzungen, Ellrich, and Heinkel-Flugzeugwerke. Liberated at Sachsenhausen by the Red Army. Youth group: Hapoel Hamizrachi. Travelled from Hungary to Italy. Was at Tradate. Married Iboya Yehudit. Divorced and remarried. Had three daughters and a son.

Klein, David *Hungary, 1922*

Klein, Erna *Poland, 1917*

Klein, Erna *Hungary, 1922*

Klein, Imra *Hungary, 1925*

Klein, Jene *Romania, 1920*

Klein, Shimon *Hungary, 1929*

Klein, Shmuel *Hungary, 1925*

Klein, Susana *Romania, 1925*

Kleinfeltz, Rachel *Poland, 1923*

Kleinman, Pinchas *Poland, 1907*

Klogir, Pola *Dobczyce, Poland, 1924*
Parents: Benjamin & Jochewed.

Kloper, Alfred Avraham *Poland, 1923*

Kloper, Henrick *Hungary, 1921*

Knishkov, Yakov *Poland, 1927*

Kochman, Hanna *Poland, 15.12.1927*

Koczova, Shlomo *Poland, 1926*

Kohane, Akiva *Katowice, Poland, 1930*
Parents: Bernard & Rachel. Father imported watch parts that were assembled in his factories in Warsaw and Katowice. In the early days of the war he went with his mother Rachel and his younger sister to Warsaw while the father tried to get to the Soviet Union. The family were briefly reunited and he spent time alternately with his parents in Wolbrom and Sosnowiec. In Sosnowiec and Bedzin ghettos and Auschwitz II on 21 July 1944, which he said everyone knew what it was about from local Poles who worked there. His mother told him to slip into the men's side as he was 15. His mother and sister were gassed immediately. Survived a death march to Mauthausen. Liberated at Gunskirchen. In the Villa Bencista in Fiesole. After a year on a kibbutz, he went to Haifa and took a part-time job while studying. Left for the USA. Died 2012.

Kohen, Frida *Ratibor, Germany (now Raciborz, Poland), 28.12.1925*
Parents: Yeshosua & Ester, who had two daughters and two sons. In the Lodz

Ghetto and Auschwitz. Transferred to Stutthof and liberated in Kiel, Germany. Made her way to Munich. Taken to Innsbruck, Klagenfurt and Udine by the Jewish Brigade. Married. Had a son and a daughter.

Kohn, Anna *Merano, Italy, 1926*
Parents: Josef, a doctor, & Gisella, were born in Czechoslovakia. Josef studied medicine in Prague and specialised in lung and heart disease as his brother and sister died of tuberculosis and heart disease when they were young. Josef was a Zionist but was told there was no need for more doctors in Palestine, so moved to Italy in the 1920s. In October 1944 the Kohns were smuggled over the border to Switzerland, near Lugano. After liberation they returned to Milan and then to Merano where Anna worked with refugees. She met Ada Sereni and Jewish Brigade soldiers who persuaded her to go to Palestine. Joined the *hachshara* Ceriana La Gueto where she met her future husband, Zvi Hoenig, who was also on the *Wedgwood*. In Kibbutz Givat Brenner, Zvi worked as a welder. Later lived in Haifa and then Tivon. Had three daughters.

Koller, Lea *Lithuania, 1894*

Koller, Yocheved *Poland, 1923*

Kollin, Almer *Czechoslovakia, 1921*

Kolner, Leah *Italy, 1925*

Komp, Shalom *Poland, 1926*

Kopchak, Sara *Poland, 1929*

Kopeelberg, Pinchas *Poland, 1920*

Koper, Avraham *Poland, 1930*

Koperard, Moshe *Poland, 1923*

Koperberg, Yakov *Poland, 1928*

Koperstein, Klara *Hungary, 1925*

Koplik, Leib *Poland, 1927*
Father: Aharon.

Koppel, Chana *Poland, 1921*

Koppel, Eli *Romania, 1919*

Koren, Harri *Poland, 1921*

Koren, Sonia *Poland, 1926*

Korenberg, Rosa *Romania, 1918*

Korenberg, Yanko *Romania, 1922*

Korenblit, Avigdor David *Zamosc, Poland, 1923*
Parents: Isaac & Hinda had six children. With sister Hinda. Married. Had three children. Died 2012.

Korenblit, Hinda *Zamosc, Poland, 1892*
Mother of Avigdor David.

Korenblit, Rosa *Poland, 1922*

Korenstein, Shulem *Husiatyn, Poland (now Ukraine), 1912*
Father: Feibush.

Kornirski, Yakov *Poland, 1913*

Kozik, Bella *Poland, 1925*

Kozniczak, Menachem *Poland, 1909*

Krakaur, David *Czestochowa, Poland, 10.6.1924*
Parents: Shmuel & Yiska. Youth Movement: Hashomer Hatzair.

Kramarski, Szulim *Lodz, Poland, 27.6.1927*
In Lodz Ghetto. On the death march from Auschwitz to Sachsenhausen 27.11.1944. Was then marched to Mauthausen.

Krantz, Chava *12.3.1923*
Parents: Moshe & Beila Stoki. Married to Yehoshua Krantz.

Krantz, Yehoshua (Shiya) *Przedecz, Kolo, Poland, 1916*
Parents: Avraham & Chaya. Wife Chava.

Krauthamer, Emanuel *Bobrka, Poland, 19.8.1925*
Parents: Yosef & Sara. Youth Movement: Beitar. In Bobrka Ghetto. Hid in Romanow forests and in Swirz, where he was hidden by Polish farmers called Jan and Katarzyna Szwed, whose daughter had been sent as forced labour to Germany and never returned. Liberated by Red Army, August 1944. One of 14 of 4,000 Jews of Bobrka to survive. Parents and his eleven-year-old sister Chaja and four-year-old Ajzyk murdered in Belzec. Emanuel had been saved by a German soldier from Gorny Sląsk (Upper Silesia) who first hid the child and then let him go, instructing him to run away. The boy had wandered around the nearby forests until he reached the Szwed home. Years later, Maria Szwed recalls that "he arrived at our door and was crying terribly". Emanuel remained with the Szwed family until the end of the War. Changed name to Kruvi.

Krawchuk, Hirsch *Poland, 1912*

Kreski, Yenia *Poland, 1921*

Kriegel, Menachem *Buczacz, Poland (now Buchach, Ukraine), 25.7.1930*
Parents: Naftali & Hanah. Had a brother and a sister, Sophie, who survived. Was hidden by Ukrainian farmers. After the liberation was found by his sister. Travelled from Lvov to Krakow with her and a cousin, Menachem Hirschorn. There passed through Lodz and using the Greek bluff moved on to Czechoslovakia. Was then in Graz and Mestre before being taken to Selvino with his cousin who

sailed on the *Wedgwood*. After Atlit they were taken to Kibbutz Ramat Yohanan. He built a career in the merchant navy. Married. Had three children. Lives in Haifa.

Krieger, Sara *Poland, 1916*

Kronenfeld, Esther *Romania, 1923*

Kucikowicz, Hersch *Poland, 1918*

Kuks, David *Poland, 1927*

Kuperwasser, Alisa *Poland, 1921*
Registered in Pabianice after the war.

Kuperwasser, Miriam *Poland, 1927*

Kuricki, Avraham *Lithuania, 1920*

Kurlander, Fira *Batia Balti, Romania, 1924*
Father: Shmuel Bronester. Wife of Nechamia. With nephew Avraham and sister Fryma.

Kurlander, Nechamia *Poland, 1917*
Wife Fira.

Kuschnir, Rachel *Romania, 1929*

Kwiat, Eliezer *Poland, 1912*

Lachovizki, Yishaya *Poland, 1924*

Lachs, Eliyahu *Poland, 1924*

Lachs, Moshe *Poland, 1925*

Lachs, Nechama *Lodz, Poland, 20.10.1926*
Youth Movement: Hashomer Hatzair.

Lachs, Yehoshua *Poland, 1927*

Lachs, Yitzhak *Poland, 1922*

Lahm, Shlomo *Poland, 1928*

Laifer, Zosia *Warsaw, Poland, 1932*
After liberation in Italy, was in Modena, Vallabrosa, Fiesole. She was sent first to Kibbutz Alumot near the Sea of Galilee.

She recalled finding it difficult to live with others who had not experienced the Holocaust. She left and went to work as a nanny in Haifa before she was drafted into the IDF. Was a children's nurse in Tel Aviv and then a teacher in Rehovot. Married. Had two children.

Laks, Efraim *Lodz, Poland, 25.7.1927*
In the Lodz Ghetto and Auschwitz. Survived the death march to Sachsenhausen that left 27.11.1944.

Laks, Rafal *Lodz, Poland, 2.1.1928*
In the Lodz Ghetto and Auschwitz. On the death march to Sachsenhausen that left 27.11.1944.

Lander, Avraham *Turobin, Poland, 1921*
Parents: Yaacov & Sara. With sister Ester Zukerman and brother-in-law Yerachmiel Zukerman and brother Yehuda Lander.

Lander, Idel *Poland, 1913*

Lander, Yehuda *Turobin, Poland, 1913*
Father: Yakov.

Landshpigel, Fishel *Poland, 1918*

Landsman, Hersch *Romania, 1922*

Landsman, Mordechai *Poland, 1924*

Langenour Yakov *Boryslaw, Poland (now Boryslav, Ukraine), 1921*
Was in Salzburg after liberation.

Langer, Lea *Radom, Poland, 1926*
Father: Reuven.

Langer, Yakov *Poland, 1924*

Langer, Zvi *Poland, 1928*

Langweiler, Mindel *Stanislawow, Poland (now Ivano-Frankivsk, Ukraine), 1925*
Father: Yosef.

Lanzner, Reuven *Poland, 1917*
Father: Yehuda.

Laster, Michael *Poland, 1922*

Lebart, Rosa *Breslau, Germany (now Wroclaw, Poland), 1914*
Father: Karl.

Lederman, Dora *Lodz, Poland, 1919*

Lehrer, Jzack Roman *Romania, 30.6.1926*
Parents: Jacob & Chana. Youth Movement: Gordonia.

Leib, Menashe *Poland, 1925*

Leibovich, Fanni *Romania, 1915*

Leibovich, Lieb *Romania, 1919*

Leibovich, Moshe *Romania, 1915*

Leibovitz, Tuvia *Novogrodek, Poland, 1923*
Father: Hanan.

Leiter, Gershon *Poland, 1920*

Leiter, Lea *Wadowice, Poland, 1924/1923*
Father: Moshe.

Leizerovich, Mordechai *Lodz, Poland, 1911*
Father: Avraham.

Leizerovich, Sofia *Poland, 1921*

Leniz, Yosef *Poland, 1923*

Lev, Pesach *Jasionowka, Poland, 1924*
Parents: Dov & Malkah Levar. Had four sisters and a brother. Family were Orthodox. Hid in barns, bunkers and forests until liberated in Spiczyn after escaping from a train heading for Auschwitz. Helped by the Polish Shloimeh and Dubenevich families. Married twice. Had a stepson and a stepdaughter.

Levar, Esther *Poland, 1924*

Levi, Avraham *Greece, 1920*
Parents: Iccak & Rywka.

Levi, Eliyahu *Poland, 1916*

Levi, Mordechai *Lithuania, 1928*

Levi, Moshe *Zgierz, Poland, [?].7.1929*
Parents: Shlomoh & Yokheved. Had three sisters and a brother. The family were Orthodox. In Lodz Ghetto and Auschwitz. Survived a death march to Mauthausen and from there to Melk and Ebensee, where he was liberated. Served in the Haganah after the war. Married. Had a son and two daughters.

Levi, Rivka *Poland, 1924*

Levi, Shlomo *Lithuania, 1898*

Levi, Yosef *Hungary, 1923*
Father: Zvi.

Levin, Golda *Vilnius, Poland (now Lithuania), 1925*

Levin, Nathan *Poland, 1929*

Levin, Rivka *Skarzysko-Kamienna, Poland, 5.7.1928*
Parents: Hanah & Eliezer. Born Regina Rashel. Had two sisters. She was in camps at Skarzysko-Kamienna, Czestochowa-Pelcery, Burgau, Ravensbrück, Türkheim and München-Allach. Liberated at Dachau by the Americans. In Feldafing and Florence after liberation. Married.

Levin, Yakov Yitzhak *Poland, 1915*

Levinson, (Lavie) Zalman *Lithuania, 31.1.1922*
Parents: Yosef & Miriam.

Levit, Aharon *Poland, 1927*

Levit, Menachem *Poland, 1911*

Levkovich, Ilonia *Czechoslovakia, 1911*

Liberbaum, Rosia *Poland, 1923*

Lieberman, Fedda *Sosnowiec, Poland, 13.12.1924*
Had attended the Hebrew gymnasium. Youth group: Hanoar Hatzioni. Active in the underground in Germany, after the first reports of mass murder were heard in the ghetto. She went to Germany with her friend Lea Diamant, who sailed with her. Both returned to Sosnowiec after the war and joined the Bricha. Travelled to Austria where the Jewish Brigade took them to Tarvisio and then to Mestre. She worked at the camp hospital as a nurse. Recruited to work for Aliyah Bet and sent to Magenta camp where she was put in charge of food supplies in the run-up to the departure. Later worked in the Israeli Embassy. Met her husband Poldek Maimon in Tarvisio, who sailed on the *Wedgwood*. On arrival in Palestine they went to Abba Kovner's kibbutz in Kibbutz Ein Hahoresh. She later worked as a nurse. Had two children.

Liberman, Rachel *Czechoslovakia, 1925*

Liberman, Sara *Czechoslovakia, 1923*

Lichtenfeld, Moshe *Poland, 1919*

Lifshits, Yehuda *Kovno, Lithuania, 7.6.1923*
Parents: Yakov & Gittel. Had two brothers and three sisters. Member of the underground. Joined the partisan group Death to the Invaders.

Lifshitz, Chana *Latvia, 1916*

Lifshitz, Michael *Czechoslovakia, 5.5.1926*
Parents: Yosef & Hinda.

Lifshitz, Yakov *Warsaw, Poland, 1919*

Ligenberg, Shmuel *Warsaw, Poland, 1922*
Father: Mendel.

Likorman, Yakov *Poland, 1922*

Lindend, Gala *Poland, 1916*

Lindenfeld, Yoel *Hungary, 1927*

Linivizki, Mordechai *Poland, 1916*

Linser, Josef Harri *Vienna, Austria, 25.1.1928*

His brother was sent on a Kindertransport. In 1942, the Linser family were deported to Theresienstadt. Linser survived typhoid disease. Deported to Auschwitz with father, who was murdered. Transferred to Kaufering, where he had to help build an underground factory site. After the liberation was in St Ottilien. Returned to Vienna but decided to go to Palestine. In Linz, Salzburg, Innsbruck, Milan. His mother survived and moved to England.

Lipkovitz, Nachum *Poland, 1920*

Litvak, Hersch *Poland, 1912*

Litvak, Rachel *Baranowicze, Poland (now Baranavichy, Belarus), 12.3.1920*
Previous name: Pinchasowicz.

Liver, Moshe *Lodz, Poland, 1.5.1925*
Youth Movement: Hashomer Hatzair. Married Miriam Weiman, who was on the *Wedgwood*.

Loel, Chava *Poland, 1927*

Loewenstein, Gershon *Poland, 1926*

Lohr, Pesach *Poland, 1924*

Londener, Avraham *Poland, 10.6.1915*
Parents: Daniel & Ruchama.

Londiner, Moshe Isar *Bedzin, Poland, 1922*
Father: Yaakov. Nakam member.

Lotner, Moshe *Lvov, Poland (now Lviv, Ukraine), 1919*
Father: Feivish.

Lustgarten, Shimon *Krakow, Poland, 4.4.1921*
Member of the Krakow underground. His apartment on 13 Jozefinska Street was the hub of the Akiva movement. In Auschwitz. Later joined Nakam.

Mack, Elchana *Latvia, 8.4.1925*

Madovich, Yosef *Poland, 1911*

Maestro, Daniel *Thessaloniki, Greece, 1923*
Parents: Icchak & Grasia.

Maestro, Yakov *Thessaloniki, Greece, 1929*
Brother of Daniel. Maestro spoke German and was given a job in the SS employment department in Auschwitz. There he saved at least a hundred lives by detailing people to work in less demanding jobs and by cancelling medical experiments. Lived in Bat Yam in Tel Aviv and worked as a car mechanic. Campaigned to have the story of the Greek Jews' experience in the Holocaust recognised.

Maimon, Yehuda 'Poldek' *Krakow, Poland, 2.2.1924*
Parents: Avi Meir & Chaya. Born Leopold Yehuda Wasserman. Studied at the Hebrew Gymnasium. Youth group: Hatzofe Pioneer. Key member of the Krakow underground. In Auschwitz. Escaped a death march in January 1945. Joined Nakam. Settled in Kibbutz Ein Hahoresh with wife Fedda Lieberman whom he met in Tarvisio. He was bitterly unhappy that the Nakam revenge plans were abandoned but he did not criticise his leader, Abba Kovner. Joined the navy. In 1963 worked for Nativ, an underground organisation which aided Russian Jews in making *aliyah* and was sent to Poland as First Secretary

at the Embassy. In 1968 was sent to Vienna as a special envoy to facilitate the *aliyah* of Polish Jews. Retired in 1972 and went into business.

Makler, Ben Zion *Poland, 12.4.1929*

Malchivski, Yakov *Poland, 1911*

Malinieski, Moshe *Lodz, Poland, 23.10.1926*
Father: Aryeh. Part of the friends' group from Auschwitz. On a death march to Sachsenhausen 27.11.1944. Arrived Mauthausen 16.2.1945.

Maltz, Rachel *Kovno, Lithuania, 1922*

Mano, Aharon *Thessaloniki, Greece, 1921*
Parents: Iccak & Lisa.

Mano, Yaakov *Thessaloniki, Greece, 4.2.1920*
Parents: Rahel & Daniel. Had two brothers and a sister. In Auschwitz. Was transferred to Warsaw to clean up the ghetto rubble, as were many of the Greeks as they did not speak Polish or Yiddish. From there he was taken to Dachau, Meldorf and Ampfing-Waldlager, where he was liberated by the US Army. In Feldafing DP camp and Santa Maria di Bagni. Married. Had two sons and a daughter.

Marchionski, David *Lithuania, 1922*

Marcus, Chaim *Greece, 1918*

Marcus, Iso *Romania, 1922*

Marcus, Mote Avraham *Romania, 1925*

Markovich, Benno *Poland, 1914*

Markovich, Frida *Czechoslovakia, 1923*
Father: Isaac.

Markovich, Mina *Kovno, Lithuania, 1917*

Markovici, Rosa *Budesti, Romania, 25.8.1922*
Parents: Leib & Bella. Had four brothers and three sisters. In the ghettos in Berbesti and Szeghed before Auschwitz II, Mühldorf and Feldafing in Germany, where she was liberated. She was then in Salzburg and Turin. Changed her name to Soshanah. Married and had two sons and a daughter.

Marmelstein, Dvora *Czechoslovakia, 1919*

Marmelstein, Efraim *Czechoslovakia, 1920*

Martinovski, Zalman *Riga, Latvia, 16.4.1923*
Parents: Tsilah & Shelomoh. Had four sisters. In Riga Ghetto and in camps in Pleskau, Lenta, Kaiserwald, Stutthof and Stolp, where he was liberated by the British. In Lubeck DP camp and was taken by the Jewish Brigade to Genoa. Married. Had two daughters and a son.

Matza, Tzado *Ioannina, Greece, 12.2.1926*
Parents: Ester & Nissim, had three sons. In Larissa, Auschwitz, Wolfsberg, Mauthausen and Ebensee, where he was liberated by the Americans. Survived a death march. In DP camps in Villach, Modena, Rome, Santa Maria di Bagni and Grottaferrata. Married. Had two daughters.

Mazparo, Tina *Romania, 1925*

Megid, Avraham *Romania, 1923*

Meiblum, Shaul *Poland, 1922*

Meir, Alexandra *Poland, 1903*
Father: Dov.

Melzer, Menachem *Lithuania, 1920*

Mendel, Chaskiel *Ostrowiec, Poland, 1929*

Mendel, Moshe *Latvia, 1921*

Mendelev, Chaim *Lithuania, 1926*

Mendelovich, Magda *Czechoslovakia, 1924*

Mendelson, Moshe *Sterdyn, Russia (now Poland), 25.12.1916*
Parents: Dov & Itah. Father a grocer. Orthodox family. Had five sisters and two brothers. Father murdered in September 1942. In Radom Ghetto but escaped. Hid near Lublin and Sterdyn, in bunkers and forests. Liberated near Dziecioly close to Lublin. Travelled to Warsaw and then to Czechoslovakia, Hungary, Romania and Italy. Married. Had a son and three daughters.

Mendelson, Sara *Sosnowiec, Poland, 1926*
Father: Gabriel.

Messing, Chedva *Poland, 1920*

Michalovsky, Mina *Lithuania, 1923*

Milgrom, Shmuel *Poland, 26.7.1919*
Parents: Baruch David & Zippora. Youth Movement: Gordonia. Husband of Wimissner, with whom he had three children. Died 1999.

Milgrom, Wimissner Genia *Baranowicze, Poland (now Baranavichy, Belarus), 6.6.1922*
Youth Movement: Gordonia.

Miller, Lea *Czechoslovakia, 12.4.1929*
Later married Ezra Steimatz, who sailed on the *Wedgwood* with his brother Shlomo and his wife Aidel.

Miller, Shimon *Novoselitsa, Czechoslovakia (now Ukraine), 8.4.1925*
Father: Yehuda.

Milstein, Mendel *Sandomierz, Poland, 7.4.1924*
Parents: Moshe & Dvora.

Mincberg, Chava *Bedzin, Poland, 1.11.1928*
Parents: Yitzhak & Pesia. Born Eva Baumgarten. Was in Mauthausen.

Minerbi, Elena Morpurgo *Milan, Italy, 20.5.1924*
Hidden by farmers, Attilio and Lidis Pigliapoco, during the German occupation, who worked on the family estate, which had been confiscated. Lived on Kibbutz Regavim. Died 2017.

Minski, Shlomo *Warsaw, Poland, 30.3.1916*
Father: Yitzhak.

Mintz, Eliezer (Leizer) *Grojec, Poland, 3.1.1921*
Parents: Zvi & Rachel. Youth Movement: Poalei Zion.

Miszok, Aharon *Poland, 1914*

Mitelman, Efter Yona Teibe *Doynark, Latvia, 1924*

Montab, Zila *Poland, 1925*

Monzik, Wolf *Poland, 1915*

Morel, Pesach *Poland, 1922*

Moshe, Chaim *Greece, 1920*
Parents: Aaron & Ester.

Moskovich, Hersch *Poland, 1926*

Moskovich, Miriam *Poland, 1926*
Father: Chaim.

Moskovich, Moshe *Poland, 25.4.1928*
Was on the death march from Auschwitz to Sachsenhausen. In the Villa Bencista in Fiesole.

Moskovich, Sara *Czechoslovakia, 1922*

Mudrik, Tzila *Sarny, Poland, 28.6.1928*
Father: Avraham.

Mulstein, Yakov *Lodz, Poland, 1928*
Parents: Hersch & Chana.

Naar, Shmuel *Thessaloniki, Greece, 1921*
Parents: Emanuel & Dina.

Nachmanovich, Moshe *Romania, 1921*

Naftalovich, Moshe *Romania, 1925*

Najman, Hersch *Poland, 15.4.1928*
Was on the death march from Auschwitz
to Sachsenhausen.

Najman, Isack *Ozorkow, Poland,*
10.9.1928
Father: Avraham. In Lodz Ghetto and Auschwitz. Survived the death march from
Auschwitz to Sachsenhausen.

Neuman, Frida *Romania, 1908*
Father: Falik.

Neuman, Lea *Hungary, 1923*

Neuman, Paula *Hungary, 1925*

Neuman, Yosef *Poland, 1925*
Father: Gershon.

Neustein, Yosef *Poland, 1921*

Nisanilevich, Senka *Poland, 1923*
Partisan and member of Nakam group.
Husband of Zelda Treger, who sailed on
the *Wedgwood*.

Nisinovic, Eliezer *Dombrowa, Poland,*
1918
Parents: Yaakov & Tojba.

Nisinovic, Kalman *Dombrowa, Poland,*
1923
Brother of Eliezer.

Nitsberg, Shraga Pavel Fajwel
Pruzhany, Poland, 1.7.1924
Parents: Eydel & Binyamin. Had one
brother. In Pruzhany Ghetto and Auschwitz, Neu-Dachs, Buchenwald, Blechhammer, Gross-Rosen, and Berga-Elster

in Germany. Liberated in Czechoslovakia.
Youth Movement: Hashomer Hatzair.
Married to Yona Wirzak, who sailed on
the *Wedgwood*.

Noigebaur, Zipora *Poland, 1925*

Nosinovich, Esther *Poland, 1925*

Nosinovich, Fella *Poland, 1925*

Nosinovich, Isaac *Poland, 1925*

Noyman, Shemuel *Kielce, Poland,*
8.5.1929
Parents: Natah & Hanah. In camps at
Sedziszow-Skarzysko, Buchenwald, Flossenbürg, Schlicben and Mauthausen,
where he was liberated by the Americans.
Taken out of Austria by the Jewish Brigade
to Modena and was in the Villa Bencista in
Fiesole. Married. Had a son.

Nussbaum, Yones *Poland, 1922*

Oberstein, Fela *Poland, 1922*

Oberstein, Leo *Netherlands, 1899*

Oezechowski, Moshe *Poland, 1928*

Offen, Aaron *Tarnow, Poland, 22.1.1923*
Parents: Wolf & Rywka. In Mauthausen.
Was at Ebensee DP camp and in Bavaria.
Was on the *Sharit Ha-Platah* list.

Offen, Chana *Tarnow, Poland, 1928*
Mother: Rywka.

Ogushevich, Nina *Poland, 1927*

Olewski, Mordechai *Poland, 1926*

Orenstein, Shaul *Romania, 1925*

Orshezer, Reuven *Krakow, Poland, 1925*
Father: Jacob.

Oshpitz, Ya'avoc *Debrecen, Hungary,*
10.10.1930
Parents: Yitzhak & Tzina. In camps in
Vienna, Graz, Mauthausen and Auschwitz.
Killed in action in 1948.

Oshrovsky, Aharon *Poland, 1926*

Paker, Yehoshua *Poland, 1927*

Paklisher, Genia *Poland, 1920*

Paklisher, Grunya *Poland 1890*

Pankowska, Frida *Pilica, Poland, 1918*
Parents: Avraham & Leah, an Orthodox couple, who had four sons and two daughters. In Sosnowiec Ghetto and camps in Blankenheim, Grünberg, Märzdorf and Schönberg. Escaped on a death march and hid until the Red Army arrived. Returned to Sosnowiec. Joined Hashomer Hatzair; went to Italy. Married. Had a son and daughter.

Parnes, Ganya *Kolbuszowa, Poland, 20.6.1924*
Parents: Moshe & Fermet Nusbaum, who were Hassids. Had two sisters and three brothers. Hid using false names. Married Yakov Parnes, who was on the *Wedgwood*. Later had a son and daughter.

Parnes, Jacob *Lvov, Poland (now Lviv, Ukraine), 1921*
Parents: Gershon & Chaja. Had a brother who was killed in 1941. Husband of Ganya Parnes.

Pat, Chaim *Bialystok, Poland, 21.10.1926*
Mother: Itka. In Auschwitz and Mauthausen. In DP camps in Ebensee and Salzburg.

Patashnik, Sara *Sosnowiec, Poland, 1926*
Parents: Josef & Chana.

Patticzer, David *Poland, 1923*

Pelcman, Rivka *Poland, 1927*

Pelta, Gershon *Pabianice, Poland, 1.3.1929*
Mother: Ester. In Lodz Ghetto. Father and sister killed at Chelmno. In Aus-chwitz, Lieberose, Sachsenhausen, Brandenburg and Gunskirchen. On the death march from Auschwitz to Sachsenhausen 27.11.1944. Was at Villa Bencista in Fiesole. Changed name to Ben Yehuda. Was in Kibbutz Alonim and then at Kivyat Amal. Best friend of Meyer Swartz, who travelled on the *Wedgwood*.

Pepper, Avraham *Poland, 1926*

Perl, Menachem *Czechoslovakia, 1919*

Perl, Rivka *Romania, 1919*

Perl, Sofia *Poland, 1920*

Perlmutter, Mordechai *Plonsk, Poland*
Parents: Faygah & Yosef. In Nosarzewo, Auschwitz, Mauthausen and Dachau. In Feldafing DP camp and in Tieringen. Changed name to Peer. Married. Had three sons.

Perlov, Ahuva *Sevlus, Czechoslovakia (now Vynohradiv, Ukraine), 1921*
Born Liba Klein. Parents: Aharon & Leah.

Perlov, Shalom *Germanowiche, Russia, 1912*

Pesach, Yakov *Greece, 1922*

Pesses, Leon *Warsaw, Poland, 2.4.1910*
Parents: Sara & Israel. Had a sister and two brothers. He was the youngest. The family were in the Warsaw Ghetto. Parents taken to Treblinka as was his sister. In the ghetto he married Laja Furcajg, who came from a wealthy family and travelled on the *Wedgwood*. Her father imported tea. They fled the ghetto and hid with false papers. As Poles they endured forced labour, he in Stettin in an aeroplane factory building the roof, and Laja in a sugar factory. Was working on a farm when the Russians arrived. Had ambitions to open a

factory in Warsaw. His father had run a hat factory making brims for caps. He made a living smuggling vodka and medicines until he was arrested by the NKVD. At this point the couple went to Lodz and joined the Bricha, travelling to Katowice. The Greek bluff was almost blown when some real Greek survivors approached them. Travelled via Bratislava to Vienna and on to Italy in covered trucks. He joined the air force and Laja sold shoes in a department store. They spent four years in Israel and had a baby son, who was sickly, and a daughter before going to Canada. They were helped by a wealthy friend of Laja's family.

Piaskevich, Arie *Poland, 1922*

Picion, Peppi Yosef *Greece, 1914*

Piciona, Ovadia *Greece, 1926*

Pinkus, Aharon *Lodz, Poland, 1926*
Parents: Shmuel & Chana.

Piotrkowski, Chaim *Lodz, Poland, 13.1.1927*
In Lodz Ghetto and Auschwitz. Survived death marches to Sachsenhausen 27.11.1944 and Mauthausen (arriving February 1945) and Lieberose. Friend of Jack Bursztain on the *Wedgwood*. Died 2008.

Pipek, Haim *Ostrowiec, Poland, 15.5.1925*
Parents: Tuvia & Nechama. Born Fishel. Brother of Efraim Porat.

Plawner, Shalom *Poland, 1929*

Plisinski, Miriam *Romania, 1926*

Pliskov, Rubin *Galatz, Romania, 1927*
Parents: Baruch & Lisa.

Plocka, Sara *Czestochowa, Poland, 10.3.1924*

Plutel, Eliezer *Siauliai, Lithuania, 1908*
Parents: Hillel & Ahuva.

Podelevich, Israel Moshe *Poland, 1922*

Polack, Chaim *Romania, 1926*

Polansky, Shoshana Rosa *Poland, 25.12.1927*
In Picciola, Italy, on the Ichud Zionist training programme.

Polansky, Moshe Fishel *Kovno, Lithuania, 9.1.1927*
Was in Picciola, Italy, on the Ichud Zionist training programme. Youth Movement: Beitar. Married to Rosa Polansky.

Pomerantz, Shaya *Lodz, Poland, 22.12.1916*

Popolawski, Reuven *Bialystok, Poland, 1927*
Father: Ephraim.

Popolevski, David *Poland, 1926*
Father: Zaccharia.

Popovich, Chaim *Romania, 1924*

Porat, Efraim *Ostrowiec, Poland, 8.11.1919*
Parents: Tuvia & Nechama Pipek. Brother of Haim Pipek, who sailed on the *Wedgwood*.

Portnoi, Yakov *Poland, 1890*

Posanski, Chaim *Poland, 1914*

Posner, David *Poland, 1926*

Postavski, Mailer *Poland, 1920*

Potash, Refael *Bedzin, Poland, 1911*
Parents: Meir & Dvora.

Potashnik, Avraham *Poland, 1908*

Potashnik, Ida *Poland, 1917*

Potashnik, Yosef *Poland, 1910*

Preminger, Yosef *Vienna, Austria, 1923*
Father: Marcus.

Prisant, Chana *Poland, 1920*

Prisant, Zelda *Stopnica, Poland, 1924*
Parents: Meir & Miriam.

Protzel, Zipora *Poland, 1921*

Pruszanowski, Mira *Lodz, Poland, 29.10.1928*
Parents: Dov & Mirjam. Had a brother. In Lodz Ghetto and then Auschwitz. Transferred to Lenzing, Austria, where she was liberated. Taken from Salzburg by the Jewish Brigade to Santa Maria di Bagni. Married. Had two daughters.

Puchtik, Isak *Manewicz, Poland, 1926*
Parents: Abraham & Reisel.

Puke, Avraham *Kovno, Lithuania, 1927*
Was in Dachau.

Rabin, Sara *Russia, 1928*

Rabinovich, Hersch *Romania, 1918*

Racholski, Yishaya *Poland, 1930*

Rafaelowich, Leib *Poland, 1924*

Rafalowich, Noach *Poland, 1902*

Raich, Feibel *Romania 1891*

Raich, Meir *Poland, 1914*

Raich, Mordechai *Hungary, 1926*

Raichman, Mordke *Poland, 1927*

Raichman, Yechiel *Poland, 1907*

Raichman, Zalek Shalom *Poland, 1917*

Rainer, Jano *Hungary, 1922*

Raisner, Shmuel *Poland, 1919*

Raiter, Peretz *Poland, 1918*

Ratner, Yitzhak *Vilnius, Poland (now Lithuania), 1923*
Partisan in the Vilnius Ghetto. Close friend of Abba Kovner. Worked for the Bricha in Italy. A Nakam member. As a chemical engineer in the group's Paris headquarters, he worked out that bread brushed with arsenic would be the best means to poison German prisoners.

Rechnitz, Willi *Vienna, Austria, 1927*
Parents: Isidor & Hunda. Was in Theresienstadt and then transferred to Auschwitz in 1943. Survived death march to Feldafing in Germany. Changed name to Zeev. Killed in action in 1948.

Reiches, Rachel *Poland, 1904*
Parents: Josef & Guna. Hid on false papers.

Reiches, Yehudit *Kovno, Lithuania, 18.3.1926*
Parents: Mordechai & Rachel. Father, an import-exporter, was murdered in August 1941 in the round-up of intellectuals. Mother was a dressmaker who made clothes for German officers' wives in the ghetto.

Reindorf, Moshe *Warsaw, Poland, 1.5.1926*
Parents: Elimehk & Sabinah. Fled to the Soviet Union. Was in Kiev and Tambov. In Tradate. A friend of David Feingold on the ship. Married. Had three daughters.

Ring, Avraham *Poland, 1910*

Rinska, Sheindel *Poland, 1920*

Robert, Andre *Hungary, 1910*

Robinstein, Binyamin *Poland, 1925*

Robinstein, Regina *Poland, 1922*

Rockman, Chana *Poland, 1923*

Rockman, Fella *Poland, 1927*

Rockman, Miriam *Poland, 1923*

Rochwald, Yitzhak *Poland, 1919*

Roden, David *Poland, 1918*

Roderman, Regina *Poland, 1908*

Roderman, Senin *Poland, 1928*

Roisman, Baruch *Poland, 1904*

Roisman, Moshe *Poland, 1919*

Rolich, Nelli *Budapest, Hungary, 1919*
Parents: Szmuel & Rosa.

Rolnik, Avraham *Poland, 1915*

Roseman, Sara *Poland, 1911*

Ronski, Aryeh *Lodz, Poland, 22.10.1928*
Born Yehuda Leib. The brothers were in Auschwitz and part of the eighty-strong friends' group. They settled in Haifa.

Ronski, Avraham *Lodz, Poland, 1926*
Parents: Chaim & Dvora. Brother of Aryeh Ronski.

Ropstein, Hersch *Poland, 1921*

Rorman, Gutta *Poland, 1921*

Rosenberg, Bernard *Poland, 1921*

Rosenberg, Leib *Poland, 1928*

Rosenberg, Sheindel *Czechoslovakia, 1924*

Rosenberg, Zvi *Baranowicze, Poland (now Baranavichy, Belarus), 1912*
Born Hersch.

Rosenblat, Meshulam *Poland, 1927*

Rosenblum, Frida *Michow, Poland, 20.12.1922*
Married Moshe Witzman, who sailed on the *Wedgwood*.

Rosenblum, Hersch *Poland, 1916*

Rosenhaft, Shumuel *Poland, 1927*

Rosensin, Nathaniel *Poland, 1919*

Rosenthal, Yakov *Poland, 1914*

Rosenwax, Esther *Poland, 1920*

Rosenwax, Rachmiel *Poland, 1916*

Rosenfeld, Anna *Romania, 1922*
Parents: Yisrael & Minlah. Had a sister. In Auschwitz, then death marched to Gross-Rosen, Sachsenhausen, death march again to Mauthausen. Survived a death march to Gunskirchen, where she was liberated by the US Army. Married. Had two daughters. Died 2004.

Rosenkroin, Henia *Poland, 1919*

Rosenman, Israel *Poland, 1916*

Rosenman, Menachem *Poland, 1914*

Rosenman, Zila *Poland, 1924*

Rosenzweig, Ada *Poland, 1926*

Rosenzweig, Asher *Poland, 1916*

Rosenzweig, Luna *Poland, 1924*

Rosenzweig, Mordechai *Romania, 1919*

Rosenzweig, Rosa *Skarzysko-Kamienna, Poland, 14.10.1923*
Was in Bergen-Belsen.

Rosenzweig, Surika *Romania, 1922*

Rosenzweig, Zweig *Poland, 1916*

Rospsza, Rachmil *Poland, 1926.*
Registered in Piotrkow after the war.

Ross, Bella *Lodz, Poland, 1924*
With Yoskovitz Sheindel. Cousin of Dvora & Meir Ross.

Ross, Dvora *Lodz, Poland, 1925*
Cousin of Bella.

Ross, Meir *Lodz, Poland, 1920*
Cousin of Bella.

Rotdogel, Josef *Lodz, Poland, 15.2.1928*
Parents: Reuben & Chana-Lea. On the 27.11.1944 death march from Auschwitz to Sachsenhausen. Died 2005.

273

Rotfink, Elkana *Poland, 1913*

Roth, Asher *Vinohradiv, Czechoslovakia (now Ukraine), 9.9.1924*
Born Zoltan. Parents: Efraim Zvi & Cilka. Youth Movement: Zionist Youth.

Roth, Leon *Romania, 1909*

Roth, Moshe *Hungary, 1926*

Roth, Rivka *Czechoslovakia, 1923*

Roth, Shimon *Poland, 1927*

Rothenberg, Pinchas *Lodz, Poland, 1923*
Parents: Szmuel & Matl.

Rothenfodem, Bella *Poland, 1922*

Rotman, Refael *Romania, 1923*
Parents: Abraham & Sofika.

Rotstein, Shmuel *Poland, 1929*

Rozenek, Henrietta *Foscani, Romania, 1927*
Parents: Natan & Chana. Married Moshe Rozenek.

Rozenek, Moshe *Dzialoszyce, Poland, 20.9.1919*
Parents: Zeev & Cypora were Orthodox. Had three sisters and two brothers. In Miechow and Krakow ghettos. In camps in Krakow-Prokocim, Krakow-Plaszow, Wieliczka, Melk and Mauthausen, where he was liberated. Was a DP in Gusen, Ebensee and Salzburg. Married Henrietta. Had three sons. President of the Dzialoszyce Society in Israel. Died 2010.

Rozensaft, Shmuel *Lodz, Poland, 5.1.1927*
Parents: Israel & Mindel. Part of the friends' group of boys who were transported to Auschwitz and liberated at Gunskirchen.

Rubin, Chaim *Poland, 1924*

Rubin, Herman *Romania, 1916*

Rubin, Shlomo *Osorkow, Poland, 1912*
Parents: Leib-Eliezer & Riwka.

Runis, Michael *Poland, 1924*

Sabath, Zila *Poland, 1905*

Sacharov, Regina *Poland, 1923*

Sadicario, Isidor *Greece, 28.12.1917*
Parents: Jehuda & Towa. Had been in Stutthof.

Sadinsky, Arje Leib *Lithuania, 1929*
Brother of Samuel.

Sadinsky, Samuel *Kovno, Lithuania, 22.7.1932*
Parents: Frida & Matisas. Had a brother, Arje Leib. Father owned a factory. He left for Vilnius to find work when the Russians confiscated the factory and was shot in the Ponar forest. When the ghetto was liquidated, the two boys went with their mother to Tiegenhof near Stutthof where they were ordered off the train. She told Samuel, who was 13, to stay with his elder brother as she knew the men would be put to work and she had a better chance of surviving without the children. If she had kept Samuel with her, she was convinced that they would both have been killed immediately. She survived Stutthof and was liberated by the Red Army. The boys carried on to Landsberg. They were marched from the station to the cement factory. Samuel got work in the kitchen. Was being transported to Dachau by train when it was attacked by the US air force. Train stopped and he and his brother ran away. The Germans tried to shoot them but they escaped and hid for three days until they heard the church bells ringing and they knew that the war was over. They hid in skeleton plane on a fake airfield

used as a decoy for the Allied bombers. The Americans billeted them in a German house where they stayed for a day or two. There were taken by the Jewish Brigade to a DP camp in Munich and then to Italy. Was in the Villa Bencista in Fiesole. In Israel, Leib worked in the arms industry in Ramat Gan and he got a job as an electrician before joining the air force. In 1952 they received a letter from their mother. She had gone back to Lithuania. She had news that they were alive, and she was then caught and sent to Siberia when she tried to escape. After this she moved to Vilnius. The boys had an aunt in New York who connected them. Mother was trapped behind the Iron Curtain until 1956 when she left for Poland and emigrated to the US. He and Leib went to America "for an easier life" and to get an education. His brother left in 1951 and was drafted and sent to Korea. He arrived in 1953 and their mother in 1958. Married. Had three sons and a daughter.

Safier, Yosef *Poland, 1926*

Safirstein, Frida *Olkusz, Poland, 1921*
Parents: Chaim & Chana.

Safirstein, Israel *Poland, 1926*
Parents: Chaim & Chana.

Safirstein, Miriam *Belchatow, Poland, 1922*
Parents: Josef-Moshe & Chana.

Salbe, Yehuda *Warsaw, Poland, 1923*
Parents: Zwi & Sara.

Salinger, Yocheved *Bedzin, Poland, 1916*
Father: Isaac.

Saloniko, Avraham *Bucharest, Romania, 1924*
Father: Yakov.

Samborski, Moshe *Lodz, Poland, 1927*
Father: Shmuel. Religious Zionist family. In Auschwitz, Jaworzno and Gleiwitz. Survived death march to Blechhammer, where he was liberated 27.1.45. Returned to Lodz to search for family.

Sandarovich, Zalman *Czechoslovakia, 1926*

Sander, Moshe *Poland, 1921*

Sandik, Etta *Czechoslovakia, 1927*

Sandik, Leib *Piotrkow, Poland, 1920*
In the Lublin Ghetto. On the *Sharit Ha-Platah* list in Bavaria.

Sandovsky, Hanah *Starachowice, Poland, 26.10.1927*
Parents: Yaakov & Chava Kaufman were Hassids. Had two daughters and a son. The family were in the Starachowice Ghetto. Hanah was in Auschwitz and endured a death march. Liberated in Czechoslovakia. She returned to Starachowice and using the Greek bluff travelled to Graz and on to Villach where the Jewish Brigade took her to Italy. With husband Avraham Sandovsky. Later had one son and a daughter.

Sammel, Rivka *Poland, 1924*

Sayevitz, Mordechai *Czechoslovakia, 1914*
Locksmith after immigration. Lived in Hadera. He had blue eyes and was 5 ft 11.

Sayovic, Avraham *Czechoslovakia, 1928*

Sayovic, Miriam *Czechoslovakia, 1928*

Schanker, Chana *Poland, 1924*

Schayewitz, Gisa *Czechoslovakia, 1923*

Schayewitz, Juli *Romania, 1924*

Schcupak, Anshel *Lututow, Poland, 6.5.1928*
Parents: Hasim & Hayah. Had one brother. Was in the Lodz Ghetto, Auschwitz and on the death march to Mauthausen. Liberated at Gusen by the US Army. Returned to Lodz. In Landsberg DP camp. Changed name to Efrayim Zeevi. Married. Had a son and two daughters.

Scheinfeld, Israel *Czechoslovakia, 1925*

Schidlavitska, Fruma *Rokitno-Wolyn, Poland, 3.4.1929*
Parents: Avraham & Miriam Barman. Youth Movement: Hashomer Hatzair. Wife of Avraham Schidlavitski. Changed their name to Shiloni.

Schidlavitski, Avraham *Poland 3.9.1923*
Youth Movement: Hasoner Hatzair. Was 6 ft tall with fair hair and blue eyes. Wife Fruma.

Schiff, Yitzhak *Poland, 2.1.1926*
Parents: Nathan & Scheindel. Youth Movement: Hashomer Hatzair. Died 2015.

Schiffeldrim, Shimon *Poland, 1914*

Schiffeldrim, Shishka *Poland, 1919*

Schifka, David *Poland, 1917*

Schifka, Sheine *Poland, 1923*

Schitenberg, Adela *Poland, 1919*

Schitenberg, Eliezer *Poland, 1914*

Schlesinger, Efraim *Poland, 1923*

Schlibovska, Sara *Poland, 1919*

Schlosberg, Bluma *Lithuania, 1921*
Parents: Godl & Fira.

Schlosberg, Yishayahu *Lithuania, 1912*

Schmit, Efraim *Poland, 1921*

Schneider, Efraim *Poland, 1881*

Schneider, Reuven *Poland, 1923*
Nakam member.

Schnisok, Leiser *Poland, 1924*

Schnitzer, Meir *Sighet, Romania, 1922*

Schnizer, Isaac *Krakow, Poland, 1926*
Sole survivor of his family. Youth group: Hashomer Hatzair. Killed 1948 defending Kibbutz Dan. Was critically injured in a burst of gunfire and died from loss of blood.

Schnizer, Sonia *Romania, 1926*

Schor, Ignetz *Romania, 1923*

Schper, Shmuel *Poland, 1917*

Schperber, Shaya *Romania, 1925*

Schperberg, Rivka *Poland, 1922*

Schperberg, Zafa *Poland, 1924*

Schperling, Rosa *Poland, 1922*
Parents: Shloma & Sara.

Schperling, Shlomo *Latvia, 1919*

Schpigel, Shmuel *Poland, 1917*

Schpir, Ruth *Poland, 1924*

Schpir, Sara *Poland, 1922*

Schpir, Tova *Poland, 1927*

Schpitz, David *Poland, 1915*

Schpitz, Shmuel *Hungary, 1920*

Schpitzer, Shaul Zvi *Poland, 1923*

Schreiber, Israel *Boryslaw, Poland (now Boryslav, Ukraine), 1.1.1927*
Parents: Bernhard & Dvora, had 14 children, two of whom were adopted. Only brother Josef survived. In Boryslaw Ghetto and camps at Wieliczka, Krakow-Plaszow, Mauthausen and Gusen. Survived a death march. Went into hiding. Was in a DP camp in Germany. Fought in the 1948 War but then moved to Germany and Sweden, and

back to Germany before settling in the USA. He was employed as a supervisor for D.A. Rosow's in Newington, and also worked for County Distributors in East Windsor. Had a son. Died 2011.

Schtrosa, Leiser *Hungary, 1927*

Schudenz, Avraham *Poland, 1922*

Schulman, Sara *Poland, 1928*

Schuster, Asher *Poland, 1906*

Schwartz, Anschel *Romania, 1927*

Schwartz, Chaviva *Romania, 1929*

Schwartz, Imra *Hungary, 1925*

Schwartz, Yosef *Romania, 1920*

Schwartz, Meir Hersch *Romania, 1912*

Schwartz, Mendel *Romania, 1921*

Schwartz, Moshe *Hungary, 1924*

Schwartz, Moshe *Poland, 1928*

Schwartz, Moshe *Poland, 1921*

Schwartz, Rosa *Poland, 1929*

Schwartz, Rivka *Romania, 1908*

Schwartz, Solomon *Hungary, 1926*

Schwartz, Shaya *Romania, 1906*

Schwartz, Yehoshua (Uzi) *Bucharest, Romania, 28.01.1925*
Parents: Yosef & Sophia. Born Oseas.

Schwartz, Yeta *Lithuania, 1918*

Schwartzbaum, Arthur *Poland, 1922*

Schwartzbaum, Mendel *Romania, 1924*

Schwartzbaum, Rosa *Poland, 1925*

Schwartzboim, David *Poland, 15.7.1919*
Parents: Yaakov & Rivka. Changed name to Shahar David. Youth Movement: Hashomer Hatzair. With wife Frania Shahar.

Schwimer, Shlomo *Poland, 1925*
Parents: Leib & Riwka.

Sega, Agnes *Hungary, 1926*

Segal, Bela *Romania*

Segal, Berl *Romania, 1925*

Segal, Frida *Poland, 1927*

Segal, Karol *Romania, 1927*
Parents: Josef & Klara.

Segal, Malka *Lithuania, 1927*
In Mariampol during the war and registered in Lodz.

Segal, Zacharia *Bucharest, Romania, 1921*
Parents: Yosef & Klara.

Segalson, Arie *Kovno, Lithuania, 9.9.1923*
Brother of Elchanan. In Landsberg-Kaufering camp in Dachau. Liberated 2.2.1945 in Waakirchen by the US Army. Endured a death march. Was in the Ichud Zionist pioneering training programme (*hachshara*) in La Picciola, Italy. Spent two years in the IDF. Studied law at Tel Aviv University and became a senior judge. Married. Had two daughters. Wrote *In the Heart of the Citadel: A View from within the Destruction of Jewish Kovno*. Died 2014.

Segalson, Elchanan *Kovno, Lithuania, 16.6.1929*
Youth group: Beitar. Active in the underground in the Kovno Ghetto, as an arms smuggler. Was a member of Irgun. Was in La Picciola, Italy, on the Ichud Zionist training programme. Killed 1948 providing cover for his retreating colleagues. Had been involved in the defence of Tel Aviv, the attack on Jaffa and conquest of Manshiya and Yehuda. Pictured with his brother Arie in Italy.

Segalson, Raya *Poland, 1900*
Father: Benjamin. Wife of Shmuel Segalson and mother of Elchanan and Arie.

Segalson, Shmuel *Kovno, Lithuania, 1899*
In Landsberg-Kaufering camp. Father of Arie & Elchanan. After liberation he was in St Ottilien. His brother Moshe was a member of the Council of the Liberated Jews of Bavaria.

Selinger, Jechezkel *Boryslaw, Poland (now Boryslav, Ukraine), 1904*
Parents: Szloma & Rywka.

Selinger, Moshe *Poland, 1910*

Selinger, Sara *Poland, 1909*

Selinsky, Tanya *Kovno, Lithuania, 3.3.1924*
Parents: Rachel & Yakov had three sons and three daughters. She fled the Kovno Ghetto and hid in Deblin until liberated by the Red Army. Travelled to Vilnius and from there to Bialystok and on to Czechoslovakia, Hungary and Austria. Jewish Brigade took her to Bari where she spent time in Santa Maria di Bagni. Married Shimon Brindt, who sailed on the *Wedgwood*, and became Yafah Brindt.

Shabasson, Avraham *Kuznitz, Poland, 1892*

Shabasson, Godel *Kuznitz, Poland, 1923*
Parents: Abraham & Zecha. In the Kozienice Ghetto.

Shabasson, Miriam *Warsaw, Poland, 1920*
Parents: Efraim & Stella.

Shalmon, Hayim *Radom, Poland, 26.11.1928*
Parents: Aharon & Dobrah Shlufman. Had a brother and a sister. In Radom Ghetto

and Szydlowiec Ghetto. In camps at Plonki and Sosnowice before being taken to Auschwitz II. Survived a death march to Mauthausen. Liberated in Gunskirchen by the US Army. In DP camp in Salzburg. Jewish Brigade took him to Italy. In Florence and Genoa. Married. Had three sons.

Shalom, Samuel *Thessaloniki, Greece, 10.12.1918*
Was in Mauthausen.

Shechner, Gabriel *Poland, 1927*
Parents: Jehoshua & Nechama.

Sheinman, Miriam *Poland, 1925*

Shimsha, Yakov *Poland, 1921*

Shinar, Zeev *Krakow, Poland, 1922*
Parents: Yisrael & Prina. Born Vilek. Family was sent to Belzec. Shinar was imprisoned in the Montelupich prison in Krakow as a forced labourer. After the war he met Shimon Lustgarten and Yehuda Maimon. They joined Nakam. Travelled to Tarvisio and joined Harmatz's group based in Nuremberg. Arrived in Italy just weeks before the *Wedgwood* sailed. On arrival in Palestine went to Kibbutz Ein Hahoresh. Joined the Palyam in 1947 and worked on the *Pan Crescent*, which brought refugees from Romania. Later went to Neve Eitan in Beit Shean Valley and worked in the sanitation department of the Emek Hefer Regional Council. Died 1983.

Shlomkovich, Basia *Poland, 1928*

Shlomovich, Shimon *Czernowitz, Romania (now Chernivtsi, Ukraine), 1923*
Was in camps in Berlovka and Varvarka.

Shmulevitch, David *Wielun, Poland, 4.05.1921*
Parents: Faygeh & Asher were Orthodox. Had three brothers and three sisters. The

family were in Wielun and Lodz ghettos. David went into hiding. He gave evidence at trials after the war. Married. Had two sons.

Sholovich, Menachem *Lodz, Poland, 15.5.1930*
Lives in Haifa.

Shtayer, Avraham *Przedmoscie, Poland, 15.7.1914*
Parents: David & Hayah were Hassids. Had seven sisters. In the Lodz Ghetto he married Helah and had a daughter Anya, who were both killed. In Auschwitz and Stutthof. Then in Dresden-Bernsdorf and Co and Theresienstadt. Escaped from a death march and was liberated in Ober-poyritz in Germany. After the war was in Salzburg, Milan, Genoa and Tradate. Remarried. Had a daughter.

Shubitz, Mordechai *Kovno, Lithuania, 1917*
Mother: Bela. Had three brothers; one called Avreymel died in the Holocaust. Married.

Shulman, Perl *Poland, 1924*
Parents: Eisig & Chana.

Shyimer, Aba *Lodz, Poland, 1.3.1921*
Parents: David & Hinda. The family were in the Lodz Ghetto. He was in camps at Markstädt, Funfteichen, Gross-Rosen and death-marched to Buchenwald. Then in Schönbeck before escaping and hiding in Gommern under a false name. He was helped by people called Schultz and Zdanek until the Russians arrived. He was then in Chrzanow, Zarki, Bedzin and Lodz. He used the Greek bluff to travel to Czechoslovakia. In Landsberg DP camp. Married. Had a son and a daughter. Changed his name to Shahiyani.

Silard, Julia *Leva, Hungary, 1919*
In Wurzen camp.

Silber, Rachel *Lithuania, 1926*
Youth Movement: Hashomer Hatzair. Married Schiff Yizak Wolf, who sailed on the *Wedgwood*.

Silberberg, Chana *Poland, 1929*

Silberman, Chana *Poland, 1912*

Silberman, David *Poland, 1911*

Silberman, Ida *Tomaszow, Poland, 1915*
Father: Yitzhak.

Silberman, Richard *Poland, 1920*

Silberman, Shimshon *Poland, 1916*

Silberman, Shulem *Poland, 1922*

Silberspitz, Eduard *Romania, 1924*

Silberstein, Leib *Poland, 1928*

Silbiger, Avraham *Poland, 1920*
Father: David.

Singer, Esther *Poland, 1924*
Father: Hadi.

Singer, Hanna *Hrubieszow, Poland, 1920*
Father: Beer.

Singer, Moshe *Yugoslavia, 1921*

Singer, Reuven *Austria, 1929*

Sirok, Pesach *Poland, 1919*

Skorziles, Israel *Poland, 1916*

Skowronski, Eliyahu *Poland, 1920*

Sliwkin, Chaim *Poland, 1927*

Smilanski, Dvora *Poland, 1922*

Sobol, David *Dubno, Poland (now Ukraine), 1922*

Solkovski, Abraham *Poland, 1912*

Solkovski, Mordechai *Poland, 1910*

Solnik, Avraham *France, 5.3.1929*
Parents: Refael & Rivka. Was in the children's home La Feuilleraie in Saint-Raphaël. Saved by a Syrian Jew, Moussa Abadi, and his future wife, Odette Rosenstock, who hid Jewish children in Catholic schools, convents and with families. They saved 527 children in all.

Solomon, Feige *Romania, 1925*

Solomon, Leiser *Romania, 1921*

Solomon, Yeshayahu *Poland, 1912*

Solomon, Yeshayahu *Czechoslovakia, 1928*
Father: Meir.

Solshenki, Pesia *Lithuania, 1921*

Sosenboim, Chaim *Romania, 1906*

Spiegel, Yosef (Gingi) *Baranowicze, Poland (now Baranavichy, Belarus), 10.5.1927*
Parents: Israel & Golda. Two of his sisters went to Palestine before the war. His parents and two brothers were murdered. He hid in the countryside. His younger sister also survived and went to Krakow after the war and joined a youth group to make *aliyah*. Youth Movement: Hashomer Hatzair. Founded Kibbutz Megiddo after the 1948 war. Married and had three children. Died 2013.

Srebrenik, Yehuda Arie *Czestochowa, Poland, 1909*

Stein, Hersch *Poland, 1924*

Stein, Yitzhak *Romania, 1929*

Steinbaum, Yosef *Poland, 1921*

Steinbock, Israel *Poland, 1902*

Steinkritzer, Baruch *Lipa Ostrog, Rivne Oblast, Poland (now Ukraine), 1920*
Killed in 1948.

Steinmatz, Aidel *Berehove, Czechoslovakia, 9.6.1920*
Parents: Asher & Persil Anschel. With husband Yosef Steinmatz.

Steinmatz, Ezra *Dubowa, Czechoslovakia, 1923/4*
Parents: Jacob & Eta. Brother of Yosef.

Steinmatz, Shlomo Yosef *Czechoslovakia, 20.5.1922*
Parents: Yaakov Shraga & Ettia Frumet. Brother of Ezra.

Steinwasser, Elsa *Germany, 1925*

Stern, Chaim *Melchow, Poland, 10.9.1924*
Was in Mauthausen and in DP camps in Linz and Munich.

Stern, Michael *Romania, 1929*

Stern, Moshe *Oradea Mare, Romania, 1923*
Parents: Leib & Gita.

Stern, Waissman Shmuel *Poland, 1915*

Stern, Yosef *Mukacevo, Czechoslovakia (now Ukraine), 8.4.1927*
Parents: Hinda & Shmuel. Had a sister, Tsiporah. Was in Sevlus Ghetto and Auschwitz. In Mauthausen, Melk, Amstetten and Ebensee, where he was liberated by the Americans. In a *hachshara aliyah* training camp in Germany after the war. Fought in 1948. Married. Had a son and daughter.

Sternberg, Chaim *Poland, 1925*

Sternberg, Michael *Lodz, Poland, 1917*
Parents: Pesach & Rina.

Sternboim, Batia *Poland, 1924*

Stolerman, Chaim *Czernowitz, Romania (now Chernivtsi, Ukraine), 1915*

Strelski, Haim *Sarny, Poland, 2.6.1926*
Parents: Yekutiel & Tseytl. Born Eliezer. Had three sisters. He spent the war in

Perm in the USSR. After the war he went to Lodz and from there went via Czechoslovakia to Biberach in Germany. In Tradate. Youth Group: Hashomer Hatzair.

Strelski, Henyah *Staszow, Poland, 8.9.1928*
Parents: Shmuel & Simhah Buchman had four daughters and one son. In camps in Kielce-HASAG and Skarzysko-Kamienna and Leipzig. Survived a death march and was liberated by the Red Army. Joined a group of Hashomer Hatzair in Czestochowa. Married Haim Strelski, she travelled with him on the *Wedgwood*. Had three daughters.

Strom, Israel *Siauliai, Lithuania, 1919*
Was in Bavaria.

Strom, Moshe *Poland, 1916*

Strosberg, Breindel *Poland, 1909*

Suchman, Shlomo *Poland, 1927*

Suzak, Hali *Poland, 1925*

Swartz, Meyer *Lodz, Poland, 25.8.1929*
Parents: David Wolf & Raja Srebrnagora. Father was a furrier. Family was Orthodox. His father wanted him to be a doctor. In Lodz Ghetto and Auschwitz. Survived a death march to Sachsenhausen and Mauthausen. In Lieberose and liberated at Gunskirchen. He left Israel for the USA in 1950, where he ran a grocery business. Part of the group of friends who ended up at the Villa Bencista in Fiesole. Married. Had two children.

Szafran, Aszer *Poland, 1929*

Szatmary, Alexandra *Czechoslovakia, 1912*

Szatmary, Rachel *Czechoslovakia, 1924*

Szirtes, Miriam Maria *Budapest, Hungary, 6.6.1932*

Szolowicz, Mendel *Lodz, Poland, 15.5.1929*
Was in Mauthausen.

Szurek, Gisela *Romania, 1922*

Szurek, Leib *Romania, 1928*

Taradaika, Feibish *Tomaszow Mazowiecki, Poland, 27.2.1926*
Changed name to Gershoni Shraga. Youth group: Dror-Habonim.

Tenenbaum, Feivel *Krasnik, Poland, 1923*
Father: Yekutiel.

Terkeltaub, Moshe *Poland, 19.2.1927*
Was on the 27.11.1944 death march from Auschwitz to Sachsenhausen.

Teitelbaum, Hersch *Poland, 1922*

Teufel, Hersch *Poland, 1920*

Tischler, Alfred *Uzhhorod, Czechoslovakia (now Ukraine), 1928*
Parents: Leopold & Miriam.

Tischler, Chaim *Camarzana, Romania, 1925* Parents: Lipa & Ester.

Tischler, Moshe *Poland, 1917*

Tischler, Yechiel *Lodz, Poland, 17.5.1921*

Tischman, Sara *Poland, 1920*

Tobias, Rivka *Lithuania, 1918*

Tobias, Yakov *Czestochowa, Poland, 1912*
Father: Beer.

Torner, Ela *Poland, 1924*
Father: Leib.

Torner, Harri *Austria, 1921*

Tosk, Hersch *Poland, 1930*

Tosk, Schmil Leib *Poland, 1926*

Traiman, Rivka *Poland, 1925*

Trakinski, Chaya *Vilnius, Poland (now Lithuania), 1925*

Traube, Fella *Poland, 1908*

Traube, Yehuda Leib *Vilnius, Poland (now Lithuania), 1916*

Treger, Zelda *Vilnius, Poland, 16.6.1920*
Parents: Zachariah, a businessman, & Genia, a dentist. When Treger was 12 years old, her father moved to Warsaw due to financial difficulties and her connection with him was severed. When she was 14, her mother died and she moved to a relative's home in Vilna. Youth group: Hashomer Hatzair. Trained as a kindergarten teacher. Her older sister Nehama went to Palestine in 1935. In 1939, she was in a youth group in Czestochowa preparing to immigrate to Palestine. She returned to Vilnius but due to illness was unable to travel east to the Soviet Union when the Germans invaded. Joined FPO partisan group in the Vilnius Ghetto and served as a company courier. In the Rudniki forest, Treger belonged to Abba Kovner's Revenge group. After the liberation Kovner sent Treger to search for surviving members of Hashomer Hatzair and organise them for immigration to Palestine. Treger worked as a founder member of the Bricha movement in Lvov and Lublin. In Lublin, Kovner recruited her to Nakam; and she and her husband, Senka Nisanilevich, who had also been a partisan, were sent to Italy, where their task was to transfer funds to the revenge units, guard the revenge activists and be responsible for getting them to safety after operations. Settled in Netanya and later Tel Aviv. Worked as a kindergarten teacher. Had a son and a daughter. Died 1987.

Tsukert, Yakov *Krasnik, Poland, 10.6.1924*
Parents: Binyamin & Soshanah, who had three sons and three daughters. Family in the Krasnik Ghetto. In camps at Budzyn, Wieliczka, Flossenbürg and Hersbruck and was liberated in Dachau. Endured a death march. In DP camps in Munich, Traunstein and Modena in Italy. Youth group: Beitar. Married. Had two sons.

Turkenich, Yehoshua *Poland, 1930*

Turkenitz, Ascher *Horodno, Poland (now Belarus), 6.7.1927*
Parents: Schmuel & Hanah. The family were Orthodox. Had two brothers. Hid in the forests. Joined Misura Otriad group of partisans. Was in the Soviet Army. Deserted in Germany. Went to Lodz, then to Landsberg. Settled in Kibbutz Kinneret. Married. Had a son and a daughter.

Turuk, Aba *Baranowicze, Poland (now Baranavichy, Belarus), 28.2.1928*
Youth Movement: Dror-Habonim. Changed name to Rotem Avinoam. Was in Abba Kovner's Nakam group.

Unterfort, Chana *Bukovina, Romania, 1921*
Parents: Jeszajahu & Perl.

Uren, Zura *Poland, 1905*

Urman, Shulem *Poland, 1928*

Valdhorn, Dobkah Tova *Gorlice, Poland, 4.7.1919*
Parents: Brish & Leah, who were Orthodox and had four daughters and five sons. She wanted to leave for Palestine and fled with her first husband, Julek Frohlich, a Zionist youth activist, trying to get to Lithuania. Her family, including her four-year-old sister, died in Belzec and she was

the sole survivor. In the Vilnius Ghetto she gave birth to a daughter, but the authorities took the child away as pregnancy was illegal in the ghetto. In her testimony she does not specify where the child was taken. Deported to Kaiserwald in Riga, where she worked in the AEG factory. Transferred to Strasdenhof, then Stutthof and Tourn. Her husband died in Klooga and his entire family perished in Belzec. Liberated in Lipno by the Red Army. After the war she went to Gorlice via Warsaw and Bialystok and from there to Krakow. Travelled with the Bricha to Prague and along the way met her second husband, Leopold Valdhorn. They went to Romania and into Italy, where they stayed at Santa Maria di Bagni. Had two sons. Youth Movement: Zionist Youth.

Valdhorn, Leopold Arie Dortmund, Germany, 6.12.1919
His family all died in the war. Was in Mauthausen. Husband of Dobkah Tova.

Valdman, Shamai Russia, 1922

Vaskovinik, Nechama Lithuania, 1929

Vladimirski, Rivka Sosnowiec, Poland, 15.1.1917

Vladimirski, Zvi Sosnowiec, Poland, 20.10.1916
Born Hersch. Youth Movement: Hashomer Hatzsair. Husband of Rivka.

Vlodavski, Chanan Poland, 1917

Volechki, Mickael Wielun, Poland, 1925
Parents: Hana & Melech, who were Orthodox Jews and had four sons and two daughters. In the Lodz Ghetto and camps at Krzesin (Poland), Eberswalde-Britz (Germany), Auschwitz, Siegmar-Schönau and Hohenstein-Ernstthal. Endured death

marches and was liberated in Czechoslovakia. In a DP camp in Salzburg. Taken by the Jewish Brigade to Italy. Was in Santa Maria di Bagni.

Volkoviski, Avraham Poland, 1925

Wachs, Bela Poland, 1924

Wachs, Moshe Poland, 1920

Wachsberg, Sara Poland, 1926

Wachselman, Tova Poland, 1927

Wail, Rosa Poland, 1925

Wainberger, Binyamin Hungary, 1928

Waissman, Shlomo Poland, 1917

Walach, Regina Rzeszow, Poland, 1916
Parents: Shalom & Berta.

Waler, Yitzhak Poland, 1919

Wand, Avraham Ternopil, Poland (now Ukraine), 1928
Father: Yehoshua.

Wasnizki, Chaim Poland, 1929

Wasserman, Yakov Poland, 1927
Youth Movement: Hashomer Hatzair.

Wasserman, Yehoshua Latvia, 1927

Wasserteil, Mordechai (Max) Shin Czechoslovakia, 26.8.1923

Wechsler, Max Poland, 1915

Wechsler, Renata Poland, 1924

Weil, Benjamin Lodz, Poland, 1921
Father: Yitzhak. In 1939 he went to Bialystok and from there to the Soviet Union. He worked in Gomel and Mogilev.

Weiman, Miriam Baranowicze, Poland (now Baranavichy, Belarus), 1.12.1928
Youth Movement: Hashomer Hatzair. Married Moshe Liver, who was on the *Wedgwood*.

283

Weimann, Rivka *Osowa Wyszka, Kostopol, Poland, 25.3.1926*
Born Taroshinska. Youth Movement: Hashomer Hatzair.

Wein, Yakov *Romania, 1924*

Weinberg, Yitzhak *Lodz, Poland, 4.6.1929*
On the death march from Sachsenhausen to Mauthausen. Was in Kibbutz Alonim.

Weiner, Mendel Hadasa *Warsaw, Poland, 1923*
Father: Moshe.

Weiner, Yitzhak *Sosnowiec, Poland, 1922*
Father: Issachar.

Weingard, Avraham *Baranowicze, Poland (now Baranavichy, Belarus)*

Weinrib, Shraga *Poland, 1924*
Changed name to Yinon Shraga.

Weinstark Dora *Poland, 1928*
Father: Leib.

Weinstein, Akiva *Poland, 1927*

Weinstein, Feige *Romania, 1901*

Weinstein, Rivka *Romania, 1923*

Weinstein Yosef *Lvov, Poland (now Lviv, Ukraine), 1.09.1924*

Weintraub, Arie *Poland, 1927*

Weintraub, Eva *Poland, 1918*
Father: Dov.

Weintraub, Rosa *Poland, 1930*

Weintraub, Yakov *Poland, 1924*

Weintraub, Zelda *Poland, 1913*

Weintraub, Zvi Moshe *Poland, 1913*

Weiss, Avraham *Hungary, 1928*

Weiss, Erna *Hungary, 1921*

Weiss, Mordechai *Hungary, 1926*

Weiss, Sultan *Romania, 1925*

Weiss, Vasili Zeev *Romania, 1924*

Weiss, Yehuda *Hungary, 1921*

Weiss, Yitzhak *Hungary, 1925*

Weissblat, Dina *Poland, 1925*

Weissblat, Ida *Poland, 1921*

Weissblat, Leib *Poland, 1927*

Weissblat, Moshe David *Poland, 1921*

Weissblat, Shlomo *Poland, 1926*

Werthaimer, Moshe *Balassagyarmat, Hungary, 1916*
Father: Yakov, a grocer. Orthodox but not Zionist upbringing and went to Jewish schools. In Mauthausen and Gunskirchen. Endured a death march. Returned home and met two surviving sisters. Went to Budapest and via Akiva religious movement to Italy.

Werthaimer, Sara *Hungary, 1905*

Werthaimer, Yakov *Bratislava, Czechoslovakia (now Slovakia), 1929*
Father: Yitzhak.

Werzberger, Ignetz *Romania, 1924*

Westelshnaider, Nathan *Poland, 1922*

Westreich, Moshe *Lasienk, Poland, 1927*
Parents: Iccak & Golda.

Westreich, Naftali *Lizensk, Poland, 1927*
Brother of Moshe. Was in Linz and Bavaria.

Widman, Pina *Romania, 1919*

Wiener, Alter *Chrzanow, Poland, 1926*
Deported to Blechhammer in Upper Silesia (modern-day Blachownia Slaska), then to Brande and Gross Masselwitz. In Klettendorf, then Waldenburg. Liberated by Red Army. Went to Krakow as he heard the JDC were helping survivors.

From there he went to Katowice and Sosnowiec where he heard there was a group organising to go to Palestine, where he had two uncles and two aunts. The Bricha took them to the Jewish Brigade in Italy. Author of *64735: From a Name to a Number*.

Wilczkowski, Eliezer *Lodz, Poland, 23.8.1927*

One of the boys in the Auschwitz friends' group and close to Meyer Swartz. He survived death marches to Sachsenhausen, Mauthausen and Gunskirchen, where he was liberated. Went to Massachusetts. Known as Larry Wilskofsky.

Wilk, Chaim *Poland, 1921*

Father: Asher.

Wilk, Ruchama *Poland, 1927*

Father: Yezekiel.

Winarnik, Shmuel *Poland, 1909*

Wirzberger, Nechama *Romania, 1925*

Wisel, Avraham *Czechoslovakia, 1926*

Witrag, Yosef *Hungary, 1927*

Witzman, Moshe *Olkusz, Poland, 20.12.1918*

With wife Frida Rosenblum.

Wolberg, Gavriel *Hajduhadhaz, Hungary, 9.9.1926*

Father: Ysrael Shlomoh. In Hajduhadhaz Ghetto, Mauthausen and Gunskirchen. In Hörsching DP camp and a *hakhsharot* in Hungary. He was in Albiate in Italy and Tradate. Changed name to Hartov. Married. Had two sons.

Wolman, Avraham *Poland, 1923*

Worm, Shulem *Poland, 1884*

Wormbrot, Dora *Poland, 1928*

Woznicki, Chaim Turek *Poland, 7.8.1929*

Was on the death march from Auschwitz to Sachsenhausen on 27.11.1944.

Wrobel, Avraham *Poland, 1921*

Wurzak, Yona *Lodz, Poland, 24.9.1928*

Parents: Henyah & Moseh Taubah. Had two brothers. Youth Movement: Hashomer Hatzair. In Lodz Ghetto, Auschwitz, Christianstadt in Germany and Kratzau in Czechoslovakia, where she was liberated by the Red Army. Went to Sosnowiec, where she met her husband, Shraga Nitsberg. They went to Föhrenwald DP camp in Bavaria. Had one son and a daughter.

Yaari, Naomi *Poland*

Born Frummerman

Yaari, Pinchas *Hungary, 1919*

Yaari, Shamai *Poland, 4.4.1922*

Previously member of Waldman Youth Movement: Dror Habonim. Fled to the Soviet Union when the war broke out. Served in the Red Army. Husband of Naomi.

Yaffa, Eta *Vilnius, Poland (now Lithuania), 1926*

Father: Avraham.

Yakobovich, Yakov *Poland, 1926*

Was in Genoa with Yehuda Erlich.

Yankalevich, Elika *Romania, 1922*

Yankalevich, Lea *Latvia, 1925*

Yankelevich, Binyamin *Romania, 1917*

Yechiel, Leon *Greece, 1910*

Yehuda, Mosze *Thessaloniki, Greece, 1925*

Parents: Szmuel & Mirkada.

Yewelewich, Mala *Poland, 1927*

285

Yitzhak, David *Greece, 1917*

Yitzhak, Moshe *Greece, 1923*

Yoffe, Feibush *Riga, Latvia, 1922*
Father: Israel.

Yoffe, Ida *Poland, 1918*

Yoffe, Rosa *Sosnowiec, Poland, 1924*
Father: Yosef.

Yoffe, Yehoshua *Novogrodek, Poland (now Navahrudak, Belarus), 1915*

Yomshtik, Hayah Kiewan *Poland, 24.3.1922*
Parents: Tsvi & Tsiporah. Had three brothers. In the Derazhne Ghetto. Escaped a death march. Hid in the forests until the Red Army arrived. On liberation, went to Rovno and from there to Lublin and Romania. From Graz the Jewish Brigade took her to Villa Bencista in Fiesole. Married and had two sons.

Yona, Yakov *Thessaloniki, Greece, 1925*
A friend of Moshe Ha-Elion with whom he had been at school. In Auschwitz. Lived in Tel Aviv. Died 1985.

Yoskovitz, Sheindel *Lodz, Poland, 7.12.1919*
Parents: Sander & Dvora Rinsky. With cousins Dvora Ross, Meir Ross and Bella Ross.

Young, Samuel *Novoselytsia, Romania (now Ukraine), 1.2.1920*

Zamsstein, Yitzhak *Poland, 1924*
Father: Yaakov.

Zauberman, Bela *Poland, 1924*

Zelik, Lea *Romania, 1928*

Zernikovski, Kalman *Poland, 1922*

Zilber, Yehudit *Janowo, Poland, 27.3.1925*
Parents: Yakov & Fridah Ashenberg, who were Hassidic Jews. They had one son and three daughters. Hid near Jarocin in farms and forests and was a member of the Kovpak partisan brigade. Travelled with her husband, Zeev Zilber. Later had two sons and a daughter.

Zilber, Zeev *Poland, 1918*
Born Wolf Silber.

Zimmerman, Chana *Poland, 1928*

Zimmerman, Yosef *Poland, 1926*

Zion, Moshe *Greece 1919*

Zmigrod, Lola *Bedzin, Poland, 1926*
Parents: Solomon & Jadwiga.

Zmigrod, Seba *Bedzin, Poland, 1926*
Parents: Solomon & Jadwiga.

NOTES ON SOURCES

I found two websites invaluable in researching this book. I am indebted to the United States Holocaust Memorial Museum, www.ushmm.org, and the USC Shoah Foundation, https://sfi.usc.edu/. I also found the websites of the Memorial and Museum of Auschwitz-Birkenau, www.auschwitz. org, the genealogy website Jewish Gen, www.jewishgen.org, the American Joint Jewish Distribution Committee (JDC), www.jdc.org, the Institute for Jewish Research (YIVO), www.yivo.org, and Israel's World Holocaust Remembrance Centre, Yad Vashem, www.yadvashem.org, a mine of information. The websites of the Palyam, www.palyam.org, and the Ghetto Fighters' House museum were key resources. Tracing the names of the *Wedgwood* people began at the Bintivey Ha'apala Clandestine Jewish Immigration and Research Centre, http://maapilim.org.il.

My thanks go to the following authors for giving me a broad understanding of the background to the stories related in this book. Yehuda Bauer's books *Out of the Ashes: The Impact of American Jews on Post-Holocaust European Jewry* (Pergamon, 1989), *Flight and Rescue: Brichah—The Organized Escape of the Jewish Survivors of Eastern Europe, 1944–1948* (Random House, 1970) and *American Jewry and the Holocaust: The American Joint Distribution Committee 1939–45* (Wayne State University Press, 2017) are the starting point for anyone interested in this topic.

Key points of reference were Ilya Ehrenburg and Vasily Grossman, *The Complete Black Book of Russian Jewry* (Transaction Publishers, 2003), Amos Ettinger, *Blind Jump: The Story of Shaike Dan* (Cornwall Books, 1992), Antol Gill, *The Journey Back from Hell: Memoirs of Concentration Camp Survivors* (Sharpe Books, 2018), Tom Segev, *The Seventh Million: The Israelis and the Holocaust* (Picador, 2000), Dan Stone, *The Liberation of the Camps: The End of the Holocaust and Its Aftermath* (Yale University Press, 2015), Ben Shepard, *The Long Road Home: The Aftermath of the Second World War* (Anchor, 2012) and Idith Zertal, *From Catastrophe to Power: Holocaust Survivors and the Emergence of Israel* (University of California Press, 1998). The information in these books allowed me to gain an understanding of the period and taught me what questions I should ask the survivors whom I interviewed.

I have always found the novels of Aharon Appelfeld inspiring and his last book, *The Man Who Never Stopped Sleeping* (Schocken Books, 2017), was especially useful when it came to understanding the survivors I was interviewing.

Finally, no journey is complete without a guidebook, and my companion was Martin Winstone's *Holocaust Sites of Europe: An Historical Guide* (I.B. Tauris, 2010).

1. RIVNE: BANDERA'S VICTORY

Yehuda Bauer's account of events in Rovno in 1944 and the memorial book for the Jews of Rovno on www.jewishgen.org were my starting points. Most of the material in this chapter is based on my interviews with Vik Chymshyt, Ephraim German and Rabbi Schneersohn in Rivne, Ukraine, in February 2017 and my interview with Yitzhak Kaplan, in Haifa, Israel, in January 2018.

2. AUSCHWITZ: WHO'S FOR LIFE?

The museums at Belzec and Treblinka and the Memorial and Museum of Auschwitz-Birkenau, www.auschwitz.org, are themselves huge resources as are their websites. I drew inspiration from Primo Levi's *If This Is a Man* and *The Truce* (Abacus, 2003). Central to this chapter are my interviews with Dani Chanoch in Karmei Yosef and Moshe Ha-Elion in Bat Yam in Israel in January 2018. Moshe Ha-Elion's book *The Straits of Hell: The Chronicle of a Salonikan Jew in the Nazi Extermination Camps Auschwitz, Mauthausen, Melk, Ebensee* (Bibliopolis, 2005) provided many background details and understanding as did Dani Chanoch's film *Pizza in Auschwitz* (2008). I also watched with interest *Numbered* (2012). Gideon Greif's *We Wept without Tears: Testimonies of the Jewish Sonderkommando from Auschwitz* (Yale University Press, 2005) provided details of the life of Eliezer Eisenschmidt but also gave me a deeper understanding of Auschwitz and Holocaust survivors.

3. VILNIUS: HARMATZ'S CHOICE

Much of the story of Josef Harmatz's life comes from his memoir *From the Wings: A Long Journey* (Book Guild, 1998) and his 1998 testimony at the

Imperial War Museum. The context was explained to me in my interviews with Rosa Bieliauskiene and Fania Brantsovskaya in Vilnius, Lithuania, in July 2017. For understanding the life of Abba Kovner, Dina Porat's *The Fall of a Sparrow: The Life and Times of Abba Kovner* (Stanford University Press, 2000) was helpful.

4. POLAND: THE HOMECOMING

Email conversations with Alter Wiener were crucial for this chapter. He gave me permission to draw on his memoir *64735: From a Name to a Number* (Author House, 2010). Key sources were interviews in Poland with Bogdan Bialek in Kielce, Robert Gadek and Olga Danek in Krakow, and Rabbi Joshua Ellis and Klara Jackl in Warsaw in July 2017. I am grateful for the help given by Piotr Nazaruk, Jagek Jeremcz and Teresa Klimowicz at the NN Teatr, Lublin, in the same month. Anyone trying to understand the Holocaust in Poland and its impact on contemporary society should read Jan T. Gross's *Neighbours: The Destruction of the Jewish Community in Jedwabne, Poland* (Arrow, 2003) and *Fear: Anti-Semitism in Poland after Auschwitz* (Random House 2007). Conversations in Warsaw and Radom with survivor Sal Bierenbaum were illuminating. I found the films *Ida* (2013) and *Aftermath* (2012) helpful.

5. BUCHAREST: AN EYE FOR AN EYE

This chapter draws on Rich Cohen's *The Avengers: A Jewish War Story* (Alfred A. Knopf, 2000), Josef Harmatz, *From the Wings: A Long Journey* (Book Guild, 1998) and Dina Porat's *The Fall of a Sparrow: The Life and Times of Abba Kovner* (Stanford University Press, 2000) as well as the testimony of Poldek Maimon. I also used information from numerous newspaper interviews with the key protagonists.

6. TARVISIO: THE GATEWAY TO ZION

Key sources for this chapter included Hanoch Bartov, *The Brigade* (Holt, Rinehart and Winston, 1965), Howard Blum, *The Brigade* (Pocket, 2002), Leonard Sanitt, *On Parade: Memoirs of a Jewish Sergeant-Major in World War II* (Spa, 1990) and Morris Beckmann, *The Jewish Brigade: An Army with Two Masters* (Spellmount, 2008).

7. DACHAU: HUMAN DEBRIS

Central to my account is the book by Abraham Klausner, *A Letter to My Children from the Edge of the Holocaust* (Holocaust Center of Northern California, 2002) and my interview with his son Amos Klausner by phone in February 2017. Abraham Klausner's archive was also illuminating and is held by the American Jewish Historical Society. Also helpful was *Dachau 29 April 1945: The Rainbow Liberation Memoirs*, edited by Sam Dann (Texas University Press, 2015).

8. ST OTTILIEN: THE DOCTOR AND HIS PATIENTS

I discovered the story of St Ottilien in Abraham Klausner's *A Letter to My Children from the Edge of the Holocaust* (Holocaust Center of Northern California, 2002) and Robert Hilliard's *Surviving the Americans: The Continued Struggle of the Jews after Liberation* (Seven Stories, 1997). My understanding of what happened here was developed in numerous conversations with Father Cyrill Schäfer, members of the Grinberg family and Robert Hilliard. Sonia Becker was a source of information about the concentration camp orchestra in which her mother sang and she gave me a copy of her book *Symphony on Fire: A Story of Music and Spiritual Resistance during the Holocaust* (2017). I listened to the testimony of Uri Chanoch at USHMM, and my interview with his brother Dani Chanoch in January 2018 gave me a picture of their family background and the story of the Kovno Ghetto. Harry Linser also gave testimony that was very helpful. Background information on the Kovno Ghetto was provided by conversation with the staff of the Sugihara House in Kaunas, Lithuania, in August 2017 and the following books: Solomon Abramovich and Yakov Zilberg, *Kaddish for Kovno: Life and Death in a Lithuanian Ghetto 1941–45* (Chicago Review Press, 1999), *Smuggled in Potato Sacks: Fifty Stories of the Hidden Children of Kaunas* (Vallentine Mitchell, 2011), Laura Mae Weinrib, *Nitzotz: The Spark of Resistance in Kovno Ghetto and Dachau-Kaufering Concentration Camp* (Syracuse, 2009) and Avraham Tory, *Surviving the Holocaust: The Kovno Ghetto Diary* (Harvard, 1991).

9. LANDSBERG: THE TOWN WHERE NOTHING HAPPENED

Much of this chapter draws on my interview with Manfried Deiler in Landsberg, Germany, in February 2017 and Abraham Klausener's *A Letter to My Children from the Edge of the Holocaust* (Holocaust Center of Northern California, 2002). The testimonies of Samuel Sadinsky and Harry Linser were also helpful. I gained much from reading Solly Ganor's extraordinary book *Light One Candle: A Survivor's Tale from Lithuania to Jerusalem* (Kodansha, 2003).

10. MUNICH: THE SURVIVORS' PASSOVER

This chapter draws on Abraham Klausner's *A Letter to My Children from the Edge of the Holocaust* (Holocaust Center of Northern California, 2002) and interviews with his son Amos Klausner as well as the papers in the Klausner Archives. There are versions of the Survivors' Haggadah online and information at USHMM but I found the edition of Yosef Dov Sheinson's *A Survivors' Haggadah* (Jewish Publication Society, 2000), edited by Saul Touster, especially helpful. Background information came from Margarete Myers Feinstein, *Holocaust Survivors in PostWar Germany 1945–57* (Cambridge University Press, 2014) and Zeev Mankowitz, *Life between Memory and Hope: The Survivors of the Holocaust in Occupied Germany* (Cambridge University Press, 2007). I found useful Avinoam Patt's *Finding Home and Homeland: Jewish Youth and Zionism in the Aftermath of the Holocaust* (Wayne State University Press, 2009). I am grateful to the guidance given to me in my research when I was starting out.

11. MILAN: PEDDLING HISTORY

Not just for this chapter but for all those set in Italy, the following were vital sources: Ruth Bondy, *The Emissary: A Life of Enzo Sereni* (Plunkett Lake Press, 2017) and Ada Sereni, *I clandestini del mare: l'emigrazione ebraica in terra d'Israele dal 1945 al 1948* (Mursia, 2006). There is little written about Raffaele Cantoni and my account is based on information in Sergio I. Minerbi, *Un ebreo fra D'Annunzio e il sionismo Raffaele Cantoni* (Bonacci, 1992) and John Davis, *The Jews of San Nicrando* (Yale, 2010). *Jews in Italy under Fascist and Nazi Rule 1922–1945*, edited by Joshua D. Zimmerman (Cambridge University Press, 2005), gave background history. Mordechai Naor's *Haapala: Clandestine Immigration 1931–1948* (Israeli Ministry of Defence, 1987) was helpful. Author interviews with Giovanni Bloisi and Daniela Tedeschi took place in March and April 2017 in Italy. I was given a flavour of the time by Primo Levi's novel *If Not Now, When?* (Penguin, 1995). Yitzhak Kaplan described life at Via dell'Unione 5 in an interview in Haifa in January 2018. I am grateful to the help and guidance of the family of Yehuda Arazi and his granddaughter Orli Bach.

12. SELVINO: THE MOST VULNERABLE PEOPLE IN THE WORLD

Without the help of historian Marco Cavallarin and campaigner Miriam Bisk, this chapter could not have been written. I relied on the information on the website *Sciesopoli—la casa dei bambini di Selvino*, www.sciesopoli. com, and was helped by Sergio Luzzatto's *I bambini di Moshe: gli orfani della Shoah e la nascita di Israele* (Einaudi, 2018). I drew on Aharon Megged's *The Story of the Selvino Children: Journey to the Promised Land* (Am Oved, 1984), and Avraham Aviel's account in *Freedom and Loneliness* (Kotarim, 2008) was a compelling read. I learned much from Sidney Zoltak's *My Silent Pledge: A Journey of Struggle, Survival and Remembrance* (Miroland, 2013). Central to this chapter were the interviews I conducted with Menachem Kriegel by telephone in November 2017 and in Haifa in January 2018.

13. FIESOLE: THE LOST BOYS OF THE BENCISTA

As far as I know, this is the only account of the children's home at the Villa Bencista. The little information I gathered on Arie Avisar was found at the synagogue in Florence. This chapter is based on the USC Shoah Foundation testimonies of Jack Bursztain, Akiva Kohane and Hayah Yomshtik. Author interviews with Dani Chanoch and Yechiel Aleksander in Israel in January 2018 and with Simone Simoni and his wife Carla in Fiesole, Italy, in February 2018 completed the picture.

14. SANTA MARIA DI BAGNI: TIME TO BREATHE

This chapter is based on interviews with the survivors Yehuda Erlich and Moshe Ha-Elion conducted in Israel in January 2018 and Alter Wiener's memoir *64735: From a Name to a Number* (Author House, 2010). My thanks go to the Museo della Memoria e dell'Accoglienza in Santa Maria di Bagni for the information they supplied and for putting me in touch with Moshe Ha-Elion. I found Sara Vinçon's *Vite in transito: gli ebrei nel campo profughi di Grugliasco (1945–1949)* (Zamorani, 2009) a good guide to the DP experience of life in the camps in Italy.

15. MAGENTA: THE SECRET CAMP

This chapter draws on the work of Lorenzo Giacchero, *Come rondine al nido: a bordo della nave Rondine* (Antica Tipografia Ligure, 2016) and *Una rondine fa primavera: un legno Arenzanese verso la Terra Promessa* (Antica Tipografia Ligure, 2013), which he kindly shared with me, and on our conversations about Aliyah Bet in Italy. I am grateful for his help. Elisabetta Bozzi and the Associazione Nazionale Partigiani d'Italia in Magenta guided my research on Camp A. Primo Levi's novel *If Not Now, When?* (Penguin, 1995) gave me a flavour of life at Camp A; and testimonies at Israel's Ghetto Fighters' House museum filled in many blanks. The picture was completed by interviews with survivors Yechiel Aleksander and Yehuda Erlich in Israel in January 2018.

16. NEW YORK: F***B SHIPPING

My research began with Murray Greenfield's *The Jews' Secret Fleet: The Untold Story of North American Volunteers Who Smashed the British Blockade of Palestine* (Gefen, 1996) and Arik Kerman's *The Jewish Refugee Warship* (CreateSpace, 2015). David Gottlieb's memoir *Almost a Mensch* (Halcyon, 2002) was a key resource as were his testimony at the USC Shoah Foundation and numerous newspaper interviews. I read many of the accounts related to the Exodus story, which provided key background information. The most helpful was by Ruth Gruber: *Exodus 1947: The Ship That Launched a Nation* (Union Square Press, 2007).

17. LA SPEZIA: MOVE OVER PAUL NEWMAN

Maria Luisa Eguez's *La Spezia, porta della speranza* (Il Nuovo Melangolo, 2016) and the website of the Exodus Prize gave me my first insight into the story of Aliyah Bet in the port of La Spezia. I drew on Helen Sendyk's account in her memoir *New Dawn: A Triumph of Life after the Holocaust* (Syracuse, 2002). The story of how the tale of the *Fede* and *Fenice* was used by Leon Uris relies on M.M. Silver's *Our Exodus: Leon Uris and the Americanization of Israel's Founding Story* (Wayne State University Press, 2010). I also found Paolo Bosso's *Ci chiesero di chiudere un occhio, ne chiudemmo due: il contributo dei cantieri navali di Porto Venere per la riuscita del'Aliyah Bet dall'Italia ad Eretz Israel* (2018) helpful. Much of my understanding of events in La Spezia comes from my interviews with Yitzhak

Kaplan in Haifa in January 2018 and with Alberto Cavanna, Marco Ferrari and the mayor Pierluigi Peracchini in La Spezia in May 2018.

18. HAIFA: THE PEOPLE'S TRAFALGAR

David Gottlieb's *Almost a Mensch* (Total Recall, 2014) was invaluable as were his testimony at the USC Shoah Foundation and interviews he gave to the press. I.F. Stone's *Underground to Palestine* (CreateSpace, 2017) was also a vital source as were Wiener's memoirs, *64735: From a Name to a Number* (Author House, 2010). The testimonies of those who travelled on the *Wedgwood* available in the USC Shoah Foundation archive added much colour and were useful in cross-referencing accounts. Josef Harmatz wrote with much humour about his arrival in Haifa in his memoir *From the Wings: A Long Journey* (Book Guild, 1998). The chapter uses material from my interviews with Yechiel Aleksander, Dani Chanoch, Yehuda Erlich, and Menachem Kriegel, and draws on Alter Wiener's account in his memoir. Fedda Lieberman's and Poldek Maimon's testimonies at the Ghetto Fighters' House website added key details. My conversations with both Dave Rich and the Rev. Alex Jacob led to an understanding of the British aspect of the story. Louise London's *Whitehall and the Jews 1933–1948: British Immigration Policy, Jewish Refugees and the Holocaust* (Cambridge University Press, 2000) provided the background to British policy. Richard Crossman's *Palestine Mission: A Personal Record* (Harper, 1947) taught me a lot.

19. TEL AVIV: ONLY YESTERDAY

In providing me with understanding of the survivors' experience, Hanna Yablonka's *Survivors of the Holocaust: Israel after the War* (Macmillan, 1999) was crucial. Survivor interviews with Dani Chanoch and Moshe Ha-Elion in Israel in January 2018, and the memoirs of Alter Wiener and Josef Harmatz, *From the Wings: A Long Journey* (Book Guild, 1998), were vital confirmation of Yablonka's findings, as were many of the testimonies I listened to at the USC Shoah Foundation. I drew on Rachel Halperin's testimony and newspaper interviews. Dina Porat's *The Fall of a Sparrow: The Life and Times of Abba Kovner* (Stanford University Press, 2000) guided me to Kovner's *Scrolls of Testimony* (Jewish Publication Society, 2001), which is deeply moving.